Oracle RAC Performance Tuning

Brian Peasland

This book is posthumously dedicated to the late Terry Richard Peasland. I am not here today or have the capability to produce this book without you. I miss you.

Brian Peasland

Oracle RAC Performance Tuning

By Brian Peasland

Copyright © 2015 by Rampant TechPress. All rights reserved.

Printed in the United States of America.

Published by Rampant TechPress, Kittrell, North Carolina, USA

Oracle In Focus Series: Book #50

Series Editor: Donald K. Burleson

Editors: Jennifer Kittleson, Donald K. Burleson,

Technical Editors: Troy Meyerink, Robert Yarbrough

Cover Design: Janet Burleson

Printing History: February 2015 for First Edition

ISBN-13: 978-0-9861194-1-5

Library of Congress Control Number:

Table of Contents

Chapter 6:

Tuning Memory... **145**

Chapter 7:

RAC Parallel Operations **173**

Chapter 8:

RAC Support Tools 207

Chapter 9:

AWR, ADDM and ASH 255

Chapter 11:

Chapter 12:

Chapter 13:

Chapter 14:

Using the Online Code Depot

Purchase of this book provides complete access to the online code depot that contains sample code scripts. Any code depot scripts in this book are located at the following URL in zip format and ready to load and use:

rampant.cc/RACTune.htm

If technical assistance is needed with downloading or accessing the scripts, please contact Rampant TechPress at rtp@rampant.cc.

Acknowledgements

When I was approached to write a book, I jumped at the chance. Sure! I'd love to write a book! I knew that it wouldn't be easy. I knew it would take lots of time. All that being said, I knew that it would be a process that I would enjoy. When I was asked to write a book about Oracle RAC performance tuning, on the inside I said "are you crazy?!?!?!" but the words that came out of my mouth was "Sure! I'd love to write that book!" which brings me to today, an Oracle RAC performance tuning book written by yours truly.

At first, I wouldn't tell anyone outside of my immediate family that I was writing a book. That way, if I failed miserably, I wouldn't have to explain myself. Eventually, word started getting out of my endeavor. The biggest question I received was "Why?" There are a few reasons for taking on this project. I get to share the knowledge in my head. I get to learn a lot in the process. I also wanted to see if I could do something like this that I had never done before. But the biggest reason I did this was for my father.

My father passed away exactly one week before the birth of my twin sons. Just like anyone who lost a loved one, I miss him terribly. I wanted to do something to commemorate his life. It took me awhile to figure out what that would be, and this book is it. My father spent a good part of his career as an instructor and developed training courses. I see so much of his traits in myself. I've been told that I have the ability to teach and explain complex material to people. I am convinced that my abilities to teach come from him. What better way to commemorate his life than to use the gifts he gave me? So for those reasons, this book is dedicated to my late father and his memory and he is the biggest reason I wanted to write this book.

I want to acknowledge the people who took a chance to hire me as a database administrator, which started me on this career path. Marty Hoag gave me my first shot as a DBA/Developer when I was in graduate school. Darrin Foell wanted me to be a full-time DBA when I was done with school. I don't know that either figured I would end up here the day that they hired me. There have been many other managers in my career. Including my current managers, they have all been supportive of my efforts to grow my career and move forward.

I appreciate the chance that Donald Burleson at Rampant TechPress took when contacting me to write a book. I hope that I did not disappoint! I would also like to thank Jennifer Kittleson at Rampant for working with me over the course of this venture. Both have been instrumental in getting this book published. I'm sure there are others at Rampant to thank, but they worked behind the scenes so I cannot name them and provide a proper word of thanks.

No technical book would be worth the paper it's written on without its technical reviewers. Thanks to both Troy Meyerink and Robert Yarbrough for their monumental efforts in going through every detail in these chapters. I know it wasn't easy and I know that I asked a lot of your time, but this book would not have been possible without your help.

In graduate school, Dr. William Perrizo (NDSU) was the first to get me thinking about how to write, how to formulate thoughts on paper. Without his teachings, I'm not sure the genesis to be an author would have been installed in me.

So many people around the world have taught me so much in so many areas. Most of them don't know me. Obviously, individuals like Tom Kyte, Jonathan Lewis, Cary Millsap, Craig Shallahamer, and others in that lofty, well-respected category have laid a foundation of technical knowledge that I have used every day in my career. There have been countless others as well. So many people I don't have space to name them all and there are so many people that I don't even know their names. I learn so much just from answering questions in various forums over my career so even people who came asking questions have taught me something. Please don't take any offense if I left your name out. If I have ever had interaction with you, or visited your blog, or read your answers, or answered your questions somewhere in the worldwide Oracle community, thank you!

Lastly, and most importantly, I want to thank my loving family for their support. My sons are not that old. Chay is just starting school and the twins Jace and Jenner aren't even in preschool yet. You boys are too young to fully realize why daddy is typing away on his laptop other than I'm doing "work". My wife, Latana, has had to put up with my constant late nights writing yet another page or two for the chapter I'm currently working on. Without her support, patience and understanding, this book doesn't get off the ground. I love all four of you and couldn't do this without you.

My sincere thanks,

Brian Peasland

Introduction TO RAC Tuning

Introduction to RAC Tuning

Many companies are deploying Oracle's Real Application Clusters (RAC) to provide high availability and high scalability for their mission-critical applications. The new Oracle 12c version has changed how RAC is being used with Oracle Multitenant, which is essentially virtualization at the database level. Oracle RAC is becoming increasingly important in today's data center. Additionally, today's Oracle database administrator is being asked to not only tune SQL statements and their Oracle database, they are also being asked to keep their clustered database performing at an optimal level. The database administrator relies on traditional single-instance tuning techniques for Oracle RAC as well as additional RAC-specific tuning.

This book does not delve into the high availability side of Oracle RAC. Rather, the focus is on achieving high degrees of performance and scalability. This book provides tools and techniques to have those mission-critical applications perform at a high level in a Real Application Clusters database. Later chapters will discuss how to tune the memory, storage, the cluster interconnect, and the application. Various tools and utilities will be examined to bolster your performance-tuning arsenal. Armed with the information in this book, you should have confidence that your company's clustered database can not only meet current workloads in place today, but also scale to meet future demands.

Readers of this book may find it helpful to have an introductory understanding of Oracle databases and Oracle Real Application Clusters. In certain places, background information will be provided as concepts are discussed. However, it would be very longwinded to explain every RAC concept in detail before discussing how to tune that concept.

As with many technical books, there often exists a circular reference that makes the book difficult to write. For example, we want to discuss statistics related to the private network as can be seen in the AWR, but we haven't explained what the AWR is yet. We could explain the AWR upfront and show examples of private network statistics, but those examples don't make much sense until we discuss the private network.

Every attempt is made to lay out the book's content in a logical order, but the circular nature of some topics means the reader may benefit from reading the book more than once.

This book offers a number of examples and metrics obtained from a variety of Oracle RAC deployments. Some examples shown will be from full production environments. Some examples shown will come from a two-node Oracle RAC deployment on a laptop. As with any examples in this book or from virtually any other source, the caveat of "your mileage may vary" comes into play. It is vital that changes be tested thoroughly before implementing in production. In the short space of this book, it is impossible to vet each change against every possible combination that might exist in the world, which means it is conceivable that your site-specific implementation has one subtle nuance that can alter the outcome. It is so important that it needs to be said again: *"It is vital that changes be tested thoroughly before implementing in production"*.

In today's world of virtual machines, there is no excuse for not having a testbed at one's disposal where the database administrator can experiment and go wild with Oracle RAC without interfering with other systems. As stated in the previous paragraph, many of the examples in this book were created on a two-node Oracle RAC database running in virtual machines on a laptop. With today's technology, it is very easy to get an Oracle RAC testbed up and running. Gone are the days where the RAC enthusiast needed to cobble together two old desktops, an old network switch or two they absconded from their network friend, and some creaky network-attached disk that they overpaid for, all to stand up an Oracle RAC cluster in their basement. Now, one can download Oracle Corporation's free Virtual Box hypervisor.

Virtual Box can help set up all of the networking, even the private network. Virtual Box even lets one define files to act as shared disk storage among multiple virtual machines. Install Linux and Oracle software and you're off and running. It shouldn't take the reader long to search the Internet for "install Oracle RAC on Virtual Box" and come up with a good document that details every step. One is not limited to using Virtual Box either. VMWare or Microsoft's Hyper-V virtual hypervisors can be used if desired. Simply change the Internet search criteria and anyone can find step-by-step instructions on how to set up Oracle RAC on a desktop or laptop. Just make sure you have enough memory on the host to support multiple virtual machines at the same time. Such a testbed will not perform extremely well but will provide a playground to test out new ideas and experiment.

Most people who stand up Oracle RAC on a desktop or laptop machine will probably be using Oracle software downloads from Oracle's Technet. Be advised that the licensing is limited with these downloads. Read the license agreement carefully to be sure that you are not violating any terms. For many companies, the Technet license is not sufficient. However, creating Oracle RAC non-production environments with your company's applications is still a very important thing to do. The database administrator may have to convince management that the investment in additional Oracle licenses is well worth it. As IT practitioners, we are all familiar with the concept that our non-production environments should match production as close as possible. However, IT budgets do not often agree with this sentiment. The database administrator can obtain some leverage in the discussion by reminding management of the cost of something going wrong leading to an unavailable production system. These costs can often be avoided if a proper non-production environment were in place. It can be terribly detrimental to a company if the database administrator has no place to practice the upgrade of Oracle Clusterware 10.2.0.3 to Oracle's Grid Infrastructure 11.2.0.4 and the upgrade goes wrong, leaving the cluster inoperable. A proper testbed would let the database administrator sort out a number of issues before attempting the upgrade in production.

Today's virtual technologies help streamline the upgrade testing with the ability to take snapshots. One can snapshot the existing system, meaning server and storage. If the upgrade goes wrong, revert the system back to the previous state, correct the issue and try the upgrade again. The database administrator should also be documenting the steps along the way. There should be at least one final run-through of the document without any issues before proceeding with the change to the production environment. Armed with proper documentation, not only will the change to production proceed with fewer incidents, it should complete much more quickly leading to a shorter downtime window.

Much of this book will discuss how to make changes to one's Oracle RAC production environment. As such, it is vitally important that the database administrator have a proper place to test the changes and ensure the change does not negatively impact the production environment. Investing in a proper non-production Oracle RAC environment can save the company money in the long run.

RAC Database vs. Instance

Many database administrators often use the terms *database* and *instance* interchangeably. Even more common is for people to use the term *database* when referring to the *instance*. In single-instance Oracle environment, it is easy to swap the terms without altering the context of the discussion. For Oracle RAC databases, it is important to understand the two terms and use them correctly.

The *database* is the collection of files on disk. One can see many of the files by querying the *dba_data_files* and *dba_temp_files* Data Dictionary views. The *v$logfile* view, the parameter file, and the password file complete the list. All of these files collectively are the *database*. The database is what persists across shutdowns. If one turns off the server, the data is still found in the files, ready to be accessed once service has been restored.

The *instance* is the collection of memory and processes running on the server. One does not start the Oracle database. Rather, one starts the Oracle instance. The instance is the gateway to the database. Without the instance, there is no access to the data file's contents, hence no access to the database.

In a single-instance database, there is a one-to-one relationship between the instance and the database. An instance can access one and only one database. With Oracle RAC, there are multiple instances for one database. Each instance runs on a separate database server, called a *node* in the cluster.

It is important to make the distinction between the database and the instance so that the material in the book makes more sense. In some cases, the book may talk about multiple instances, which may or may not be all of the instances associated with a particular database.

RAC Tuning Methodology

Just because we will be dealing with Oracle RAC databases does not mean that we don't have to perform proper tuning.

1. **Tune the application**. Chapter 3 devotes significant time to RAC-specific application tuning issues.
2. **Tune the instances**. Chapters in this book discuss how to tune Oracle's memory, leverage parallel operations, and how to address the database's files.
3. **Tune the server**. Chapter 4 discusses how to tune the Cluster Interconnect to ensure it is not a major bottleneck to application performance.

Normally, the tuning methodology one will see is to tune the application first, then the database, then the server. In that workflow, we would tune the Cluster Interconnect in the last section. As we will see in the next chapter, Cache Fusion and cross-instance communication is vital to the health and performance of an Oracle RAC database. This book will depart from the normal conventions and discuss tuning the private network early in the list of topics.

The fact that the database is clustered does not change the database administrator's approach to tuning. At a high level, performance tuning is concerned with maximizing *throughput* and minimizing *response time.* Oracle RAC performance tuning is no different.

Throughput is the amount of work that can be accomplished over a period of time. For example, a teller at a bank can handle 15 customer transactions per hour. Maximizing throughput is engineering the system to handle more work in the same period of time. If the bank teller works faster and can handle 20 customer transactions per hour, throughput is increased. A second teller could be added, doubling the throughput. At some point in computer systems, demands on the machine's resources reaches a saturation point that defines the system's maximum throughput.

Response time is defined as *the service time* plus *wait time.* The response time for the bank's customer is the total time from when the customer says "hello" to the teller to the time the customer's interaction with that teller is complete. From the customer's perspective, the *service time* is the time spent talking with the teller. The *wait time* is when the customer is standing there idle while the teller types information into the bank's computer system and the teller counts money. From a computer system tuning perspective, the service time is the time spent processing on the CPU and the wait time is time spent waiting for something to happen. Wait times may be waiting for data to be read from disk, waiting for data to be sorted, or waiting for another transaction to release a lock. Since *response time = service time + wait time,* the way to reduce response time is to reduce one or the other or both.

When Oracle performance tuning specialists first started tuning by wait event analyses, as opposed to the ratio based, antiquated tuning methods, the focus was on reducing wait time. While this is an admirable goal, reducing service time may also be necessary. Consider a query that takes 1 minute to complete and it is determined that the SQL statement spent 55 seconds executing on the CPU and 5 seconds waiting for events to complete. If the wait time is reduced to zero seconds, the query's overall runtime is reduced by only 8.3%, not a significant difference.

It is very common to see a query in an Oracle instance that mimics this behavior: large service time and low wait time. In many of these cases, the query is performing too much logical I/O. *Physical I/O* is when a block of data is read from disk. Once in the instance's Buffer Cache, the next execution of the query reads the data from memory, which is called *Logical I/O.* Accessing data from memory, i.e. logical I/O operations, are CPU actions. Reducing the response time in this scenario means reducing the logical I/O, hence reducing the service time.

A *bottleneck* is anything that slows down the process. It is vitally important to understand that there will always be a bottleneck. Some database administrators get focused on eliminating the "Top 5" wait events to tune application performance.

Because there will always be a bottleneck, even if the database administrator is successful at eradicating all five of the wait events at the top of the list, those events will be replaced by five more events at the top of the list. Without knowing when to stop tuning, the database administrator could keep on tuning forever. So how do we know when to stop tuning? It comes down to the end user's perspective. All users want all processes to complete in record time, but that goal is unobtainable. More realistically, end user may want the first results from a search returned to the application in less than one second.

They may be willing to wait up to 30 seconds from the time they press the Complete Order button until the time they get an order confirmation page. The end user may be willing to wait up to five minutes for a long report to complete. Armed with response time goals like this, we know when to stop. If a report is taking thirty minutes to complete, the end user is experiencing pain. Pain will go away when the report completes in five minutes. The performance-tuning specialist spots a bottleneck and reduces the wait time. The report now runs in fifteen minutes. While the response time was reduced by 50%, the goal has not been met. So the performance tuner goes back to work. Two more bottlenecks are spotted and addressed. The report now runs in four minutes. At this point, the performance tuning activity should cease. As soon as the accepted response time is met, the performance tuning work is done.

RAC Tuning for a Single Instance

Oracle RAC can help you get more performance out of your application but it is not a silver bullet for your performance woes. There have been many occurrences of an application that did not perform well in a single-instance configuration performing much better once deployed on Oracle RAC. Those who are initially pleased with the application's improved response time will often find disappointment when their application does not scale well for the future, even though Oracle RAC is being leveraged.

It will probably be no surprise that there have been occurrences where applications perform worse once deployed on Oracle RAC. Oracle RAC adds layers of complexity that can hamper application performance if not handled properly. The applications that perform worse running in Oracle RAC are often applications that are not properly tuned and will not scale well in a single-instance database. Oracle RAC can act as a magnifying glass for some performance problems. Before tuning an application for Oracle RAC, the application should be tuned as if it were deployed on a single-instance database. Applications that are well tuned and scalable should perform even better and scale even higher on Oracle RAC.

Most of the readers of this book will be familiar with Oracle performance tuning for single-instance databases. Oracle tools you already use like Explain Plan, wait events, tuning advisors, and the Automated Workload Repository still work with Oracle RAC databases. The performance tuning tools in non-RAC databases are often the first tools to be employed even if the application is running on a clustered database. Tune the application to work well on a single-instance database and it will make your Oracle RAC performance tuning easier.

RAC Scalability

Scalability is the ability of a system to handle an increased workload as the number of user's increases. When you only have one server, the only way to raise the server's capacity is to increase the resources available in the server. The server can be outfitted with more CPUs with more cores. Physical memory can be increased. We say that adding resources to a server is *scaling up* or *vertical scaling*.

One of the biggest problems with vertical scaling is that hard limits exist in any server. You can only add a certain number of CPU cores to the server. The server has a finite number of memory slots that have a physical limit on the size of the memory chips that can be used. If the workload increases sufficiently, a server that is outfitted to the maximum may still be overburdened and not be able to handle the end user demands.

Another issue with vertical scaling is the cost. As more and more memory is added to the system, the cost increases very rapidly. As an analogy, think of constructing a building and your requirement is to have 10,000 square feet. Such a large building will cost more if it is built as a ten story structure with each story sized at 1,000 square feet than if it were built as a single story building. The taller the building, the more it costs to create. Similarly, a server outfitted with lots of CPU cores and very large amounts of physical memory will cost more than buying lots of smaller servers together provide the same number of cores and RAM.

Oracle RAC offers the ability to *scale out*, or perform *horizontal scaling*. Horizontal scaling is normally much cheaper than vertical scaling. Back to the analogy, in scaling out, we can erect ten 1,000 square foot single story buildings to achieve our total resource requirement. A ten-story building is much, much more expensive than ten smaller one-story buildings even if the end result is the same square footage. Oracle RAC horizontal scaling is typically accomplished by implementing low-cost commodity hardware. Today's data centers are now filled with inexpensive servers rather than the big iron systems of the past. We typically scale our Oracle RAC configurations by adding a new server rather than buying a larger server. Back to our analogy, if the workload dictates that we need to grow from 10,000 square feet to

12,000 square feet, we do that by creating two more 1,000 square foot buildings. Similarly, if our Oracle RAC cluster needs to scale to meet demands, we simply add another low-cost server to the cluster.

Oracle RAC offers the ability to both scale up and scale out. You are not limited to one or the other. This gives the company great flexibility is designing their database infrastructure to suit their specific needs. It is possible to incorporate high-end servers into a RAC cluster. However, this is rarely done in practice as the company often saves money by using commodity hardware, but it is always nice to have options and not be constrained in a single direction.

Another option is to have some nodes in the cluster with more resources than other nodes. In this way, we can mix and match nodes to specific needs across the cluster. Be very careful in architecting your RAC systems where nodes may have different resources. If you use any application failover within the cluster, you may find that sessions connecting to a different node in the cluster do not have enough resources to be able to perform adequately.

A node in the cluster should not only have enough resources to handle a normal workload, it should have enough resources to handle the additional demands placed on it when the number of sessions increases due to failure in another node. For this reason, it is rare to have an Oracle RAC cluster where nodes do not have all the same resources available to it. While possible to have nodes with different configurations, doing so would be rare and requires a proper understanding of the risks involved.

Summary

This first chapter provided an introduction to Oracle RAC performance tuning. The chapter started with a discussion of using testbeds to understand the effect of a change on a system, made even easier with today's virtualization techniques. The conversation turned to tuning the application for a single instance. Oracle RAC is not a silver bullet for an application's performance woes. A properly tuned, scalable application can be taken to the next level with Oracle RAC, but it is possible to have worse performance on Oracle RAC.

Next, we discussed scale up and scale out. Oracle RAC is primarily a scale out solution, often leveraging commodity hardware to scale with reasonable costs. Yet Oracle RAC does not limit the infrastructure to one scaling direction as the systems can be configured to scale up as well.

This chapter also discussed a tuning methodology that works for single-instance as well as Oracle RAC databases. Tune the application first, the database second, and the server last. Bottlenecks always exist in any system and it is impossible to eliminate them all. Response time is defined as service time plus wait time. Oracle's wait events tell us where processes are spending their time.

In the next chapter we will discuss Cache Fusion, the secret sauce to make Oracle RAC databases perform very well. The Cache Fusion operations discussed will be important, as those operations will be illustrated throughout the remainder of the book.

Cache Fusion

Introduction to Cache Fusion

Understanding Cache Fusion and how it works is an important prerequisite to learning Oracle RAC performance tuning. This chapter will give a history of Cache Fusion and provide a high-level overview of how Cache Fusion works to help improve Oracle RAC database performance. However, in order for the material in other chapters to make sense, we need to have a deeper understanding of Cache Fusion operations.

Oracle RAC relies heavily on Cache Fusion to achieve high performance for its clustered database. Cache Fusion is not a specific feature in Oracle RAC. Rather it is a collection of memory structures and process, many that exist in single instance databases, that work together efficiently in a clustered environment.

History of Cache Fusion

In the 1960's, as people began to discuss how to extend the processing power of a computer system, some IT practitioners latched on to the idea of splitting a given workload among multiple systems. If one system could not handle the workload, then split the work over two systems. The only hard part becomes how to put the two results back together into one final solution. It was not until 1977 that Datapoint released ARCnet, the first commercial clustered computing system. In 1984, Digital Equipment Corporation (DEC) released its first VAXCluster and ever since, clustered computing has been available for business use.

In the same year that ARCNet was released, Larry Ellison and others founded Software Development Laboratories (SDL). In 1978, the first version of the Oracle database engine was created to run on the DEC PDP-11 although this version was never officially released. Early on, the Oracle database software was available on DEC equipment. The company known as SDL changed its name to Relational Software, Inc. (RSI) and then in 1982 it changed its name once again, this time to Oracle Corporation. At this time, the Oracle database software was running on DEC VAX systems. It should be no surprise that if Oracle databases were running on VAX and DEC was also working on clustered VAX systems, that the Oracle Corporation would create a clustered database system. In 1988, Oracle Corporation announced the first commercially clustered database product when Oracle Version 6 was released. Oracle's clustered database ran on, you guessed it, DEC VAX clustered systems. Oracle called their first clustered database Oracle Parallel Server (OPS).

Oracle Parallel Server worked well, but it also had its drawbacks, as do many young computer technologies. In 1999, Oracle Corporation released the Oracle 8i version. Oracle Parallel Server would get a new name, Oracle Real Application Clusters (RAC). This new name was warranted because of major changes in the clustered database architecture. Chief among those changes was the introduction of Cache Fusion.

In OPS, servers in the cluster (called *nodes*) would not talk to each other very much even though they were networked together. A major problem with OPS was a concept known as "disk pinging". If a session on Node 1 of the cluster needed to access a record in a table, but a transaction in Node 2 of the cluster had modified that row, the changed data needed to be written from Node 2 to the shared disk storage.

In turn, the session on Node 1 had to wait for this write to complete, after which Node 1 could then read the changed data. The only communication between the instances on the two nodes was to request the change to be written to disk and to acknowledge the write had completed. The shared storage became the middleman facilitating transmission of changed data blocks between nodes in the cluster.

In sum, disk pinging was a performance killer for OPS systems. Cache Fusion solved this problem by leveraging the *cluster interconnect*, a high-speed private network used exclusively by the clustered database servers. Instead of using the shared storage middleman, Oracle RAC's Cache Fusion transfers changed data blocks from one node to another via this network. Transferring a data block across the cluster interconnect is much, much faster than disk pinging.

Cache Fusion Overview

If data were never changed, life would be easier. Each node in the cluster would just read the data block from disk. Sadly, things become more difficult when we have to deal with transactions that modify data in the database. Since this in an Oracle database, we live in a world where writers never block readers, which is a very good thing. A transaction modifying a row in a table is not allowed to block another session that needs to read that row. Yet the session reading the row is not allowed to see the other transaction's changes until those changes are committed.

In a single instance database, Oracle generates a *consistent read*, an image of the data block before the transaction started. Oracle uses the information in the Undo tablespace to generate the consistent read image. When Oracle 8i introduced Cache Fusion, the only block transfers across the cluster interconnect were to transfer consistent read images from the node that changed the block to the node that needed to read the block. Oracle 8i's Cache Fusion alleviated read/write contention issues for Oracle RAC. However, write/write contention still required disk pinging. Oracle 9i's Cache Fusion improved write/write block contention. If one node modified a block and another instance needed to modify the same block, instead of writing the dirty buffer to disk, the dirty block is transferred to the requesting node through the cluster interconnect.

In order to facilitate Cache Fusion, we still need the Buffer Cache, the Shared Pool and the Undo tablespace just like a single-instance database. However, for Oracle RAC, we need the Buffer Caches on all instances to appear to be global across the cluster.

Hence, extra coordination is needed in the cluster to make a collection of instances work together. For starters, we need a Global Resource Directory (GRD) to be able to keep track of the resources in the cluster. There is no true concept of a master node in Oracle RAC. Instead, each instance in the cluster becomes the *resource master* for a subset of resources. The Global Cache Services (GCS) are responsible for facilitating the transfer of blocks from one instance to another. A single-instance database relies on *enqueues* (locks) to protect two processes from simultaneously modifying the same row. Similarly, we need enqueues in Oracle RAC but since the Buffer Cache is now global, the enqueues on the resources must be global as well.

It should be no surprise that the Global Enqueue Services (GES) is responsible for managing locks across the cluster. As a side note, GES was previously called the Distributed Lock Manager (DLM). When Oracle introduced their first cluster on DEC VAX systems, the clustered database used VAX's cluster lock manager but it was not designed for the demands of a transactional database and did not scale well. Oracle designed the DLM to have a scalable global lock manager. The DLM still persists in many publications.

The processes running to support an Oracle RAC instance include:

- **LMS**: This process is GCS. This process used to be called the Lock Manager Server.
- **LMON**: The Lock Monitor. This process is the GES master process.

- **LMD:** The Lock Manager Daemon. This process manages incoming lock requests.

- **LCK0:** The instance enqueue process. This process manages lock requests for library cache objects.

Now, let's take a look at cache coherency.

Cache Coherency

The Oracle data blocks are a global resource that is available to any user or process in the clustered database, and each instance needs to work with the other instances in a cohesive effort to manage the blocks.

Coherency is defined in many dictionaries as "the act of uniting or sticking together". For Oracle RAC databases, *cache coherency* is defined as the collective effort of the instances to appear as if the Buffer Caches are one larger, logical unit. Implementing cache coherency in a clustered environment is no small task. There is a lot of overhead involved in making sure that each instance knows what is in the other caches. This process overhead increases overall response time.

The trick, (which Oracle RAC performs very well), is keeping cache coherency impacts to a minimum for most applications. Unfortunately, cache coherency can also act as a magnifying glass and make some performance problems worse than if the application were run on a single-instance database.

At the heart of Oracle RAC's cache coherency is *Global Cache Services* (GCS). GCS manages resources and everything in Oracle RAC is a resource. If a row needs to be modified in a table, that table resource needs to be acquired before the transaction is allowed to make the change. If this were a single-instance database and a simultaneous transaction needed to modify the same row, the second transaction would need to wait for the transaction lock (TX) to be released. In Oracle RAC, the TX locks still exist in all instances.

Consider the scenario where the second transaction is executing in a different instance than the first transaction. GCS and its partner, *Global Enqueue Services* (GES) need to ensure that the second transaction cannot be performed until the first session releases its TX lock in the first instance. GCS tracks the locations of the blocks in all of the collective buffer caches. To do this, all blocks in the Buffer Cache have a *master copy* of the block in only one instance, but other instances may have copies of the block as well. The GCS ensures cache coherency by keeping track of these copies and ensuring the blocks are consistent across the cluster. There can be multiple versions of a block to support consistent reads for end users. GES is responsible for keeping track of the block versions.

In order to keep track of the blocks and their versions, Oracle RAC sets up a *Global Resource Directory* (GRD). Each instance's *Shared Global Area* (SGA) sets aside a portion of memory for the GRD. Whenever a resource is used, GCS will assign one instance as the *resource master* for that resource. All of the instances can then determine the resource master for any particular resource. Remember, it is not necessary that the master copy of the block be in the same instance as the resource master. All of these working components, GCS, GES, and GRD, combine to form cache coherency for the cluster.

Now let's take a look at the current read requests.

RAC Current Read Tracing

In a single-instance database, whenever the data block is not in the Buffer Cache, a disk read must be performed. Later, when another session needs the same data block, that session just accesses the data block from the RAM in the Data Buffer Cache.

In an Oracle RAC database, we still have the block being read from disk when it is not in any Buffer Cache. If another session in the same instance needs the data block, the session just accesses the block from the Buffer Cache. If another session in another instance needs the data block, Cache Fusion will perform a global cache transfer of the block from one Buffer Cache to the other Data Buffer Cache.

A *current read* is one where a session reads the current value of the data block from another instance's Data Buffer Cache. This current value contains the most up-to-date committed data. The current read would happen when a second instance needs a data block that has not been changed. This is often thought of as a read/read situation. The current read will be seen as any wait event that starts with *gc current*. It is easy to simulate the situation by querying the same row of data in each instance. In the first instance, the following is issued.

```
SQL> select
  2      instance_name
  3  from
  4      v$instance;

INSTANCE_NAME
---------------
orcl1

SQL> select
  2      first_name
```

```
3  from
4      employees
5  where
6      employee_id=100;

FIRST_NAME
-------------------
Steven
```

In the second instance, a trace of the session will be started so that the wait events can be captured. The following script is used to start a trace in the current session.

💾 trace_my_session.sql

```
declare
   v_sid     number;
   v_serial number;
begin
   select
      sid,
      serial#
   into
      v_sid,
      v_serial
   from
      v$session
   where
      sid=SYS_CONTEXT('USERENV','SID');

   dbms_monitor.session_trace_enable(v_sid,v_serial,TRUE,TRUE);
end;
/
```

If a trace needs to be stopped, the following script will do the trick.

💾 no_trace_my_session.sql

```
declare
   v_sid     number;
   v_serial number;
begin
   select
      sid,
      serial#
   into
      v_sid,
      v_serial
   from
      v$session
   where
      sid=SYS_CONTEXT('USERENV','SID');

   dbms_monitor.session_trace_disable(v_sid,v_serial);
end;
/
```

In the second session on the second instance, a trace is started and the same query is issued.

```
SQL> select
  2      instance_name
  3  from
  4      v$instance;

INSTANCE_NAME
----------------
orcl2

SQL> @trace_my_session.sql

PL/SQL procedure successfully completed.

SQL> select
  2      first_name
  3  from
  4      employees
  5  where
  6      employee_id=100;

FIRST_NAME
--------------------
Steven
```

Since no blocks were modified in this tightly controlled environment, it is safe to assume that a current block was requested. The trace file generated from the second session is examined. The trace file can be determined with the following script.

💾 my_trace_file.sql

```
SQL> select
  2      pm.value||'/diag/rdbms/'||d.name||'/'||i.instance_name||
  3      '/trace/'||i.instance_name||'_ora_'||pr.spid||'.trc' as trace_file
  4  from
  5      (select
  6          p.spid
  7       from
  8          v$session s
  9       join
 10          v$process p
 11          on s.paddr=p.addr
 12       where
 13          s.sid=SYS_CONTEXT('USERENV','SID')) pr
 14      cross join
 15          (select
 16              value
 17           from
 18              v$parameter
 19           where
 20              name='diagnostic_dest') pm
```

```
21      cross join
22        (select
23            instance_name
24         from
25            v$instance) i
26      cross join
27        (select
28            lower(name) as name
29         from
30            v$database) d
31 /

TRACE_FILE
--------------------------------------------------------------------
/u01/app/oracle/diag/rdbms/orcl/orcl1/trace/orcl1_ora_8554.trc
```

Another easy way to identify the session's trace file is to use a trace file identifier.

```
SQL> alter session set tracefile_identifier=my_trace;

Session altered.

SQL> alter session set sql_trace=true;

Session altered.
```

Whatever is provided as the *tracefile_identifier* is added to the trace file name. If the above were executed, the trace file's name might be something like "orcl1_ora_8924_MY_TRACE.trc".

With the trace file created, it is now time to run it through the tkprof utility, the output of which can be seen below.

```
********************************************************************************
select
   first_name
from
   hr.employees
where
   employee_id=100

call     count       cpu    elapsed       disk      query    current       rows
------- ------  --------  ---------- ---------- ---------- ---------- ----------
Parse        1      0.00       0.03          0          0          0          0
Execute      1      0.00       0.00          0          0          0          0
Fetch        2      0.00       0.01          0          2          0          1
------- ------  --------  ---------- ---------- ---------- ---------- ----------
total        4      0.00       0.05          0          2          0          1

Misses in library cache during parse: 1
Optimizer mode: ALL_ROWS
Parsing user id: 61
```

```
Number of plan statistics captured: 1

Rows (1st) Rows (avg) Rows (max)  Row Source Operation
---------- ---------- ----------  ------------------------------------------
         1          1          1  TABLE ACCESS BY INDEX ROWID EMPLOYEES
         1          1          1    INDEX UNIQUE SCAN EMP_EMP_ID_PK


Elapsed times include waiting on following events:
  Event waited on                            Times    Max. Wait  Total Waited
  ------------------------------------------ Waited   ---------  ------------
  SQL*Net message to client                      2       0.00          0.00
  gc current block congested                     1       0.00          0.00
  gc current block 2-way                         1       0.00          0.00
  SQL*Net message from client                    2       9.51          9.51
```

The wait events in the tkprof output show global cache current blocks were needed. Since the raw trace file will contain additional information, we can examine the portion of the raw trace file pertaining to these two events.

```
WAIT #140457422331544: nam='gc current block congested' ela= 4091 p1=5
p2=179 p3=1 obj#=80224 tim=1405697028587410
WAIT #140457422331544: nam='gc current block 2-way' ela= 1216 p1=5 p2=167
p3=1 obj#=80222 tim=1405697028588843
```

The obj# value is the object identifier of the block involved in the wait event. We can verify the objects affected by these wait events from the *dba_objects* view.

```
SQL> select
  2      owner,
  3      object_name
  4  from
  5      dba_objects
  6  where
  7      object_id=80224;

OWNER                           OBJECT_NAME
------------------------------  ------------------------------
HR                              EMP_EMP_ID_PK

SQL> select
  2      owner,
  3      object_name
  4  from
  5      dba_objects
  6  where
  7      object_id=80222;

OWNER                           OBJECT_NAME
------------------------------  ------------------------------
HR                              EMPLOYEES
```

According to the Explain Plan for this query in the tkprof output, the index was used to access the table and these wait events prove that the index was used. The index was used first and then the table was accessed. The P1 and P2 values for these events point to the file id and block number respectively. A quick check of the *dba_extents* view further proves that the index and table were accessed. The first wait event had values P1=5 and P2=179. The second wait event had values P1=5 and P2=167.

```
SQL> select
  2      owner,
  3      segment_name
  4  from
  5      dba_extents
  6  where
  7      file_id=5
  8      and
  9      179 between block_id and block_id+blocks-1;

OWNER                            SEGMENT_NAME
-------------------------------- --------------------------------
HR                               EMP_EMP_ID_PK

SQL> select
  2      owner,
  3      segment_name
  4  from
  5      dba_extents
  6  where
  7      file_id=5
  8      and
  9      167 between block_id and block_id+blocks-1;

OWNER                            SEGMENT_NAME
-------------------------------- --------------------------------
HR                               EMPLOYEES
```

This example illustrates how a *gc current read* performs. Instead of reading the index and table blocks from disk, the gc current wait events prove that Cache Fusion assisted us. There are a number of events related to global cache current reads.

```
SQL> select
  2      name
  3  from
  4      v$event_name
  5  where
  6      name like 'gc current%'
  7  order by
  8      name;

NAME
----------------------------------------------------------------
gc current block 2-way
gc current block 3-way
gc current block busy
gc current block congested
```

```
gc current block lost
gc current block unknown
gc current cancel
gc current grant 2-way
gc current grant busy
gc current grant congested
gc current grant unknown
gc current multi block request
gc current request
gc current retry
gc current split
```

Throughout the course of this book, many of these events will be discussed. What is important to take away from this section is the understanding of what a current read is from the global cache.

RAC Consistent Reads Tracing

Enterprise database engines ensure that transactions are ACID compliant: Atomic, Consistent, Isolated, and Durable. Each database vendor's product handles the ACID properties differently. Oracle databases implement transaction control with a central premise that "writers never block readers". The "I" in ACID needs to ensure that each transaction appears as an isolated event in the system. The transaction moves the data from one consistent state to another as if the transactions occurred serially when in fact the transactions are executing concurrently.

Oracle's method of implementing transaction control is one of its greatest strengths and without it, Oracle RAC would not scale very well. At the heart of making sure that writers do not block readers is Oracle's *consistent read* mechanism. For example, assume that a transaction starts and modifies a row of data. The transaction has not yet committed when another session needs to read that same row of data. Some database vendor products will block the read of the row until the first session commits its transaction, but Oracle takes a different approach. Instead, Oracle provides the user a *read consistent image* of how the row looked before the other transaction began. In plain English, the session reading the row sees the data as if the uncommitted transaction has never taken place. The concept of a consistent read applies to both single-instance databases and Oracle RAC databases.

Oracle relies heavily on the information in the Undo tablespace to create read consistent images. When a transaction modifies a row, the data block containing the row will be changed in the Buffer Cache and information to roll back the change is written to the Undo tablespace. Whenever a different session reads the same row of data, Oracle will automatically detect that the block is "dirty" and that it contains uncommitted data. Oracle will then create a copy of this block and rollback the transaction just in that copy. The session performing the read now uses the copy of the block with the rolled back change. The session initiating the change has one version of the block. The session that is reading the data after the change started will use another version of the block. In Oracle RAC databases, a difference from single-instance databases is that the consistent read image may need to be transmitted across the Cluster Interconnect. Another difference is that each instance has their own Undo tablespace but all instances can read from that tablespace.

We can illustrate consistent reads similar to the section above on current reads. To demonstrate, a transaction is started in the first instance.

```
SQL> select
  2      instance_name
  3   from
  4      v$instance;

INSTANCE_NAME
----------------
orcl1

SQL> update
  2      hr.employees
  3   set
  4      commission_pct=.15
  5   where
  6      employee_id=200;

1 row updated.
```

Note that the transaction has not yet committed or rolled back. A second session queries this same row.

```
SQL> select
  2      instance_name
  3   from
  4      v$instance;

INSTANCE_NAME
----------------
orcl2

SQL> @trace_my_session.sql

PL/SQL procedure successfully completed.

SQL> select
  2      nvl(commission_pct,0)
  3   from
  4      hr.employees
  5   where
  6      employee_id=200;

NVL(COMMISSION_PCT,0)
---------------------
                    0
```

In the second instance, we do not see the change initiated by the first session. A trace was started in the session and the trace file is run through tkprof to produce a more readable report as seen below.

```
****************************************************************************

select
    nvl(commission_pct,0)
from
    hr.employees
where
    employee_id=200

call     count      cpu    elapsed       disk      query    current       rows
------- ------  ------  ---------- ---------- ---------- ---------- ----------
Parse        1     0.00        0.01          0          0          0          0
Execute      1     0.00        0.00          0          0          0          0
Fetch        2     0.00        0.02          2          2          0          1
------- ------  ------  ---------- ---------- ---------- ---------- ----------
total        4     0.00        0.04          2          2          0          1

Misses in library cache during parse: 1
Optimizer mode: ALL_ROWS
Parsing user id: 61
Number of plan statistics captured: 1

Rows (1st) Rows (avg) Rows (max)  Row Source Operation
---------- ---------- ----------  ---------------------------------------------------
         1          1          1  TABLE ACCESS BY INDEX ROWID EMPLOYEES
         1          1          1  INDEX UNIQUE SCAN EMP_EMP_ID_PK


Elapsed times include waiting on following events:
  Event waited on                                 Times   Max. Wait  Total Waited
  ------------------------------------------      Waited  ---------- ------------
  SQL*Net message to client                            2        0.00         0.00
  gc cr multi block request                            1        0.00         0.00
  SQL*Net message from client                          1        0.00         0.00
```

The output above shows the wait event named *gc cr multi block request* in the tkprof output from the session's trace file. All global cache transfer wait events involving consistent reads start with "gc cr"

We can confirm, as we did in the preceding section, that the wait event is indeed for the table in question. The wait event is found in the raw trace file so that the object number can be determined.

```
WAIT #139943706210584: nam='gc cr multi block request' ela= 4924 file#=5
block#=163 class#=1 obj#=80222 tim=1405711132002055
```

Verification is needed to ensure that the object mentioned is the correct table.

```
SQL> select
  2      owner,
  3      object_name
  4  from
  5      dba_objects
  6  where
  7      object_id=80222;

OWNER                           OBJECT_NAME
------------------------------  ------------------------------
HR                              EMPLOYEES
```

Just like the "gc current" wait events, there are multiple types of global cache consistent read events.

```
SQL> select
  2      name
  3  from
  4      v$event_name
  5  where
  6      name like 'gc cr%'
  7  order by
  8      name;

NAME
----------------------------------------------------------------
gc cr block 2-way
gc cr block 3-way
gc cr block busy
gc cr block congested
gc cr block lost
gc cr block unknown
gc cr cancel
gc cr disk read
gc cr disk request
gc cr failure
gc cr grant 2-way
gc cr grant busy
gc cr grant congested
gc cr grant unknown
gc cr multi block request
gc cr request
```

Notice how similar the wait event names are to the ones for *gc current* events. This should not be a surprise as a transaction may experience similar reasons for the wait no matter if they are waiting for a current or a consistent read block.

RAC 2-way and 3-way Global Cache Fusion Transfers

Up to three RAC instances can be involved in the global cache transfer of a block.

- One instance must be requesting the block. If the no other instance has a copy of the block, the instance requesting the block reads the block from disk and no global cache transfer is performed.
- If another instance has the master copy of the block, a copy is transferred across the private network to the requesting instance.
- A third instance may serve as the resource master for the block. It is possible that the resource master is not the instance requesting the block or the one holding the master copy of the block.

If a transaction needs to modify the contents of a block and the transaction is running on the instance that has the master copy of the block and it is also the resource master for the block, then no global cache transfer needs to take place. If a transaction needs a copy of a block and the master copy is on the instance that also has the block's resource master, then Oracle only needs to transfer the master copy. Only two instances are involved in this scenario. In this case, there are two actions, a call to the resource master and the transfer of the block. As such, these wait events are called 2-way events. We have already seen examples with the *gc current block 2-way* and *gc cr block 2-way* wait events.

When three instances are involved in the global cache transfer, the wait events are 3-way event, i.e. *gc current block 3-way* and *gc cr block 3-way*. The 3-way events often have a request to the master copy's instance, a request to the resource master's instance, and the transfer of the block. With the extra work, it shouldn't be any surprise that 3-way events require more work than 2-way events, but this additional time may be negligible.

If the clustered database only has two instances, then 3-way wait events will not be seen. The global cache transfers will be 2-way events or there will be no global cache transfer need as everything is in one instance. If the clustered database has three instances, we can see both 2-way and 3-way events. If the clustered database has more than three instances, there will still be only 2-way or 3-way events, as four or more instances will not participate in the global cache transfer. A higher number of total instances will increase the chances of seeing 3-way events as the odds of the resource master and master copy being on different instances can increase.

There are not too many 2-way events in RAC, and this chapter has already shown half of them. The complete list of 2-way RAC events is below.

```
SQL> select
  2      name
  3  from
  4      v$event_name
  5  where
  6      name like '%2-way%'
  7  order by
  8      name;

NAME
------------------------------------------------------------------
gc cr block 2-way
gc cr grant 2-way
gc current block 2-way
gc current grant 2-way
```

The events with 'grant' in their name will be discussed in the next section. However, the grant events are only 2-way events. There are no equivalent 3-way grant events.

```
SQL> select
  2      name
  3  from
  4      v$event_name
  5  where
  6      name like '%3-way%'
  7  order by
  8      name;

NAME
------------------------------------------------------------------
gc cr block 3-way
gc current block 3-way
```

The *gv$instance_cache_transfer* view contains metrics on 2-way and 3-way global cache transfers. This view calls the transfers "hops". To see the metrics for 2-way consistent read block transfers a query similar to the following can be used.

```
SQL> select
  2      inst_id,
  3      instance,
  4      class,
  5      cr_2hop,
  6      cr_2hop_time
  7  from
  8      gv$instance_cache_transfer
  9  where
 10      instance in (select
 11                      inst_id
 12                   from
 13                      gv$instance)
 14      and
 15      inst_id <> instance;

INST_ID   INSTANCE CLASS                   CR_2HOP    CR_2HOP_TIME
--------- ---------- -------------------- ---------- -------------
```

```
   1             2 data block         528      312851
   1             2 undo header         27       12614
   1             2 undo block           0           0
   2             1 data block         837      459306
   2             1 undo block           0           0
   2             1 undo header         32       13377
```

Some of the output was removed from the above example for brevity. The results form this query show the global cache transfers from instance 1 to instance 2 and vice versa. In this particular example, we can see exactly how many 2-way transfers were performed and how much time those transfers took. The view contains similar columns for 3-way transfers as well as current block transfers, both 2-way and 3-way. The Oracle documentation refers to the 2-way and 3-way events as *block-oriented* wait events.

Oracle RAC Global Resource Manager Grants

In the cache coherency section of this chapter, it was mentioned that the GCS manages resources and everything in Oracle RAC is a considered a resource. RAC resources include, but are not limited to data blocks. Before a resource can be modified a lock must be obtained. In Oracle RAC, the Global Resource Manager (GRM) is responsible for managing locks of resources across the cluster.

The GRM maintains a list of locks that are currently granted to sessions in the instances. This list is called the *grant queue*. Conversely, the *convert queue* is the list of processes waiting for the resource. Remember that each resource has a resource master, which could be on any of the instances. If a session needs a lock and the resource master is in another instance, the session requesting the lock must wait for cross instance communication to complete for the global cache grant operation. There are only two instances involved in this activity, the instance requesting the lock and the instance that serves as the resource master. So if a session needs a lock, (shared or exclusive), on a consistent read image, the session will experience the wait event named *gc cr grant 2-way*. A complete list of global cache grant wait events can be seen below.

```
SQL> select
  2      name
  3  from
  4      v$event_name
  5  where
  6      name like 'gc%grant%'
  7  order by
  8      name;

NAME
```

```
----------------------------------------------------------------
gc cr grant 2-way
gc cr grant busy
gc cr grant congested
gc cr grant ka
gc cr grant unknown
gc current grant 2-way
gc current grant busy
gc current grant congested
gc current grant ka
gc current grant unknown
```

The current grant wait events are similar to the consistent read grant events. Since only two instances will participate in the grant wait event, there is no 3-way grant wait event. The Oracle documentation refers to the grant events as *message-oriented* wait events.

RAC Dynamic Resource Manager (DRM)

The *gc cr grant 2-way* and *gc current grant 2-way* wait events occur when locks need to be obtained in one instance but the resource master is in another instance. The GRD keeps track of the number of times a lock was requested from an instance other than where the resource master is located.

If the requests frequently come from the same instance, *Dynamic Resource Mastering* (DRM) will relocate the resource master to the instance dominating the requests.

By re-mastering the resource to another instance, the number of *gc cr grant 2-way* and *gc current grant 2-way* wait events are reduced.

The end users will not have to wait for cross-instance messaging to complete to be able to obtain the lock. GRD calls this technique *resource affinity* where a resource and its master have a strong attraction to one instance in the cluster. Resource affinity is often seen in Oracle RAC deployments where application partitioning is performed, a topic discussed in the next chapter. The *gv$gcspfmaster_info* view shows which objects have been the subjects of DRM:

```
SQL> select
  2     data_object_id,
  3     gc_mastering_policy,
  4     current_master+1 as current_mast_inst,
  5     remaster_cnt
  6  from
  7     gv$gcspfmaster_info;

DATA_OBJECT_ID GC_MASTERIN CURRENT_MAST_INST REMASTER_CNT
```

```
              57 Affinity               1            1
              58 Affinity               2            1
              59 Affinity               3            1
```

The *data_object_id* column can be joined to *dba_objects.object_id* to know which database object is involved.

It should be noted that the *current_master* and *previous_master* columns are one number off the instance identifier as they start counting from zero. The example query above adds one to obtain the instance id. Also, these current and previous master columns may show a value of 32767. If *current_master* is 32767, then the object was subject to DRM but no longer is. If *previous_master* is 32767, then the object was not subject to DRM, but now is.

RAC Session Blockers

If a session is holding on to locks too long, other sessions may have to wait excessively, and the end user waiting on the lock will see that their performance is slow. It is often helpful to understand how GES locks in Oracle RAC can be viewed to determine the sessions that are blocked and their blockers.

To start, it is interesting to note if a resource is on the grant queue and which instance is the resource master. The *gv$ges_resource* view can provide this information. Resource names have the format "[0xblock_id][0xfile_id],BL" with BL meaning the Block Lock or sometimes called the Buffer Lock. The block id and file_id are in hexadecimal format. The query below shows a table that resides in file 5 from blocks 160 to 167.

```
SQL> select
  2     file_id,
  3     block_id as start_block,
  4     block_id+blocks-1 as end_block
  5  from
  6     dba_extents
  7  where
  8     owner='HR'
  9     and
 10     segment_name='EMPLOYEES'
 11  order by
 12     file_id,
 13     block_id;

   FILE_ID START_BLOCK END_BLOCK
---------- ----------- ----------
         5         160        167
```

The file and block numbers need to be converted to hexadecimal. File 5 is 0x5. Block 160 is 0xA0 and block 167 is 0xA7. The resource name for the first block would be "[0xA0][0x5],BL" and we can look in *gv$ges_resource* for more information on any of the resources for this table similar to the following query.

```
SQL> select
  2       resource_name,
  3       on_grant_q,
  4       master_node+1 as master_inst
  5   from
  6       gv$ges_resource
  7   where
  8       resource_name like '[0xA%][0x5],BL%';

RESOURCE_NAME                        ON_GRANT_Q MASTER_INST
------------------------------------ ---------- -----------
[0xA2][0x5],[BL][ext 0x0,0x                   1           2
```

The output above shows that one of the blocks is on the grant queue. The resource master is instance 2 of the clustered database. Note that the *master_node* column has a value of zero for instance id 1 so the query above adds one to obtain the instance identifier.

Now that a resource name can be determined, it can be used in the *gv$ges_blocking_enqueue* view to see blockers and those that are blocked.

🖫 ges_blockers.sql

```
SQL> select
  2       inst_id,
  3       pid,
  4       resource_name1 as resource_name,
  5       blocker,
  6       blocked,
  7       owner_node
  8   from
  9       gv$ges_blocking_enqueue
 10   order by
 11       resource_name;

INST_ID     PID RESOURCE_NAME                       BLOCKER   BLOCKED OWNER_NODE
-------- ------- ----------------------------------- ------- --------- ----------
       2   30421 [0xA7][0x5],[RS][ext 0x0,0x0]             1         0          1
       1   29102 [0xA7][0x5],[RS][ext 0x0,0x0]             0         1          0
       2   14494 [0x2000e][0x65a],[TX][ext 0x2,            0         1          1
       1   29086 [0x2000e][0x65a],[TX][ext 0x2,            1         0          0
```

The first two lines show the resource being blocked on instance 1 from a session on instance 2. Note the resource name conforms to the *hr.employees* table as shown earlier in this section. The blocker and blocked columns identify that instance 2 has the lock and is blocking the session on instance 1.

Oracle RAC Performance Tuning

The last two lines show a transaction (TX) lock that is probably familiar to most readers of this book. What is interesting are the participants involved with the TX lock. Joining *gv$ges_blocking_enqueue* to *gv$process* and *gv$session* gives us insight.

ges_blocking_programs.sql

```
SQL> select
  2      s.inst_id,
  3      p.spid,
  4      s.program
  5  from
  6      gv$session s
  7  join
  8      gv$process p
  9      on s.inst_id=p.inst_id
 10          and
 11          s.paddr=p.addr
 12  join
 13      gv$ges_blocking_enqueue e
 14      on p.inst_id=e.inst_id
 15          and
 16          p.spid=e.pid;

  INST_ID SPID  PROGRAM
--------- ----- ------------------------------------------------
        1 29102 oracle@host01 (CKPT)
        1 29086 oracle@host01 (LMD0)
        2 30421 oracle@host02 (CKPT)
        2 14494 sqlplus@host02 (TNS V1-V3)
```

Comparing the *spid* column of this output to the *pid* column of the previous output, it is clear that the checkpoint process on each instance holds the two RS resource locks. The holder of the TX lock (pid 29086) is the Lock Manager Daemon process (LMD). The waiter of the TX (pid 14494) is the SQL*Plus session. From the GES perspective, the LMD process holds the lock on the resource, not a user's session in the instance. Keep in mind that the *gv$ges_blocking_enqueue* view is showing resource locks, not transactional locks in the Oracle database engine.

The TX resource locks are named "[0x2000e][0x65a],[TX]" with the first parameter being hexadecimal 2000E. Converting to decimal, this becomes number 131086. This value can be used to query the *id1* column of the *gv$lock* view for TX locks.

```
SQL> select
  2      inst_id,
  3      sid,
  4      type,
  5      lmode,
  6      request
  7  from
  8      gv$lock
  9  where
 10      id1=131086;
```

```
INST_ID     SID TY     LMODE     REQUEST
--------  ---------- --  ---------- ----------
       1      31 TX         6          0
       2      33 TX         0          6
```

The query above is similar to one that readers may already be familiar with. The TX locks are identified in the instance, one has a lock mode of 6 and the other is waiting for the exclusive lock to be released so that it can obtain the same lock mode. The next queries verify that the TX locks are held by SQL*Plus sessions.

```
SQL> select
  2      program
  3  from
  4      gv$session
  5  where
  6      inst_id=1
  7      and
  8      sid=31;

PROGRAM
--------------------------------------------------
sqlplus@host01 (TNS V1-V3)

SQL> select
  2      program
  3  from
  4      gv$session
  5  where
  6      inst_id=2
  7      and
  8      sid=33;

PROGRAM
--------------------------------------------------
sqlplus@host02 (TNS V1-V3)
```

As was expected, both sessions participating in the output from *gv$lock* are the SQL*Plus sessions running this test.

RAC Block Busy Events

It is common to see the *gc cr block busy* and *gc current block busy* wait events in Oracle RAC systems. These events occur when a consistent read or current block is needed from another instance yet it is taking some time to receive that block, and the sending of the block has been delayed by the other instance. These events are often accompanied with *gc cr block 2-way/3-way* and *gc current block 2-way/3-way* wait event. A request is made to another instance for a data block. That instance is not able to send the block right now so the block busy event is raised. When the other instance is able to send the block, the wait event becomes a 2-way or 3-way event while the block is being transferred on the private network.

Many times, these events are due to slow I/O writing redo changes to the online redo logs in the remote instance. These events can also be raised when there is a high degree of write/write activity for the blocks involved in the event. Consider an example of a 3-node Oracle RAC database that has simultaneous requests to modify the same block in all three instances.

The block is locked on instance 1 and instance 1 is waiting to write redo to the online redo logs. Instances 2 and 3 are waiting on the block busy wait event. Instance 2 now has its turn to make the change and write the change vectors to the online redo log. Instance 3 is still waiting on the block busy wait event. Instance 3 finally gets its chance to obtain the block and can work on making its change.

There are only two block busy wait events, both related to global cache transfers of current or consistent read blocks.

```
SQL> select
  2     name
  3  from
  4     v$event_name
  5  where
  6     name like 'gc%block busy%'
  7  order by
  8     name;

NAME
------------------------------------------------------------
gc cr block busy
gc current block busy
```

The Oracle documentation calls these two waits *contention oriented* events. Like all of the gc wait events in this chapter, the P1 and P2 values will point to the file and block involved, respectively. If there are a few "hot" blocks causing this contention, it may be worthwhile to limit write access to those blocks to as few instances as possible. If the application is seeing a high occurrence of these events, it is an application that may not scale well in Oracle RAC as will be discussed in the next chapter.

Summary

This chapter started off with a history of Cache Fusion. Knowing its history helps us understand why Cache Fusion works as well as it does today. A high level overview was provided to understand the basics of Cache Fusion.

We now know that Cache Fusion relies heavily on block transfers across the private network. There are current and consistent read blocks that need to be transferred, often times in 2-way or 3-way communications.

Everything in Oracle RAC is a resource and blocks are no different. This chapter illustrated how grants are made at the resource level. One instance becomes the resource master. Dynamic Resource Mastering may relocate the resource master to become more efficient.

This chapter discussed block transfers, grants, block busy events and other Cache Fusion operations. One could definitely expand on these topics in more detail as the inner workings of Oracle RAC and Cache Fusion is very complicated. The minutia of Cache Fusion operations is very interesting but can often bog down the learning process by overwhelming the reader with too many details. A conscious decision was made to provide sufficient information to understand the remainder of the book's material without offering too much information. The reader is encouraged to seek out other sources after completing this book.

Chapter 1 discussed a tuning methodology that stated that tuning begins at the application layer before proceeding to the database and finally the server. With that in mind, the next chapter discusses topics for tuning applications that run on Oracle RAC systems.

RAC Application Tuning

As we stated in Chapter 1, an application that is not well tuned and scalable for a single-instance Oracle database will not necessarily magically run well just because an Oracle RAC database runs on a cluster and gives the application more resources. A poorly tuned application may actually perform worse on Oracle RAC. If the poorly tuned application should perform well on Oracle RAC, it may not scale well over the long term. It is so important that it must be stated again; you must tune an application well before deploying them on Oracle RAC. This includes making sure SQL statements are using efficient execution plans, and that queries can benefit from proper indexes. The application should also be able to leverage partitioning or Materialized Views to reduce processing time. These are just a few examples of application tuning that apply to applications even if RAC is not used. This chapter helps tune applications for RAC-specific issues.

SQL Trace and RAC

Armed with Oracle's SQL Trace facility, (also called the 10046 trace), the database administrator can start a trace of a user's session and obtain a vast amount of information on the SQL statements executed by that session. This book assumes that most readers of this book already have a rudimentary understanding of SQL Trace. As such, this book will be covering SQL Trace as it pertains to Oracle RAC databases.

Even with Oracle RAC databases, a trace is started at the session level. First, we need to identify the *sid* and *serial#* of the session. We also need to know which instance the session is connected to.

```
SQL> select
  2      instance_number,
  3      instance_name
  4  from
  5      v$instance;

INSTANCE_NUMBER INSTANCE_NAME
--------------- ----------------
              2 orcl2
```

```
SQL> select
  2      inst_id,
  3      sid,
  4      serial#
  5  from
  6      gv$session
  7  where
  8      username='SCOTT';

  INST_ID        SID     SERIAL#
---------- ---------- ----------
         1         42        219
```

The first query shows that the current session is connected to the second instance, *orcl2*. We need to identify a session for the user SCOTT but do not know to which instance the user is connected. A query of the *gv$session* view can search to find all sessions across all instances. The example above gives us the instance id, session identifier, and serial number of the session.

Just like a single-instance database, the *dbms_monitor* supplied package is used to start a trace in a session. The only difference with Oracle RAC is that calls to *dbms_monitor* must be executed in the instance of the session that needs to be traced. In the example above, the current session was connected to instance *orcl2* but the session to be traced is in *orcl1*. We need to connect to *orcl1* to start the trace, similar to the following.

```
SQL> connect system@orcl1
Enter password:
Connected.

SQL> begin
  2      dbms_monitor.session_trace_enable(42,219);
  3  end;
  4  /

PL/SQL procedure successfully completed.
```

To end the trace, the *disable* procedure of *dbms_monitor* is used.

```
SQL> begin
  2      dbms_monitor.session_trace_disable(42,219);
  3  end;
  4  /

PL/SQL procedure successfully completed.
```

Another item to remember is that the trace file will be created on the node of the traced session's instance. The trace file will be found in the *diag/rdbms/db_name/instance_name/*trace subdirectory of the *diagnostic_dest* initialization parameter. For single instance databases, the instance name will equal the database name. For Oracle RAC databases, the instance name will be the database name appended with the instance ID. Your life can be made easier if the diagnostic destination is on shared storage accessible by all instances. This way, all trace files will be on the same disk, no matter which RAC instance generated the file.

The *dbms_monitor* supplied package additionally provides the ability to start SQL traces for a specific service with the *serv_mod_act_trace_enable* procedure.

```
SQL> begin
  2     dbms_monitor.serv_mod_act_trace_enable('hr_svc');
  3  end;
  4  /

PL/SQL procedure successfully completed.
```

With the command above, all connections to the *hr_svc* service will automatically be traced. Tracing can be turned off for the service with the *serv_mod_act_trace_disable* procedure:

```
SQL> begin
  2     dbms_monitor.serv_mod_act_trace_disable('hr_svc');
  3  end;
  4  /

PL/SQL procedure successfully completed.
```

The *serv_mod_act_trace_enable* procedure has additional parameters for the module name, action name, and instance name. The module and action names are set by the *dbms_application_info* supplied package if the application is coded to set the module and action names. Tracing can be restricted to a specific RAC instance by specifying that instance name as a parameter. Any combination of these parameters can be used to refine the sessions to be traced. For example, all connections using a specific service on a specific instance can be traced, leaving sessions using that service on another instance untraced. Services are discussed in more detail later on in this chapter.

When tracing a service, the end result will most likely have multiple trace files being generated. Most readers should be familiar with using the *tkprof* utility to turn a raw trace file into a more readable format. One of the problems with *tkprof* is that it will take one trace file as input and generate one output file. This limitation is perfectly acceptable when dealing with only one trace file but multiple trace files would need numerous runs of the *tkprof* utility. Furthermore, the results from all of those *tkprof* output files may have to be manually combined. Handling multiple trace files is where the *trcsess* utility can be used. An example can illustrate how to use the *trcsess* utility to combine multiple trace files. In one session, the following SQL statements are executed.

```
alter session set sql_trace=true;

select
   first_name,
   last_name
from
   hr.employees
where
   employee_id=100;

select
   department_id,
   department_name,
   manager_id
from
   hr.departments;

select
   first_name,
   last_name
from
   hr.employees
where
   employee_id=200;
```

In another session, additional SQL statements are executed.

```
alter session set sql_trace=true;

select
   first_name,
   last_name
from
   hr.employees
where
   employee_id=100;

select
   city,
   state_province,
   country_id
from
   locations
where
   location_id=1700;
```

Notice that each session queried for the same employee but the rest of the SQL statements were different. The two resulting trace files will be combined into one file. The SQL statements were executed in SQL*Plus. As such, the trace file contains similar lines near the top.

```
*** 2014-07-22 23:40:05.205
*** SESSION ID:(31.459) 2014-07-22 23:40:05.205
```

```
*** CLIENT ID:() 2014-07-22 23:40:05.205
*** SERVICE NAME:(SYS$USERS) 2014-07-22 23:40:05.205
*** MODULE NAME:(SQL*Plus) 2014-07-22 23:40:05.205
*** ACTION NAME:() 2014-07-22 23:40:05.205
```

SQL*Plus automatically uses the *dbms_application_info* package to set the module name. Knowing this, we can instruct *trcsess* to look for any trace files that were generated with the SQL*Plus module.

```
trcsess output=trcsess.out module="SQL*Plus"
```

The *trcsess* utility will comb through the current directory. If there is a trace file with this defined module, *trcsess* will add its contents to the output file. Now that the trace files have been combined into a single file, the *tkprof* utility can be invoked to make the combined trace file more readable.

```
tkprof trcsess.out tkprof.out aggregate=yes
```

Examining the *tkprof* output file shows all of the SQL statements are executed once except for the one query that was executed twice.

```
********************************************************************************
select
    first_name,
    last_name
from
    hr.employees
where
    employee_id=100
```

call	count	cpu	elapsed	disk	query	current	rows
Parse	2	0.01	0.04	0	0	0	0
Execute	2	0.00	0.00	0	0	0	0
Fetch	4	0.00	0.00	1	4	0	2
total	8	0.01	0.04	1	4	0	2

The execute count is 2 as expected.

The trcsess utility has other useful parameters. If the *dbms_application_info* supplied package is used to define the module or action, the *trcsess* utility can combine trace files with those parameters. The *trcsess* utility can also be given a specific service name, a very common way to use *trcsess* in Oracle RAC traces. We will discuss services in more detail later in this chapter. Note that the *trcsess* parameters accepts the asterisk wildcard symbol. The following is a list of parameters for the trcsess utility.

```
output=<output file name >
session=<session ID >
clientid=<clientid>
```

```
service=<service name>
action=<action name>
module=<module name>
<trace file names>
```

As was discussed earlier in this section, the *dbms_monitor.serv_mod_act_trace_enable* procedure is used to start traces for sessions based on any combination of service, action, and/or module. Once those trace files have been generated, the database administrator will most likely want to use the *trcsess* utility to aggregate the trace files into one large output file by executing one simple, easy command.

With Oracle RAC, each instance maintains its own diagnostic dump destination for its trace files. There is no requirement to have the diagnostic dump destination on shared storage. That being said, the database administrator's life will be easier if all trace files are available on all nodes otherwise they will end up moving trace files generated on one node to another node to be able to combine the files together. Remember, the *trcsess* utility will not cross nodes in the cluster.

Sequence Cache and RAC

The sequence database object needs special attention for applications running on Oracle RAC. It is common for an Oracle sequence to be a point of contention when the application is deployed on Oracle RAC. Most applications create a sequence similar to the following example.

```
SQL> create sequence
  2      emp_pk_id_seq
  3      start with 1000
  4      increment by 1
  5      nocache;

Sequence created.
```

It has become a standard practice for many sequences to have the *nocache* directive. The main reason for specifying *nocache* is so that the next sequence value is not lost when the instance abnormally terminates. If both *cache* and *nocache* are omitted, the default is to cache 20 sequence values in memory.

In the next example, a sequence is created with the default cache value and the first two values are selected.

```
SQL> create sequence
  2      cache_example_sequence
  3      start with 1
  4      increment by 1;
```

```
Sequence created.

SQL> select
  2       cache_example_sequence.nextval
  3  from
  4      dual;

   NEXTVAL
----------
         1

SQL> select
  2       cache_example_sequence.nextval
  3  from
  4      dual;

   NEXTVAL
----------
         2
```

The database is abnormally terminated and after startup, the next value of the sequence is selected.

```
SQL> select
  2       cache_example_sequence.nextval
  3  from
  4      dual;

   NEXTVAL
----------
        21
```

It's important to note that a gap now exists in the values generated by this sequence. The sequence has generated values 1, 2, and 21. The first twenty values were in the cache but only the first two were actually used. When the instance abnormally terminated, sequence values 3 through 20 were lost.

For sequences that are used to generate primary key values, the gap in ID values is inconsequential, as most end users won't notice the gap. Sequence gaps are most noticeable for entities like invoices or check numbers. Accountants determine if a check has yet to clear the bank by gaps in the check number sequence. Unless you are dealing with accountants, almost every other occurrence of missing numbers in a sequence is irrelevant. Yet humans tend to like order and gaps in the numbers mean disorder, chaos. It often takes training to educate users that gaps in sequences are truly meaningless. It is easier for the database designer to use *nocache* so that there will be no missing sequence values than it is to take the time to teach users that sequence gaps are perfectly acceptable. There are other reasons for ensuring no gaps in the sequence numbers, but most are for convenience not factual business requirements.

Over time, the database designer simply started using *nocache* without any second thoughts. For many, *nocache* is now a simple habit.

The problem with *nocache* sequences in Oracle RAC lies with the sequence being a global database object. Any node in the cluster can generate the next value. In a database where the sequence is used frequently by many sessions, the sequence can become a bottleneck. While a session is generating the sequence's next value, other sessions must wait, and coordinate through the Cluster Interconnect for access to the resource. In a single-instance database, all of this coordination is done locally, entirely in memory. In an Oracle RAC database, processes on different nodes need to talk to each other through the private network, which can really slow the process down.

To show the effect of *nocache* on sequences in Oracle RAC, we will have two sessions, each of which will select from the same sequence in a loop, over and over again. The sequence is altered to use *nocache*.

```
SQL> alter sequence
  2      cache_example_sequence
  3      nocache;

Sequence altered.
```

Next, an anonymous PL/SQL block is executed concurrently in two sessions, one session attached to instance *orcl1* and the other session attached to instance *orcl2*.

```
SQL> set timing on
SQL> declare
  2      curr_val number;
  3      cnt   number;
  4  begin
  5      cnt := 0;
  6      while cnt <= 100000
  7      loop
  8        select cache_example_sequence.nextval
  9          into curr_val
 10        from
 11          dual;
 12        cnt := cnt + 1;
 13      end loop;
 14  end;
 15  /

PL/SQL procedure successfully completed.

Elapsed: 00:19:59.61
```

The elapsed runtime of 19:59.61 is from the session on the *orcl1* instance. The code executed on the *orcl2* instance completed in 20:43.22. Each session required approximately 20 minutes to gather 100,000 sequence values when run concurrently.

Next, the sequence is modified to cache 20 values. The instances are bounced to eliminate any memory caching in the instances from skewing the results.

```
SQL> alter sequence
  2      cache_example_sequence
  3      cache 20;

Sequence altered.
```

The same anonymous PL/SQL block is executed concurrently in both instances.

```
SQL> set timing on
SQL> declare
  2      curr_val number;
  3      cnt   number;
  4  begin
  5      cnt := 0;
  6      while cnt <= 100000
  7      loop
  8          select cache_example_sequence.nextval
  9              into curr_val
 10          from
 11              dual;
 12          cnt := cnt + 1;
 13      end loop;
 14  end;
 15  /

PL/SQL procedure successfully completed.

Elapsed: 00:00:41.19
```

The first session completed in 00:41.19 and the second session completed in 00:49.18. Just by making a simple, small change in the sequence's cache value (setting "cache 20"), the runtime of this sample program decreased from 20 minutes to less than 1 minute!

To further illustrate the effect of the sequence's cache value, the sequence will be modified with larger cache sizes and the same PL/SQL block will be executed concurrently in two instances. When the cache value was increased to 100, the PL/SQL block completed in 00:10.98 for the first session and 00:11.57 for the second session, now around 10 seconds. When the sequence's cache value was increased to 1000, the PL/SQL block's run times were 00:01.06 and 00:02.62, each less than 3 seconds. The following table summarizes the results.

Cache Value	Node 1 Session Runtime	Node 2 Session Runtime
None	19:59.61	20:43.22
20	00:41.19	00:49.18
100	00:10.98	00:11.57
1000	00:01.06	00:02.62

Table 3.1 Sequence Runtimes With Caching

It should be obvious from these results the effect the sequence's cache value. These results were obtained on a two-node RAC database running on a laptop, definitely not production hardware. Your results will most likely differ depending on the system's configuration. No matter the resources available to the RAC cluster, this simple test can be used to illustrate the effect of the *cache* values for a sequence.

Some readers may be thinking, "When am I ever going to code a loop that does nothing more than select the sequence's next value?" This is a fair question. The simple example above is only meant to demonstrate sequence contention. This example had only two concurrent sessions running on two Oracle RAC nodes. In practice, there may be more than 100 concurrent sessions on three or four nodes. Sequence contention can certainly exist and can exhibit performance not that different than this simple example.

While a real application would never code selecting the sequence's next value in a loop like this example, other than as an academic exercise, an application would code a statement similar to the following.

```
insert into
   destination_table
select
   my_sequence.next_val,
   column
from
   source_table;
```

In the case of the sample insert statement above, the sequence's next value will be generated for each row of the result set which is not that different from a loop as used in this example. Insert 100,000 rows into a table that gets one column populated from a sequence database object and we have effectively leveraged the sequence similar to our example. Alternatively, there could be a trigger on the destination table that generates the sequence's next value for every row inserted into that table with a similar effect.

Using *nocache* for a sequence in an Oracle RAC database can lead to poor application performance. It is best to set a high cache value. Most sequences will benefit from a cache value of 100 or higher. Obviously, the more contention for this resource, the higher its cache value should be. It is not out of the ordinary to see a cache value of 1,000 for a sequence in an Oracle RAC database. The following query can be used to determine which sequences have *nocache* specified.

```
select
    sequence_owner,
    sequence_name
from
    dba_sequences
where
    cache_size = 0;
```

Any sequences owned by application users should be checked to ensure the cache value would not cause the sequence to be an application bottleneck. Note that we never attempt to change any sequences that are part of the Oracle Data Dictionary.

Examining the wait events for a session can identify contention for sequences objects. Querying *v$session_wait* will show all of the events our session waited on. It is often useful to see the top 5 wait events. The script below shows the top five wait events for one of the sessions involved in the sequence example.

current_session_top5_waits.sql

```
SQL> select
  2      *
  3  from
  4      (select
  2          event,
  3          total_waits,
  4          time_waited
  5      from
  6          v$session_event
  7      where
  8          sid=SYS_CONTEXT('USERENV','SID')
  9      order by
 10          time_waited desc)
 11  where
 12      rownum <= 5;

EVENT                                 TOTAL_WAITS TIME_WAITED
------------------------------------- ----------- -----------
row cache lock                              94154       40306
gc cr block lost                              393       17826
gc current block lost                         371       17462
gc cr block busy                            37397        6731
gc current block 2-way                      93214        5587
```

Four of the top five wait events for this session all start with "gc". The previous chapter reviewed some of these global cache wait events seen above. The remainder of these Cache Fusion waits will be discussed in a later chapter.

The top wait event is the *row cache lock* event. So how does this wait event prove the contention is for a sequence database object? To know for sure, the specific parameter values of the row cache lock wait event need to be examined for that session. While the session was running and experiencing contention, this session's specific wait event was captured.

🖫 current_session_wait.sql

```
SQL> select
  2      event,
  3      p1,
  4      p2,
  5      p3
  6  from
  7      v$session_wait
  8  where
  9      sid=SYS_CONTEXT('USERENV','SID');

EVENT                                 P1          P2          P3
------------------------    ----------  ----------  ----------
row cache lock                        13           0           5
```

In the output above, the session is experiencing the *row cache lock* wait event. Notice the P1 value is 13. Examining the *v$rowcache* view shows the Data Dictionary object type that is involved. For the *row cache lock* wait event, the P1 value links to the *cache#* column of the *v$rowcache* view

```
SQL> select
  2      parameter,
  3      gets,
  4      getmisses
  5  from
  6      v$rowcache
  7  where
  8      cache#=13;

PARAMETER                  GETS   GETMISSES
--------------------  ----------  ----------
dc_sequences               64740       64283
```

The output above shows that the session is experiencing contention for the *dc_sequences* object type. Also notice that the number of *get misses* is very high compared to the number of *gets*. However, the metric shown in this query may have a low *get misses* ratio compared to total *gets* and the application can still have sequence contention. The *v$rowcache* metric shown is for all sequence database objects, even ones that have little or no contention. In the end, the above has shown that our session was experiencing a bottleneck, a wait, on something in the row cache which subsequently confirmed this to be the part of the row cache that deals with sequences.

What has yet to answered is which sequence is involved in the bottleneck. To answer that question, one would have to look at the code being executed for that session. If access to the code is not available, then one can always start a SQL trace in session to determine the sequence involved.

It should be noted that some versions of Oracle RAC that are experiencing contention for sequences may not manifest themselves as the *row cache lock* wait event shown in this chapter. These examples were run on Oracle 11.2.0.4 and Oracle 12.1.0.1 and obtained similar results. Some versions may show the wait event to be *enq: SQ – contention* which is a fancy way of indicating sequence (SQ) enqueues (lock) contention.

Sequence ORDER clause

Worse than not caching values of a sequence in Oracle RAC is using the *order* clause when creating a sequence database object. For the discussion in this section, the example sequence is dropped and recreated with the *order* clause.

```
SQL> drop sequence
  2      cache_example_sequence;

Sequence dropped.

SQL> create sequence
  2      cache_example_sequence
  3      start with 1
  4      increment by 1
  5      order;

Sequence created.
```

Many people have never seen the *order* clause when used in conjunction with a sequence database object. The reason why this clause is rarely used is because the clause only has relevance for Oracle RAC databases, and even then, it is normally a bad idea to use the clause, as will be shown in this section.

The *order* clause guarantees that the sequence's next value is the next one in line, no matter the instance that received the request. To illustrate, assume a sequence defined with *cache=20*. Instance 1 has sequence values 1 through 20 in its cache. Instance 2 has sequence values 21 through 40 in its cache. Normally, concurrent sessions might generate sequence values in this order: 1, 2, 21, 3, 22, 4, 23, and 24. It can easily be determined which values were generated in which instance in this example. Each sequence value is larger than the one that preceded it only in that instance. However, when examined chronologically, the values are not in order.

If the purpose of the sequence is to generate unique values, as is often done for synthetic primary keys, the fact that the values jump around when viewed over time is of little concern. Yet some applications need the sequences to denote time ordering, i.e. a sequence value of 11 occurred at some time prior to the record with the sequence value of 12. In those cases, Oracle RAC applications must use the *order* clause to guarantee the sequence's values are generated in order, no matter which instance the next value was generated. An example of such a sequence is seen next.

```
SQL> create sequence
  2      example_order_seq
  3      start with 1
  4      increment by 1
  5      cache 20
  6      order;

Sequence created.
```

Notice in the example above that the sequence is defined with *cache=20* and *order*. Now let's look at sessions in two instances generating some next set of values from this sequence.

```
SQL> select
  2      instance_name,
  3      example_order_seq.nextval
  4  from
  5      v$instance;

INSTANCE_NAME         NEXTVAL
---------------- ----------
orcl1                      1

SQL> select
  2      instance_name,
  3      example_order_seq.nextval
  4  from
  5      v$instance;

INSTANCE_NAME         NEXTVAL
---------------- ----------
orcl2                      2

SQL> select
  2      instance_name,
  3      example_order_seq.nextval
  4  from
  5  v$instance;

INSTANCE_NAME         NEXTVAL
---------------- ----------
orcl1                      3
```

```
SQL> select
  2      instance_name,
  3      example_order_seq.nextval
  4  from
  5      v$instance;

INSTANCE_NAME        NEXTVAL
---------------- ----------
orcl2                      4
```

Even though the sequence was denoted to cache sequence values and those values were selected from one instance, then the next and so on, the *order* clause ensured each subsequent value would be in numerical order. The *order* clause effectively makes the sequence have a *nocache* setting.

Similar to examining the performance of a sequence in the previous section, the performance of the sequence using the *order* clause can be easily determined. To do this, the sequence is dropped and then recreated.

```
SQL> drop sequence
  2      cache_example_sequence;

Sequence dropped.

SQL> create sequence
  2      cache_example_sequence
  3      start with 1
  4      increment by 1
  5      nocache
  6      order;

Sequence created.
```

Now that the sequence has been created, the same PL/SQL block as before is executed in two sessions connected to the two instances of the RAC cluster.

```
SQL> set timing on
SQL> declare
  2      curr_val number;
  3      cnt   number;
  4  begin
  5      cnt := 0;
  6      while cnt <= 100000
  7      loop
  8          select cache_example_sequence.nextval
  9              into curr_val
 10          from
 11              dual;
 12          cnt := cnt + 1;
 13      end loop;
 14  end;
 15  /
```

```
PL/SQL procedure successfully completed.

Elapsed: 00:18:54.95
```

The PL/SQL block took about 19 minutes to complete in the first instance. The same block took almost the same identical time to complete in the second instance. These results are similar to the *nocache* example seen previously. The tests will be repeated for cache values of 20, 100, and 1000 as was previously performed. The following table shows the cache values and the effect with the *order* clause compared to the earlier tests without explicit ordering of the sequence values.

Cache Value	NOORDER		ORDER	
	Node 1	Node 2	Node 1	Node 2
None	19:59.61	20:43.22	18:54.95	18:55.34
20	00:41.19	00:49.18	01:17.34	01:19.75
100	00:10.98	00:11.57	00:33.41	00:32.45
1000	00:01.06	00:02.62	00:29.30	00:28.74

Table 3.2 Sequence Runtimes With Caching and ORDER

From the results in the table above, it is easy to see that with no caching of sequence values, the *order* clause had slightly better results. As the cache value increased slightly, requiring a specific order to the sequence values started to have a negative effect. Instead of running in less than fifty seconds, the order clause made the sequence run in less than eighty seconds. When the cache value was set to 100, the ordered sequence performed three times worse than with no order. Most significantly was when the caching was increased to 1000, great improvement occurred with *noorder*, but no improvement with *order*.

Next, let's examine the top wait events for one of these sessions.

```
SQL> @current_session_top5_waits.sql

EVENT                          TOTAL_WAITS TIME_WAITED
------------------------------ ----------- -----------
gc cr block 2-way                    66167        7710
gc cr block busy                     31606        5130
gc cr block lost                         1          28
db file sequential read                 12           1
Disk file operations I/O                 3           0
```

Surprisingly, the *row cache lock* wait event is not seen here. Instead, the top wait events are Cache Fusion related.

The Data Dictionary can be queried to easily find those sequences that are defined to order the values.

```
select
   sequence_owner,
   sequence_name
from
   dba_sequences
where
   order_flag='Y'
order by
   sequence_owner,
   sequence_name;
```

The query above will return a number of sequences owned by SYS and SYSTEM. With one exception that will be discussed in the next section, the database administrator should not modify the sequences that are part of the Data Dictionary.

For those sequences returned from the above query that belong to application owners, the database administrator needs to determine if the ordering of sequence values is truly necessary. If the *order* clause is not a business requirement, it should be removed.

In this section, a simple example showed how using the *order* clause quickly negates any benefits of caching sequence values. This should be no surprise as the clause serializes access to the sequence's next values across all instances. As such, the *order* clause should only be used for those sequences that have specific business requirements stating that the sequence's values are to denote a time ordering. The absence of such a requirement would negate the need for the *order* clause. It is a good practice to use the *order* clause sparingly and only when completely necessary.

SYS.AUDSES$ Sequence

There is one special Data Dictionary sequence worth of mention, *sys.audses$*. This sequence is used in computing the audit session identifier as seen in the *audsid* column of the *v$session* view. In Oracle RAC, it is possible for a high degree of concurrent logon requests to exhibit waits while accessing this sequence's next value. Prior to Oracle 10.2.0.3, the cache value for this sequence was 20. In Oracle 10.2.0.3 and higher, the *cache* value for this sequence is now 10,000 as can be seen from this Oracle 12.1.0.1 database.

```
SQL> select
  2     cache_size
  3   from
```

```
   4      dba_sequences
   5   where
   6      sequence_owner='SYS'
   7      and
   8      sequence_name='AUDSES$';

CACHE_SIZE
----------
     10000
```

If the Oracle RAC database is at a version lower than 10.2.0.3, then Oracle Support recommends increasing the cache value of this sequence.

```
SQL> alter sequence
  2      sys.audses$
  3      cache 10000;

Sequence altered.
```

Hopefully, most readers of this book are using an Oracle RAC version higher than the 10.2.0.3 release and the information in this section is not necessary.

RAC Row Insert Contention

One issue that is often seen in Oracle RAC databases is contention when inserting rows to a table. The contention is not necessarily with the new row being placed into the table, but rather with updating the table's index. To understand the issue, examine the following illustration of a table's index.

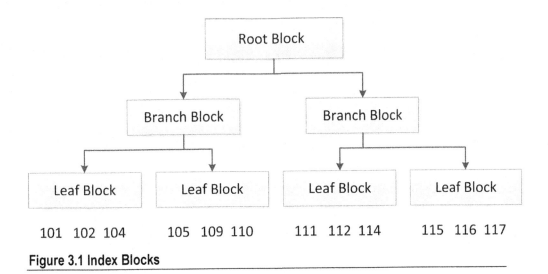

Figure 3.1 Index Blocks

In the diagram above, we can traverse the index from the root block, through branch blocks until the process arrives at a leaf block. Under the leaf blocks, the column's values are noted, just for illustration purposes. The right-most leaf block contains values 115, 116, and 117.

Many times, but not always, the indexed column receives increasing values. The values are often time-related or populated from a database sequence. Newly inserted values will be larger than any of the existing values and as such will be added to the right side of the index. In the example above, assume that a user in instance 1 is adding the value 118 to the table while a concurrent user in instance 2 is adding the value 119 to the table. In this case, both users will be attempting to add values to the same leaf block. Trying to simultaneously update the same leaf block will require Cache Fusion to copy that leaf block from one instance to another and handle locking on a global scale. This type of index contention is more problematic in Oracle RAC than in a single-instance database.

The index contention described in this section can be illustrated with a simple example. First, a table is created with an index. Next, a sequence used to populate the ID column of the table.

```
SQL> create table
  2      index_contention_examp (
  3          id_val    number);

Table created.

SQL> create index
  2      index_cont_ix1
  3  on
```

```
   4        index_contention_examp (id_val);

Index created.

SQL> create sequence
  2        index_cont_seq
  3        start with 1
  4        increment by 1
  5        cache 1000;

Sequence created.
```

Now that the table, index and sequence have been created, two concurrent sessions insert rows into the table with the following code.

```
set timing on

declare
   cnt number;
begin
   cnt := 0;
   while (cnt <= 5000000)
   loop
      insert into
         index_contention_examp
      select
         index_cont_seq.nextval
      from
         dual;
      cnt := cnt + 1;
   end loop;
end;
/

commit;
```

The first session completed in 00:30:10.15 and the second session completed in 00:29:45.31 or approximately 30 minutes each. After the two sessions have finished, the top wait events for one of these sessions is seen below.

```
SQL> @current_session_top5_waits.sql

EVENT                           TOTAL_WAITS TIME_WAITED
------------------------------- ----------- -----------
SQL*Net message from client              24       43596
gc current block busy                129556       38066
gc current split                       9427        20955
gc buffer busy release               106335       14192
gc current grant busy                 16803        10092
```

In the above listing, note that it is normal to see the *gc current block busy* and *gc current split* among the top wait events when there is index contention as was forced, as it was in this example.

Reverse Key Indexes in RAC

If right-side index leaf contention is an issue, (i.e. you are loading ascending high values into an ascending index) one way to reduce contention is to create a Reverse Key index. A Reverse Key index takes the column value and simply reverses it before storing it in a leaf block. A key value of "book" becomes "koob". A key value of 12345 becomes 54321. Figure 3.1 showed a regular index with specific leaf values. The same values would appear in a Reverse Key index as shown in the next figure.

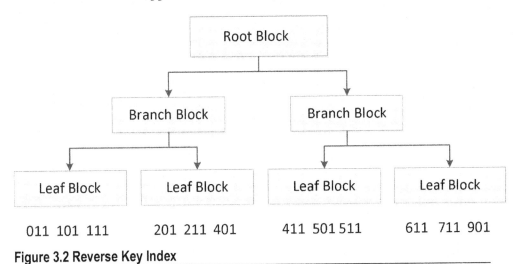

Figure 3.2 Reverse Key Index

With a reverse key index, there will no longer be contention on the right-side leaf blocks of the index. Newly inserted data will be spread out among the leaf blocks. When the values 119 and 120 are added to the column of the table, those values will get reversed to 911 and 021 respectively. The new values will be inserted into the last and the first leaf blocks of the index, instead of both being inserted into the last block.

Using a Reverse Key index is not always a sure-fire way to reduce contention as it may introduce more blocks being transferred from one instance to another for non-insert activity on the table. Test carefully before making this change in a production environment to ensure that solving one performance problem will not cause a new one. For instance, when converting the index to a reverse key index, index range scans will no longer be possible as the index keys are no longer in sorted order. While you may improve insert performance into the table, it may come at a cost of application performance using index range scans when selecting data from that table. It is important to understand the application and the queries that access the table before making the change to a reverse key index.

A second method to reduce the right-side leaf contention is to partition the index with a hash-partitioning scheme. Similar to using reverse key indexes, hash partitioning of an index will spread out the subsequent insert values over different partitions. One could say that reversing the keys is one type of hashing algorithm so it would be easy to understand how hash partitioning accomplishes the same goal. It should then be no surprise that hash partitioning of the index may be an easy change but it can have the same issues as a reverse key index. Additionally, partitioning an index requires you to have licensed Oracle Enterprise Edition as well as the Partitioning Option.

A third method to reducing right-handed leaf block contention is to have all insert statements executing on the same instance. If the insert statements execute on the same instance, there is no need for cross-instance block transfers. The primary method to force the application to the same instance is to leverage services, which will be discussed later in this chapter. However, for many Oracle RAC deployments, forcing the bothersome insert statements to the same instance may not be possible. For purposes of this discussion, we will force all inserts to the same instance by opening a second SQL*Plus session on that host. The table is truncated and the sequence is recreated before the next test is performed.

```
SQL> truncate table
  2       index_contention_examp;

Table truncated.

SQL> drop sequence
  2       index_cont_seq;

Sequence dropped.

SQL> create sequence
  2       index_cont_seq
  3       start with 1
  4       increment by 1
  5       cache 1000;

Sequence created.
```

The test is run again with both sessions connected to the same instance. Instead of 30 minutes per session, the tests completed in approximately 20 minutes per session. The wait events are examined for one of the sessions.

```
SQL> @current_session_top5_waits.sql

EVENT                           TOTAL_WAITS TIME_WAITED
------------------------------- ----------- -----------
SQL*Net message from client              13       55661
events in waitclass Other             45420        4198
library cache: mutex X                11961        3040
buffer busy waits                     33541        1573
enq: TX - index contention             2299         401
```

From the information above, the top wait events are no longer Cache Fusion related. The sessions finished in approximately 67% of the time of the original test. Without cross-instance transfers, the work was completed in less time. Note that it may not be possible to force all insert statements to one instance, so this option may not be available to all Oracle RAC deployments.

When a column is indexed and the newly inserted values of that column will be "monotonically increasing", as mathematicians would say, there can be contention for the right-side leaf blocks of the index. This index contention will manifest itself with the *gc current block busy* and *gc current split* wait events. To reduce that contention, consider hash partitioning of the index, converting the index to a reverse key index, or performing the inserts on the same instance if possible. Each alternative has its pros and cons and the application should be tested so that the change does not negatively impact performance of other application areas.

RAC TNS Services

When there is only one application using the Oracle RAC database, the application will most likely connect to all instances of the database. Distributing the application workload across the cluster is often desired as it allows the application to scale out over the nodes. High performance and scalability is one reason for deploying Oracle RAC. The tradeoff for distributing the workload over multiple servers is that resources need to be managed on a global scale that can introduce a bottleneck of its own. This section will discuss how to leverage database services to reduce the instances used by the application. The database administrator needs to walk a fine line when configuring the instances in use by a service. Too many instances and the application may suffer from too much cross-instance communication. Too few instances and the application may suffer from lack of system resources to complete the database requests in a timely fashion.

Another reason for using Oracle RAC is to consolidate applications. Letting multiple applications use the same Oracle RAC database can help a company reduce their

Oracle database footprint in the data center. Oracle 12c helps application and database consolidation with the Oracle 12c Multitenant option, or virtualization at the database level. If there are multiple applications using an Oracle RAC database, then it is beneficial to employ *application partitioning*, also called *application segregation* or *application affinity*.

The idea behind application partitioning is to point one application (or a module of that application) to one Oracle RAC instance and another application (or module) to a separate Oracle RAC instance. If the application is contained to just one Oracle RAC instance, the need for cross-instance communication can be significantly reduced. We saw an example of this concept earlier in the previous section when two concurrent sessions performed their insert operations using only one instance. If multiple applications are using the same Oracle RAC database, then consider segregating those applications across the nodes in the cluster. In the old Oracle Parallel Server days, (before the creation of Cache Fusion), application partition was a "must" because the only way a block could be transferred from one instance to another was by disk pinging. Cache Fusion has greatly improved block transfers and many Oracle RAC implementations have worked well without application partitioning. However, a large number of application performance issues can be resolved by proper application partitioning.

Application partitioning may be counter-intuitive to leveraging Oracle RAC to scale-out an application. One often implements Oracle RAC for high performance and spreads out an application load across multiple nodes in the cluster. Yet application partitioning is reducing the number of instances used by the instance, all in the name of better performance by reducing cross-instance operations. So which is it? Do we improve performance by adding more nodes or improve performance by reducing the number of nodes in use?

Both approaches may be correct depending on the situation. Applications that are not well tuned can have their performance flaws magnified and would become candidates for application segregation. Applications that are already well-tuned can certainly benefit from the scale-out capabilities of Oracle RAC. One can always mix and match the concepts in the design of the Oracle RAC deployment. For instance, a six-node RAC implementation may use three nodes for the first application and the remaining three nodes for the second application. The two applications are partitioned but still have scale-out characteristics.

The primary mechanism to achieve application partitioning is to leverage *services*. A service is a gateway to a specific instance, or multiple instances, depending on how the service is configured. As an example, the Oracle RAC database might have a service named "hr_svc" as the service for our Human Resource application. The service named "hr_svc" will only be running on instance 1 of the RAC database. Another service named "accntg_svc", the service for the Accounting application, will run only on instance 2 of the RAC database. By segregating the services in this manner, the database administrator has ensured that the HR application will connect only to instance 1 and the Accounting application will connect only to instance 2. The two applications are now segregated across the Oracle RAC instances.

Creating RAC TNS Services

Before applications can use RAC services, the service must be created. Oracle does not automatically create application services. Which services to create and which instances will operate the services is a decision left to the database administrator.

Out of the box, an Oracle RAC database is created with four services, two of which are internal to the database. Even single instance databases have these four default services. Running services can be discovered in the *gv$services* view.

```
SQL> select
  2      inst_id,
  3      name
  4  from
  5      gv$services
  6  order by
  7      inst_id,
  8      name;

  INST_ID NAME
---------- --------------------------------------------------------------------
        1 SYS$BACKGROUND
        1 SYS$USERS
        1 orcl
        1 orclXDB
        2 SYS$BACKGROUND
        2 SYS$USERS
        2 orcl
        2 orclXDB
```

The *sys$background* services is used internally for the instance's background processes. The *sys$users* service is for all local database connections that did not go through the Oracle Listener. If you sign on to the database host and from that host use SQL*Plus to make a local connection to the instance, you are using the *sys$users* service. The *v$session* view shows the service name in use by the session.

```
SQL> select
  2      username,
  3      program,
  4      service_name
  5  from
  6      v$session;
```

```
USERNAME     PROGRAM                                         SERVICE_NAME
----------   ----------------------------------------------  ----------------
             oracle@host01.localdomain (PMON)                SYS$BACKGROUND
             oracle@host01.localdomain (DIAG)                SYS$BACKGROUND
             oracle@host01.localdomain (LMON)                SYS$BACKGROUND
             oracle@host01.localdomain (DBW0)                SYS$BACKGROUND
             oracle@host01.localdomain (LGWR)                SYS$BACKGROUND
             oracle@host01.localdomain (CKPT)                SYS$BACKGROUND
             oracle@host01.localdomain (SMON)                SYS$BACKGROUND
             oracle@host01.localdomain (RECO)                SYS$BACKGROUND
             oracle@host01.localdomain (CJQ0)                SYS$BACKGROUND
SCOTT        sqlplus@host01.localdomain (TNS V1-V3)          SYS$USERS
```

The output from the query above has been trimmed for brevity. The sessions utilizing the *sys$background* service are actually background processes most readers should already be familiar with, i.e *pmon, lgwr, smon*, etc. The last line of output shows one user connected as SCOTT. The program is SQL*Plus running right on the database host and is connected to the *sys$users* service.

In addition to the two internal services, Oracle RAC also creates two other services. One service has the same name as the database name. The other service has a name of the form *db_name*XDB. These last two default services are accessible from applications external to the database servers. The services are registered with the listener. A status of the listener reveals all services and the instance they are registered with.

```
[oracle@host01 ~]$ lsnrctl status

LSNRCTL for Linux: Version 12.1.0.1.0 - Production on 03-JUL-2014 14:00:01

Copyright (c) 1991, 2013, Oracle.  All rights reserved.

Connecting to (ADDRESS=(PROTOCOL=tcp)(HOST=)(PORT=1521))
STATUS of the LISTENER
------------------------
Alias                     LISTENER
Version                   TNSLSNR for Linux: Version 12.1.0.1.0 - Production
Start Date                03-JUL-2014 11:01:31
Uptime                    0 days 2 hr. 58 min. 29 sec
Trace Level               off
Security                  ON: Local OS Authentication
SNMP                      OFF
Listener Parameter File   /u01/app/crs12.1.0.1/network/admin/listener.ora
Listener Log File
/u01/app/oracle/diag/tnslsnr/host01/listener/alert/log.xml
Listening Endpoints Summary...
  (DESCRIPTION=(ADDRESS=(PROTOCOL=ipc)(KEY=LISTENER)))
  (DESCRIPTION=(ADDRESS=(PROTOCOL=tcp)(HOST=127.0.0.1)(PORT=1521)))
  (DESCRIPTION=(ADDRESS=(PROTOCOL=tcp)(HOST=192.168.56.81)(PORT=1521)))
Services Summary...
Service "+ASM" has 1 instance(s).
  Instance "+ASM1", status READY, has 1 handler(s) for this service...
Service "orcl" has 1 instance(s).
```

```
   Instance "orcl1", status READY, has 1 handler(s) for this service...
Service "orclXDB" has 1 instance(s).
   Instance "orcl1", status READY, has 1 handler(s) for this service...
The command completed successfully
```

In the output above, the *orcl* and *orclXDB* services are clearly registered with the *orcl1* instance. The status output also shows a service for the ASM database instance. The status command of the listener shows much more information than just the services involved. The *lsnrctl* utility also includes a *services* command to focus on that specific status item.

```
[oracle@host01 ~]$ lsnrctl services

LSNRCTL for Linux: Version 12.1.0.1.0 - Production on 03-JUL-2014 14:00:05

Copyright (c) 1991, 2013, Oracle.  All rights reserved.

Connecting to (ADDRESS=(PROTOCOL=tcp)(HOST=)(PORT=1521))
Services Summary...
Service "+ASM" has 1 instance(s).
  Instance "+ASM1", status READY, has 1 handler(s) for this service...
    Handler(s):
      "DEDICATED" established:0 refused:0 state:ready
         LOCAL SERVER
Service "orcl" has 1 instance(s).
  Instance "orcl1", status READY, has 1 handler(s) for this service...
    Handler(s):
      "DEDICATED" established:0 refused:0 state:ready
         LOCAL SERVER
Service "orclXDB" has 1 instance(s).
  Instance "orcl1", status READY, has 1 handler(s) for this service...
    Handler(s):
      "D000" established:0 refused:0 current:0 max:1022 state:ready
         DISPATCHER <machine: host01.localdomain, pid: 3877>
         (ADDRESS=(PROTOCOL=tcp)(HOST=host01)(PORT=36099))
The command completed successfully
```

Most Oracle RAC database administrators use the "lsnrctl status" command because it is second nature to them.

One way to create a service is to use the srvctl utility. Following the example earlier in this section, two services will be created, *hr_svc* and *accntg_svc*. To partition the applications using these services, *hr_svc* will run on the first instance, *orcl1*. The service *accntg_svc* will run on the second instance, *orcl2*.

```
[oracle@host01 ~]$ srvctl add service -d orcl -service hr_svc \
> -preferred orcl1 -available orcl2
[oracle@host01 ~]$ srvctl add service -d orcl -service accntg_svc \
> -preferred orcl2 -available orcl1
```

The *-preferred* parameter denotes the primary instance for the service. If the preferred instance is down, the service will fail over to any *-available* instance. After the services are created, the status is checked.

```
[oracle@host01 ~]$ srvctl status service -d orcl
Service accntg_svc is not running.
Service hr_svc is not running.
```

The services need to be started after their initial creation.

```
[oracle@host01 ~]$ srvctl start service -d orcl -s hr_svc
[oracle@host01 ~]$ srvctl start service -d orcl -s accntg_svc
[oracle@host01 ~]$ srvctl status service -d orcl
Service accntg_svc is running on instance(s) orcl2
Service hr_svc is running on instance(s) orcl1
```

The services are now running, on the preferred instances. When the database is bounced, the services will automatically start.

```
[oracle@host01 ~]$ srvctl stop database -d orcl -o immediate
[oracle@host01 ~]$ srvctl start database -d orcl
[oracle@host01 ~]$ srvctl status service -d orcl
Service accntg_svc is running on instance(s) orcl2
Service hr_svc is running on instance(s) orcl1
```

A quick check of *gv$services* shows the services running in the proper instances.

```
SQL> select
  2      inst_id,
  3      name
  4  from
  5      gv$services
  6  order by
  7      inst_id,
  8      name;

  INST_ID NAME
---------- -------------------------------------------------
        1 SYS$BACKGROUND
        1 SYS$USERS
        1 hr_svc
        1 orcl
        1 orclXDB
        2 SYS$BACKGROUND
        2 SYS$USERS
        2 accntg_svc
        2 orcl
        2 orclXDB
```

The *tnsnames.ora* configuration file helps to denote the service the application will connect. Sample entries in the *tnsnames.ora* file might look like the following.

```
HR_APPL =
  (DESCRIPTION =
    (ADDRESS = (PROTOCOL = TCP)(HOST = rac-scan)(PORT = 1521))
    (CONNECT_DATA =
      (SERVER = DEDICATED)
      (SERVICE_NAME = hr_svc)
    )
  )
ACCNTG_APPL =
  (DESCRIPTION =
    (ADDRESS = (PROTOCOL = TCP)(HOST = rac-scan)(PORT = 1521))
    (CONNECT_DATA =
      (SERVER = DEDICATED)
      (SERVICE_NAME = accntg_svc)
    )
  )
```

The HR application would make a connection to the *hr_appl* alias in the tnsnames.ora configuration file. Similarly, the accounting application would use the *accntg_appl* alias. Notice that both aliases are contacting the same Scan Listeners in the *host* field, the same Oracle RAC system.

The database administrator has complete control when configuring where a service runs. The service may run as the only service on an instance, or the service may run with other services on that instance. The service may run on multiple instances. By mixing and matching combinations of services to instances, the database administrator has utmost flexibility in segregating applications to reduce cross-instance traffic as well as scaling out an application across multiple database servers. If the Oracle RAC database supports multiple applications, it would be irresponsible to have all applications use the default database service. Using only one service for all applications eliminates flexibility and manageability and significantly reduces the options at the database administrator's disposal. A good practice is to have at least one service per application that will use the Oracle RAC database. A application that is broken down into modules may use one service per module.

Service Partitioning with RAC 12c

It is worthy to note that Oracle RAC12c makes application partitioning very easy with the Oracle Multitenant option. The database administrator can place each application's schema in its own Pluggable Database (PDB). Oracle Multitenant may actually be preferred when consolidating applications in Oracle RAC. Consider the case where one application has a database role named "admin_role". Privileges are granted to this role to allow application administrators to have privileged access to database objects. Adding a second application can be problematic if that application has a role with the same name. With Oracle Multitenant, each application would be in its own PDB and the two application roles will never cross paths. When PDBs are deployed, each PDB gets its own service name. Oracle Multitenant provides de facto application partitioning in this regard.

RAC Buffer Cache Effect

This section has already pointed out that application partitioning reduces the cross-instance "chatter". Another positive effect of application partitioning is the impact on the Buffer Cache. To illustrate the effect, let's assume each node has a 6GB Buffer Cache. It will further be assumed that 1GB of the Buffer Cache is needed for blocks common to all Oracle instances, leaving 5GB of the cache for the application. If we were able to determine the application's usage of the cache, we might find that of the 5GB available to the application, the human resources and accounting applications are using equal amounts of the cache, 2.5GB each. If each application has a buffer cache hit ratio of 98%, then 2.45GB of the HR application's blocks in the first instance's cache are probably identical to 2.45GB of the second instance's cache.

In other words, if the application is split across multiple nodes, a significant amount of the buffer cache in each instance will contain the same data blocks. The collective Buffer Caches are not being used as effectively as they could be. If the applications are partitioned, the HR application will be able to use all 5GB of the buffer cache in the first instance and the accounting application will be able to use all 5GB of the buffer cache in the second instance. It is important to note that the Buffer Cache Hit Ratio (BCHR) is not being used to make any performance tuning recommendations. The BCHR is only being used to illustrate how the two caches can to contain the same blocks.

The *gv$bh* view provides a glimpse of the contents of the Buffer Cache. Let's look at a three-node production Oracle RAC database. First, the count of total object blocks in the Buffer Cache is determined.

buffer_cache_blocks.sql

```
SQL> select
  2      count(*) as num_blocks
  3  from (
  4      select distinct
  5          file#,
  6          block#
  7      from
  8          gv$bh
  9      where
 10          inst_id=1);

  NUM_BLKS
----------
    522681
```

```
SQL> select
  2      count(*) as num_blks
  3  from (
  4      select distinct
  5          file#,
  6          block#
  7      from
  8          gv$bh
  9      where
 10          inst_id=2);

   NUM_BLKS
----------
   537001

SQL> select
  2      count(*) as num_blks
  3  from (
  4      select distinct
  5          file#,
  6          block#
  7      from
  8          gv$bh
  9      where
 10          inst_id=3);

   NUM_BLKS
----------
   542963
```

The purpose of the "distinct" clause on line 4 of each query is to eliminate duplicate blocks in the cache that have been constructed for consistent read purposes. Now let's see how many blocks are in all three Buffer Caches.

💾 buffer_cache_blocks.sql

```
SQL> select
  2      count(*) as num_shared_blocks
  3  from (
  4      select distinct
  5      file#,
  6      block#
  7  from
  8      gv$bh
  9  where
 10      inst_id=1
 11  intersect
 12  select distinct
 13      file#,
 14      block#
 15  from
 16      gv$bh
 17  where
 18      inst_id=2
 19  intersect
 20  select distinct
```

```
21      file#,
22      block#
23 from
24      gv$bh
25 where
26      inst_id=3);

NUM_SHARED
----------
   345753
```

There are 345,753 blocks that are the same in each instance's Buffer Cache.

The effect on the Buffer Cache can be summarized in the following table.

Instance ID	Total Blocks	Shared Blocks	Ratio
1	522681	345753	66.15%
2	537001	345753	64.39%
3	542963	345753	63.68%

Table 2.3 Buffer Cache Efficiency – No Application Partitioning

The numbers shown above are from a production Oracle RAC database that does not have application partitioning. All applications have an equal chance at connecting with any of the instances. The three instances have 63% to 66% of the same blocks in their caches. From SQL*Plus, the total Buffer Cache size is shown.

```
SQL> show sga

Total System Global Area 1.3896E+10 bytes
Fixed Size                  2241624 bytes
Variable Size            8522828712 bytes
Database Buffers         5335154688 bytes
Redo Buffers               36093952 bytes
```

In this example the Buffer Cache is about 5.3GB in size. For the first instance, if the calculated ratio holds across the cache, then 3.5GB (66.15% * 5.3GB) of the Buffer Cache contains blocks that are also found in instance 2 and instance 3. It can be extrapolated from this information that each cache is about 3.5GB the same across all instances with approximately 1.8GB unique to that instance. For three instances, a total of 15.9GB has been allocated to the Buffer Caches, but the system is effectively using only 7.2GB (1.8GB * 3 + 3.5GB) by not partitioning the application. It may be perfectly acceptable to use the Buffer Caches in this manner because the workload scales very well when spread over multiple nodes, but keep in mind the impact to the collective caches in each instance.

The whole point of examining the Buffer Cache contents of this Oracle RAC database is to show how the lack of application partitioning is not utilizing every bytes of the collective Buffer Caches from all instances in the cluster. Many people think if the Buffer Cache is X GB in size and there are Y instances, the total Buffer Cache is X*Y GB. In reality, the total Buffer Cache across all instances is effectively less due to duplication of blocks in the caches.

Looking at a different three-node Oracle RAC database where application partitioning is in effect, we can see the effect on the Buffer Cache.

The same queries were run on a different 3-node RAC database and summarized in the table below.

Instance ID	Num Blocks	Num Blocks Shared	Ratio
1	79622	13469	16.92%
2	80919	13469	16.65%
3	78462	13469	17.17%

Table 2.4 Buffer Cache Efficiency – Application Partitioning

From the table above, we see that there is a much better use of the Buffer Caches. In this Oracle RAC database, approximately 17% of each cache has blocks found in the other caches. With application partitioning, the applications have more cache to use. The database administrator needs to understand the impact on the Buffer Caches of each instance when leveraging services and deciding how to distribute the applications workloads over the Oracle RAC database.

The Resource Manager and RAC

Oracle RAC implementations often serve multiple workload types, especially if applications have been consolidated into a single Oracle RAC database. The different workloads will often be competing for the same computing resources, namely CPU and disk I/O. End users will see this competition for scarce resources as manifesting as slow performance. The Oracle database Resource Manager helps limit and constrain a given workload from consuming more than its allocated share of resources.

Previously in this chapter, two services were created, *hr_svc* and *accntg_svc*. The services were defined so that they run on two different instances. The Human Resource application is resource intensive while the Accounting application has a small workload, primarily because the Accounting department only has 5 staff members. A new business requirement came in to host a new application for the Marketing department. The Marketing department only has 2 staff members and the application can coexist alongside the Accounting application. Now, assume that management wants to ensure the Accounting department is not negatively impacted and should take priority over the Marketing department needs. Management agrees that keeping track of the company's current cash flow is more important than landing new clients. The database administrator knows the solution lies in the Resource Manager. The first thing to do is to create a new service for the new application.

```
[oracle@host01 ~]$ srvctl add service -d orcl -service mktg_svc \
> -preferred orcl2 -available orcl1
```

Next, a Resource Manager consumer group is created.

```
SQL> exec dbms_resource_manager.create_pending_area();

PL/SQL procedure successfully completed.

SQL> exec dbms_resource_manager.create_consumer_group( -
>           'MARKETING_GROUP', 'Consumer Group for Marketing');

PL/SQL procedure successfully completed.
```

The next step is where the Oracle RAC piece comes into play. The database administrator will want to have all sessions that connect to the Marketing service to use this new consumer group. The database administrator needs to map the service to that group. The *set_consumer_group_mapping* procedure of the *dbms_resource_manager* package links the service to the consumer group.

```
SQL> exec dbms_resource_manager.set_consumer_group_mapping( -
>           attribute=>DBMS_RESOURCE_MANAGER.SERVICE_NAME, -
>           value=>'MKTG_SVC', -
>           consumer_group=>'MARKETING_GROUP');

PL/SQL procedure successfully completed.
```

The next step is to create a resource plan. The goal here is to limit the Marketing application to using at most 20% of the CPU. The *create_plan* procedure is needed to define the resource plan. After the plan is created, it is given a directive to limit the CPU usage.

```
SQL> exec dbms_resource_manager.create_plan( -
>           'MARKETING_PLAN', -
>           'Resource Plan for Marketing');

PL/SQL procedure successfully completed.

SQL> exec dbms_resource_manager.create_plan_directive( -
```

```
>               plan=>'MARKETING_PLAN', -
>               group_or_subplan=>'MARKETING_GROUP', -
>               mgmt_p1=>20);

PL/SQL procedure successfully completed.
```

All is said and done so the database administrator submits the pending area.

```
SQL> exec dbms_resource_manager.submit_pending_area();

PL/SQL procedure successfully completed.
```

There is a lot more to the Resource Manager than is shown in this section. The goal of this section was to show how to implement the Resource Manager by leveraging services that were set up in an Oracle RAC database. Without the Resource Manager, all services in the instance will run unconstrained which could negatively impact performance of an important application. The database administrator can use the Resource Manager to keep applications in check.

Real Application Testing and RAC

If a single-instance application needs to be ported to Oracle RAC, then Oracle's Real Application Testing (RAT) product with Database Replay can help determine how well this application will work in a clustered database environment. Database Replay is an additional cost option; as such it may not be available in many organizations unless the company has licensed the product. If this product is licensed, the database administrator can leverage RAT to help understand how well the single-instance application will react once deployed in an Oracle RAC environment.

To use Database Replay, the following steps are performed.

1. The production instance is often restarted to start with a clean slate.
2. The Database Replay capture process is started. Enough disk space needs to be available to hold the capture files.
3. The production application is run against the single-instance database to generate the production workload.
4. The Database Replay capture process is stopped.
5. The capture files are copied to the Oracle RAC database.
6. The capture files are preprocessed on the new system.
7. The workload is replayed against the Oracle RAC database.
8. Reports are generated for analysis.

The Oracle RAC database should not be actively used as a production environment when the workload is replayed against it. The activity of using Database Replay should be performed to determine how well the application reacts in the new environment and what changes need to be made to have the application perform optimally.

In addition to the Database Replay reports, the database administrator is encouraged to generate Automated Workload Repository (AWR) or Statspack reports for the capture and replay periods to obtain a behind-the-scenes look at overall database performance. Note that AWR requires the optionally licensed Diagnostics Pack. A future chapter will discuss AWR in more detail.

Table Compression and RAC

Another option to consider is leveraging Oracle's table compression features. Basic table compression is included in Enterprise Edition for both Oracle 11g and 12c. Online Transaction Processing (OLTP) compression is part of Oracle Enterprise Edition's optional Advanced Compression, which does require extra licensing. Compressing tables saves on storage costs and has been known to reduce the required I/O to satisfy SQL statements. The advantages of compression come at the expense of extra CPU usage. Oracle RAC and single-instance databases may all benefit from the reduce I/O requirements. Oracle RAC database, in particular, can see a reduction in the blocks transferred across the cluster interconnect to support Cache Fusion's global cache transfer operations. A simple example can illustrate table compression's impact in Oracle RAC. First, a table is created and populated with rows of data.

```
SQL> create table
  2      precompress
  3  as
  4      select
  5          owner,
  6          object_type,
  7          object_name
  8      from
  9          dba_objects;

Table created.

SQL> insert into
  2      precompress
  3  select
  4      *
  5  from
  6      precompress;

19546 rows created.
```

```
SQL> insert into
  2      precompress
  3  select
  4      *
  5  from
  6      precompress;

39092 rows created.

SQL> insert into
  2      precompress
  3  select
  4      *
  5  from
  6      precompress;

78184 rows created.

SQL> commit;

Commit complete.
```

Next, a compressed version of the table is created.

```
SQL> create table
  2      compress_example
  3  compress for all operations
  4  as
  5  select
  6      *
  7  from
  8      precompress;

Table created.
```

Rowcounts are verified to ensure both tables contain the same number of rows.

```
SQL> select
  2      count(*)
  3  from
  4      precompress;

  COUNT(*)
----------
    156368

SQL> select
  2      count(*)
  3  from
  4      compress_example;

  COUNT(*)
----------
    156368
```

The number of blocks and extents for each table are shown below.

```
SQL> select
  2      segment_name,
  3      blocks,
  4      extents
  5  from
  6      user_segments;

SEGMENT_NAME             BLOCKS      EXTENTS
-------------------- ----------- -----------
COMPRESS_EXAMPLE             640          20
PRECOMPRESS                  896          22
```

Here we see that the compressed table uses 71% of the total blocks of the uncompressed version. The impact of the compression on global cache transfers can easily be determined. First, the database is bounced to start with a clean slate.

```
[oracle@host01 trace]$ srvctl stop database -d orcl -o immediate
[oracle@host01 trace]$ srvctl start database -d orcl
```

The following SQL statement is executed in the first instance to populate the Buffer Cache. The same SQL statement is executed in the second instance that will generate transfers across the cluster interconnect.

```
SQL> select
  2      count(distinct owner)
  3  from
  4      precompress;

COUNT(DISTINCTOWNER)
--------------------
                  13
```

The instances are bounced again, and a similar SQL statement is used against the compressed table and run on both instances.

```
SQL> select
  2      count(distinct owner)
  3  from
  4      compress_example;

COUNT(DISTINCTOWNER)
--------------------
                  13
```

The Cache Fusion-related wait events each test experienced in the second instance are summarized in the following table.

Event	Waits w/o compression	Waits w/compression
gc current block 2-way	3	1
gc cr multi block request	28	23

Table 2.5 Compression Wait Events Summary

In a controlled environment, the session in the second instance had to wait for Global Cache wait events less if the table was compressed.

Admittedly, the example in this section is very rudimentary but it does illustrate how to reduce global cache transfers in an Oracle RAC database by compressing the table. A well-compressed table fits the same data in fewer blocks. Another way to look at it is that one block will contain more rows of data if compressed. Many companies will not be purchasing the Oracle Advanced Compression option just to reduce Cluster Interconnect traffic but if this option is available to the database administrator, it should be considered. Thorough testing should be performed to determine if the table compresses well and to ensure that the additional CPU demands are not detrimental to application performance.

Partitioning and RAC

Similar to compressing tables to reduce global cache transfers, partitioning tables may also help reduce traffic on the cluster interconnect. Oracle's Partitioning option is an extra cost feature available for Oracle Enterprise Edition so it may not be available to everyone.

One way that partitioning helps performance, even in single-instance databases, is with a concept called *partition pruning*. Let's assume a table of interest holds more than 1 million rows of data. The table is populated with new rows for a 7 year time period. If the end user is interested in last year's data from this table, an index on the date column may not be selective enough as it will return approximately one seventh of the rows, which means a full table scan of a million-row table would be required. If the table were partitioned on the date column, such that each partition contains one year's worth of data then querying for last year's data would only involve one partition. The other 6 partitions would be automatically eliminated, pruned, from consideration by the cost-based SQL optimizer.

Anything in Oracle that reduces I/O operations, including partition pruning, can benefit Oracle RAC databases by lowering global cache transfers. Similar to Oracle's Advanced Compression, it is most likely not cost effective to purchase the Partitioning option as a means of reducing traffic on the private network but if this option is already available to the database administrator, it should be considered for usage in an Oracle RAC database.

Summary

As with any Oracle database, performance tuning should start with the application before tuning the Oracle instance or the database server. This chapter discussed many topics related to tuning applications that use an Oracle RAC database.

- One of your strongest tools is the ability to start a trace in a session. This chapter discussed how to start SQL traces with Oracle RAC databases and how to use the trcsess utility to combine multiple trace files into one file.

- Oracle sequences require special handling in Oracle RAC databases. This chapter illustrated the effect of the *cache* and *order* clauses used when creating a sequence.

- Application partitioning is a great methodology to employ for Oracle RAC databases to segregate demand for shared, global resources. This chapter discussed how to employ services to facilitate application partitioning. Once services are created, the Database Resource Manager can be leveraged to control competing resource demands.

- A large part tuning global cache transfers is to reduce the I/O demands on tables. This chapter showed how compression could be used to this end. Oracle's Partitioning option can also be leveraged to reduce I/O, and potentially reduce traffic on the private network.

Normally, the next performance tuning steps would be to focus on tuning the database. On the other hand, the cluster interconnect is so vital to the performance of Cache Fusion, which in turn is vital to the performance of Oracle RAC, that the next chapter will focus on tuning the network.

Tuning the Cluster Interconnect

The second chapter of this book offered a brief history of Cache Fusion as well as a summary of how Cache Fusion works in a RAC environment. Central to the performance of Cache Fusion is the cluster's private network, known as the *Cluster Interconnect*. The third chapter devoted a few sections to techniques for reducing cross-instance traffic on the private network. It is not always possible for global cache transfers to be reduced. This chapter focuses on the next step, which is to tune the Cluster Interconnect to be more efficient.

The cluster_interconnects parameter

Since this chapter is devoted to the Cluster Interconnect, it is important to know which network interfaces on the host are configured for the private network. The *gv$cluster_interconnects* view provides this information.

```
SQL> select
  2     inst_id,
  3     name
  4  from
  5     gv$cluster_interconnects;

 INST_ID NAME
---------- ---------------
        1 eth1:1
        2 eth1:1
```

The Cluster Interconnect definition normally comes from the Oracle Cluster Registry (OCR). On rare occasions, the *cluster_interconnects* initialization parameter is used to override the OCR setting. We would set this *cluster_interconnects* parameter to define multiple private networks to be used by the RAC database. However, Highly Available IP (HAIP) was introduced in Oracle 11gR2 that negates the need for the *cluster_interconnects* parameter to be used for this purpose. A later section in this chapter will discuss HAIP in more detail. Another reason to use the *cluster_interconnects* parameter is if the database administrator wants to use one private network for one Oracle RAC database and another private network for a second Oracle RAC database running on the same cluster. In this case, the first Oracle RAC database will use the private network defined in the OCR and the second database will need to be pointed to the second private network via the *cluster_interconnects* parameter. Doing so may initially sound like a good idea. Each RAC database gets their own private network so high rates of global cache transfers from one RAC database will not dominate usage and negatively impact the other Oracle RAC database. However, if HAIP is employed, one Oracle RAC database may benefit from the extra private network similar to the way virtualization benefits systems from oversubscribing resources.

Private Network

The Cluster Interconnect is also referred to as the *private network*. This is a private interconnect and the only traffic on this network should be for cluster operations, including Cache Fusion. There is a misconception that the private network is used only for the cluster heartbeat, a pulse sent from one node to another to signify that the node is alive. A heartbeat is a lightweight operation on a network so why devote a network switch only usable for the private network?

This incorrect line of thinking leads to some Oracle RAC deployments that combine the public and private networks on the same switch. Other RAC deployments may separate the public and private networks, but put the private network on a switch that is used for other network purposes. Each of these configuration options is a mistake that many people later regret when Oracle RAC performance suffers. The private network needs to remain private, solely and exclusively for the use of the Cluster Interconnect.

Chapter 2 has already shown how the private network is used for so much more than just a cluster heartbeat, and it should be clear that the private network is used for any cross-instance communications. When two sessions on different instances want to modify the same block, Global Enqueue Services "talk" across the Cluster Interconnect. Global cache transfers of data blocks will dominate the private network traffic. Examine these metrics from an AWR report.

```
Global Cache Load Profile
~~~~~~~~~~~~~~~~~~~~~~~~~~~         Per Second      Per Transaction
                                  ---------------   ---------------
    Global Cache blocks received:      1,279.68               79.62
      Global Cache blocks served:        637.30               39.65
          GCS/GES messages received:   4,367.95              271.76
              GCS/GES messages sent:   7,440.72              462.94
                  DBWR Fusion writes:      21.15                1.32
   Estd Interconnect traffic (KB)    17,642.23
```

The metrics above were taken from one instance of a three-node RAC database over a one-hour period of time. The metrics above show an average of 1,916.98 global cache blocks sent and received per second. The database block size is 8 Kbytes, which means there are 15,335.84 kilobytes of traffic each second on the private network just to perform global cache transfers. The total private network traffic is 17,642.23 kilobytes is for all cross-instance traffic including the global cache transfers. The total Cluster Interconnect traffic for this one-hour snapshot is about 17.6 megabytes. These metrics prove that the Cluster Interconnect is used for so much more than just heartbeat traffic. These metrics should also reinforce the notion that the private network needs to remain private, as it can be busy. It is not uncommon to see some Oracle RAC deployments that have many gigabytes per hour of traffic on the Cluster Interconnect.

On the Oracle RAC nodes, it is very easy to determine which interfaces support the public and private networks for the cluster. The Oracle Interface Configuration Tool (*oifcfg*) can provide that information.

```
[root@host02 oracle]# cd /u01/app/crs12.1.0.1/bin

[root@host02 bin]# ./oifcfg getif

eth0  192.168.56.0  global  public
eth1  192.168.10.0  global  cluster_interconnect
```

From the output above, we can see that device *eth0* is for the public network and *eth1* is for the Cluster Interconnect. It is a requirement that the device names be the same on all nodes so if we execute the same commands on another node, the output should be the same. If another node has a different interface, cluster communications will not work correctly. It is also a requirement that the public and private interfaces be on different subnets.

Using iperf with RAC

Before any configuration change is made, it is helpful to document baseline performance prior to the change and then run the same benchmark after the test to note the effect of the change. Did the change improve or hurt performance? The *iperf* utility is a tool for measuring network performance. The *iperf* utility will measure both TCP and UDP performance, which is important to us because the public network uses TCP and the Cluster Interconnect uses a lot of UDP data transfers.

Iperf can be downloaded at *https://iperf.fr* and *iperf* is available for many different platforms. The web site includes documentation and examples. From the web site, we can see that *wget* can be used to easily install the utility to the host.

```
[root@host01 ~]# wget --no-check-certificate

https://iperf.fr/download/iperf_2.0.5/iperf_2.0.5-2_amd64 ; chmod +x
iperf_2.0.5-2_amd64 ; sudo mv iperf_2.0.5_2_amd64 /usr/bin/iperf
--2014-07-11 10:54:07--  https://iperf.fr/download/iperf_2.0.5/iperf_2.0.5-
2_amd64
Resolving iperf.fr... 89.84.127.53
Connecting to iperf.fr|89.84.127.53|:443... connected.
WARNING: certificate common name "www.iperf.fr" doesn't match requested host
name "iperf.fr".
HTTP request sent, awaiting response... 200 OK
Length: 66840 (65K)
Saving to: "iperf_2.0.5-2_amd64"

100%[=============================================================>] 66,840
116K/s   in 0.6s

2014-07-11 10:54:09 (116 KB/s) - "iperf_2.0.5-2_amd64" saved [66840/66840]

[root@host01 ~]# which iperf

/usr/bin/Iperf

[root@host01 ~]# iperf -h

Usage: iperf [-s|-c host] [options]
       iperf [-h|--help] [-v|--version]
```

> 🔔 Note" The "--no-check-certificate" directive was not mentioned on
> the *iperf* web site, yet it was needed to complete the install.

With *iperf* installed, we need to start its server mode on one of the hosts. In server
mode, *iperf* will log output to the terminal window:

```
[root@host01 ~]# iperf -s

------------------------------------------------------------
Server listening on TCP port 5001
TCP window size: 85.3 KByte (default)
------------------------------------------------------------
```

Iperf can also be started as a daemon with the –D parameter. Output will need to be
logged to a file.

```
[root@host02 ~]# iperf -s -D > /tmp/iperf.log
```

With *iperf*'s server running on *host01*, we can initiate a TCP test from *host02* to *host01's*
private network.

```
[root@host02 ~]# iperf -c host01-priv

------------------------------------------------------------
Client connecting to host01-priv, TCP port 5001
TCP window size: 22.9 KByte (default)
------------------------------------------------------------
[  3] local 192.168.10.2 port 27847 connected with 192.168.10.1 port 5001
[ ID] Interval        Transfer     Bandwidth
[  3]  0.0-10.0 sec  1.52 GBytes  1.31 Gbits/sec
```

The output shows that 1.52 gigabytes were transferred with a bandwidth of 1.31 gigabits per second. The output also shows that the transfer was initiated from the 192.168.10.2 IP address to the 192.168.10.1 IP address. Next, we verify these IP addresses. The nslookup utility is attempted, but since this is done on a test system, the IP addresses are not registered with DNS. So the information must be in the system's hosts file.

```
[root@host02 ~]# nslookup 192.168.10.2

Server:           192.168.0.1
Address:       192.168.0.1#53

** server can't find 2.10.168.192.in-addr.arpa.: NXDOMAIN

[root@host02 ~]# cat /etc/hosts |grep 192.168.10.2

192.168.10.2 host02-priv.localdomain host02-priv
[root@host02 ~]# cat /etc/hosts | grep 192.168.10.1

192.168.10.1 host01-priv.localdomain host01-priv
```

We have verified that 192.168.10.2 is *host02-priv*, or the private network from *host02*. Similarly, 192.168.10.1 is *host01-priv*.

The *iperf* utility is then used to see the effect of using a larger TCP window. The server needs to be started with a larger window. The default window size is overridden with the –w parameter.

```
[root@host01 ~]# iperf -s -w 256k

------------------------------------------------------------
Server listening on TCP port 5001
TCP window size:  512 KByte (WARNING: requested  256 KByte)
------------------------------------------------------------
```

The test is repeated, also with a larger window.

Using iperf with RAC

```
[root@host02 ~]# iperf -c host01-priv -w 256k
------------------------------------------------------------
Client connecting to host01-priv, TCP port 5001
TCP window size:  512 KByte (WARNING: requested  256 KByte)
------------------------------------------------------------
[  3] local 192.168.10.2 port 28348 connected with 192.168.10.1 port 5001
[ ID] Interval       Transfer     Bandwidth
[  3]  0.0-10.0 sec  2.00 GBytes  1.72 Gbits/sec
```

This small change in the test parameters increased the bandwidth from 1.31 gigabits per second to 1.72 gigabits per second. For normal testing, the TCP window size would not be modified in this manner. Instead, the network configuration settings would be altered and the same test would be run again.

As mentioned previously in this section, *iperf* can also test UDP performance. The server needs to be started with –u for DUP. A display interval of 10 seconds is chosen.

```
[root@host01 ~]# iperf -s -u -i 10
------------------------------------------------------------
Server listening on UDP port 5001
Receiving 1470 byte datagrams
UDP buffer size:  256 KByte (default)
------------------------------------------------------------
```

On the other host, the test is initiated. Again, the –u parameter defines this as a UDP test.

```
[root@host02 ~]# iperf -c host01-priv -u
------------------------------------------------------------
Client connecting to host01-priv, UDP port 5001
Sending 1470 byte datagrams
UDP buffer size:  256 KByte (default)
------------------------------------------------------------
[  3] local 192.168.10.2 port 59332 connected with 192.168.10.1 port 5001
[ ID] Interval       Transfer     Bandwidth
[  3]  0.0-10.0 sec  1.25 MBytes  1.05 Mbits/sec
[  3] Sent 893 datagrams
[  3] Server Report:
[  3]  0.0-10.0 sec  1.25 MBytes  1.05 Mbits/sec   0.315 ms    0/  893 (0%)
```

Above, we can see 1.25 megabytes were transferred with a bandwidth of 1.05 megabits per second.

This section shows how to install and use the *iperf* utility to help metric network performance. This chapter is concerned primarily with the private network's performance. There are other utilities one can use as well. The *ping* and *traceroute* commands still have their place as does other tools such as *netstat* and *netperf*. What is important is that network tools are used to baseline network performance prior to the change. After the change is implemented, the same test is run with the same tools to understand the impact of the change.

Infiniband or Gig-E Cluster Interconnects with RAC

The Cluster Interconnect requires a high speed, low latency infrastructure in order to be successful. When creating the Cluster Interconnect, there are two choices widely in use in today's RAC deployments. The two choices for the interconnect include Infiniband (IB) and Gigabit Ethernet (Gig-E). The system architect should decide the network platform that will be the backbone of the private network.

Standard network switches deployed in most data centers can provide the Gigabit Ethernet networks infrastructure. Every network administrator has experience with Gig-E switches. As such, using Gig-E is an easy choice to make. The company already has experienced staff on hand that will not require any additional training to implement the Cluster Interconnect. The hardware is very low cost as well. A sixteen-port Gig-E switch can be purchased for around $100. Since the switch is used for the private network, the switch does not need a large number of ports, as only the cluster nodes will be plugged into the device. A low-cost device already familiar with the current staff makes Gig-E switches the first choice for most RAC private networks. By today's standards, gigabit switches may not be fast enough. Oracle Corporation recommends 10-gigabit switches with 1- gigabit switches being the minimum. The cost of the 10-gigabit switches has dropped dramatically over the years so these switches are still a top choice.

When Gig-E is not fast enough, the system architects often turn to Infiniband. Infiniband can leverage bandwidths up to 25 Gbps, or 2.5x more than 10 Gbs Ethernet switches and that is in just one lane of traffic! If twelve lanes are used, the Infiniband solution can enjoy 300 Gbps of throughput.

Oracle Corporation's fastest database machine, Oracle Exadata, is a multi-node RAC cluster that uses Infiniband for the Cluster Interconnect. When the Cluster Interconnect needs to perform better, people turn to Infiniband with its higher speeds and lower latency. However, faster speed comes at a cost, and Infiniband hardware has a higher cost than Gig-E. In addition, many network administrators are not familiar with Infiniband so they may need training and have to overcome a learning curve. If you are implementing Infiniband, you might consider employing Reliable Datagram Sockets (RDS) over Infiniband. Oracle recommends RDS because it has lower latency and uses less CPU than IP over Infiniband (IPoIB).

Jumbo Frames and RAC

By default, Ethernet has a variable frame size up to 1,500 bytes. The Maximum Transmission Unit (MTU) defines this upper bound and defaults to the 1,500 byte limitation. If data is sent across the network, the data is broken into pieces no larger than the MTU frame size. Right away, we can see a problem with the MTU limitation for Oracle RAC's Cluster Interconnect. Many Oracle databases are configured with a database block size of 8KB. If one block needs to be transferred across the private network for Cache Fusion purposes, the 8KB block will be broken into six frames. Even with a 2KB block size, the block will be broken into two frames. Those pieces need to be assembled back together when arriving at the destination. To make matters worse, the maximum amount of data Oracle will attempt to transmit is defined by multiplying the *db_block_size* initialization parameter by the *db_file_multiblock_read_count* parameter. A block size of 8KB taken 128 blocks at a time leads to 1 megabyte of data needing to be transferred.

Jumbo Frames allows a MTU value of up to 9,000 bytes. Unfortunately, Jumbo Frames is not allowed in all platforms. Not only does the OS need to support Jumbo Frames, but the network cards in the servers and the network switch behind the private network need to support Jumbo Frames. Many of today's NICs and switches do support Jumbo Frames, but Jumbo Frames is not an IEEE standard, and as such, there may be different implementations that may not all work well together. Not all configurations will support the larger MTU size. When configuring the network pieces, it is important to remember that the smallest MTU of any component in the route is the maximum MTU from point A to B. You can have the network cards configured to support 9000 bytes, but if the switch is configured for a MTU of 1,500 bytes, then Jumbo Frames won't be used. Infiniband supports Jumbo Frames up to 65,000 bytes.

It is out of scope of this book to provide direction on how to enable Jumbo Frames in the network switch. You should talk with their network administrator, who may, in turn, have to consult the switch vendor's documentation for more details. On the OS network interface side, it is easy to configure the larger frame size. The following examples are from Oracle Linux 6. First, we need to determine which device is used for the Cluster Interconnect.

```
[root@host01 ~]$ oifcfg getif

eth0  192.168.56.0  global  public
eth1  192.168.10.0  global  cluster_interconnect
```

The *eth1* device supports the private network. Now we configure the larger MTU size.

```
[root@host01 ~]# ifconfig eth1 mtu 9000

[root@host01 ~]# vi /etc/sysconfig/network-scripts/ifcfg-eth1
```

In the *ifcfg-eth1* file, one line is added that says "MTU=9000" so that the setting persists when the server is restarted.

The interface is verified to ensure the larger MTU is used.

```
[root@host01 ~]# ifconfig -a

eth0      Link encap:Ethernet  HWaddr 08:00:27:98:EA:FE
          inet addr:192.168.56.71  Bcast:192.168.56.255  Mask:255.255.255.0
          inet6 addr: fe80::a00:27ff:fe98:eafe/64 Scope:Link
          UP BROADCAST RUNNING MULTICAST  MTU:1500  Metric:1
          RX packets:3749 errors:0 dropped:0 overruns:0 frame:0
          TX packets:3590 errors:0 dropped:0 overruns:0 carrier:0
          collisions:0 txqueuelen:1000
          RX bytes:743396 (725.9 KiB)  TX bytes:623620 (609.0 KiB)
eth1      Link encap:Ethernet  HWaddr 08:00:27:54:73:8F
          inet addr:192.168.10.1  Bcast:192.168.10.255  Mask:255.255.255.0
          inet6 addr: fe80::a00:27ff:fe54:738f/64 Scope:Link
          UP BROADCAST RUNNING MULTICAST  MTU:9000  Metric:1
          RX packets:268585 errors:0 dropped:0 overruns:0 frame:0
          TX packets:106426 errors:0 dropped:0 overruns:0 carrier:0
          collisions:0 txqueuelen:1000
          RX bytes:1699904418 (1.5 GiB)  TX bytes:77571961 (73.9 MiB)
```

Notice that device *eth1* has the larger MTU setting. The *traceroute* utility can be used to verify the largest possible packet size.

```
[root@host01 ~]# traceroute host02-priv --mtu

traceroute to host02-priv (192.168.10.2), 30 hops max, 9000 byte packets
 1  host02-priv.localdomain (192.168.10.2)  0.154 ms F=9000  0.231 ms  0.183
ms
```

Next, a 9,000 byte packet is sent along the route. The –F option ensure the packet is not broken into smaller frames.

```
[root@host01 ~]# traceroute -F host02-priv 9000

traceroute to host02-priv (192.168.10.2), 30 hops max, 9000 byte packets
 1  host02-priv.localdomain (192.168.10.2)  0.495 ms  0.261 ms  0.141 ms
```

The route worked successfully.

Now a packet one byte larger is sent along the route.

```
[root@host01 ~]# traceroute -F host02-priv 9001

too big packetlen 9001 specified
```

The error from the traceroute utility shows the packet of 9,001 bytes is too big. These steps verify that Jumbo Frames is working. Let's verify that the change improved the usable bandwidth on the cluster interconnect. To do that, the *iperf* utility is used. The *iperf* utility can force a specific packet length with the –l parameter. The public interface is not configured for Jumbo Frames and no applications are connecting to the nodes so the public network can be used as a baseline.

```
[root@host02 ~]# iperf -c host01 -l 9000

------------------------------------------------------------
Client connecting to host01, TCP port 5001
TCP window size: 22.9 KByte (default)
------------------------------------------------------------
[  3] local 192.168.56.72 port 18222 connected with 192.168.56.71 port 5001
[ ID] Interval       Transfer     Bandwidth
[  3]  0.0-10.0 sec   923 MBytes   774 Mbits/sec
```

The same test is repeated for the private network with Jumbo Frames enabled.

```
[root@host02 ~]# iperf -c host01-priv -l 9000

------------------------------------------------------------
Client connecting to host01-priv, TCP port 5001
TCP window size: 96.1 KByte (default)
------------------------------------------------------------
[  3] local 192.168.10.2 port 40817 connected with 192.168.10.1 port 5001
[ ID] Interval       Transfer     Bandwidth
[  3]  0.0-10.0 sec  1.28 GBytes  1.10 Gbits/sec
```

Here we see that the bandwidth increased from 774 Mbs/sec to 1.10 Gbs/sec, a 42% increase! For the same 10 second interval, the number of bytes transferred increased from 923 megabytes to 1.28 gigabytes, a 65% increase!

If the Oracle RAC systems are using Ethernet (Gig-E or 10Gig-E) for the Cluster Interconnect, then the recommendation is to leverage Jumbo Frames for the private network. It is less common to employ Jumbo Frames for the public network interfaces. Jumbo Frames requires that all network components from end to end support the larger MTU sizes. In some cases, it may be tricky to diagnose issues where Jumbo Frames will not work in the system, but even then, the effort is well worth the cost.

Block Size and RAC

The choice of the database block size can have an impact on the Cluster Interconnect. One normally considers the block size parameter, *db_block_size* in relation to disk I/O operations. For Oracle RAC databases, Cache Fusion will also be performing cross-instance I/O as well. It should come as no surprise that the database block size can impact global cache transfers as well.

The general rule of thumb is that databases in support of data warehouses should use large blocks sizes and databases in support of online transaction systems should use smaller block sizes. Oracle RAC database often follow this convention as well.

The smaller the database block, the quicker a block can be read from disk. Just like disk I/O, the smaller the database block, the quicker it is transferred from one instance to another via Cache Fusion. This is just a matter of physics. No matter how fast the Cluster Interconnect is, 2 kilobytes of data can transfer across the network faster than 8 kilobytes. There are studies found which indicate transfer rates similar to the following.

Block Size	Gigabit Ethernet	Infiniband
2K	300 microseconds	100 microseconds
4K	350 microseconds	150 microseconds
8K	450 microseconds	200 microseconds

Table 4.1 Block Size Transfer Times

The actual transfer times do not matter and may vary considerably from environment to environment. The numbers in the table above are just meant to illustrate the effect of larger block sizes on global cache transfers.

Initially, one might look at the table above and conclude that for Oracle RAC databases, we should always choose the smaller block size. While a 2KB block transfers faster than a 4KB block, the amount of data being transferred per millisecond is improved as the block size increases. Using the figures from the table above, easy mathematics calculates the transfer rate as shown in the next table.

Block Size	Gigabit Ethernet	Infiniband
2K	0.00667 KB/ μ s	0.020000 KB/ μ s
4K	0.01142 KB/ μ s	0.026667 KB/ μ s
8K	0.01778 KB/ μ s	0.040000 KB/ μ s

Table 4.2 Block Size Throughput

The values in the table above were derived by simple math, i.e. block size divided by time in microseconds. In any case, the larger the block size, the more data per microsecond is transferred.

So based on the information in both tables, which block size should be used? The answer all depends on the application and how it accesses data. If the application accesses few rows at a time, then the smaller block size is preferred as it returns the data back to the application quicker than larger block sizes. If the application regularly accesses multiple rows or large amounts of data then a larger block size is preferred.

To illustrate the concept using the example times above, consider an online transaction processing system where a query selects one row from the table and the table has an average row length of 148 bytes. A database block size of 8KB would contain, on average, 55 rows of data. A database block size of 2KB would contain, on average, 13 rows of data. If the application is seeking 1 row, the 8KB block size would force a read of 54 unneeded rows of data while the 2KB block size would force a read of 12 unneeded rows of data. The one row would be returned in 300 microseconds if the 2KB block size is used or 450 microseconds for the 8KB block size. For applications that exhibit this behavior, a smaller block size is preferred. The application would benefit from the metrics seen in the first table of this section.

On the flip side is the application that processes many rows of data and each row is larger than as described in the previous paragraph. Assume the application selects thousand rows of the table at a time and each row in the table averages 533 bytes. The typical data access pattern would seek 533,000 bytes at a time. For the 2KB block size, 261 blocks would be needed whereas for the 8KB block size, 66 blocks would be needed. In this example, the application would benefit from the metrics in the second table of this section.

The examples above assumed that each data block was completely full, i.e. no space reserved for future update or insert operations. The examples further assume that all rows were the average size and they packed nicely into the block. Data in blocks rarely cooperate in this fashion in the real world. The examples are used to illustrate the points made in this section. However, the main ideas of each example will hold true even if a parameter like *pctfree* is used to reserve space for future updates. In the end, the only thing that matters is end user application performance. If you are considering the block size to be used, perform adequate testing of the application with different block sizes to determine the most optimal setting. Remember that Oracle has one default block size but you can also employ non-default block sizes as well to have the best of all worlds. Many of today's applications do not exhibit true OLTP or DW behavior but have characteristics of both. One could choose a block size that is in the middle of allowable values or one could deploy multiple block sizes for their application.

Sizing UDP in RAC

Oracle's Grid Infrastructure uses the User Datagram Protocol (UDP) for private network traffic. Most IT practitioners are already familiar with the Transmission Control Protocol over Internet Protocol (TCP/IP). UDP is a different protocol over IP. UDP is leveraged for the private network because it has lower overhead than TCP. There is no handshaking involved to ensure the sender is ready to receive data. With UDP, there is no guarantee that data will be delivered. The lower overhead does make UDP faster, which is exactly what is needed from the cluster's private network. The Oracle documentation states that the public network uses TCP/IP and the private network needs UDP.

Configuring UDP on the cluster nodes is OS-specific. Oracle supports too many platforms for Grid Infrastructure to talk about all certified platforms in this chapter. This book will discuss UDP settings for Linux. Other platforms will have different configuration settings so refer to platform-specific documentation for additional information.

The easiest way to configure the UDP-related kernel settings in Linux is to implement the Oracle-validated RPM. Doing so will automatically update the /etc/sysctl.conf file with the following lines.

```
# oracle-rdbms-server-12cR1-preinstall setting for net.core.rmem_default is
262144
net.core.rmem_default = 262144

# oracle-rdbms-server-12cR1-preinstall setting for net.core.rmem_max is
4194304
net.core.rmem_max = 4194304

# oracle-rdbms-server-12cR1-preinstall setting for net.core.wmem_default is
262144
net.core.wmem_default = 262144

# oracle-rdbms-server-12cR1-preinstall setting for net.core.wmem_max is
1048576
net.core.wmem_max = 1048576
```

These lines can also be added manually. The values in /etc/sysctl.conf are exported to network configuration files in /proc/sys/net/core as seen below. The /proc/sys/net/core values are also overwritten on reboot so changes need to be made to */etc/sysctl.conf* to persist across server shutdowns.

```
[root@host01 core]# cd /proc/sys/net/core

[root@host01 core]# cat rmem_default

262144

[root@host01 core]# cat rmem_max

4194304

[root@host01 core]# cat wmem_default

262144

[root@host01 core]# cat wmem_max

1048576
```

The "rmem" parameter settings are for the receive socket memory. The "wmem" parameters are for the send (write) socket memory.

When data is being sent on the network, the sockets are initially sized with the default value. The socket sizes are dynamically adjusted to meet demands. The sockets can increase up to the maximum defined size and can be decreased below the starting, default socket size.

The usual settings have 256KB for the default socket size and 4GB for the maximum receive socket and 1GB for the maximum write socket. For most Oracle RAC implementations, these socket settings will work just fine. Occasionally, the maximum socket sizes may need to be increased. The default socket sizes should never be different than the Oracle recommendation.

The big question becomes how does the database administrator know when to raise the maximum socket size? The /usr/sbin/ss utility can help answer the question. The old tried and true netstat command is obsolete. A number of programs are replacing it. For instance, "netstat –r" shows routing information and it is replaced by the "ip route" command. The /usr/sbin/ss command shows socket statistics. In Oracle Linux 6, the UDP sockets can be seen with a command similar to the following:

```
[root@host01 ~]# /usr/sbin/ss -m|grep mem

     mem:(r0,w0,f0,t0)
     mem:(r0,w0,f0,t0)
     mem:(r0,w0,f0,t0)
     mem:(r0,w0,f0,t0)
     mem:(r0,w0,f0,t0)
     mem:(r0,w0,f0,t0)
```

```
mem:(r0,w0,f0,t0)
mem:(r0,w0,f0,t0)
mem:(r0,w0,f0,t0)
mem:(r0,w0,f0,t0)
mem:(r0,w0,f0,t0)
mem:(r0,w0,f0,t0)
mem:(r0,w0,f0,t0)
mem:(r0,w0,f0,t0)
mem:(r0,w0,f0,t0)
mem:(r15446,w0,f938,t0)
mem:(r0,w0,f0,t0)
mem:(r0,w0,f0,t0)
mem:(r0,w0,f0,t0)
mem:(r0,w0,f0,t0)
mem:(r0,w0,f0,t0)
mem:(r0,w0,f0,t0)
mem:(r0,w0,f0,t0)
mem:(r0,w0,f0,t0)
mem:(r0,w0,f0,t0)
mem:(r0,w0,f0,t0)
mem:(r34588,w0,f2276,t0)
mem:(r0,w0,f0,t0)
mem:(r0,w1297,f2799,t0)
```

The outputs from this command is showing the read and write socket sizes in use.
Any lines with 0 bytes for read and write (r0 and w0) can be ignored. Instead, focus
on the lines of output that have non-zero values for read and write. The database
administrator needs to compare the bytes in use to the *rmem_max* and *wmem_max*
socket settings. If any of these approach the maximum limits for the read and write
sockets, the database administrator may need to consider raising the maximum socket
sizes. In the example above, the maximum read socket is 34,588 bytes, well below
rmem_max. The maximum write socket is 1,297 bytes, again, well below *wmem_max*.

Be very careful before raising either *rmem_max* or *wmem_max*. Increasing these values
can cause higher CPU usage, as larger datagrams need to be handled. If these values
are raised too high, then there is an increased risk in datagram loss, which means data
loss on the Cluster Interconnect. It is very rare to need to increase the maximum
socket sizes outside of the Oracle recommendations for Oracle RAC systems. Before
raising the maximum read and write socket sizes in production, it is vitally important
that thorough testing be performed to understand the impact.

GC Block Lost

No network is perfect. Data transmitted from point A to point B may occasionally get lost. The same is true for global cache transfers along the Cluster Interconnect. Global cache block transfers can get lost. If a requested block is not received by the instance in 0.5 seconds, the block is considered to be lost. When most block transfers complete in milliseconds, too many lost global cache block transfers can hamper application performance because the block needs to be re-sent, thus wasting time for the second transfer to complete.

Lost global cache block transfers can be seen in two different areas. Wait events named *gc cr block lost* and *gc current block lost* will be raised when a consistent read block transfer is lost, or when a current block transfer is lost, and the session must wait for the block to be resent. The other area is for the Oracle statistics named *gc blocks lost* as can be seen on the system or session level. Examples of these two metrics are seen below.

🖫 gc_blocks_lost.sql

```
select
    inst_id,
    event,
    total_waits,
    time_waited
  from
    gv$system_event
  where
    event in ('gc current block lost',
              'gc cr block lost')
  order by
    event,
    inst_id;

   INST_ID EVENT                                     TOTAL_WAITS TIME_WAITED
---------- ----------------------------------------- ----------- -----------
         1 gc cr block lost                                   50        3029
         2 gc cr block lost                                   75        4516
         1 gc current block lost                              26        1467
         2 gc current block lost                              36        2060
select
    sn.inst_id,
    sn.name,
    ss.value
  from
    gv$statname sn,
    gv$sysstat ss
  where
    sn.inst_id = ss.inst_id
    and
    sn.statistic# = ss.statistic#
```

```
    and
    sn.name = 'gc blocks lost'
 order by
 sn.inst_id;

  INST_ID NAME                           VALUE
--------- ---------------------  ----------
        1 gc blocks lost                    90
        2 gc blocks lost                   164
```

The output above shows the metrics on a per-instance basis. One can certainly summarize the values across all instances if desired.

The presence of blocks lost in wait events or a system statistic is not sufficient to cause us great concern. Just like any network, there may be an occasional hiccup that would lead to lost block transfers and would appear in the *gv$sysstat* view. As with any wait event, the wait event metric by itself is essentially meaningless as there is no context from the output above. Is the wait event a "Top 5" wait event? Where the wait events generated over a 1-hour time period or 1 month? Since we do not know the answers to these questions, we cannot determine if the metrics are indicating a problem or not. More information is needed. An AWR report from a 1-hour snapshot of time can be more indicative that a real problem exists.

```
Top 5 Timed Foreground Events
~~~~~~~~~~~~~~~~~~~~~~~~~~~~~~~
                                                 Avg
                                                wait    % DB
Event                        Waits    Time(s)   (ms)   time Wait Class
---------------------------  ---------  ---------  ------  ------  ----------
DB CPU                                     6,975           32.1
db file sequential read    3,831,277     5,809       2   26.8 User I/O
gc current block lost          3,819       942     247    4.3 Cluster
db file parallel read        145,588       854       6    3.9 User I/O
gc cr multi block request    535,685       498       1    2.3 Cluster
```

Above, the *gc current block lost* wait event is in the Top 5 list. The listing above now provides context to the wait event in question. This event contributes the second longest total wait time for the instance during the one-hour time period. However, if the wait event were totally eliminated, only 4.3% of the total processing time would be recovered. From a performance tuning perspective, where the end goal is often to reduce processing time, it would be better to focus on the *db file sequential read* wait event that is contributing 26.8% of the total database time or determining if the CPU utilization can be decreased as that is contributing to 32.1% of the total time. That being said, it is never a good sign when any global cache blocks being lost are a top wait event.

The most common reason for lost global cache blocks is a faulty private network, i.e. one that is dropping packets. If global cache lost blocks are seen as a problem, then work with the network administrator to ensure the switch is valid, cables are secure and seated properly, firmware levels are up to date, and that other network configuration issues are not a problem. The network administrator should be able to use network tools like netstat and anything else in their arsenal to check for dropped packets on the private network.

```
[root@host01 ~]# netstat -su

IcmpMsg:
    InType0: 91
    InType3: 723
    InType8: 23
    OutType0: 23
    OutType3: 928
    OutType8: 103
Udp:
    664034038 packets received
    983 packets to unknown port received.
    20080 packet receive errors
    654621700 packets sent
UdpLite:
IpExt:
    InMcastPkts: 18041
    OutMcastPkts: 8745
    InBcastPkts: 102377
    OutBcastPkts: 119
    InOctets: 4678332299675
    OutOctets: 2652878623355
    InMcastOctets: 1401313
    OutMcastOctets: 636504
    InBcastOctets: 19312376
    OutBcastOctets: 49090
```

The *netstat* utility is reporting UDP packet receive errors, indicating global cache lost block transfers for this node of the cluster. In addition to verifying the hardware is correct, the network administrator should investigate the following:

- Private network is truly private
- Oversaturated bandwidth due to too much traffic on the network
- Quality of Service (QoS) settings that may be downgrading performance
- Incorrect Jumbo Frames configuration
- Multiple hops between the nodes and the private network switch
- Mismatched MTU settings between devices
- Mismatch in duplex mode settings between devices
- Incorrect bonding/teaming configuration

If everything on the network side checks out, then look to sizing the UDP settings to have larger socket sizes as discussed in the previous section of this chapter. Global cache lost blocks are not always a network issue. After the network has been verified and UDP socket sizes are correct, look to see if CPU resources are in short supply.

Top GC Transfers

In tuning the Cluster Interconnect, it is often desirable to know which database objects are involved in the most global cache transfer operations. A simple query to the *gv$segment_statistics* view looking for all segments involved in "gc" operations will do the trick.

gc_top_5_segments.sql

```
select
   *
from (
   select
      owner||'.'||object_name as segment_name,
      sum(value) as total_gc_ops
   from
      gv$segment_statistics
   where
      statistic_name like 'gc%'
   group by
      owner||'.'||object_name
   order by
      sum(value) desc)
where
   rownum <= 5;
```

SEGMENT_NAME	TOTAL_GC_OPS
HOBBES.DATA_SUPPRESSION_EXCHANGE	9324769
ACCTG.ACCTS_RCVBL	6947711
ACCTG.ACCTS_PAYBL	6750072
HOBBES.APPLICATION_HEART_BEAT	6481296
HOBBES.TRANSFER_RATES	5596916

The output above shows the five segments most involved in global cache operations. The primary mechanism to reduce global cache operations, thus reducing the demands placed on the Cluster Interconnect, is to partition the applications using the Oracle RAC database as was discussed in Chapter 2 of this book. From the output above, the database administrator may guess that the applications using the *hobbes* and *acctg* schemas are not partitioned. There is no query that can be run to determine with 100% certainty if the applications are segregated or not but the database administrator can get a good idea by querying *gv$services* to see which services are being used.

🖫 db_services.sql

```
select
    inst_id,
    name
from
    gv$services
where
    name not in ('SYS$BACKGROUND',
                 'SYS$USERS')
    and
    name not like '%XDB'
    and
    upper(name) not in (select
                            name
                        from
                            v$database);
```

```
   INST_ID NAME
---------- -----------------------------------------
         1 hobbes_svc
         1 acctg_svc
         2 hobbes_svc
         2 acctg_svc
```

Both application services are on all nodes of the cluster so it looks like the applications could benefit from partitioning on the cluster nodes. Once segregated correctly, the global cache related waits should drop significantly, but will not be reduced entirely. If application partitioning is in effect or is not possible, then other methods in Chapter 2 can be used to reduce the global cache transfers such as reverse key indexes, etc.

Details of the top-5 global cache segments can easily be determined from *gv$segment_statistics* as well. From the same system, but at a different time, the database administrator can see details on the top-5 segments in the output below.

🖫 gc_top_5_segment_details.sql

```
select
    top5.owner,
    top5.object_name,
    stats.statistic_name,
    sum(stats.value) as total_value
from (
        select
            owner,
            object_name
        from (
```

```
      select
        owner,
        object_name,
        sum(value)
      from
        gv$segment_statistics
      where
        statistic_name like 'gc%'
      group by
        owner,
        object_name
      order by
        sum(value) desc)
    where
        rownum <= 5) top5
join
   gv$segment_statistics stats
   on top5.owner = stats.owner
   and
   top5.object_name = stats.object_name
where
   stats.statistic_name like 'gc%'
group by
   top5.owner,
   top5.object_name,
   stats.statistic_name
order by
   top5.owner,
   top5.object_name,
   stats.statistic_name;
```

OWNER	OBJECT_NAME	STATISTIC_NAME	TOTAL_VALUE
ACCTG	ACCTS_PAYBL	gc buffer busy	13865
ACCTG	ACCTS_PAYBL	gc cr blocks received	14481
ACCTG	ACCTS_PAYBL	gc current blocks received	7987430
ACCTG	ACCTS_RCVBL	gc buffer busy	103746
ACCTG	ACCTS_RCVBL	gc cr blocks received	3468327
ACCTG	ACCTS_RCVBL	gc current blocks received	3406565
HOBBES	APPLICATION_HEART_BEAT	gc buffer busy	12068
HOBBES	APPLICATION_HEART_BEAT	gc cr blocks received	58261
HOBBES	APPLICATION_HEART_BEAT	gc current blocks received	7155963
HOBBES	DATA_SUPPRESSION_EXCHANGE	gc buffer busy	682
HOBBES	DATA_SUPPRESSION_EXCHANGE	gc cr blocks received	22976
HOBBES	DATA_SUPPRESSION_EXCHANGE	gc current blocks received	6274004
HOBBES	TRANSFER_RATES	gc buffer busy	16521
HOBBES	TRANSFER_RATES	gc cr blocks received	78158
HOBBES	TRANSFER_RATES	gc current blocks received	11564921

```
15 rows selected.
```

The detailed information can be helpful to not only see which segments are at the top of the list, but also what kind of contention exists for those segments.

This section has discussed the top segments involved in global cache transfers. A few scripts were provided to help the database administrator understand the segments using the most global cache transfers in the system. One way to reduce the block transfers is to tune SQL statements to perform the fewest reads possible to satisfy the query. Application partitioning is another method. However, keep in mind that application partitioning may reduce the available resources for the application's end users. It is possible that global cache wait events are preferable to reduced resources. Careful testing must be performed before throwing a switch to partition applications.

Cluster Interconnect Performance

It is often helpful to know how well the Cluster Interconnect is performing. Previous sections discussing Jumbo Frames and the correct sizing of UDP socket sizes show how to configure the private network, which should be done correctly even if performance is currently sufficient. An incorrect configuration may not scale over time. The next section of this chapter discusses how to leverage Highly Available IP (HAIP) to improve interconnect throughput but prior to that discussion, this chapter will discuss how to measure the Cluster Interconnect performance.

There are many metrics that can be examined through various $gv\$$ views will be shown in this section. The AWR report aggregates the metrics in nice little summaries. On a side note, the AWR report is part of the extra cost Diagnostics Pack and Performance Pack options. Many companies do not feel the need to license this option. However, the Diagnostics Pack and Performance Packs are well worth the cost. It saves the database administrator a lot of time and over the long run, pays for itself many times over. Earlier in this chapter, the following section of the AWR report was shown.

```
Global Cache Load Profile
~~~~~~~~~~~~~~~~~~~~~~~~~~~~          Per Second        Per Transaction
                                     ---------------    ---------------
    Global Cache blocks received:        1,279.68                 79.62
      Global Cache blocks served:          637.30                 39.65
         GCS/GES messages received:      4,367.95                271.76
           GCS/GES messages sent:        7,440.72                462.94
              DBWR Fusion writes:           21.15                  1.32
Estd Interconnect traffic (KB)           17,642.23
```

Above, we see that the estimated Interconnect traffic shown above is 17,642 kilobytes per second. If the Cluster Interconnect uses Gigabit-Ethernet, then the maximum transfer speed of 1 gigabit per second or approximately 125,000 kilobytes per second. The AWR report shows an average that is much less than the theoretical maximum of the switch. If the metric reaches values close to the private network's maximum speed, it is time to consider augmenting the Cluster Interconnect with HAIP.

The AWR report gives additional metrics for the Cluster Interconnect performance.

```
Global Cache and Enqueue Services - Workload Characteristics
~~~~~~~~~~~~~~~~~~~~~~~~~~~~~~~~~~~~~~~~~~~~~~~~~~~~~~~~~~~~~~~~
                  Avg global enqueue get time (ms):     0.0

        Avg global cache cr block receive time (ms):     0.6
   Avg global cache current block receive time (ms):     0.9

          Avg global cache cr block build time (ms):     0.0
           Avg global cache cr block send time (ms):     0.0
     Global cache log flushes for cr blocks served %:    42.0
          Avg global cache cr block flush time (ms):     1.3

      Avg global cache current block pin time (ms):     0.0
      Avg global cache current block send time (ms):     0.0
 Global cache log flushes for current blocks served %:    0.1
     Avg global cache current block flush time (ms):     2.6
```

The average block receive time is reported in milliseconds. Anytime these metrics are more than a few milliseconds, it could be an indicator that the private network is having problems keep up with demand. In the example above, the average times are less than 1 millisecond. The *gv$sysstat* view can provide similar information.

💾 gc_read_waits.sql

```
select
        a.inst_id,
        a.value as read_waits,
        b.value as read_wait_time,
        b.value/a.value as "AVG_TIME_PER_WAIT(ms)"
   from
      (select
         inst_id,
         name,
         value
      from
         gv$sysstat
      where
         name ='gc read waits') a,
      (select
         inst_id,
         name,
         value
         from
         gv$sysstat
         where
         name ='gc read wait time') b
   where
      a.inst_id=b.inst_id
   order by
      a.inst_id;
```

```
INST_ID READ_WAITS READ_WAIT_TIME AVG_TIME_PER_WAIT(ms)
---------- ---------- --------------- ----------------------
        1     201317          111036            .551548056
        2     194547           79916            .410779914
        3     158460           84841            .535409567
```

Again, each instance is showing less than 1 millisecond per wait, on average. Keep in mind that *gv$* views have metrics that are only collected since instance startup time. Peak periods of activity may not be seen in an overall average taken over a period of days, weeks, or months. A smaller sample window may be more desirable depending on the performance problem that has been encountered.

Near the end of the AWR report, there are additional metrics on Global Cache Transfer Statistics.

```
Global Cache Transfer Stats    DB/Inst: ORCL/orcl1   Snaps: 47609-47610

-> Immediate (Immed) - Block Transfer NOT impacted by Remote Delays
-> Busy      (Busy)  - Block Transfer impacted by Remote Contention
-> Congested (Congst)- Block Transfer impacted by Remote System Load
-> ordered by CR + Current Blocks Received desc


                          CR                         Current
            ------------------------------- -------------------------------
Inst Block     Blocks     %      %      %    Blocks     %      %      %
No   Class   Received  Immed  Busy Congst  Received  Immed  Busy Congst
---- -----   -------- ------ ------ ------  -------- ------ ------ ------
   2 data block  118,751   75.5   20.9    3.6 2.30E+06   86.4     .2   13.4
   3 data block  111,713   83.3   14.1    2.5 1.92E+06   86.7     .1   13.1
   2 Others        9,816   96.1    1.9    2.0   45,260   85.2     .5   14.4
   3 Others       10,849   95.6    2.0    2.3   41,024   89.2     .6   10.2
   2 undo header  16,319   93.3    5.5    1.1    1,301   94.9    3.3    1.8
   3 undo header   5,087   88.5   10.3    1.1    1,209   94.8    4.0    1.2
   2 undo block    4,282   97.9     .7    1.4        0    N/A    N/A    N/A
   3 undo block    3,686   96.2    2.5    1.4        0    N/A    N/A    N/A
```

The AWR report above is from instance 1 of a three node clustered database. As such, the report shows transfers between instance 1 and the other two instances. This explains why the Inst No column only shows instances 2 and 3. This summary is showing the block transfer classifications. The output shows data blocks, undo transfers, and anything else is lumped into the "Others" category. It is not surprising that the data block classification accounts for the bulk of the transfers. Of the data block transfers, 75.5% CR blocks were received from instance 2 immediately and 83.3 CR blocks were received from instance 3 immediately. Approximately 86% of the current blocks were received immediately.

As it relates to Cluster Interconnect performance, the next summary in the AWR report shows the transfer times in milliseconds.

```
Global Cache Transfer Times (ms)   DB/Inst: ORCL/orcl1   Snaps: 47609-47610

-> Avg Time - average time of all blocks (Immed,Busy,Congst) in ms
-> Immed, Busy, Congst - Average times in ms
-> ordered by CR + Current Blocks Received desc

                    CR Avg Time (ms)              Current Avg Time (ms)
                -------------------------      -----------------------------
Inst Block
  No Class      All   Immed  Busy  Congst      All   Immed  Busy  Congst
---- --------  -----  -----  -----  ------     -----  -----  -----  ------
   2 data blo   0.8    0.4    1.9    1.5        0.9    0.8    1.1    1.8
   3 data blo   0.6    0.4    1.7    1.1        0.9    0.7    1.6    1.8
   2 others     0.4    0.4    1.9    0.7        0.8    0.7    1.8    1.2
   3 others     0.4    0.4    1.9    1.7        0.6    0.6    1.6    0.9
   2 undo hea   0.3    0.3    1.4    0.5        0.4    0.3    1.5    0.4
   3 undo hea   0.4    0.3    1.8    0.7        0.4    0.3    1.5    0.3
   2 undo blo   0.3    0.3    1.3    0.8        N/A    N/A    N/A    N/A
   3 undo blo   0.3    0.3    1.2    0.6        N/A    N/A    N/A    N/A
               ----------------------------------------------------------
```

Again, this summary breaks down the metrics by requests served immediately and those where remote contention was an issue. Ideally, the metrics should be below one millisecond for the immediate requests. If longer than a few milliseconds, the private network may not be fast enough.

Immediate requests from other instance are often a good indicator of the private network performance. The next summary in the AWR report captures the metrics on just Immediate block transfer request, those not impacted by delays on the other instances.

```
Global Cache Transfer (Immediate)  DB/Inst: ORCL/orcl1   Snaps: 47609-47610

-> Immediate  (Immed) - Block Transfer NOT impacted by Remote Processing
Delays
-> % of Blocks Received requiring 2 or 3 hops
-> ordered by CR + Current Blocks Received desc

                               CR                        Current
                    -------------------------    ----------------------------
Src Block    Blocks  Immed Blks    %       %    Immed Blks    %        %
Inst Class    Lost    Received    2hop    3hop   Received    2hop     3hop
---- --------  ------ ----------  ------  ------ ----------  ------   ------
   2 data blo    0      89,668    64.8    35.2  1,984,898    78.8     21.2
   3 data blo    0      93,098    70.1    29.9  1,668,142    78.5     21.5
   2 others      0       9,433    65.6    34.4     38,540    73.6     26.4
   3 others      0      10,375    68.4    31.6     36,574    75.4     24.6
   2 undo hea    0      15,227   100.0     0.0      1,235    96.6      3.4
   3 undo hea    0       4,504   100.0     0.0      1,146    99.4      0.6
   3 undo blo    0       4,194   100.0     0.0          0    N/A      N/A
   2 undo blo    0       3,545   100.0     0.0          0    N/A      N/A
                -------------------------------------------------------------
```

One important metric to look at is the *Blocks Lost* column. If there are non-zero values, than it can be indicative of datagram loss on the UDP transfers as discussed in an earlier section of this chapter. This summary also includes breakdowns on 2-hop and 3-hop transfers.

An important summary section in the AWR report is the Interconnect Ping Latency section.

```
Interconnect Ping Latency Stats     DB/Inst: ORCL/orcl1  Snaps: 47609-47610

-> Ping latency of the roundtrip of a message from this instance to ->
target in
-> The target instance is identified by an instance number.
-> Average and standard deviation of ping latency is given in miliseconds
-> for message sizes of 500 bytes and 8K.
-> Note that latency of a message from the instance to itself is used as
-> control, since message latency can include wait for CPU

   Target 500B Pin Avg Latency    Stddev  8K Ping Avg Latency   Stddev
  Instance   Count    500B msg  500B msg    Count     8K msg    8K msg
 --------- -------- ----------- ---------- -------- ----------- -----------
         1      285         .21        .10      285         .22         .10
         2      285         .26        .11      285         .33         .24
         3      285         .21        .09      285         .27         .24
 -----------------------------------------------------------------------
```

The grid Infrastructure regularly pings all of the instances in the cluster. It uses a 500-byte ping size and an eight-kilobyte ping size. These pings occur approximately every five seconds. The ping times should be in the sub-millisecond range as is shown above. One important thing to note is that this summary gives a baseline. The Ping Latency Stats includes a ping from the instance to itself as the baseline. This AWR report was generated on instance 1 of the database. The average ping time to the other instances should be near the average ping time to itself otherwise there may be private network contention.

At times, the database administrator may need to know what type of traffic is on the Cluster Interconnect. The following script will break down the private network traffic by transfer type. This script is one of the rare ones that will access a *x$* fixed view and will most likely need to be executed by a sysdba user.

interconnect_traffic_breakdown.sql

```
select
    name,
    trunc(bytes_sent/1024/1024) as mb_sent,
    trunc(bytes_rcv/1024/1024) as mb_recv,
```

```
    trunc((bytes_sent+bytes_rcv)/1024/1024) as mb_total,
    to_char(round(100*(((bytes_sent+bytes_rcv)/1024/1024)/
      sum((bytes_sent+bytes_rcv)/1024/1024) over ()),2),'990.00') as
total_perc
  from
    sys.x$ksxpclient
  order by
    total_perc desc;
```

NAME	MB_SENT	MB_RECV	MB_TOTAL	TOTAL_P
cache	268609	236650	505259	59.48
ipq	94032	98765	192797	22.70
dlm	62596	78489	141085	16.61
diag	991	2375	3366	0.40
ksxr	505	2518	3024	0.36
cgs	1130	1112	2243	0.26
ping	808	808	1616	0.19
ksv	0	0	0	0.00
streams	0	0	0	0.00
internal	0	0	0	0.00
osmcache	0	0	0	0.00

The output from the script shows various traffic types. The top entry, accounting for 59.48% of all traffic, is for global cache transfers. The second entry, accounting for 22.70% of all traffic, is for parallel query execution transfers. The third entry shows traffic just to satisfy Distributed Lock Manager information exchange. Note that the output of this script is just the private network to and from this node. Other nodes may have different values. For those environments that have licensed the Diagnostics Pack, the *dba_hist_ic_client_stats* view shows the same information and this view does collect the statistics for all instances.

HAIP

Oracle 11gR2 introduced the Highly Available IP (HAIP) for the Cluster Interconnect to help eliminate a single point of failure. If the node in the cluster only has one network adapter for the private network, and that adapter fails then the node will no longer be able to participate in cluster operations. It will not be able to perform its heartbeat with the cluster. Eventually, the other nodes will evict the failing node from the cluster. If the cluster only has a single network switch for the Cluster Interconnect and the switch fails, then the entire cluster is compromised. Examine the diagram below which shows one public network and two private networks.

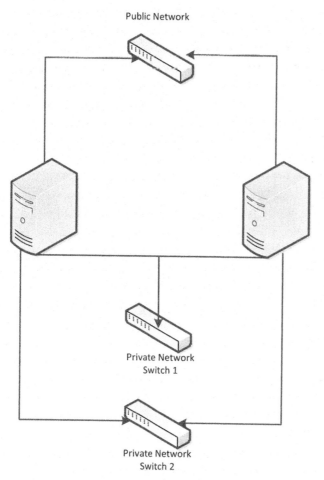

Public Network

Private Network
Switch 1

Private Network
Switch 2

Figure 4.1 Redundant Private Networks

Each node in the cluster has access to dual private networks. The single points of failure have been eliminated. Note that dual network adapters serve as the interfaces to dual network switches.

One cannot simply stand up a second private network and expect the clusterware software to start utilizing both networks. Without any additional configuration, only one private network would be used and the other would sit idle.

Prior to Oracle 11gR2, system architects that were concerned with the single point of failure would leverage *link aggregation*. The terms *NIC bonding*, *NIC teaming*, or *port trunking* are also used for the same concept. The central idea behind link aggregation is to have two private networks act as one. The two private networks are combined together to appear to the operating system as one unit. To the OS, the network adapters look like one adapter. If one of the physical network adapters were to fail, the OS would hardly notice and network traffic would proceed through the remaining adapter.

This is not a book on maximum availability architecture and at this point you may be asking what link aggregation has to do with Oracle RAC performance tuning? In addition to higher availability for the cluster, link aggregation improves the private network throughput. Two private networks have twice the capacity, and thus, twice the throughput of a single private network. When the traffic on the Cluster Interconnect saturates a singular private network, another option is to leverage link aggregation to improve the global cache transfer performance.

Oracle Grid Infrastructure now provides HAIP, which is link aggregation moved to the clusterware level. Instead of bonding the network adapters on the OS side, Grid Infrastructure in instructed to use multiple network adapters. Grid Infrastructure will still start HAIP even if the system is configured with only one private network adapter. The following shows the resource name *ora.cluster_interconnect.haip* is online.

```
[oracle@host01 bin]$ ./crsctl stat res -t -init
-------------------------------------------------------------------------
Name            Target  State      Server              State details
-------------------------------------------------------------------------
Cluster Resources
-------------------------------------------------------------------------
ora.asm
      1         ONLINE  ONLINE     host01              Started,STABLE
ora.cluster_interconnect.haip
      1         ONLINE  ONLINE     host01              STABLE
ora.crf
      1         ONLINE  ONLINE     host01              STABLE
ora.crsd
      1         ONLINE  ONLINE     host01              STABLE
ora.cssd
      1         ONLINE  ONLINE     host01              STABLE
ora.cssdmonitor
      1         ONLINE  ONLINE     host01              STABLE
ora.ctssd
      1         ONLINE  ONLINE     host01              OBSERVER,STABLE
ora.diskmon
      1         OFFLINE OFFLINE                        STABLE
ora.evmd
      1         ONLINE  ONLINE     host01              STABLE
ora.gipcd
      1         ONLINE  ONLINE     host01              STABLE
ora.gpnpd
      1         ONLINE  ONLINE     host01              STABLE
ora.mdnsd
      1         ONLINE  ONLINE     host01              STABLE
ora.storage
      1         ONLINE  ONLINE     host01              STABLE
-------------------------------------------------------------------------
```

Furthermore, only one adapter is defined for the Cluster Interconnect.

```
[oracle@host01 bin]$ ./oifcfg getif

eth0  192.168.56.0  global  public
eth1  192.168.10.0  global  cluster_interconnect
```

The *ifconfig* command shows that network device *eth1* is part of two subnets.

```
[oracle@host01 bin]$ ifconfig -a
eth0      Link encap:Ethernet  HWaddr 08:00:27:98:EA:FE
          inet addr:192.168.56.71  Bcast:192.168.56.255  Mask:255.255.255.0
          inet6 addr: fe80::a00:27ff:fe98:eafe/64 Scope:Link
          UP BROADCAST RUNNING MULTICAST  MTU:1500  Metric:1
          RX packets:947 errors:0 dropped:0 overruns:0 frame:0
          TX packets:818 errors:0 dropped:0 overruns:0 carrier:0
          collisions:0 txqueuelen:1000
          RX bytes:100821 (98.4 KiB)  TX bytes:92406 (90.2 KiB)

eth1      Link encap:Ethernet  HWaddr 08:00:27:54:73:8F
          inet addr:192.168.10.1  Bcast:192.168.10.255  Mask:255.255.255.0
          inet6 addr: fe80::a00:27ff:fe54:738f/64 Scope:Link
          UP BROADCAST RUNNING MULTICAST  MTU:9000  Metric:1
          RX packets:406939 errors:0 dropped:0 overruns:0 frame:0
          TX packets:382298 errors:0 dropped:0 overruns:0 carrier:0
          collisions:0 txqueuelen:1000
          RX bytes:445270636 (424.6 MiB)  TX bytes:202801222 (193.4 MiB)

eth1:1    Link encap:Ethernet  HWaddr 08:00:27:54:73:8F
          inet addr:169.254.225.190  Bcast:169.254.255.255  Mask:255.255.0.0
          UP BROADCAST RUNNING MULTICAST  MTU:9000  Metric:1
```

The entry for *eth1* with IP address 192.168.10.1 is the way the NIC was configured on this system for the private network. Notice the device listed as eth1:1 in the output above. It has been given the 169.254.225.190 IP address.

Device eth1:1 is HAIP in action even though only one private network adapter exists. HAIP uses the 169.254.*.* subnet. As such, no other network devices in the cluster should be configured for the same subnet.

When Grid Infrastructure is stopped, the ifconfig command will no longer show the eth1:1 device. The *gv$cluster_interconnects* view shows the HAIP subnets for each instance.

```
select
    inst_id,
    name,
    ip_address
  from
    gv$cluster_interconnects;
```

```
INST_ID NAME          IP_ADDRESS
---------- --------------- ----------------
        1 eth1:1        169.254.225.190
        2 eth1:1        169.254.230.98
```

Notice that for instance 1, the name of the interconnect device and the IP address seen in *gv$cluster_interconnects* is the same as shown with the *ifconfig* command. The alert log also shows HAIP being configured on instance startup.

```
Private Interface 'eth1:1' configured from GPnP for use as a private
interconnect.
  [name='eth1:1', type=1, ip=169.254.225.190, mac=08-00-27-54-73-8f,
net=169.254.0.0/16, mask=255.255.0.0, use=haip:cluster_interconnect/62]
Public Interface 'eth0' configured from GPnP for use as a public interface.
  [name='eth0', type=1, ip=192.168.56.71, mac=08-00-27-98-ea-fe,
net=192.168.56.0/24, mask=255.255.255.0, use=public/1]
```

While HAIP is running, there is no redundancy or additional network bandwidth because only one network interface is configured. If a second network interface is available for the private network, it will need to be added to Grid Infrastructure. The device needs to be a well-configured network adapter in the operating system. The new network interface needs to have the same configuration as the current interface, i.e. both must be on the same subnet, have the same MTU size, etc. The oifcfg command is used to set the new interface as a *cluster_interconnect* device.

```
[oracle@host01 bin]$ ./oifcfg setif –global \
eth3/192.168.10.0:cluster_interconnect

[oracle@host01 bin]$ ./oifcfg getif

eth0  192.168.56.0  global  public
eth1  192.168.10.0  global  cluster_interconnect
eth3  192.168.10.0  global  cluster_interconnect
```

The device *eth3* is now part of the Cluster Interconnect. The commands do not need to be repeated on all nodes as Grid Infrastructure takes care of that for us. On *host02*, the device is already configured.

```
[oracle@host02 bin]$ ./oifcfg getif

eth0  192.168.56.0  global  public
eth1  192.168.10.0  global  cluster_interconnect
eth3  192.168.10.0  global  cluster_interconnect
```

Grid Infrastructure needs to be restarted on all nodes.

```
[root@host01 bin]# ./crsctl stop crs
[root@host01 bin]# ./crsctl start crs
```

Once the cluster nodes are back up and running, the new interface will be part of the HAIP configuration.

```
[root@host01 ~]# ifconfig -a
eth0      Link encap:Ethernet  HWaddr 08:00:27:98:EA:FE
          inet addr:192.168.56.71  Bcast:192.168.56.255  Mask:255.255.255.0
          inet6 addr: fe80::a00:27ff:fe98:eafe/64 Scope:Link
          UP BROADCAST RUNNING MULTICAST  MTU:1500  Metric:1
          RX packets:5215 errors:0 dropped:0 overruns:0 frame:0
          TX packets:6593 errors:0 dropped:0 overruns:0 carrier:0
          collisions:0 txqueuelen:1000
          RX bytes:2469064 (2.3 MiB)  TX bytes:7087438 (6.7 MiB)

eth1      Link encap:Ethernet  HWaddr 08:00:27:54:73:8F
          inet addr:192.168.10.1  Bcast:192.168.10.255  Mask:255.255.255.0
          inet6 addr: fe80::a00:27ff:fe54:738f/64 Scope:Link
          UP BROADCAST RUNNING MULTICAST  MTU:9000  Metric:1
          RX packets:3517 errors:0 dropped:0 overruns:0 frame:0
          TX packets:2771 errors:0 dropped:0 overruns:0 carrier:0
          collisions:0 txqueuelen:1000
          RX bytes:789056 (770.5 KiB)  TX bytes:694387 (678.1 KiB)

eth1:1    Link encap:Ethernet  HWaddr 08:00:27:54:73:8F
          inet addr:169.254.21.30  Bcast:169.254.127.255  Mask:255.255.128.0
          UP BROADCAST RUNNING MULTICAST  MTU:9000  Metric:1

eth3      Link encap:Ethernet  HWaddr 08:00:27:6A:8B:8A
          inet addr:192.168.10.3  Bcast:192.168.10.255  Mask:255.255.255.0
          inet6 addr: fe80::a00:27ff:fe6a:8b8a/64 Scope:Link
          UP BROADCAST RUNNING MULTICAST  MTU:9000  Metric:1
          RX packets:857 errors:0 dropped:0 overruns:0 frame:0
          TX packets:511 errors:0 dropped:0 overruns:0 carrier:0
          collisions:0 txqueuelen:1000
          RX bytes:158563 (154.8 KiB)  TX bytes:64923 (63.4 KiB)

eth3:1    Link encap:Ethernet  HWaddr 08:00:27:6A:8B:8A
          inet addr:169.254.170.240 Bcast:169.254.255.255 Mask:255.255.128.0
          UP BROADCAST RUNNING MULTICAST  MTU:9000  Metric:1
```

The new interface is also found in the *gv$cluster_interconnects* view.

```
select
    inst_id,
    name,
    ip_address
 from
    gv$cluster_interconnects;


  INST_ID NAME            IP_ADDRESS
--------- --------------- ----------------
        1 eth1:1          169.254.21.30
        1 eth3:1          169.254.170.240
        2 eth1:1          169.254.75.234
        2 eth3:1          169.254.188.35
```

In the end, setting up HAIP was as simple as using the "oifcfg setif" command to add a new network adapter as part of the Cluster Interconnect and restarting Grid Infrastructure. In addition to removing a single point of failure in the Cluster Interconnect, additional bandwidth is now available to the private network that can help improve cluster performance.

In Summary

This chapter has discussed many aspects related to tuning the Cluster Interconnect. The chapter started with a section talking about the private network and its need to truly be private. Not only should the private network not have any application traffic on it, the network should not be shared with other non-RAC related network traffic.

- When making changes to any part of the system configuration, it is desirable to have a utility that can benchmark the system before and after the change. This chapter shows how to use the iperf utility although other utilities can be used. Iperf works well because it can test both TCP and UDP traffic, both of which Oracle RAC uses.

- The chapter then discussed aspects in configuring Jumbo Frames and UDP for the Cluster Interconnect. While many might not think it important for network tuning, the Chapter provided a section on how the *db_block_size* parameter is important, not only for the database configuration but also for the private network.

- This chapter discussed the effect of losing global cache transfer blocks and how to identify the top segments involved in those transfers. A number of AWR report sections were shown as they can help analyze Cluster Interconnect performance.

- The chapter finished by discussing network adapter aggregation to provide not only high availability but also higher private network throughput. Oracle 11gR2 introduced HAIP to simplify link aggregation at the Grid Infrastructure level.

This chapter discussed one shared RAC component, the Cluster Interconnect. The next chapter moves to the other shared RAC component, the shared storage.

Tuning RAC Storage

CHAPTER

5

Central to every instance of an Oracle RAC database is the storage system. Remember, all nodes in the RAC cluster need access to the same shared storage devices, and it is important to tune the storage system sufficiently. Otherwise performance will suffer not just for one user or for one instance, but for all instances serving the clustered database.

While the Cluster Interconnect is the glue that holds the instances together to form one cohesive unit, the shared storage is the town hall, the one place everyone goes to get information. This chapter will discuss various storage-related areas that need to be tuned for Oracle RAC databases.

Tuning storage for Single Instance RAC

Don't forget that the best approach for disk I/O tuning is to tune as if the database were of the single-instance variety. This was mentioned in the first chapter and most people think it applies just to the application side. But Oracle RAC storage needs to be tuned with all of the storage-related techniques as if this were a single-instance database.

For example, tuning concepts such as separating hot spots on disk and keeping write-intensive files away from RAID levels that introduce a write penalty are still tops on the list of storage tuning items to apply to an Oracle RAC database. It is even more important in Oracle RAC to tune the storage well. Poor storage tuning practices that one may be able to get away with in a single-instance database may be magnified once multiple instances are involved hitting the same files.

Consider the fact that that in an Oracle RAC configuration, multiple servers exist to parallelize the workload. As was discussed in the previous chapter, HAIP or NIC Bonding lets us implement parallel networks to improve the Cluster Interconnect throughput. Many Oracle RAC implementations forget about providing parallel pathways to the shared storage or scaling the storage subsystem's IOPs capacity to handle the extra workload.

The choice of the *db_block_size* parameter is an important consideration. Databases that deal with transactions short in duration and with small amounts of data, like online transaction processing systems, will work best with a smaller block size. Databases that deal with larger amounts of data, like Data Warehouses, will work best with larger block sizes. The previous chapter discussed the impact of the *db_block_size* on global cache transfers on the private network. However, long before Oracle RAC, the *db_block_size* choice was about the impact on disk I/O operations. We can now see that with Cache Fusion, the choice of the *db_block_size* setting is even more important because it affects multiple areas, disk I/O and Cluster Interconnect traffic.

Disk I/O patterns are just as important as if this were a single-instance database. Online redo logs are write-intensive. When the log fills up, the archive process creates a copy of the log file in the archive log destination. If the archive log destination is on the same physical disk as the online redo logs, disk head contention can significantly slow down the time to archive the log file. It is normal to have the archive log destination segregated from the online redo logs.

The undo tablespace is write-intensive as well. A transaction will cause write operations to occur to both the online redo logs and the undo tablespace with one change. As such, the online redo logs should be separated from the undo tablespace. For some systems, the temporary tablespace can also see lots of write activity. Application tablespaces vary in their I/O patterns depending on the application. Some application's tablespaces are read only or even read mostly while other tablespaces have high degrees of write activity. The database administrator needs to understand the read/write patterns on the various files that comprise an Oracle database and segregate I/O patterns accordingly to ensure optimal performance. In should go without saying that a properly tuned application where SQL statements perform a minimum of disk activity always helps an Oracle database perform better.

RAC Disk Architecture

Lots of options are available to one designing the disk subsystem to support an Oracle RAC database. It can be daunting to wade through all of the options to arrive at a high-performing shared storage architecture. This section provides an overview of the disk architecture options.

It is beneficial to work with the storage vendor of choice when implementing an Oracle RAC shared storage solution. We try to work with vendors who have experience with Oracle RAC implementations. Good vendors can help us wade through the myriad of options in their portfolio as well as provide documentation on how to configure their hardware solution for optimal Oracle RAC performance.

The first option to consider is the disk devices. Many of today's options include Fibre Channel (FC), Serial ATA (SATA), and Serial Attached SCSI (SAS) interfaces. Fibre Channel disks offer high speed, but also come with a high price. SATA disks are high capacity but much slower than FC disks. SAS disks bridge the gap between FC and SATA disks. If performance is our goal, we should consider the fastest disks available.

Disk speed is comprised of multiple factors: the seek time, the rotational delay, and the time to read from disk. The seek time is the time it takes for the disk head to move into position above the sector that contains the data. Rotational delay is the amount of time it takes for the disk to spin into position so that the data is under the disk head. Since rotational delay and the time to read the data from disk are influenced by how fast the disk platter spins, the faster the platter rotates, the faster the disk. The Revolutions Per Minute (RPM) metric is one metric of the disk's speed. Another disk speed metric is the data transfer rate, it's throughput, often expressed in megabytes per second.

The Solid State Disk (SSD) is the newest player to the market offering excellent disk performance and it is maturing every day as a viable enterprise-level disk platform. Basically, a SSD is physical memory that acts like a disk drive. The SSD has no moving components and is not subject to the same wear and tear as a normal disk drive. That being said, the SSD drive is typically rated to support a certain number of write operations over its lifetime. Not only is the SSD fast, it typically requires less energy and does not run as hot so it does not need to be cooled. The SSD device works great for reads and writes.

 Tip! New research has shown that sequential writes are not that much faster in a SSD than traditional disks. This means that it is not cost effective to put online redo logs on SSD devices.

Most of today's storage vendors offer SSD devices in their portfolio. We recommend that you work with the vendor to determine how to best implement their SSD platform for your Oracle RAC deployment.

Disk devices can be placed in a Storage Area Network (SAN). The server needs a Host Bus Adapter (HBA) card. The HBA is like a NIC, but for storage. The HBA connects the database server to a SAN fabric switch, which in turn is connected to disk controllers. The SAN should have redundant controllers and fabric switches for high availability. The redundant components also provide additional throughput similar to the way HAIP provides additional throughput for the Cluster Interconnect. The SAN is often an expensive piece of infrastructure to build. As such, the Oracle RAC database often has to share the SAN with other non-database IT infrastructure needs. Care needs to be taken to ensure the storage administrator has not over-provisioned the SAN in such a manner that the Oracle RAC database performance suffers. This often means that the storage administrator needs to zone the SAN properly.

The storage architect has a wide range of options for the SAN. Many SAN deployments use Fibre Channel (FC) switches with Fibre Channel over IP (FCoIP) and iSCSI becoming more popular for RAC systems. In order to keep the SAN up and running and performing optimally, it is recommended:

> 1 - Have a storage expert on staff (temporarily) so that you do not not burden the DBA with storage optimization work.

> 2 - It is also recommended to work with the storage vendor for their specific instructions on how to set up the SAN for Oracle RAC. Many storage vendors have documentation for running Oracle RAC on their product. If the vendor does not have such documentation and is not helpful with setting up their product to support Oracle RAC, then choose another storage vendor.

Network Attached Storage (NAS) is a very good alternative to using a SAN. The Network File System (NFS) protocol allows NAS devices to be used as shared storage for Oracle RAC. One major appeal of NAS disk storage is that is does not require special fabric switches or special HBA cards in the server. NAS disk storage works with traditional network switches already in place in the data center.

> **Tip!** It is a RAC best practice for the server to have Network Interface (NIC) cards devoted just to the server to storage network connection. Do not use the public or private network interfaces of an Oracle RAC node to access the NAS storage devices, otherwise Oracle RAC performance can suffer.

Furthermore, it is a very good idea to have separate redundant NIC cards to provide redundancy and higher throughput for NAS storage access. This would mean a minimum of five NIC cards in the server; one for the public network, two for the redundant private network, and two for the redundant storage network.

The disks can be configured for redundancy and performance as well by specifying RAID levels. The Redundant Array of Independent Disks (RAID) level controls how data is mirrored and/or striped across disk volumes. Mirroring duplicates one disk onto another disk. Changes to either disk are automatically applied to the other disk so that the two disk units are mirror images of each other. RAID 1 is the level for disk mirroring. The downside to RAID 1 is that the level of redundancy comes at a high cost. Implementing RAID 1 cuts the total available disk space in half. If company buys a 20-terabyte storage solution, RAID 1 will make that into 10 terabytes of usable space. Even though disk is cheap, as the saying goes, it is a bitter pill to swallow to lose half of your enterprise disk solution before any data is stored on it. Also, some shops will triple mirror disks for mean time between failures expressed in centuries.

RAID 5 and RAC

Many storage administrators tend to favor RAID 5 that stripes data across multiple disk units (more on striping in a little bit) and also distributes parity information among those disk units. The computed parity is used to reconstruct data in the event one disk unit is unavailable. A typical RAID 5 configuration would use approximately fifteen to twenty percent of the disk space in the RAID group to support parity bits, depending on the number of disk units in that group.

While using less space to support redundancy compared to RAID1, The downside to RAID 5 is the time for write operations to complete. When a block of data is changed on RAID 5 disk, the disk needs to read the current value and read the current parity information. Then the new value is written to disk and then the new parity is written to disk. Two write operations occur for every write request received. As such, write operations on RAID 5 can take twice as long to complete compared to RAID 1.

 Warning! Never place write-intensive database files on RAID 5 disk devices otherwise performance may suffer. Write intensive files include online redo logs, archived redo logs, tempfiles, the undo tablespace, and any other tablespace that has anything more than a small amount of change.

It is common to see 1 terabyte, or larger, high-capacity disk drives being sold today. With the larger capacity drives used in the disk subsystem, RAID 6 is becoming more popular. Where RAID 5 protects against loss of one disk in the RAID group, RAID 6 protects against the loss of two disks in the RAID group by using double parity.

Using double parity adds one more write operation than seen in RAID 5 so RAID 6 should not be used to support Oracle RAC databases.

RAID striping and RAC

Different RAID levels stripe data across multiple disks for higher performance. Instead of placing a single file on one disk drive, that file may be broken up into multiple chunks. The first chunk would be placed on the first disk drive. The second chunk would be placed on the second drive, and so on. When a chunk is written to the last drive in the RAID group, the next chunk is written to the first disk drive and so on. The size of the chunk is called the *stripe size* or *stripe length*. The number of disks in the group is called the *stripe width*.

Striping helps performance by using multiple disks in parallel. If there are five disks in the RAID group, reading a file should complete in about one-fifth of the time a single disk would take. RAID 0 stripes data on the disks in the group. There is no redundancy so RAID 0 isn't technically "RAID" but we live with the RAID 0 designation. RAID 5, which as discussed above, is not good for write performance but is great for read performance due to striping on multiple disk volumes.

Tablespaces that are read only or "read mostly" can be placed on RAID 5 disk groups with great success so long as the application can tolerate the slower writes to the tablespace. Many database administrators like RAID 0+1 or RAID 1+0, which combines RAID 0 with RAID 1. In RAID 0+1, the data is striped first and then mirrored. RAID 1+0 mirrors first and then stripes. Both of these RAID levels offers great all-around performance for both read and write operations, but comes at the high cost as RAID 1 does. This is the Oracle "standard" solution called S.A.M.E. (Stripe And Mirror Everywhere).

Most of this section is not specific to Oracle RAC. It is meant as a primer to disk architecture terminology to help understand material later in this chapter. It would not be surprising if the reader is already familiar with the material in this section. While this section does contain some common-sense information for disk systems supporting Oracle databases, it also provides a few rules of thumb for Oracle RAC implementations: redundant paths from nodes to storage and zoning storage.

Next, let's examine the Oracle Orion I/O testing utility.

Oracle Orion testing utility

In the previous chapter, the *iperf* utility was used to obtain performance metrics of the Cluster Interconnect. However, many other network performance tools exist. For Oracle databases, there is one disk performance tool that today's Oracle database administrators typically use, called "Orion". While many utilities can measure disk performance, Orion is the only tool engineered to simulate Oracle database disk calls using the same I/O software as the Oracle database engine. Prior to Orion, one used other available disk performance utilities. However, those utilities never quite come close to mimicking Oracle database I/O. So the next tactic was to use a performance tool that would generate a load on an Oracle instance. However, things like the Buffer Cache can often skew the results as to make the test metrics unusable for measuring just disk performance. Orion combines the best of both worlds. Oracle Corporation supplies Orion for a very good price, free.

Orion stands for ORacle I/O Numbers. The utility does not need an Oracle database created on the server. The documentation says that Orion does not need the Oracle RDBMS software installed. However the easiest way to obtain the utility is by installing Oracle 11.2 and higher.

Orion can simulate a variety of workloads including:

- Small random I/O similar to OLTP applications.
- Large sequential I/O similar to data warehouse applications.
- Large random I/O to test striping across multiple disk units.
- A mixed workload of small random I/O and either large sequential I/O or large random I/O.

We use Orion to test the storage system that will be most representative of the application type to be deployed against the database on that storage.

An easy way to understand Orion is to see it in action. This first example will test NFS disk storage. The NFS storage must be mounted to the server. A file needs to be created to use in the test. The file should be at least 1 gigabyte in size. If the file is too small, it can negatively impact the results. The *dd* command can be used to pre-create a file for testing.

```
[oracle@host01 orion_test]$ dd if=/dev/zero of=test.file bs=1G count=1

1+0 records in
1+0 records out
1073741824 bytes (1.1 GB) copied, 114.455 seconds, 9.4 MB/s
```

```
[oracle@host01 orion_test]$ ls -l

total 1052712
-rw-r--r-- 1 oracle oinstall 1073741824 Jul 24 22:16 test.file
```

If there are multiple NFS mounts to be tested, create a file on each mount point. Orion needs to know the test file names so a parameter file will be created containing the file names, one to a line. The parameter file's name must be of the format "*testname*.lun" where *testname* is defined at runtime. If no test name is provided, it defaults to "orion". The file created above is the only line in the file named "firsttest.lun" as can be seen below.

```
[oracle@host01 ~]$ cat firsttest.lun

/u01/app/oracle/orion_test/test.file
```

All that's left is to start Orion. The first test will simulate a small random I/O workload so the run type will be "oltp". The test system is Linux but does not have huge pages configured. Orion's default is to use huge pages. So Orion needs to be instructed to not use huge pages with the *–hugenotneeded* parameter. For systems that do have huge pages configured, use the default setting. Running the Orion utility produces output similar to the following.

```
[oracle@host01 ~]$ $ORACLE_HOME/bin/orion -run oltp \
> -testname firsttest -hugenotneeded

ORION: ORacle IO Numbers -- Version 11.2.0.4.0
firsttest_20140724_2232
Calibration will take approximately 22 minutes.
Using a large value for -cache_size may take longer.


Maximum Small IOPS=13018 @ Small=15 and Large=0
Small Read Latency: avg=1152 us, min=312 us, max=11984 us, std dev=390 us @
Small=15 and Large=0

Minimum Small Latency=921 usecs @ Small=11 and Large=0
Small Read Latency: avg=921 us, min=304 us, max=85692 us, std dev=462 us @
Small=11 and Large=0
Small Read / Write Latency Histogram @ Small=11 and Large=0
    Latency:                   # of IOs (read)      # of IOs (write)
        0 - 1      us:              0                    0
        2 - 4      us:              0                    0
        4 - 8      us:              0                    0
        8 - 16     us:              0                    0
       16 - 32     us:              0                    0
       32 - 64     us:              0                    0
       64 - 128    us:              0                    0
      128 - 256    us:              0                    0
      256 - 512    us:           2102                    0
```

```
     512 -    1024       us:    603335                                    0
    1024 -    2048       us:     91864                                    0
    2048 -    4096       us:     16386                                    0
    4096 -    8192       us:      2090                                    0
    8192 -   16384       us:        71                                    0
   16384 -   32768       us:        10                                    0
   32768 -   65536       us:         3                                    0
   65536 -  131072       us:         1                                    0
  131072 -  262144       us:         0                                    0
  262144 -  524288       us:         0                                    0
  524288 - 1048576       us:         0                                    0
 1048576 - 2097152       us:         0                                    0
 2097152 - 4194304       us:         0                                    0
 4194304 - 8388608       us:         0                                    0
 8388608 - 16777216      us:         0                                    0
16777216 - 33554432      us:         0                                    0
33554432 - 67108864      us:         0                                    0
67108864 - 134217728     us:         0                                    0
134217728 - 268435456    us:         0                                    0
```

Right after the Orion test starts running, it will provide an estimate of how long the test will take to complete. After the test is complete, metrics on IOPS and latency are provided. The last part of the output on the screen shows a histogram of latency.

In the output above, the latency for read operations fell between 256 microseconds to 131072 microseconds with the bulk in the 512 to 1024 microsecond range. The OLTP test did not perform any write operations. While the output on the screen is good information to know, the best output is provided in some in the comma-separated values (CSV) files Orion creates. The file names will contain the test name and the date and time of the test. Two important CSV files are the one that shows IOPS and the other that shows megabytes per second. Visualization of data points is often better than raw data. The IOPS CSV file contents are loaded into a spreadsheet and the output is graphed as seen in the graph below.

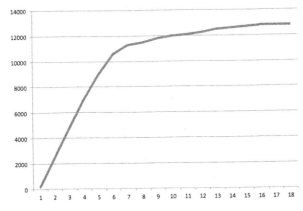

Figure 5.1: Orion IOPS Graph

Throughput graphs often level off as the data points move to the right side of the graph. Where the graph levels off, the system being measured is saturated. In the graph above, this disk storage becomes saturated around 13,000 IOPS.

The OLTP test provided IOPS metrics for the disk subsystem. The data warehouse test provides MBPS metrics by performing large sequential I/O operations. The only difference in the way the second test is executed lies with the *–run* parameter to define the run type.

```
[oracle@nau-rac01 ~]$ $ORACLE_HOME/bin/orion -run dss \
> -testname secondtest -hugenotneeded

ORION: ORacle IO Numbers -- Version 11.2.0.4.0
secondtest_20140725_0948
Calibration will take approximately 65 minutes.
Using a large value for -cache_size may take longer.

Maximum Large MBPS=66.85 @ Small=0 and Large=6
```

The output on the screen for the DSS, or data warehouse test, is much smaller than for the random I/O, OLTP test. Only one item of note is provided on the screen, the maximum megabytes per second. Similar to the OLTP test, a CSV file (comma delimited spreadsheet file) is generated which can be visualized in a Excel spreadsheet graph.

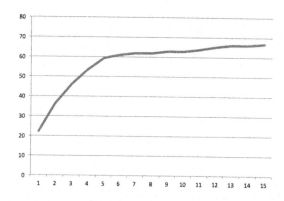

Figure 5.2: Orion MBPS Graph

Not surprisingly, the graph levels off as it travels to the right. This shape is a classic throughput profile. This book could have shown the data points, but the visual representation provides a much clearer picture. The figure above clearly shows the throughput levels off once the disk subsystem crosses 60 MBPS.

Orion can be a very useful tool in determining the throughput and performance of the disk subsystem. This section is only meant as a primer on Orion's capabilities. More information on Orion can be found in the Oracle Performance Tuning Guide in the I/O Configuration and Design chapter.

Many storage systems have a variety of configuration parameters to tune the disk access for optimal performance. Use Orion to obtain a performance baseline. As disk system parameters are tweaked, Orion can be run again to determine if the change will improve performance for an Oracle database. For instance, later in this chapter there is a section discussing mount point options for NAS storage. Orion can be used to obtain a baseline of the NAS storage performance. Then change a mount point option and run the same Orion test again. Comparing to the baseline will help understand if the change helped or hurt storage performance for an Oracle RAC database.

Migrations from a single-instance database system to Oracle RAC can benefit greatly from using Orion before the RAC migration takes place. We use Orion to obtain a baseline on the single-instance disk units. When running Orion, it is important to make sure the disk units have no other activity because it can skew the Orion results. With the Oracle RAC shared storage up and running, run Orion again and compare the results to the single-instance baseline. In sum, the RAC shared storage should perform no worse than the single-instance database's disk subsystem.

ASM and RAC

For Oracle RAC databases, the files need to be accessed concurrently by multiple processes on multiple nodes. Even as far back as the Oracle Parallel Server days, the shared storage of the clustered database could use a third party Clustered File System (CFS) or raw disks that had no file system. Without a CFS or raw disks, multiple processes could not simultaneously open and modify shared files without causing file corruption. The CFS would look and appear just like any normal file system and one can interact with the files with traditional OS file commands like *cp* and *mv*. Two downsides exist with using a CFS for Oracle RAC.

1. One, the company had to buy a CFS before it could be implemented.

2. Two, implementing a third party's solution between the storage and the Oracle database was not always seamless and did not always work flawlessly.

At one point, Oracle Corporation released the Oracle Cluster File System (OCFS) but the product is at the end of its life in favor of ASM. Using raw disks saved the cost associated with a CFS. Raw disks generally perform faster than a CFS because there is no overhead associated with managing the files. However, raw disks are more difficult to work with. Traditional OS file commands do not work with data files stored on raw disk. Furthermore, starting with Oracle 12c, raw disks are no longer supported for use with an Oracle database.

As an alternative to raw devices, Oracle introduced Automatic Storage Management (ASM) with the 10g release. ASM is Oracle's file system implementation that can be used in place of a CFS or raw disk. Oracle Corporation recommends ASM for Oracle RAC implementations. ASM provides file system and volume management built right into the Oracle kernel.

Right off the bat, using ASM reduces latency time because there is no interaction between the Oracle kernel and the OS and a traditional file system and therefore ASM exhibits performance similar to raw disks. ASM not only provides optimal performance for Oracle RAC databases, it also has very good manageability aspects as well, making ASM a wise choice. Also, ASM is required for Oracle RAC Standard Edition deployments but Enterprise Edition deployments can use a clustered file system.

ASM is not limited to Oracle's clustered databases. Single-instance databases can be deployed on ASM file systems as well. The database administrator looking to migrate from a single-instance environment to Oracle RAC may already be familiar with ASM.

In Oracle 11g, ASM is part of the Grid Infrastructure software stack. Using ASM on a single-instance database means adding another software installation to the mix. Oracle RAC deployments require Grid Infrastructure anyway so using ASM for Oracle RAC does not require anything that isn't already installed on the cluster nodes.

ASM is in use for many Oracle databases around the world so ASM is very familiar to many DBA's. This section will not discuss how to implement, use, and manage ASM for Oracle databases simply to save space. This section will show how to configure Oracle RAC databases using ASM, providing information the database administrator may not be familiar with.

All nodes in the cluster should have multipathing enabled for access to ASM disk units. Multipathing provides redundant routes from the host to the disk. Should a disk controller or host bus adapter card fail, multipathing will route the I/O request along the other route. Implementing multipathing ensures the high availability side of Oracle RAC. Multipathing also provides a higher level of performance similar to HAIP for the Cluster Interconnect as discussed in the previous chapter. Two paths to the shared storage mean twice the throughput.

When using ASM, some additional tuning needs to be performed. Oracle recommends increasing the *processes* parameter by 16 to support ASM needs in the SGA. The Shared Pool should be increased by 600 kilobytes. The Large Pool will hold ASM extent maps and needs to be increased as well. The following script will determine the Large Pool increase depending on the ASM redundancy level.

🖫 asm_large_pool_recommendations.sql

```
set serveroutput on
declare
    db_file_size    number;
    log_file_size   number;
    temp_file_size  number;
    tot_file_size   number;
    recommend_size  number;
begin
    select
        sum(bytes) into db_file_size
    from
        v$datafile;

    select
        sum(bytes) into log_file_size
    from
        v$log;

    select
        sum(bytes) into temp_file_size
    from
        v$tempfile;

    tot_file_size := db_file_size+log_file_size+temp_file_size;
    tot_file_size := tot_file_size/1024/1024/1024;
    dbms_output.put_line('Total DB Size (GB):
'||round(tot_file_size,2)||chr(10));

        -- external redundancy
    recommend_size := round(2 + floor(tot_file_size/100),2);
    dbms_output.put_line('For External Redundancy increase Large Pool by
'||recommend_size||' MB');

        -- normal redundancy
    recommend_size := round(4 + floor(tot_file_size/50),2);
    dbms_output.put_line('For Normal Redundancy increase Large Pool by
'||recommend_size||' MB');
```

```
    -- high redundancy
    recommend_size := round(6 + floor(tot_file_size/33),2);
     dbms_output.put_line('For High Redundancy increase Large Pool by
'||recommend_size||' MB');

  end;
/
```

Total DB Size (GB): 7.35

For External Redundancy increase Large Pool by 2 MB
For Normal Redundancy increase Large Pool by 4 MB
For High Redundancy increase Large Pool by 6 MB

PL/SQL procedure successfully completed.

Oracle Corporation make some important recommendations about ASM on RAC:

1. A minimum of four LUNs for each ASM disk group be used to ensure optimal performance.

2. Use no more than two ASM disk groups per instance, one for the database's files and the other for the flash recovery area.

However, multiple disk groups should be used to support different storage tiers in support of Information Lifecycle Management (ILM) where less frequently used data is stored on slow, low-cost disk and the most frequently used data is stored on high-speed disk. Many database administrators often find having a few diskgroups to help segregate I/O hot spots helps, so Oracle recommendation of only two diskgroups is often ignored in practice.

ASM includes dynamic performance views to help collect performance statistics. The *v$asm_disk_stat* view shows statistics broken down by disk group.

🖫 asm_diskgroup_stats.sql

```
select
    '+'||g.name as diskgroup,
    s.bytes_read,
    s.reads/s.read_time as avg_read_time,
    s.bytes_written,
    s.writes/s.write_time as avg_write_time
 from
    v$asm_disk_stat s
    join
    v$asm_diskgroup g
    on s.group_number = g.group_number;
```

DISKGROUP	BYTES_READ	AVG_READ_TIME	BYTES_WRITTEN	AVG_WRITE_TIME
+DATA	7167120896	2.03586	1619842560	1.31321153
+REDO	43447808	.494166224	392464384	.541298912
+VOTE	6473881600	.865554	4196446720	1.83263873

The database administrator can use the metrics above to indicate if a diskgroup is acting "slow". We need historical metrics to understand a well-behaved ASM diskgroup's performance. From the information above, you might ascertain that the +DATA diskgroup is performing terribly because its average read time is much higher than the other disk groups.

This line of thinking, with only the information above, can be dangerous.

The database administrator needs a baseline of good performance to know if the output above is cause for concern. If a baseline of good performance shows the +DATA diskgroup to have an average read time of 6.5, then the metrics above are showing much better read performance than the baseline.

Automatic Storage Management is Oracle's recommended and future direction for Oracle RAC databases. If using ASM, increase the RAC instance's SGA settings as described in this section. If using Automatic Memory Management (AMM), increase the *sga_target* or *memory_target* parameter instead of increasing the Shared Pool and Large Pool individually. Next, let's look at NFS and RAC.

NFS and RAC Tuning

A Network File System (NFS) is becoming a popular choice for Oracle RAC shared storage. In the past, NFS storage units were best suited for department-level file shares but that sentiment has changed, as NFS has become a viable shared storage platform for Oracle RAC. Part of the appeal of NFS is the storage is attached to the cluster nodes through standard networks. NFS does not require special hardware like host bus adapters for each node or Fibre Channel switches between the nodes and the storage making it a much cheaper connectivity model compared to Storage Area Networks.

It's important to note that when implementing NFS for shared storage of a clustered database, we should use dedicated Network Interface Cards for the NFS storage. If the NFS storage does not have its own NIC in the host, disk I/O requests can negatively impact performance of the network it shares, public or private. Additionally, redundancy for the network path to the NFS storage should be implemented. If the host loses access to the storage, the node will be evicted from the cluster, as it won't be able to maintain contact with the voting disks. Just like the Cluster Interconnect uses multipathing for SAN disks, NIC bonding or similar approaches not only provides needed redundancy, it also provides additional throughput.

On Unix and Linux servers, many of the NFS-related performance parameters are defined in the *fstab* configuration file.

```
[oracle@host01 ~]$ cat /etc/fstab

LABEL=/boot                      /boot              ext3     defaults          1 2
tmpfs                            /dev/shm           tmpfs    defaults          0 0
devpts                           /dev/pts           devpts   gid=5,mode=620    0 0
sysfs                            /sys               sysfs    defaults          0 0
proc                             /proc              proc     defaults          0 0
/dev/VolGroup00/LogVol01 swap                       swap     defaults          0 0

192.168.10.3:/vol/rac_crsdata        /u01/app/crs_data        nfs
rw,bg,hard,nointr,rsize=32768,wsize=32768,vers=3,tcp,noac,nointr,suid,timeo=
600,actimeo=0   0 0
192.168.10.3:/vol/rac_data           /u01/app/oracle/oradata     nfs
rw,bg,hard,nointr,rsize=32768,wsize=32768,vers=3,tcp,noac,nointr,suid,timeo=
600,actimeo=0   0 0
```

The last two lines of the above listing shows the NFS mounts. The NFS server is located at 192.168.10.3 on the network. After the IP address is a colon followed by the folder on the NFS server. Following the NFS folder is the mount point name on the database server, then the keyword "nfs" to denote this as a NFS disk volume. What follows the "nfs" keyword are the performance parameters. This /etc/fstab file is from a 64-bit Linux system. Oracle recommends the following parameters for NFS mounts on 64-bit Linux.

Type	Mount Options
Oracle Binaries	rw,bg,hard,nointr,rsize=32768,wsize=32768,tcp,vers=3, timeo=600, actimeo=0
OCR and Voting Disks	rw,bg,hard,nointr,rsize=32768,wsize=32768,tcp,noac,vers=3, timeo=600,actimeo=0
Datafiles	rw,bg,hard,nointr,rsize=32768,wsize=32768,tcp,actimeo=0, vers=3,timeo=600

Table 5.1 64-Bit Linux NFS Mount Options

The mount options above are for Linux 2.6 and higher and for Oracle RAC installations. For additional platforms, other Linux versions or single-instance systems, refer to MOSC Note 359515.1 in My Oracle Support Community.

The Oracle Binaries classification is for volumes that will hold the Grid Infrastructure and RDBMS home directories. These options are only necessary if the home directories are shared on the nodes, and the OCR and Voting disks may have their own options.

The Datafiles type includes data files, temp files, online redo logs, and control files. For RMAN and Data Pump files, any NFS mounts should not include the *noac* option as specifying this can cause poor performance for RMAN backups and Data Pump exports.

Just from looking at the information above, it can be difficult to discern what all of those options mean. The following table summarizes the mount options.

Mount Option	Description
rw	Mounts file system as Read Write.
bg	Mount attempts are performed in the background. Can also be *fg* but not desired.
noac	Disables data and attribute caching. Same as setting both *sync,actimeo=0*".
actimeo=0	Disables attribute caching on the client.
hard	Prevents NFS from returning *short write* errors. A *short write* error will retry every *timeo* intervals. A *short write* error would be detrimental to Oracle RAC systems, so use *hard* not *soft*.
tcp	Forces TCP and will restrict NFS from using UDP.
vers=3	Specifies the NFS protocol version. Version 2 is obsolete.
rsize	This specifies the file systems block size for read operations. Should be an integer multiple of the *db_block_size* parameter. Use Oracle's recommendation for this parameter shown in Table 5.1.
wsize	This specifies the file systems block size for write operations. Should be an integer multiple of the *db_block_size* parameter. Use Oracle's recommendation for this parameter shown in Table 5.1.
nolock	Disables file locking. Do not use this for Oracle RAC.
nointr	If *intr* is specified, allows NFS requests to be interrupted for server failures, which would be detrimental for Oracle RAC. Use *nointr* instead.

Table 5.2 NFS Mount Options

Oracle's recommendations for platform-specific mount options are a great starting point. However, some database administrators have found benefits in deviating from these recommendations. The Orion test tool is a great asset here. Initially, we define the NFS mount points as suggested by Oracle. Then we run the Orion tool to obtain baselines, focusing on the expected database type. With these resulting baseline metrics, the system is ready for testing.   Note that we change one, and only one mount option, and then run the same exact tests again. It is useful to place the tests inside scripts so that testing becomes a push-button operation. After each iteration, we capture metrics and compare to the baseline to see if and how performance improves. Next, we can mix a few changes together and then compare to the baseline.

Many NFS storage vendors have documentation for Oracle RAC on their product. If the vendor does not have such documentation and is not willing to assist with setting up their product to support Oracle RAC, then it might be wise to choose another storage vendor. Oracle Corporation cannot certify every possible NFS product out there so it is incumbent on those designing the Oracle RAC system to verify the storage product works well for their needs. The vendor should be willing to help assist and should have other customers who are deploying Oracle RAC on their products. Following the recommendations in this section, and those of the NFS storage vendor, should help the NFS shared storage system perform very well for Oracle RAC databases.

Direct NFS and RAC Tuning

NFS shared storage for Oracle RAC relies on the NFS protocols in the operating system. The Oracle kernel communicates the I/O request to the OS. Oracle 11g introduced Direct NFS that places the NFS client protocols directly in the Oracle kernel. Standard NFS client protocols in the OS are designed for general purpose I/O needs. Oracle's Direct NFS client protocols are optimized for an Oracle database's I/O needs.

Oracle Corporation recommends Direct NFS for shared storage on NAS devices. Direct NFS provides higher reliability by allowing up to four different network paths from the node to the disk storage. Direct NFS will detect a failure on one of the paths and automatically reissue the I/O request on another available path, relieving the kernel from the failure resolution responsibilities.

This chapter already discussed how Direct NFS has NFS client protocols to optimize Oracle database performance. Additionally, Direct NFS provides asynchronous I/O so that processes do not have to wait for an I/O request to complete before moving on to the next task. Direct NFS also bypasses any OS memory set aside for file caching. Bypassing the OS file cache means one less hop between the I/O request and the disk storage system. Another benefit of bypassing the OS file cache is that is eliminates CPU resources to copy data from the OS file cache into the SGA. Lastly, bypassing the OS file cache reduces RAM consumption. Direct NFS not only performs better than the operating system's NFS client protocols, it uses fewer resources as well.

To implement Direct NFS, the database administrator needs to shutdown the Oracle RAC instances.

```
[oracle@host01 ~]$ srvctl stop database -d orcl -o immediate
```

In the *$ORACLE_HOME/lib* directory on all nodes, we issue the following commands:

```
[oracle@host01 ~]$  cd $ORACLE_HOME/lib

[oracle@host01 lib]$ mv libodm11.so libodm11.so.bkup

[oracle@host01 lib]$ ln -s  libnfsodm11.so libodm11.so

[oracle@host01 lib]$ l libodm*
```

```
-rw-r--r-- 1 oracle oinstall  7402 Apr  4 10:55 libodm11.a
lrwxrwxrwx 1 oracle oinstall    14 Jul 26 15:28 libodm11.so ->
libnfsodm11.so
lrwxrwxrwx 1 oracle oinstall    12 Apr  4 10:50 libodm11.so.bkup ->
libodmd11.so
-rw-r--r-- 1 oracle oinstall 12291 Apr  4 10:55 libodmd11.so
```

Note above that the libodm11.so softlink now points to the Direct NFS library file. Next, the database administrator starts the instances.

```
[oracle@host01 lib]$ srvctl start database -d orcl
```

To verify the Direct NFS is being used, look for this entry in the Oracle Alert Log when the instance is started.

```
Oracle instance running with ODM: Oracle Direct NFS ODM Library Version 3.0
```

Later in the Alert Log, messages similar to the following will appear.

```
Direct NFS: channel id [0] path [192.168.10.3] to filer [192.168.10.3] via
local [] is UP
Direct NFS: channel id [1] path [192.168.10.3] to filer [192.168.10.3] via
local [] is UP
```

Direct NFS usage can also be seen in the *v$dnfs_servers* view.

```
select
    svrname,
    dirname
from
    v$dnfs_servers;
```

```
SVRNAME                 DIRNAME
------------------      --------------------
192.168.10.3            /vol/rac_data
```

If Direct NFS is not being used, the above query will return zero rows. Files under Direct NFS control can be seen in the *v$dnfs_files* view.

```
select
    filename
from
    v$dnfs_files;
```

```
FILENAME
-----------------------------------------
/u01/app/oracle/oradata/orcl/control01.ctl
/u01/app/oracle/oradata/orcl/control02.ctl
/u01/app/oracle/oradata/orcl/system01.dbf
/u01/app/oracle/oradata/orcl/sysaux01.dbf
/u01/app/oracle/oradata/orcl/undotbs01.dbf
/u01/app/oracle/oradata/orcl/undotbs02.dbf
/u01/app/oracle/oradata/orcl/users01.dbf
/u01/app/oracle/oradata/orcl/temp01.dbf
/u01/app/oracle/oradata/orcl/redo01.log
/u01/app/oracle/oradata/orcl/redo02.log
/u01/app/oracle/oradata/orcl/redo03.log
/u01/app/oracle/oradata/orcl/redo04.log
```

Direct NFS also keeps performance statistics on read and write activity with the *v$dnfs_stats* view.

🖫 dnfs_disk_stats.sql

```
select
    p.program,
    d.nfs_readbytes + d.nfs_writebytes as nfs_totalbytes
from
    v$dnfs_stats d
    join
    v$process p
    on d.pnum = p.pid;
```

```
PROGRAM                                   NFS_TOTALBYTES
----------------------------------------  --------------
oracle@host02.naucom.com (DBW0)               1387520
oracle@host02.naucom.com (LGWR)               1217024
oracle@host02.naucom.com (CKPT)              26903552
```

```
oracle@host02.naucom.com  (SMON)          27377664
oracle@host02.naucom.com  (RECO)              8192
oracle@host02.naucom.com  (MMON)           4229120
```

Many of the rows were trimmed from the output above for brevity. The script above works for Oracle 12c and beyond. In Oracle 11g, the columns *nfs_readbytes* and *nfs_writebytes* are changed to *nfs_read* and *nfs_write* respectively.

As a summary, if the shared storage is on NAS disk storage, Oracle recommends using Direct NFS over traditional NFS protocols. Direct NFS is very easy to implement. Direct NFS performs better than regular NFS by bypassing the OS file system cache and using asynchronous I/O calls.

OCR and Voting Disks with RAC Tuning

There really isn't a lot for the Oracle Cluster Registry (OCR) and Voting Disks on the topic of performance tuning. All nodes need access to these two otherwise the node will be evicted from the cluster and rebooted. Any disk subsystem that is capable of handling database disk I/O should be more than capable enough to handle the I/O requirements for the OCR and Voting Disks. Neither of these is very I/O intensive. It is good practice to separate the OCR and Voting disks from other files. Intensive I/O for other files should not impact performance accessing the OCR or Voting disks.

Starting in Oracle release 11.2 we began the process of deprecating "raw" disk devices. Prior to Oracle 11.2, it was possible for Oracle RAC deployments to place the OCR and Voting Disks on raw disk. While still possible in 11.2, the Oracle Universal Installer (OUI) would not allow these files to be placed on raw disk but upgrades from previous versions still allowed it. Starting with Oracle 12c, using raw disk devices is de-supported so it may be time to move the OCR and Voting Disks to ASM, Oracle's preferred disk storage location.

Tuning Online Redo Logs in a RAC environment

The Online Redo Log (ORL) for Oracle RAC is slightly different than a single-instance database. Most database administrators know that it is good practice to have at least three ORL groups for the database. What may not be obvious is that in a single-instance database, it is good practice to have at least three redo log groups *per thread*. Many people incorrectly think of threads as an Oracle RAC concept but even in a single-instance database, there is one *thread* of redo. All Oracle databases have one thread per instance.

Database administrators working on single-instance databases should strive for three to four redo log switches per hour. Switching too frequently can cause performance problems.

The same is true for Oracle RAC databases except that each instance should have three to four redo log switches per hour. The following script can be used in Oracle RAC databases to determine the max number of log switches in any one hour.

max_hourly_log_switches.sql

```
declare
    cursor c1 is
    select
        inst_id,
        count(*)
    from
        gv$log
    group by
        inst_id,
        to_char(first_time,'YYYY-MM-DD HH24')
    order by
        inst_id;

    v_inst number;
    v_curr number;
    v_cnt  number;
    v_max  number;
    v_name varchar2(16);

begin

    open c1;
    v_curr:=0;

    loop
        fetch c1 into v_inst,v_cnt;
        exit when c1%notfound;
        if (v_curr<>v_inst) then
            if (v_curr<>0) then
                select
                    instance_name into v_name
                from
                    gv$instance
                where
                    inst_id=v_curr;
            dbms_output.put_line('Instance: '||v_name||
                    '    Max Hourly Switches: '||v_max);
            end if;
            v_max := -1;
            v_curr := v_inst;
        end if;
```

```
        if (v_max < v_cnt) then
            v_max := v_cnt;
        end if;

    end loop;
    select
        instance_name into v_name
    from
        gv$instance
    where
        inst_id=v_curr;
    dbms_output.put_line('Instance: '||v_name||
                '    Max Hourly Switches: '||v_max);

  end;
/

Instance: orcl1    Max Hourly Switches: 5
Instance: orcl2    Max Hourly Switches: 8
Instance: orcl3    Max Hourly Switches: 3

PL/SQL procedure successfully completed.
```

The script above will work for any number of instances supporting the Oracle RAC database. Since each instance has its own thread of redo, we need to examine the maximum number of log switches per hour in each instance.

As previously stated, the online redo logs should be sized to see three or four log switches per hour at peak DML load. In the sample output above, there was at least one hour in one instance that experienced eight log switches. It may be a good idea to resize the online redo logs to twice the size so that the target of four log switches in an hour can be obtained. Unfortunately, it is very common to see some Oracle RAC deployments that are experiencing sixty or more log switches in their busiest hours! Databases exhibiting this behavior should have the redo logs resized to be larger.   It is a best practice to have all redo logs sized the same for each thread and for each group in that thread.

Sizing the redo logs to meet the target of three or four log switches works well for the hour that has the highest redo generation rate. But what about the hour timeframe that has a very low redo generation rate? Some database administrators translate the three or four log switches per hour to a requirement that the redo logs should switch every fifteen or twenty minutes. As such, they often set the *archive_lag_target* parameter to 900 or 1200.

From a performance perspective, there is little reason to ensure the redo logs switch every fifteen or twenty minutes even during period of low redo generation. The only reason to force a log switch regularly, even when the redo log group is not full, is for archiving the redo on a regular schedule, not to improve performance.

If the services are configured differently for each instance, then it is likely each instance experiences different redo generation rates. For example, one instance may have 20GB of redo generated in one hour and another instance only has 1GB of redo generated in one hour. The database administrator may create redo logs of 5GB each for the first thread and 300MB each for the second thread.

Note that having different redo log group sizes for each thread can be problematic when the service fails over due to instance failure. If the first instance terminates, the second instance will find itself trying to handle 21GB of redo generated in one hour and will perform approximately 70 log switches in that hour. It is a good practice for the redo logs to be sized to handle the maximum redo generation rate imparted on it by any application workload taking into account service relocations due to instance failures. This also means that all threads would have the same size redo logs groups. If You are worried that the second instance with 1GB of redo in its busiest hour would need five hours with the 5GB redo log groups, then turn to the *archive_lag_target* parameter to ensure the logs switch more often. Again, this parameter is not needed for performance reasons. It is needed for backup and recovery reasons to ensure an archived copy of the redo log is written to a backup location for disaster recovery purposes.

For those databases configured in archive log mode, the redo log switch will prompt the archiver process to copy the redo log to the archive log destination. We need to keep in mind that for Oracle RAC, there are multiple threads of redo, and there will be multiple archives being generated simultaneously. There is a natural tendency to use only one archive log destination for all threads, but for databases that have a high rate of redo generation (high DML activity), a single archive log destination for all threads may become a bottleneck. It may be more beneficial if each thread has its own archive log destination but that is not always the case.

Undo Tablespaces in RAC

Just like with the Online Redo Logs, each thread needs its own undo tablespace. Redo and undo go hand in hand. Every transaction causes writes operations to both. For Oracle RAC databases that undergo high rates of change, the undo should be on separate disks from the redo. Additionally, each instance's undo tablespace may need to be separated from each other to avoid I/O contention.

In the previous section, it was mentioned that the size of the ORL groups should be the same for all threads. Similarly, the *undo_retention* parameter should be set the same in all instances. This parameter should be sized to handle any application service on any instance. If the parameters have different values for each instance and a service fails over, the instance may not have sufficient undo to support the application. The database administrator should size the undo tablespace large enough to handle service failover. The *gv$undostat* view can help us determine a minimum size for the *undo_retention* parameter.

```
select
    max(maxquerylen)
from
    gv$undostat;
```

```
MAX(MAXQUERYLEN)
----------------
            4929
```

From the output above, the *undo_retention* parameter needs to be at least 5000 seconds.

Oracle 12c introduces a new parameter named *temp_undo_enabled*. When this parameter is set to TRUE, all undo generated on Global Temporary Tables (GTT) is written to the temporary tablespace rather than the undo tablespace. If the application has large amounts of activity against a global temp table, then this parameter can reduce the impact to undo tablespace. The *gv$tempundostat* view provides statistics on the performance of undo in the temp tablespace, similar to the *gv$undostat* view.

Temporary Tablespaces and RAC

In many Oracle RAC systems, the strong majority of sorts are performed in-memory. For those databases, one temporary tablespace is often sufficient. The demands placed on the temporary tablespace are low.

The *gv$sysstat* view can help determine how often the temporary tablespace is being used.

```
select
    inst_id,
    name,
    value
from
    gv$sysstat
where
    name like 'workarea%'
order by
    inst_id,
    name;
```

```
  INST_ID NAME                                                VALUE
--------- --------------------------------------------- ----------
        1 workarea executions - multipass                        0
```

```
1 workarea executions - onepass                      0
1 workarea executions - optimal                  59989
1 workarea memory allocated                          0
2 workarea executions   multipass                    0
2 workarea executions - onepass                      0
2 workarea executions - optimal                  41297
2 workarea memory allocated                          0
```

The *workarea executions – optimal* statistic shows how many operations are performed in memory. The *workarea executions – onepass* and *workarea executions – multipass* statistics are operations that were performed with the assistance of the temporary tablespace. In the output from above, there are no occurrences of the temp tablespace being used. If the output above is representative of normal operations, then a single temporary tablespace may be satisfactory. Consider the sample output below.

```
INST_ID NAME                                        VALUE
------- -----------------------------------------  ----------
      1 workarea executions - multipass              3734
      1 workarea executions - onepass               98175
      1 workarea executions - optimal             6386047
      2 workarea executions - multipass                10
      2 workarea executions - onepass                 643
      2 workarea executions - optimal             5894282
```

The output above shows much higher usage of the temporary tablespace. At this point, you may be thinking that the *pga_aggregate_target* parameter needs to be increased, and in many cases, they would be correct. What is missing from the output above is the context in which these statistics were generated.

The output above is from a decision support system that runs large analytic queries. The servers do not have enough physical memory to eliminate the usage of the temporary tablespace. Also notice that instance 2 has 653 onepass and multipass operations. Instance 1 has 101,909 onepass and multipass operations. Such an imbalance is indicative of a distributed workload, probably due to application partitioning. In this case, it may be beneficial to create two temporary tablespaces. Undo tablespaces can be denoted for use in a specific instance but temporary tablespaces do not have this capability. However, by using services, the database administrator can assign all users of a service to use one temporary tablespace and users of the other service to use the second tablespace.

In Oracle RAC, the temporary tablespace is a global resource. The temporary tablespace is allocated as a series of extents. When a user needs temp space, extents are *soft reserved* in the instance's SGA. Once an extent is reserved for an instance, other instances cannot use that extent. When a session is done with the extents from the temp tablespace, the instance does not return the soft reserved extents to be used by other instances. The extents soft reserved by an instance that are no longer being used are held by that instance. If another instance needs to soft reserve extents but none are available, control of unused extents will be transferred from one instance to another. The *gv$temp_extent_pool* view shows how many extents are soft reserved (cached) and in use for each instance.

```
select
    inst_id,
    file_id,
    extents_cached,
    extents_used
from
    gv$temp_extent_pool
order by
    inst_id,
    file_id;
```

```
   INST_ID    FILE_ID EXTENTS_CACHED EXTENTS_USED
---------- ---------- -------------- ------------
         1          3           8764            6
         1          4           7434           46
         1          5          19841           39
         2          3           2931           19
         2          4           4284           59
         2          5             40           38
         3          3           8247           11
         3          4           8213           74
         3          5            118           29
```

The output above shows each instance has soft reserved a number of extents from each temp file. Of the extents cached, few are being used. If an instance needs more extents, it will obtain them from one of the other instances if the temporary tablespace does not have any more available. The act of transferring unused extents from one instance to another can be seen by the presence of the *enq: SS - contention* wait event, where SS stands for Sort Segment. This event will often be accompanied by the *enq: TS - contention* and the *DFS lock handle* wait events.

When creating temporary tablespaces for Oracle RAC databases, it is a best practice to have one temp file for each instance. If a single-instance database is being migrated to Oracle RAC, make the temp tablespace larger to support the soft reserved extent allocation method between instances.

ASSM and RAC

Automatic Segment Space Management (ASSM) was introduced in Oracle 9i. Prior to ASSM, the only way to manage space in a segment was by specifying *freelists*, *freelist groups*, *pctfree*, and *pctused* when creating a segment. ASSM replaces the old one-way linked lists freelists with bitmap freelists to help identify which blocks of the segment have room for additional rows of data. ASSM performs faster. As such, ASSM scales better. It should be no surprise that Oracle Corporation recommends using ASSM for Oracle RAC databases.

We declare ASSM at the tablespace level, and any segments created in the tablespace will automatically use ASSM. Any *pctfree* or *pctused* parameters are largely ignored on segment creation. A tablespace using ASSM must be a Locally Managed Tablespace (LMT), which are also recommended. Dictionary Managed Tablespaces are hopefully becoming a thing of the past in the data center. The last line of the following *create tablespace* statement defines ASSM.

```
create tablespace
    assm_example
datafile
    '+DATA/orcl/assm_example01.dbf'
size
    100M
extent management local
segment space management auto;
```

Tablespace created.

The *segment_space_management* column of the *dba_tablespaces* view shows if ASSM is being used for the tablespace.

```
select
    tablespace_name,
    segment_space_management
from
    dba_tablespaces
order by
    tablespace_name;
```

TABLESPACE_NAME	SEGMEN
ASSM_EXAMPLE	AUTO
SYSAUX	AUTO
SYSTEM	MANUAL
TEMP	MANUAL
UNDOTBS1	MANUAL
UNDOTBS2	MANUAL
USERS	AUTO

As shown above, the system-related tablespaces are using manual segment space management. Do not attempt to modify these tablespaces unless directed to do so by Oracle Support. Application tablespaces should be declared with ASSM in use.

A simple example can show the power of ASSM in Oracle RAC. To illustrate ASSM's benefits we cannot use Orion because we need to perform DML operations. For this example, we will use Swingbench to simulate an Order Entry application. A future chapter will discuss Swingbench in more detail. For this test, 40 concurrent users were evenly distributed across a 2-node RAC cluster. The only variable in our control that was changed was the segment space management scheme of the tablespace holding the application tables. The following table shows the maximum Transactions Per Minute (TPM) as measured by Swingbench.

With ASSM	Without ASSM
6753 TPM	3639 TPM

Table 5.3 ASSM Test Results

While Swingbench may not be representative of your application, this test does show the power of using ASSM when performing a high degree of concurrent DML activity. It would be very surprising if a tablespace without ASSM would perform concurrent DML with higher throughput than a tablespace with ASSM. It is a best practice to use ASSM for Oracle RAC databases.

Hot Segments in RAC Tuning

When tuning storage, it is often beneficial to be able to identify hot spots in the databases, i.e. tables with more I/O activity than others. The *v$segment_statistics* view can be used to generate a list of objects order by read and write operations similar to the following:

hot_segments.sql

```
select
    owner,
    object_name,
    sum(value) as total_ios
 from
    gv$segment_statistics
where
   (statistic_name like 'physical%read%'
    or statistic_name like 'physical%write%')
    and
    owner not in ('SYS','XDB','SYSTEM','APEX_030200','MDSYS',
        'WMSYS','DBSNMP','EXFSYS','AUDSYS','GSMADMIN_INTERNAL')
 group by
    owner,
    object_name
 order by
    sum(value) desc;

OWNER        OBJECT_NAME      TOTAL_IOS
```

```
- - - - - - - - - -   - - - - - - - - - - - - - - -   - - - - - - - - - -
SCOTT          DEPTS                    6574
SCOTT          DEPTS_PK                  354
HR             EMPLOYEES                 184
HR             EMP_EMP_ID_PK              18
HR             DEPARTMENTS                 8
```

Even in single-instance databases, the above query is beneficial to be able to identify hot spots. Tables and indexes at the top of the list are candidates to be on separate disks so as to reduce disk contention. For Oracle RAC databases, one may also want to consider using application partitioning to access the segments from different instances, if possible. In the example above, there are two schemas shown and those applications may use different services. While separating the segments to different instances will not cut down on the I/O operations, it will reduce global cache transfers between instances.

Hot Services

For those licensed to use the AWR report, there is a section of the AWR report that details the I/O usage per service.

```
Service Statistics                       DB/Inst: ORCL/orcl1  Snaps: 181-182
-> ordered by DB Time

                                                        Physical        Logical
Service Name              DB Time (s)  DB CPU (s)      Reads (K)       Reads (K)
------------------------  -----------  ----------    ------------    ------------
orcl                           22,283         256              58           1,970
SYS$BACKGROUND                     14           3               1             155
SYS$USERS                           4           0               0               0
SYS.SCHEDULER$_EVENT_QUEUE          0           0               0               0
accntg_svc                     11,987         116             134           2,776
hr_svc                         48,945       1,764           1,138          10,893
mktg_svc                       55,930         982           2,226          17,483
                          ------------------------------------------------------
```

If the AWR report is not licensed, the *gv$service_stats* view can provide similar information.

🖫 **service_io_stats.sql**

```
select
    service_name,
    stat_name,
    sum(value) as total_val
from
    gv$service_stats
where
```

```
    stat_name like 'physical%'
    and
    service_name not like 'SYS%'
group by
    service_name,
    stat_name
order by
    service_name,
    stat_name;
```

SERVICE_NAME	STAT_NAME	TOTAL_VAL
accntg_svc	physical reads	134
accntg_svc	physical writes	178
hr_svc	physical reads	1138
hr_svc	physical writes	55
mktg_svc	physical reads	2226
mktg_svc	physical writes	5371
orcl	physical reads	58
orcl	physical writes	17
orclXDB	physical reads	0
orclXDB	physical writes	0

The *hr_svc* and *mktg_svc* services have the highest physical I/O operations. The database administrator may choose to place these two services on different nodes. Segregating services based on physical I/O rates is often done to leverage I/O related resources on the nodes. For instance, if two services have high rates of physical write activity, the Database Writer processes on multiple nodes can provide higher write throughput.

Information Lifecycle Management (ILM) and RAC

Oracle 12c introduces automated Information Lifecycle Management (ILM), part of the optionally licensed Advanced Compression option. The goal of ILM is to provide good stewardship of disk resources. Hot segments, those most recently used, are placed on high-speed disk, possibly on Solid State Drives (SSDs). Cold segments are placed on low-speed disk, typically Serial ATA (SATA) disk devices. Data can be compressed as it is moved to the cold tier as well. Before any ILM activities can take place, one needs to know which segments are cold or hot.

Oracle 12c uses a new feature call the Heat Map to be able to track the last time segments have been used. Automatic Data Optimization (ADO) automates the compression and movement between storage tiers based on policies defined by the database administrator. The fastest disk tier is expensive and with today's very sizable databases, the high-speed disk is cost prohibitive for the entire database.

ILM lets the database administrator maximize performance for a subset of the database. The savings from purchasing the low-speed disk units often offset the cost of the high-speed disk. Performance is improved for the most recently used segments at the expense of segments that are rarely accessed. Automated ILM works best with Oracle Partitioning whereby portions of a table can be moved to cold disk storage at the partition level.

The Heat Map provides the basis of information to define the objects involved in ILM actions. By default, the Heat Map is off and needs to be turned on by modifying the *heat_map* initialization parameter.

```
SQL> alter system set heat_map=on scope=both;

System altered.
```

Once the Heat Map is turned on, a number of views can be used to show how segments are used. The *dba_heat_map_segment* view shows the last time a segment was accessed.

```
select
    owner,
    object_name,
    full_scan,
    lookup_scan
  from
    dba_heat_map_segment
  where
    owner in ('HR','SCOTT');
```

OWNER	OBJECT_NAME	FULL_SCAN	LOOKUP_SC
HR	DEPARTMENTS	29-JUL-14	
HR	EMPLOYEES	29-JUL-14	
HR	EMP_EMP_ID_PK		29-JUL-14
SCOTT	DEPTS	29-JUL-14	
SCOTT	DEPTS_PK		29-JUL-14

The *full_scan* and *lookup_scan* columns show the last time the segment was accessed with a full table scan or an index lookup, respectively. This view does not show how many times a segment has been accessed during any given time period.

Before automated ILM policies can be created, a cold tablespace on lower-tier disk needs to be created.

```
create tablespace
    cold_storage_ts
  datafile
    '+COLD/orcl/cold_storage_ts01.dbf'
  size
    30g
  extent management local autoallocate;

Tablespace created.
```

Next, a partitioned table is created.

```
create table
    hr.assest_401k_alloc_history
        (emp_id number,
         asset_type varchar2(30),
         allocation_unit varchar2(10),
         allocation_amt  number,
         allocation_date date)
  tablespace users
  partition by range
     (allocation_date)
     (partition alloc_2010
       values less than (to_date('01-JAN-2011','DD-MON-YYYY'))
       tablespace users,
      partition alloc_2011
       values less than (to_date('01-JAN-2012','DD-MON-YYYY'))
       tablespace users,
      partition alloc_2012
       values less than (to_date('01-JAN-2013','DD-MON-YYYY'))
       tablespace users,
      partition alloc_2013
       values less than (to_date('01-JAN-2014','DD-MON-YYYY'))
       tablespace users,
      partition alloc_2014
       values less than (to_date('01-JAN-2015','DD-MON-YYYY'))
       tablespace users,
      partition alloc_max
       values less than (maxvalue)
       tablespace users
  );

Table created.
```

ADO policies need to be implemented. The first policy will be to compress data in the segment if data has not been modified for 3 months.

```
SQL> alter table
  2      hr.assest_401k_alloc_history
  3  ilm add policy
  4      compress for archive high segment
  5      after 3 months of no modification;

Table altered.
```

The next policy is to move old partitions to the cold storage tablespace.

```
SQL> alter table
  2      hr.assest_401k_alloc_history
  3  ilm add policy
  4      tier to cold_storage_ts;

Table altered.
```

So when does the segment get migrated to tiered storage? The *dba_ilmparameters* view shows the default values that determine ILM segment movement.

```
SQL> select
  2      name,
  3      value
  4  from
  5      dba_ilmparameters
  6  where
  7      name like 'TBS%';

NAME                    VALUE
-------------------- ----------
TBS PERCENT USED            85
TBS PERCENT FREE            25
```

When a tablespace reaches 85% used, the ILM tiering policy will kick in. Segments will be migrated until the tablespace falls to 25% utilization. If those values are not sufficient, they can be modified similar to the following.

```
SQL> begin
  2      dbms_ilm_admin.customize_ilm(
  3          dbms_ilm_admin.tbs_percent_used,80);
  4      dbms_ilm_admin.customize_ilm(
  5          dbms_ilm_admin.tbs_percent_free,50);
  6  end;
  7  /

PL/SQL procedure successfully completed.

SQL> select
  2      name,
  3      value
  4  from
  5      dba_ilmparameters
  6  where
  7      name like 'TBS%';

NAME                    VALUE
-------------------- ----------
TBS PERCENT USED            80
TBS PERCENT FREE            50
```

The automatic movement of segments to the cold storage tablespace will now kick in when the primary tablespace becomes 80% full and will stop once the utilization falls below 50%.

The information, while specific to the new Oracle 12c release, is not only applicable to Oracle RAC databases. This section can also apply to single-instance Oracle 12c databases as well. However, when using Oracle RAC to consolidate applications especially with Oracle 12c's Multitenant option, the amount of disk storage needed can be at a premium. As such, it may be best to implement an Information Lifecycle Management policy to compress old data and move it to low-cost disk devices.

Summary

This chapter focuses on performance tuning for Oracle RAC databases. Many single-instance performance tuning concepts apply to Oracle RAC storage as well including separating disk hot spots and using disk fast enough to support the required I/O operations. Oracle RAC relies on two things heavily; the Cluster Interconnect and the shared storage, the former being the subject of the previous chapter. This chapter discusses performance tuning for the latter.

When looking at disk performance, it is beneficial to have a tool to benchmark the performance. Oracle provides the Orion tool for these purposes. Orion uses the Oracle kernel code to simulate disk I/O operations without having the Buffer Cache skew the results.

This chapter has discussed ASM, NFS, and Direct NFS and how they can be configured and leveraged for an Oracle RAC database. Online Redo Logs, undo tablespaces and temporary tablespaces were discussed next.

The chapter finished with a discussion of Oracle 12c's new automated Information Lifecycle Management. The ILM features built into this new version of Oracle not only maximize storage space by compressing unused data, but also can automatically move segments to low-cost but slower disk storage units. Prior to Oracle 12c, the database administrator would have to perform these tasks manually.

The next chapter discusses how to tune Oracle RAC memory structures. Not surprisingly, some of the information applies to single-instance databases, but the chapter focuses on RAC-specific memory issues.

Tuning Memory

The previous chapters have discussed tuning the ever-important Cluster Interconnect and the shared storage used by Oracle RAC databases, both of which are central components of the infrastructure and shared by all nodes in the cluster. This chapter is the first one that takes the topic to the instance level. Each instance has its own memory structures that need to be sized correctly or database performance can suffer. As you will see in this chapter, while each instance can have different memory configurations, it is a good idea to RAM size all instances equally. Additionally, you should factor in the costs of failover of sessions in support of Transparent Application Failover (TAF).

Tuning For Single Instance Databases

As with many aspects of Oracle RAC performance tuning, tuning for a single-instance database helps with Oracle RAC as well. When talking about tuning memory, the same techniques we use for a single-instance database will work for Oracle RAC. For example, the System Global Area (SGA) and Program Global Area (PGA) both need to be sized correctly to match the database workload. The DBA can still use the *v$pga_target_advice* and *v$sga_target_advice* views to help size those components or automate it using Automatic Memory Management (AMM). The only difference is that the global views would be used instead, namely *gv$pga_target_advice* and *gv$sga_target_advice* respectively.

The *sga_target*, *memory_target*, and *pga_aggregate_target* initialization parameters are still used to define the memory footprints. Each instance needs to be sized correctly for optimal overall performance. This chapter will help the reader understand the differences involved when tuning memory areas for Oracle RAC.

The Data Buffer Cache

The Data Buffer Cache is a big part of Oracle RAC Cache Fusion. The global cache transfers, at a basic level, move blocks from the Buffer Cache of one instance to another. The Buffer Cache needs to be sized adequately to support the application demands, just like in a single-instance database. Where Oracle RAC instances differ is that the Buffer Cache appears to be more of a global resource to the cluster. The Buffer Cache is not truly global because one instance cannot read from another instance's cache directly but Cache Fusion helps make the collective caches cooperate together as if they were one entity.

Unfortunately, the effects of Cache Fusion often result in similar blocks being located in more than one instance's Buffer Cache. As such, Oracle Corporation recommends adding ten percent to the Buffer Cache size when converting from a single-instance database to Oracle RAC. In reality, this rule of thumb may not be sufficient. Chapter 3 discussed application partitioning and had a section illustrating the effect on the Buffer Cache. An application that is not isolated to a single instance can require extra blocks in the Buffer Cache as a result of *gc current* and *gc cr* read requests.

It can, of course, be very beneficial to spread the workload over multiple instances. We just to remember to increase the size of the Buffer Cache to accommodate the extra blocks that are needed for global cache transfers; otherwise the application performance may suffer. The ten percent increase as recommend is a good starting point but don't be surprised if the Buffer Cache still needs to be increased further to adequately support the workload over multiple instances.

The *v$db_cache_advice* view includes two columns when created for Oracle RAC instances, *estd_cluster_reads* and *estd_cluster_read_time*. These columns are not present in this view on single-instance databases. In addition to providing the estimated number of disk reads for various Buffer Cache sizes, the *v$db_cache_advice* view also estimates how many global cache transfers will be performed as seen in the next example.

```
SQL> select
  2      size_for_estimate,
  3      size_factor,
  4      estd_physical_reads,
  5      estd_cluster_reads
  6  from
  7      v$db_cache_advice;

SIZE_FOR_ESTIMATE SIZE_FACTOR ESTD_PHYSICAL_READS ESTD_CLUSTER_READS
----------------- ----------- ------------------- ------------------
              448        .094           387024742          150761248
              896       .1879           323102226          125860936
             1344       .2819           270348503          105311304
             1792       .3758           229019356           89211984
```

2240	.4698	197199001	76816720
2688	.5638	172868136	67338888
3136	.6577	154302062	60106680
3584	.7517	140152607	54594916
4032	.8456	129354116	50388484
4480	.9396	121082545	47166380
4768	**1**	**116685119**	**45453412**
4928	1.0336	114717835	44687076
5376	1.1275	109826272	42781624
5824	1.2215	106110954	41334364
6272	1.3154	103321208	40247648
6720	1.4094	101188238	39416772
7168	1.5034	99486432	38753852
7616	1.5973	97935451	38149684
8064	1.6913	96481904	37583472
8512	1.7852	95079821	37037304
8960	1.8792	93702628	36500832

When interpreting the output from *v$db_cache_advice*, it is beneficial to start where the *size_factor* column contains a value of '1'. The *size_for_estimate* value on this line represents the current buffer cache size. In the above example, when the Buffer Cache is increased by 87.9%, the number of physical reads decreases from 116,685,119 to 93,602,628, a drop of 19.8%. The number of global cache reads decreases from 45,453,412 to 36,500,832, a drop of 19.7%. Especially if application partitioning is in effect, use the *gv$db_cache_advice* view as each instance's Buffer Cache will have different performance characteristics.

As will be a recurring theme throughout this chapter, the memory areas should be sized to handle any additional workload in the event one node is unavailable and the remaining nodes need to support any sessions that have failed over. If a node goes down, the demands on the Buffer Cache will surely increase as application connections either failover or subsequently connect to a surviving node. We increase the Buffer Cache to be able to handle the workload to facilitate the disaster recovery for RAC one node.

Next, let's look at the RAM sizing for the shared pool.

Shared Pool

Beyond the standard contents for the shared pool for a single-instance database (e.g. SQL statements), the Shared Pool area of the SGA is used to store Global Resource Directory (GRD) information for the instance. With a single-instance database, the Oracle instance does not have to worry about keeping track of database resources on a global scale. In Oracle RAC, the Shared Pool needs to be increased to handle the GRD information, namely the Global Cache Services (GCS) and Global Enqueue Services (GES) components. A good starting point is to add twenty percent to the Shared Pool size when moving from a single-instance database to Oracle RAC. As with the Buffer Cache, this recommendation is just a starting point. The optimal Shared Pool increase may differ, depending upon the individual workload. The more the applications are partitioned across the cluster, the less global cache transfers need to take place which translates to a smaller increase in the Shared Pool, maybe as little as five percent. If there is no application partitioning and the application's sessions can connect to any and all instance which means that the Shared Pool will need to be sized larger than a five percent increase.

The following output shows the memory allocated to support GCS and GES components in the Shared Pool. The output from this script can help you understand the impact of the Oracle RAC portions of the Shared Pool that a single-instance database would not have.

🖫 shared_pool_grd.sql

```
select
    round(sum(bytes)/1024/1024,2) as total_mb
from
    v$sgastat
where
    pool='shared pool';

  TOTAL_MB
----------
       288

select
    round(sum(bytes)/1024/1024,2) as grd_mb
from
    v$sgastat
where
    name like 'gcs%'
    or
    name like 'ges%';

    GRD_MB
----------
     47.56

select
    pool,
    name,
    bytes
from
    v$sgastat
where
    name like 'gcs%'
    or
    name like 'ges%'
order by
    name;
```

POOL	NAME	BYTES
shared pool	gcs I/O statistics struct	48
shared pool	gcs affinity object	504
shared pool	gcs commit sga state	106512
shared pool	gcs delta freelist	8
shared pool	gcs mastership buckets	3072
shared pool	gcs opaque info freelist	200
shared pool	gcs opaque info freelist	8
shared pool	gcs process descriptor ar	8
shared pool	gcs procsss descriptor	9624
shared pool	gcs res hash bucket	1048576
shared pool	gcs res latch table	16384
shared pool	gcs resource freelist	264
shared pool	gcs resource freelist arr	8
shared pool	gcs resource freelist seg	8
shared pool	gcs resource segmented ar	48
shared pool	**gcs resources**	16924888
shared pool	gcs scan queue	176
shared pool	gcs scan queue array	8
shared pool	gcs shadows	10415312
shared pool	gcs shadows freelist	288
shared pool	gcs shadows freelist arra	8
shared pool	gcs shadows seg array	8
shared pool	gcs shadows segmented arr	48
shared pool	ges big msg buffers	3977128
shared pool	ges deadlock xid hash tab	15664
shared pool	ges enqueue cur. usage pe	16
shared pool	ges enqueue max. usage pe	16
shared pool	ges enqueue multiple free	480
shared pool	**ges enqueues**	6993264
shared pool	ges ipc instance maps	384
shared pool	ges lmd array	32
shared pool	ges msg pool watchlist	288
shared pool	ges process array	540160
shared pool	ges process descriptor	9624
shared pool	ges process descriptor ar	8
shared pool	ges process hash table	14080
shared pool	ges recovery domain table	176
shared pool	ges regular msg buffers	808648
shared pool	ges res mastership bucket	3072
shared pool	ges reserved msg buffers	3977128
shared pool	ges resource dynamic	610256
shared pool	ges resource hash table	819672
shared pool	ges resource permanent	3363504
shared pool	ges resource pools	936
shared pool	ges scan queue array	176
shared pool	ges shared global area	162344

The first query of the script shows the total Shared Pool size. This instance is using Automated Memory Management (AMM) so we cannot simply look at the *shared_pool_size* initialization parameter value. No matter which memory management scheme is employed, querying from *v$sgastat* as done in the script shows the current Shared Pool size. This instance is using 288 megabytes for the Shared Pool. The next query in the script shows the GCS and GES components total 47.56 megabytes in the Shared Pool. This is not a trivial amount and amounts to 16.5% of the total shared pool size. The last query in the script shows the memory breakdown for all of the GCS and GES components within the Shared Pool. The *gcs resources* component is where GCS is keeping track of all of the global resources. In the output above, this component is sized at approximately 16.9 megabytes. The *ges enqueues* component helps keep track of locking on the global scale. In the output above, this component is sized at approximately 7 megabytes. It should be obvious from this script output that the Shared Pool for an Oracle RAC instance needs additional memory above what is seen for a single-instance database. You will need to adjust the shared pool size accordingly.

The Shared Pool resizes its many components to meet workload demands throughout the lifetime of the instance. The *v$resource_limit* view shows the current setting and maximum setting for some of these components.

🖫 grd_resource_utilizations.sql

```
select
    resource_name,
    current_utilization,
    max_utilization
from
    v$resource_limit
where
    resource_name like 'gcs%'
    or
    resource_name like 'ges%'
order by
    resource_name;
```

RESOURCE_NAME	CURRENT_UTILIZATION	MAX_UTILIZATION
gcs_resources	373707	490739
gcs_shadows	331087	389839
ges_big_msgs	31	1200
ges_cache_ress	8162	11449
ges_locks	31576	48813
ges_procs	314	820
ges_reg_msgs	280	2728
ges_ress	56917	79328
ges_rsv_msgs	0	0

As stated, the Shared Pool adjusts its component sizes to meet a changing workload. One needs to establish a baseline to know what *max_utilization* values in *v$resource_limit* are within normal bounds. The figures above do not necessarily represent a problem. However, if we had a baseline that showed a *gcs_resources* maximum utilization of approximately 250,000 was "normal" and we saw that the maximum utilization is reached 490,000 then we know the demands placed on have increased significantly and the Shared Pool may need to be increased as a result. Without increasing the Shared Pool, other components may now be short of the memory the instance needs for optimal performance.

If you own a license for the Oracle Diagnostics Pack and Oracle Performance Pack, you can query the *dba_hist_sgastat* view to show historical information from *v$sgastat*. The following script can be used to see the minimum, average, and maximum values for the GRD components in the SGA.

💾 shared_pool_grd_hist.sql

```
select
    round(min(grd_bytes)/1024/1024,2) as min_grd_mbytes,
    round(avg(grd_bytes)/1024/1024,2) as avg_grd_mbytes,
    round(max(grd_bytes)/1024/1024,2) as max_grd_mbytes
from (
    select
        snap_id,
        sum(bytes) as grd_bytes
    from
        dba_hist_sgastat
    where
        pool='shared pool'
        and
        (name like 'gcs%'
        or
        name like 'ges%')
    group by
        snap_id);


MIN_GRD_MBYTES AVG_GRD_MBYTES MAX_GRD_MBYTES
-------------- -------------- --------------
    568.72         667.9          736.69
```

The output above shows a minimum size of 569 megabytes, an average of 668 megabytes and a maximum of approximately 737 megabytes. If the minimum and maximum values are wide apart, it can be indicative of a Shared Pool that is too small to support the application demands on the Oracle RAC instances and the Shared Pool is compensating by resizing the GRD components to a wide degree.

As more instances are added to the RAC cluster, the Shared Pool in all instances (RAC nodes) will need to be increased. More instances equates to more global resources that need to be tracked, hence more room is needed in the Shared Pool. A good starting point is to increase the Shared Pool by five percent for each instance, but like any rule of thumb, the best value may differ depending on a variety of factors. Unlike the Buffer Cache, the Shared Pool does not need to be increased to handle application failover should a node go down. The reason is that with a node being down, less global cache transfers and global locking is needed, which results in less demand on Shared Pool resources.

PGA Sizing for RAC

In the past, a session's Program Global Area (PGA) was sized by a number of initialization parameters including *sort_area_size* and *hash_area_size*. Most of today's database administrators now use the *pga_aggregate_target* parameter to size the PGA memory allocation. The big downside to this parameter is that the value defined is a target and not a hard limit. It is too common to have all session's collective PGA sizes exceed the target value, thus consuming too much memory on the server.

In Oracle RAC, sessions often perform parallel operations, a subject that will be discussed in more detail in the next chapter, to split the processing for a SQL statement over multiple nodes. The parallel server slave processes read data blocks directly into the session's PGA. Due to the increased parallelization seen in Oracle RAC systems, it is too easy for all sessions to exceed the *pga_aggregate_target* value. You may need to increase the PGA memory to support Oracle RAC parallel processing across the nodes. You will still want to use the *v$pga_target_advice* view to assist with correctly sizing the PGA on an instance-by-instance basis. Similar to sizing the Buffer Cache, you will need to handle the PGA needs of any sessions that failover due to instance failure on another node.

pga_aggregate_limit

Oracle 12c introduced the *pga_aggregate_limit* initialization parameter to constrain PGA memory usage. The default value of this parameter is the maximum of the following:

* 2 gigabytes
* 2 * *pga_aggregate_target*
* 3 megabytes * *processes*

If the total PGA consumption on a server reaches the *pga_aggregate_limit* value, sessions consuming the most memory will have their current calls terminated. If this action does not reduce the total PGA consumption below the limit, those sessions will be wholly terminated. Database administrators running Oracle RAC instances on nodes that do not have an abundance of physical memory may want to configure the *pga_aggregate_limit* value so that parallel operations do not consume too much memory leading to swapping and slower performance. However, you may want to implement the *pga_aggregate_limit* initialization parameter with a high degree of caution. If a node fails and connections are now hitting a surviving instance, the *pga_aggregate_limit* limit may be reached easily if not sized to handle the additional workload.

Huge Pages

In a computer, a *page* is a contiguous chunk of virtual memory. The virtual memory can exist in one of two places, the computer's physical memory or in a holding place on disk. For Windows systems, this holding place is called the *pagefile*. For Unix or Linux, it is called the *swap space*.

The page is the smallest unit of memory. On Linux, the page size is typically 4 kilobytes in size. A program that allocates memory will consume multiple pages. For example, if a process needs 1 megabyte of memory, 256 pages will be allocated to the process. It is possible for all running processes to allocate more memory than is physically available on the system. When the physical memory is exceeded, pages not currently in use will be relocated to disk. This movement is why the page is called virtual memory. The page may exist in real memory or on disk and move back and forth over its lifetime. The process of the page moving to and from disk is called *paging* or *swapping*.

Each process contains a *page table* that keeps track of the pages in use by that process. The operating system has its own page table that keeps track of all pages used by all processes. It is easy to see that a computer with a large amount of physical memory can have a very large page table. A server configured with 64 gigabytes of RAM and a page size of 4 kilobytes will need 16.8 million entries in the page table just for keeping track of the RAM contents. It is common for systems to have the same amount of swap space, which means another 16.8 million entries in the page table.

With so many entries in the page table, looking for a single page can be time consuming. To facilitate searching the page table, the Translation Lookaside Buffer (TLB) was created. The TLB is always cached in the computer's physical memory and is much smaller in size compared to the page table. If a process requests a page, the TLB is first searched to find the page's location. If the page is not found in the TLB, called a *TLB miss*, the much larger page table is searched.

The TLB and the page table contain pointers to a page. If larger page tables are used, then the TLB can address more memory with the same number of pointers. The page table can have fewer entries for the same amount of virtual memory. In our previous example, 64 gigabytes of RAM with a page size of 4 kilobytes will need 16.8 million entries in the page table. However, if the page size were increased to 1 megabyte, the same 64 gigabytes only need 65,536 entries in the page table.

If Oracle RAC is deployed on Linux nodes, Oracle Corporation's recommendation is to use Huge Pages for managing memory on the host. In addition to leading to smaller page tables, Huge Pages have the added benefit that the larger pages cannot be paged out to disk. Using Huge Pages for the SGA means the SGA will never be swapped out.

Before Huge Pages can be configured, the total number of required pages needs to be calculated and the database may need to be changed to stop using Automated Memory Management (AMM). AMM is incompatible with Huge Pages. You may want to use Huge Pages because it needs to eliminate the usage of the *memory_target* and *memory_max_target* initialization parameters.

In the steps that follow, Huge Pages will be configured to support the Oracle RAC instances. First, the number of required pages is calculated. To calculate the number of pages, we need to know the current page size configured for the server. Most recent Linux kernels have a 2-megabyte Huge Page size but a quick check can confirm the setting.

```
[oracle@host01 ~]$ cat /proc/meminfo | grep Hugepagesize

Hugepagesize:        2048 kB
```

All of the instances should be running, including the ASM and Management Databases instances if applicable. If they are not running, they will need to be started before proceeding.

```
[oracle@host01 ~]$ ps -ef|grep _smon_

oracle    3558    1  0 14:53 ?        00:00:00 asm_smon_+ASM1
oracle    3972    1  0 14:53 ?        00:00:00 mdb_smon_-MGMTDB
oracle    4075    1  0 14:53 ?        00:00:00 ora_smon_orcl1
oracle    7541 7434  0 15:04 pts/1    00:00:00 grep _smon_
```

With the instances up and running, all of the shared memory segments are now allocated. The ipcs command is used to see the shared memory segment usage.

```
[oracle@host01 ~]$ ipcs -m

------ Shared Memory Segments --------
key        shmid      owner      perms      bytes      nattch     status
0xcad7b97c 12419086   oracle     640        4096       0
0x00000000 12451855   oracle     640        4096       0
0x0c7c2960 26378256   oracle     640        10485760   78
0x00000000 26411025   oracle     640        515899392  39
0x3e836b60 29196306   oracle     640        14680064   136
0x00000000 29229075   oracle     640        1035993088 68
```

For each row returned from the ipcs command, calculate the number of pages needed based on the Huge Page size. This system has a Huge Page size of 2048 kilobytes which equals 2097152 bytes. Divide the number of bytes returned from the ipcs command by the larger page size and round up any fractional values. The following table shows the calculations done based on the ipcs output above.

Bytes	Number of Pages	Rounded Up
4096	4096/2097152 = 0.00195	1
4096	4096/2097152 = 0.00195	1
10485760	10485760/2097152 = 5	5
515899392	515899392/2097152 = 246	246
14680064	14680064/2097152 = 7	7
1035993088	1035993088/2097152 = 494	494
	Total Pages:	754

Table 6.1 Huge Pages Calculations

The 4096-byte pages will need one page each since they cannot use a partial page. The other shared memory segments fit nicely into their pages without any excess. On Linux 2.4 the *vm.hugetbl_pool* kernel parameter will need to be set to the total number of Huge Pages needed. On Linux 2.6 and higher, the *vm.nr_hugepages* kernel parameter is set instead. It is a good practice to allocate at least a few extra pages to the kernel setting. One may also want to consider adding extra pages so that the SGA can be grown in the future without having to reconfigure the number of Huge Pages.

Keep in mind that when raising the SGA, you need to check if the new SGA will fit into the number of Huge Pages defined on the system. In this example, the calculation is pretty easy. Every page is 2 megabytes so raising the SGA a total of 1 gigabyte will require 512 more pages. According to our calculations, we should allocate at least 754 pages but we should raise this at least a little to allow for future growth. Keep in mind that other processes on the server may not use be able to use the extra pages and if SGA is not using the extra pages, allocating too many huge pages can lead to unused memory on the system. For this example, we will configure 1,000 huge pages.

```
echo "vm.nr_hugepages = 1000" >> /etc/sysctl.conf
```

The configuration change will not take effect until the server is rebooted. Prior to the reboot, the Oracle memory allocation is reconfigured to avoid another downtime.

```
SQL> show parameter memory_target

NAME                                 TYPE        VALUE
------------------------------------ ----------- ------------------------
memory_target                        big integer 1400M

SQL> show sga

Total System Global Area  1043886080 bytes
Fixed Size                   2296280 bytes
Variable Size              322962984 bytes
Database Buffers           713031680 bytes
Redo Buffers                 5595136 bytes
```

The instances are configured with AMM using 1400 megabytes of total memory. The *show sga* command tells us that of the 1400 megabytes, 1000 megabytes is used for the SGA so the rest must be allocated to the PGA. The database needs to stop using AMM and instead use the *sga_target* and *pga_aggregate_target* initialization parameters.

```
SQL> alter system reset memory_target scope=spfile;


System altered.


SQL> alter system reset memory_max_target scope=spfile;

alter system reset memory_max_target scope=spfile
*
ERROR at line 1:
ORA-32010: cannot find entry to delete in SPFILE

SQL> alter system set sga_target=1000m scope=spfile;


System altered.


SQL> alter system set pga_aggregate_target=400m scope=spfile;


System altered.
```

The *memory_target* parameter is reset in the parameter file. When the *memory_max_target* parameter is reset, the ORA-32010 error is raised because this parameter is not defined in the parameter file. The *sga_target* and *pga_aggregate_target* parameters are given correct values. The nodes can now be rebooted.

Prior to using Huge Pages, the instance's alert log will show zero pages in use.

```
*********************** Large Pages Information ********************
Tue Jul 08 03:12:06 2014
Per process system memlock (soft) limit = UNLIMITED
Tue Jul 08 03:12:06 2014

Total System Global Area in large pages = 0 KB (0%)
Tue Jul 08 03:12:06 2014

Large pages used by this instance: 0 (0 KB)
Tue Jul 08 03:12:06 2014
Large pages unused system wide = 0 (0 KB)
Tue Jul 08 03:12:06 2014
Large pages configured system wide = 0 (0 KB)
```

After Huge Pages is configured, the alert log will show non-zero values in this section.

```
*********************** Large Pages Information ********************
Thu Aug 07 15:47:51 2014
Per process system memlock (soft) limit = UNLIMITED
Thu Aug 07 15:47:51 2014

Total System Global Area in large pages = 1002 MB (100%)
Thu Aug 07 15:47:51 2014

Large pages used by this instance: 501 (1002 MB)
Thu Aug 07 15:47:51 2014
Large pages unused system wide = 248 (496 MB)
Thu Aug 07 15:47:51 2014
Large pages configured system wide = 1000 (2000 MB)
```

The last line shows the 1000 pages were configured. This instance is using 501 of these large pages with 248 total pages free on the node. If 501 pages are used and 248 pages are free, that is a total of 749 pages. Where did the other 251 pages go? They are being used by the other instances on the node.

The OS side can confirm the same information that was seen in the Alert Log.

```
$ cat /proc/meminfo | grep Huge
```

```
HugePages_Total:      1000
HugePages_Free:        249
HugePages_Rsvd:          1
HugePages_Surp:          0
Hugepagesize:         2048 kB
```

The output above shows 1000 total pages configured with 249 free The Alert Log indicated 248 free but notice that one page is reserved out of the number of free pages. With 248 free pages, the SGA size can be increased by at most 500 megabytes of additional space without having to reconfigure the total number of Huge Pages. If the *HugePages_Total* count is less than was configured the system does not have enough free memory to support the total number of pages or there are not enough physically contiguous pages available.

If the Oracle version is less than 11.2.0.3, then the instance will fit the entire SGA into Huge Pages or not use them at all. For example, with a 2 kilobyte Huge Page size and a 1 gigabyte *sga_target* parameter setting, 512 byte pages would be needed for the SGA. If only 500 Huge Pages were available when the instance started up, then the instance would use small pages instead. If 512 or more Huge Pages were available on instance startup, then Huge Pages would be used.

Starting with Oracle 11.2.0.3, mixed pages can be used. If only 500 Huge Pages are available, they will be used by the instance and the remainder will be spread among regular memory pages. If mixed pages are used, it may be hard to detect. One would have to read the Alert Log on instance startup to know. See the following example.

```
*********************** Large Pages Information ********************
Thu Aug 07 15:47:51 2014
Per process system memlock (soft) limit = UNLIMITED
Thu Aug 07 15:47:51 2014

Total System Global Area in large pages = 1002 MB (100%)
Thu Aug 07 15:47:51 2014

Large pages used by this instance: 490 (980 MB)
Thu Aug 07 15:47:51 2014
Large pages unused system wide = 0 (0 MB)
Thu Aug 07 15:47:51 2014
Large pages configured system wide = 1000 (2000 MB)
```

Notice that the Total SGA size is 1002 megabytes but this instance is only using 980 megabytes of Huge Pages. The other 22 megabytes are using the normal page size.

Using mixed pages is not desirable. If the *use_large_pages* initialization parameter is set to a value of ONLY, the instance will start only if the entire SGA will fit into available Huge Pages on the server. The default value of this parameter is TRUE which allows Huge Pages to be used by the SGA. Setting this parameter to FALSE will cause the SGA to use regular pages even if Huge Pages are available, but it would be very rare to see this value being used.

If Huge Pages are configured, you may additionally set the *pre_page_sga* initialization parameter to TRUE. When this parameter is turned on, the entire SGA must be loaded into memory at instance startup. With regular page sizes and a large SGA footprint, setting this parameter to TRUE can cause high CPU usage on the server when the instance is started. With Huge Pages, the impact is much less as a fewer number of pages are used. Oracle Corporation recommends for large SGA's that this parameter be set to FALSE or Huge Pages be employed.

Using Huge Pages can help SGA memory performance on Oracle Linux systems. A larger page size leads to a smaller page table and a smaller TLB. Additionally, the Huge Pages cannot be swapped out when the system is under memory pressure. It is recommended to use Huge Pages if the Oracle RAC system supports it. The larger the SGA and the larger the physical memory on the server, the more important it is to implement Huge Pages.

Result Cache and RAC

Oracle 11g introduced the Result Cache to significantly speed up frequently executed queries or PL/SQL functions. Instead of actually executing the query or function, the results stored in the cache are returned to the user. The Result Cache is available in single-instance databases as well as Oracle RAC. Using the Result Cache is the same in both. Later parts of this section will discuss RAC-specific information related to the Result Cache.

For those not familiar with the Result Cache, it is natural to ask how this differs from the Buffer Cache. A simple example can show the benefits of the Result Cache. First, the maximum department id value is selected from the invoices table. The query is executed once to populate the Buffer Cache and then again with blocks in the cache.

```
SQL> @trace_my_session.sql

PL/SQL procedure successfully completed.

SQL> select
  2     max(det.invoice_date)
  3  from
  4     invoices i
  5  join
  6     invoice_detail det
  7     on i.dept_id=det.dept_id;

MAX(DET.I
---------
09-AUG-14

SQL> select
  2     max(det.invoice_date)
  3  from
  4     invoices i
  5  join
  6     invoice_detail det
  7     on i.dept_id=det.dept_id;

MAX(DET.I
---------
09-AUG-14
```

Since a trace was started in the session, we can look at the results from the trace file that has been run through the *tkprof* utility.

```
select
    max(det.invoice_date)
from
    invoices i
join
    invoice_detail det
on i.dept_id=det.dept_id
```

call	count	cpu	elapsed	disk	query	current	rows
Parse	1	0.00	0.00	0	0	0	0
Execute	1	0.00	0.00	0	0	0	0
Fetch	2	2.77	6.66	75521	75583	0	1
total	4	2.77	6.67	75521	75583	0	1

The query executed in 6.67 seconds, read over 75 thousand blocks from disk and returned one row of data. The second execution of the same query had similar numbers.

```
select
    max(det.invoice_date)
from
    invoices i
join
    invoice_detail det
    on i.dept_id=det.dept_id
```

call	count	cpu	elapsed	disk	query	current	rows
Parse	1	0.00	0.00	0	0	0	0
Execute	1	0.00	0.00	0	0	0	0
Fetch	2	3.31	5.62	75521	75583	0	1
total	4	3.31	5.62	75521	75583	0	1

Even though the Buffer Cache is in place, subsequent executions of the same query took about the same time to complete.

To use the Result Cache, one simply uses the *result_cache* optimizer hint. The following output is from a session that ran the same exact query with the optimizer hint in place.

```
select
   /*+ result_cache */
   max(det.invoice_date)
from
   invoices i
join
   invoice_detail det
   on i.dept_id=det.dept_id
```

call	count	cpu	elapsed	disk	query	current	rows
Parse	1	0.00	0.00	0	0	0	0
Execute	1	0.00	0.00	0	0	0	0
Fetch	2	0.00	0.00	0	0	0	1
total	4	0.00	**0.00**	0	0	0	1

The query ran so fast, the elapsed time was computed as zero. No disk reads were needed and still one row was returned.

Without the result cache, the next time the query is submitted, it must still be executed. Blocks in the Buffer Cache can help subsequent executions complete faster but the query is still executed. With the Result Cache, the Oracle engine recognizes that the result has already been calculated and stored in the cache. The query is not actually executed the next time. Instead, the result is passed to the user.

The Explain Plan output for the query verifies that the Result Cache was used in processing the SQL statement.

Id	Operation	Name	Rows	Bytes	Cost
0	SELECT STATEMENT		1	18	20790
1	**RESULT CACHE**	cmp9mq9vt0qwmd7uax			
2	SORT AGGREGATE		1	18	
3	HASH JOIN		5159K	88M	20790
4	INDEX FAST FULL SCAN	INVOICES_PK	20328	99K	14
5	TABLE ACCESS FULL	INVOICE_DETAIL	5187K	64M	20753

Most of the Explain Plan output shows regular operations like a full table scan and using an index, all to feed a hash join operation. But notice the second line indicates the Result Cache was used. The Hash Join, full table scan, and index access never took place.

The Result Cache is split into two areas, the SQL Query Result Cache and the PL/SQL Function Result Cache. The SQL Query Result Cache works best for SQL statements that access a high number of rows but return a small number of them. The

Result Cache is not good for queries that have frequently changing return values. If the tables involved in the query are modified, the entry in the Result Cache is invalidated and needs to be recomputed.

The Result Cache is enabled whenever the *result_cache_max_size* initialization parameter is set to a non-zero value. The default value is derived from the *shared_pool_size*, *sga_target*, and *memory_target* initialization parameters, as such it will default to a value larger than zero. In Oracle RAC, is it possible for each instance to have different values for the *result_cache_max_size* parameter. If application partitioning is employed, you may very well want to size each instance's Result Cache differently to adequately handle the workloads that will vary on each instance.

However, you also needs to keep in mind the effect on the Result Cache should connections failover due to instance failure. It is a good practice to size the Result Cache's the same on all instances to be able to handle the largest workload. If the *result_cache_max_size* parameter is set to zero, the Result Cache is disabled. In Oracle RAC, it is not possible to disable the Result Cache on one instance but have it enabled on another instance. If AMM is used, the *result_cache_max_size* parameter defaults to 0.25% of the *memory_target* parameter setting else it defaults to 1% of the Shared Pool size.

Each instance has its own Result Cache area. A change to a dependent object that invalidates the result in the cache in one instance will do the same for the other instances as well. Cache Fusion will transfer results from one instance's Result Cache to another. A session waiting on the Cache Fusion transfer of the result will experience the *gc cr block 2-way* wait event. Also keep in mind the example in this section where 75 thousand disk reads were required to satisfy the query but only 1 row is returned. Without the Result Cache, global cache transfers may be performed of the 75 thousand blocks. The Cluster Interconnect will perform better if the one row of data is transferred rather than all of those blocks. The Result Cache can help reduce global cache transfers for queries that can benefit from it.

The *v$result_cache_statistics* view can be used to help determine how well the Result Cache is performing.

```
SQL> select
  2      name,
  3      value
  4  from
  5      v$result_cache_statistics
  6  order by
  7      name;
```

```
NAME                            VALUE
------------------------------  --------------------
Block Count Current                               32
Block Count Maximum                             5120
Block Size (Bytes)                              1024
Create Count Failure                               0
Create Count Success                               1
Delete Count Invalid                               0
Delete Count Valid                                 0
Find Copy Count                                    7
Find Count                                         7
Global Hit Count                                   0
Global Miss Count                                  0
Hash Chain Length                                  1
Invalidation Count                                 0
Latch (Share)                                      0
Result Size Maximum (Blocks)                     256
```

The Block Size is important in helping understand some of the other statistics. In the output above, the block size is 1,024 bytes. Now that the block size is known, the top two lines from the query result makes more sense. The Result Cache is currently using 32 blocks which equates to 32,768 bytes. The maximum number of blocks allowed is 5,120 blocks or 5,242,880 bytes. The Block Count Maximum corresponds to the *result_cache_max_size* initialization parameter.

```
SQL> show parameter result_cache_max_size

NAME                            TYPE        VALUE
------------------------------  ----------- -----------------------------------
result_cache_max_size           big integer 5M
```

To know if the Result Cache is too small, one should query the *v$result_cache_statistics* view. The Result Cache will grow to meet demand but will not shrink. If the Block Count Current * Block Size is near or equal to the *result_cache_max_size* value, the Result Cache may be too small. Increase the Result Cache's maximum size and check again. Also, the Delete Count Valid statistics should be zero or close to it. If this statistic is high, it is an indicator of items being aged out of the Result Cache.

The Result Cache is a great way to improve performance for applications. The Result Cache works well for both single-instance and Oracle RAC databases. For Oracle RAC, Cache Fusion will transfer results from one instance to another. Transferring results, and not the data blocks to execute the query can often result in much less Cluster Interconnect traffic.

In Memory Database

As luck would have it, Oracle Corporation released the 12.1.0.2 patchset the week this chapter was being written. Aside from being the first patchset for Oracle 12c, this version's major claim to fame is quickly becoming the In Memory database option. Because In Memory is a new Oracle database option, exactly how it works for various applications is still being explored. Database administrators around the world are learning more and more about this highly touted feature each day. As such, it is important for you to test this option very carefully with their application.

The In Memory option is not intended to replace Oracle's Times Ten, which holds the entire database's contents in physical memory. The In Memory option works differently to help improve the performance of analytic queries. This acceleration of performance requires no application changes. Data Warehouses run lots of lots of analytic queries and may benefit from leveraging Oracle's In Memory functionality. The Oracle documentation states that the In Memory option will benefit the following:

- SQL statements involving analytic functions to aggregate data.
- SQL statements that return a small number of columns from a table that has lots of columns.
- SQL statements that join large tables to small tables.

Increasingly, today's OLTP systems are also asked to run a variety of resource-intensive reports making the database a mixed-workload environment. Using In Memory will help improve reporting performance while reducing the resource requirements. The In Memory option does require an extra license so it may not be available to everyone.

The reader is already aware that Oracle stores a table's data in rows. The rows are packed into a database block. This physical storage scheme works well for many applications. The storage organization does not work so well when the table contains millions of rows and the query is only interested in one column. The normal storage scheme requires that the entire row be read into the Buffer Cache no matter how many columns are involved in the query.

An alternative storage structure would be to store the table's data in columns, and not in rows. *Columnar storage* makes querying one column of a table much faster than the traditional row-based storage organization. Columnar storage does not work so well when trying to query many or all of the columns of a row. To illustrate column storage, examine the following table's data.

```
SQL> select
  2      *
  3   from
  4       t;

A       B       C
-----   -----   -----
a1      b1      c1
a2      b2      c2
a3      b3      c3
a4      b4      c4
a5      b5      c5
a6      b6      c6
a7      b7      c7
a8      b8      c8
a9      b9      c9
a10     b10     c10
a11     b11     c11
a12     b12     c12
```

This table was purposely populated with dummy data to help illustrate the concepts. Column C has values that all start with the letter 'c'. Each row is given a different number in that column value and so on. With the data denoted this way, we can easily tell which column and row a data value came from.

The DBA is probably familiar with how the data is physically arranged in a table. The following diagram illustrates four rows per block.

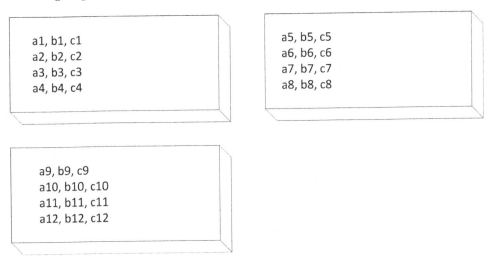

Figure 6.1 Row Format

If a query tries to access all values from the B column, all of the blocks would need to be read. The Oracle engine cannot read just the B values without also reading the A and C values as well. For three data blocks, this may not seem like much, but imagine if the table holds millions of rows of data. Looking for one column's worth of data can require extraordinary amounts of I/O. Enter the columnar format where the column values are stored together. The columnar format would store the values in blocks similar to the following illustration.

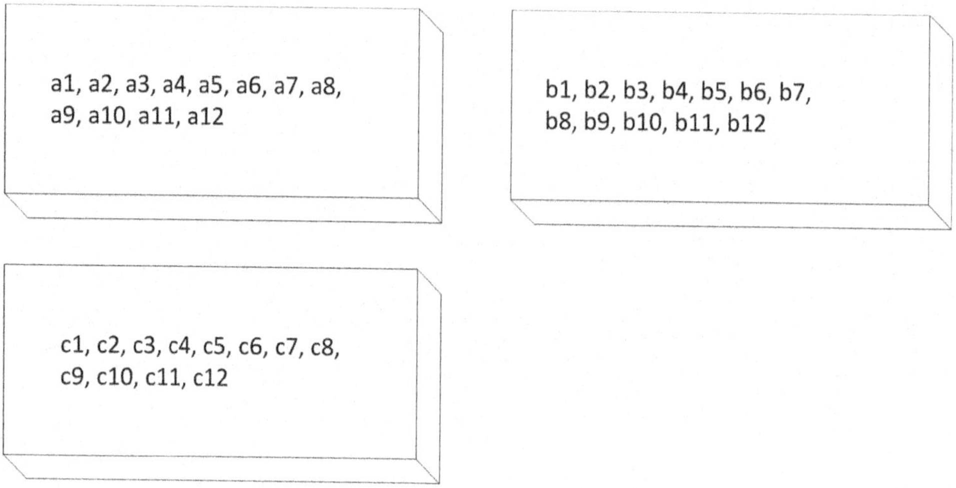

Figure 6.2 Columnar Data Storage Format

Now, to read the values from column B, only one disk block is needed. The database engine keeps track of the row pieces, as they will be spread out over multiple blocks. While the columnar format is helpful when looking for values just from a few columns of the table, it hampers operations that involve the entire row. If the row with the value '3' is needed, all of the blocks in the diagram above would need to be read from disk. The row and columnar formats are in direct opposition to each other. When designing the physical data model, you determines which storage format will provide the most benefit to the application with the understanding that some queries may not work well in with the chosen storage structure.

Oracle's In Memory database option leverages the best of both worlds. The physical storage is unchanged. The table's data is still stored in row format. The row format data block is still read into the instance's Buffer Cache. A new In Memory cache area will store the same table data converted into columnar format. The data is transparently available in both formats to provide the best access path to quickly support mixed workloads. The Oracle engine automatically handles transaction consistency across both formats. To illustrate the In Memory database option, examine the query shown below.

```
select
   min(order_date) as min_date,
   max(order_date) as max_date
from
   order_details;
```

The query is executed a number of times in a regular Oracle 12c database. Output from a trace of the session shows the following metrics.

```
Call       count      cpu    elapsed      disk      query    current        rows
-------   ------   ------  ---------  --------- ---------  ----------  ----------
Parse          3     0.00       0.02          0          0           0           0
Execute        3     0.00       0.00          0          0           0           0
Fetch          6     0.86      15.41     243817     243834           0           3
-------   ------   ------  ---------  --------- --------   ----------  ----------
total         12     0.86      15.43     243817     243834           0           3
```

The query was executed three times with a total elapsed time of 15.43 seconds, or about 5.1 seconds per execution. Also notice that this example used approximately 80,000 disk reads per execution.

Now that a baseline has been generated, the In Memory option is enabled. You sets the *inmemory_size* initialization parameter to a value sufficient large enough to hold tables that need to be stored in columnar format. The In Memory cache is part of the SGA so the SGA will need to be increased as well else other SGA components will be negatively impacted.

```
SQL> show parameter inmemory_size
```

```
NAME                                     TYPE          VALUE
---------------------------------------- -----------   -------------------------
inmemory_size                            big integer                           0
```

```
SQL> show parameter sga_target
```

```
NAME                                     TYPE          VALUE
---------------------------------------- -----------   -------------------------
sga_target                               big integer                       1000M
```

```
SQL> alter system set inmemory_size=1g scope=spfile;
```

```
System altered.
```

```
SQL> alter system set sga_target=2g scope=spfile;
```

```
System altered.
```

The *inmemory_size* parameter is set to 1 gigabyte. The *sga_target* parameter was initially set to 1000 megabytes so it was increased to 2 gigabytes. The instances need to be bounced for the parameter changes to take effect. After the instances are back up, the In Memory cache availability is verified.

```
SQL> show sga
```

```
Total System Global Area    2147483648 bytes
Fixed Size                      2926472 bytes
Variable Size                 553650296 bytes
Database Buffers              503316480 bytes
Redo Buffers                   13848576 bytes
In-Memory Area               1073741824 bytes
```

The In Memory area is divided into two sections, a 1 megabyte pool to store the column format data and a 64 kilobyte pool to store metadata about objects in the cache. The *v$inmemory_area* view shows how much memory is allocated to each pool and how much is in use.

```
SQL> select
  2     pool,
  3     alloc_bytes,
  4     used_bytes,
  5     populate_status
  6  from
  7     v$inmemory_area;
```

```
POOL                        ALLOC_BYTES USED_BYTES POPULATE_STATUS
--------------------------  ----------- ---------- --------------------------
1MB POOL                      854589440          0 DONE
64KB POOL                     201326592          0 DONE
```

The majority of the memory allocation is for the 1MB pool, but keep in mind that the 64K pool adds overhead to the memory structure and the *inmemory_size* parameter needs to be a little larger than what is needed for the table data. Notice in the above output that the *used_bytes* column shows values of zero for both pools. The In Memory cache is created but nothing is in it. Oracle needs to be instructed as to which tables to place In Memory as can be seen below.

```
SQL> alter table
  2     order_details
  3     inmemory;
```

```
Table altered.
```

When table is being loaded to the In Memory area, the *v$inmemory_area* view will show a *populate_status* of "populating".

```
SQL> select
  2       pool,
  3       alloc_bytes,
  4       used_bytes,
  5       populate_status
  6    from
  7       v$inmemory_area;
```

POOL	ALLOC_BYTES	USED_BYTES	POPULATE_STATUS
1MB POOL	854589440	31457278	POPULATING
64KB POOL	201326592	262144	POPULATING

Also notice that the *used_bytes* column is non-zero indicating objects are now in the In Memory cache. The *v$im_segments* view shows the segments defined for the In Memory area.

```
SQL> select
  2       owner,
  3       segment_name,
  4       inmemory_size
  5    from
  6       v$im_segments;
```

OWNER	SEGMENT_NAME	INMEMORY_SIZE
SCOTT	ORDER_DETAILS	3342336

With the segment now using the In Memory area, the same query is run again just like the baseline test. The tkprof metrics are shown below.

Call	count	cpu	elapsed	disk	query	current	rows
Parse	3	0.00	0.00	0	0	0	0
Execute	3	0.00	0.00	0	0	0	0
Fetch	6	0.15	0.23	0	99849	0	3
total	12	0.15	0.23	0	99849	0	3

Without the In Memory area configured, the query executed three times in 15.43 seconds and consumed 243,817 disk reads. With the table in the In Memory area, the three executions of the same query executed in 0.23 seconds using zero disk reads!

The Explain Plan for the query now shows the In Memory operation.

```
Rows (1st) Rows (avg) Rows (max)  Row Source Operation
---------- ---------- ----------  ------------------------------------------------
         1          1          1  SORT AGGREGATE
     81272      81272      81272     TABLE ACCESS INMEMORY FULL ORDER_DETAILS
```

This simple example shows the power of the new Oracle 12c In Memory option. Granted, a simple example was used to illustrate how the new In Memory option works, but with proper application testing, you can ensure the option works well for your applications as well.

Everything in this section so far applies to both Oracle RAC and single-instance databases. In Oracle RAC, it is possible for each instance to have a different size for the In Memory area however it is recommended that the area be sized identically in all instances. Furthermore, you need to keep in mind the effect of application failover should a node become unavailable. With application partitioning, the In Memory area of each instance may contain different segments. Should failover be necessary, the In Memory area of surviving instances may need to accommodate additional segments.

Oracle RAC means scalability, and one way to help achieve scalability is to spread out the resource demands across nodes. Oracle 12c's In Memory option helps by providing the capability to spread a large segment over multiple In Memory areas with the *distribute* and *duplicate* clauses. The *duplicate* clause is only applicable to RAC on Oracle engineered systems like Exadata.

Without specifying how to allocate the segment to the In Memory areas, the default action is to load the segment into each In Memory area in all instances. However, if the table is partitioned, the default action is to spread the partitions over the instances as seen below.

🖬 inmemory_segments.sql

```
select
    inst_id,
    owner,
    segment_name,
    partition_name,
    bytes,
    populate_status,
    inmemory_distribute
  from
    gv$im_segments;


INST_ID OWNER SEGMENT_NAME  PARTITION_NAME           BYTES POPULATE_ INMEMORY_D
------- ----- ------------- ---------------- ------------- --------- ----------
      1 SCOTT ORDER_DETAILS ORDER_DETAILS_P1     343932928 COMPLETED AUTO
      2 SCOTT ORDER_DETAILS ORDER_DETAILS_P2     335544320 COMPLETED AUTO
```

The output above shows the first partition is in instance 1 and the second partition is in instance 2. You can state a number of distribution schemes to the multiple In Memory areas for Oracle RAC. Those schemes include:

- *distribute by partition* – Spread the partitions over the instances.
- *distribute by rowid range* – Use for non-partitioned tables
- *distribute by subpartition* – Spread the subpartitions over the instances.

You should use *distribute by partition* or *distribute by subpartition* especially if tables will be participating in partition-wise join operations. Oracle will put similar partitions on the same instance so that partition-wise joins will be more efficient. The database engine will not have to perform global cache transfers to join two partitions if they are in the same instance's In Memory area. Oracle will start parallel slave processes on the instances that hold the needed partition within the In Memory area and process portions of the SQL statement on the other instances. Parallel operations will be discussed in more detail in the next chapter.

The Explain Plan of the query is worth taking a look at when involving partitioned tables that are held within the In Memory area.

```
Rows (1st) Rows (avg) Rows (max)  Row Source Operation
---------- ---------- ----------  ------------------------------------------
         1          1          1  SORT AGGREGATE
     81272      81272      81272  PARTITION RANGE ALL PARTITION: 1 2
     81272      81272      81272    TABLE ACCESS INMEMORY FULL
                                     ORDER_DETAILS PARTITION: 1 2
```

The second line is no different than a normal SQL statement accessing a partitioned table. This second line indicates all partitions are used which just happens to be partitions 1 and 2. The third line shows the In Memory area in use and that the table partitions were accessed. This does not show which nodes were involved. To know which instances participated in the query, the *gv$im_segments* view must be queried as shown earlier.

Oracle 12c's new In Memory database option gives us the best of both worlds, row format storage and columnar storage. Leveraging this extra cost option can dramatically improve performance of analytic queries. This section provided additional information on how the In Memory database option works with Oracle RAC databases.

Summary

This chapter discussed a number of areas to help tune the memory of instances of an Oracle RAC database. Much of what the database administrator's memory tuning skills in a single instance database are still applicable to Oracle RAC. This chapter does describe the additional items you need to be concerned with when tuning memory.

The Shared Pool needs to be sized larger to hold GRD information. A good starting point is to increase the Shared Pool by twenty percent compared to a single-instance database. The Buffer Cache will also need to be increased as well. Oracle Corporation recommends increasing the Buffer Cache by ten percent, but this should be just a starting point as it may not be enough.

Where possible, you should configure Linux Huge Pages because the Oracle RAC instance will perform better due to smaller page tables. Additionally, Huge Pages cannot be swapped to disk when the node is experiencing memory pressure.

This chapter finished with a brand new feature, the Oracle 12c In Memory database option. The In Memory option seamlessly handles both row and columnar formats to provide excellent performance transparent to the application.

The next chapter discusses how to leverage parallel operations in Oracle RAC. Parallel operations can be used in a single-instance database. Oracle RAC provides additional scalability involving multiple nodes in the operation.

RAC Parallel Operations

Previously in this book, we took a look at a brief history of Oracle RAC. We mentioned that the product was first introduced under the name Oracle Parallel Server (OPS). The OPS product was built for high performance by spreading the workload over multiple systems. In addition to distributing many processes over several machines, OPS allowed a single SQL statement to be executed in parallel across the cluster as well.

Parallel operations are not restricted to Oracle RAC systems, and it is most common to see a SQL statement in parallel on a single-instance database, but in Oracle RAC, a parallel SQL statement can leverage more resources, a sort of "parallel parallelism". Just like other chapters, this chapter will provide additional material with RAC-specific details included.

Parallel execution in Oracle RAC is a great way to process millions or billions of rows of data in short order. However, not all SQL statements will benefit from parallel execution. Some SQL statements will complete in a shorter duration if run serially. The only true way to know if parallel or serial executions are faster is to try the SQL statement both ways. You should also take special care with SQL statements that work just fine with parallel execution in a single instance database and verify that the SQL statement works just as well, or better, with parallel execution over multiple instances in Oracle RAC. As will be discussed in this chapter, parallel execution in Oracle RAC involves cross-instance transfer of information, different than parallel SQL in a single-instance database, which could be just enough to slow down the overall parallel SQL execution runtime.

Parallel SQL statements will not run faster if the Oracle RAC nodes performing the processing do not have adequate resources available. If a node is short on CPU or disk I/O resources, or does not have enough memory to support multiple processes, then parallel execution has a very high chance of performing slower than serial execution. Traditional OS utilities to monitor resources can be used to help determine if server resources are in short supply. On Windows, you can use PerfMon. On Unix or Linux, utilities like *sar*, *top*, and *vmstat* can be used to see the resource utilization.

Parallel Example

The idea behind parallel operations is to break down the serial operation into smaller pieces, each executed concurrently or in parallel, to reduce the overall execution time. This section provides an example of a parallel query. First, the query is executed with the *no_parallel* hint so as to ensure a serial execution.

```
SQL> set timing on
SQL> set autotrace on explain
SQL> select
  2      /*+ NO_PARALLEL */
  3      status,
  4      max(order_date)
  5  from
  6      order_details
  7  group by
  8      status;
```

```
STATUS                  MAX(ORDER
--------------------    ---------
IN PROGRESS             14-AUG-14
FULFILLED               14-AUG-14

Elapsed: 00:01:29.38

Execution Plan
-----------------------------------------------------------
Plan hash value: 3673013235
```

```
-------------------------------------------------------------------
|Id |Operation           | Name          |Rows|Bytes | Cost| Time |
-------------------------------------------------------------------
| 0 |SELECT STATEMENT    |               |   1|   14| 22353| 00:00:01 |
| 1 | HASH GROUP BY      |               |   1|   14| 22353| 00:00:01 |
| 2 |  PARTITION RANGE ALL|              |81272|1111K| 22349| 00:00:01 |
| 3 |   TABLE ACCESS FULL |ORDER_DETAILS|81272|1111K| 22349| 00:00:01 |
-------------------------------------------------------------------
```

```
Note
-----
   - Degree of Parallelism is 1 because of hint
```

The output above shows that the query completed in 1 minute and 29 seconds (89 seconds). With autotrace enabled, the Explain Pan is provided, some of which was removed to fit better on the page. The output concludes with information that the degree of parallelism is 1, or a serial execution. The degree of parallelism will be discussed later in this chapter.

The same query is run, this time with the hint that instructs the optimizer to use parallel processing.

```
SQL> select
  2      /*+ PARALLEL */
  3      status,
  4      max(order_date)
  5  from
  6      order_details
  7  group by
  8      status;


STATUS                  MAX(ORDER
--------------------    ---------
IN PROGRESS             14-AUG-14
FULFILLED               14-AUG-14

Elapsed: 00:00:49.69
```

With parallel operations, the query completes in 49.69 seconds, a little more than half the serial runtime. The execution plan is much more complicated showing a number of parallel operations, which will be discussed later in this chapter.

```
Execution Plan
----------------------------------------------------------------
Plan hash value: 3262344915

----------------------------------------------------------------

| Id | Operation            | Name          | Rows  | Bytes| Cost |
----------------------------------------------------------------

|  0 | SELECT STATEMENT     |               |     1 |   14 | 198K |
|  1 |  PX COORDINATOR      |               |       |      |      |
|  2 |   PX SEND QC (RANDOM)| :TQ10001      |     1 |   14 | 198K |
|  3 |    HASH GROUP BY     |               |     1 |   14 | 198K |
|  4 |     PX RECEIVE       |               |     1 |   14 | 198K |
|  5 |      PX SEND HASH    | :TQ10000      |     1 |   14 | 198K |
|  6 |       HASH GROUP BY  |               |     1 |   14 | 198K |
|  7 |        PX BLOCK ITERATOR |           | 81272 | 1111K| 198K |
|  8 |         TABLE ACCESS FULL| ORDER_DETAILS | 81272 | 1111K| 198K |
----------------------------------------------------------------

Note
-----
   - dynamic statistics used: dynamic sampling (level=AUTO)
   - automatic DOP: Computed Degree of Parallelism is 2
```

All of the Explain Plan entries with "PX" are Parallel Execution operations. The end of the Explain Plan shows that the Degree of Parallelism is 2. Because the Degree of Parallelism is 2, the SQL statement completed in about half the time as the serial execution. This ratio does not always hold so careful testing needs to be performed to ensure the parallel SQL statement is showing benefits, i.e. a faster runtime.

The example in this section was chosen to ensure that the query run with parallel operations performed faster than the same query executed serially. As stated previously, not all queries will benefit from parallel execution. The reasons why some parallel SQL statements will actually perform slower than a serial execution will be explained in the next section.

How Parallel Query Works

The basic premise of parallel execution is to break down a large body of work into smaller units that will be performed simultaneously. After completion, the smaller units of work are merged into one final result.

Multiple CPU cores can be used to perform each unit of work. If a SQL statement takes X minutes to complete serially, then breaking the work in four equally sized pieces, each performed in parallel, would ideally complete the same SQL statement a little more than one quarter of the serial execution time.

Why a little more? The extra time is due to the effort required to put the results back together.

The number of concurrent processes is called the *Degree of Parallelism* (DOP). The process performing the smaller units of work is called the parallel *slave*. The process that puts the results back together is called the *Query Coordinator* (QC).

The following diagram illustrates performing a disk I/O on a database file serially as many database administrators should be very familiar with.

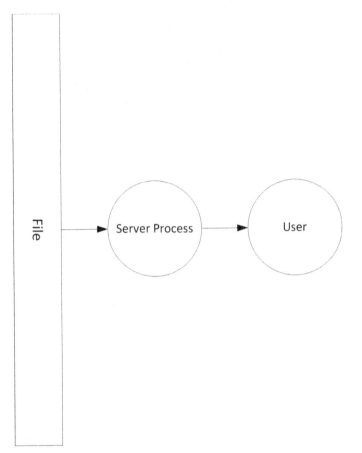

Figure 7.1 Serial Disk Read

The user's server process reads the data from the file before it is passed on to the end user. The diagram above is simplistic in that it removes the SGA and other components from the picture, but this was intentionally done so as to focus on just the parallel aspects discussed in the next diagram.

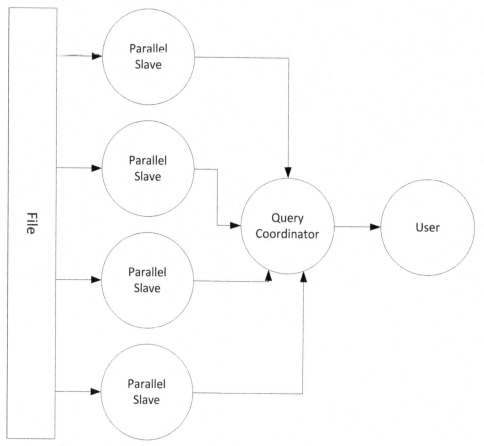

Figure 7.2 Parallel Operations

In diagram 7.2 above, the same file is read, this time with a parallel degree of 4. Each slave will ideally be responsible for one-fourth of the I/O activity. The results are passed on to the Query Coordinator before the data is ready for the end user. Notice that this diagram shows an extra level of work, that of the QC process. This diagram should help illustrate why parallel processing is not always faster than serial processing. If the time saved by the slaves executing the disk I/O in parallel is more than the time taken by the QC to do its job, the overall execution will be faster than if run serially. At this point, it should be obvious that multiple slave processes reading from the same file can perform worse if the file system does not have enough resources to support the concurrent I/O operations from the slaves. A lack of sufficient resources will hamper parallel SQL statement execution.

The Query Coordinator (QC) has a few jobs to do. The QC acquires slave processes from a pool. The QC then doles out pieces of the work to each slave process. As the slave processes complete their work, the QC combines the results. Finally, the QC returns the slave processes to the pool and sends the final result to the end user. Don't feel bad that the slave processes appear to be doing all the work. The QC has enough work to do on its own as well. All this extra work can add up. The ultimate goal is that the extra work performed by the QC is significantly less than the time saves by the slaves working in parallel, otherwise the parallel execution will not perform well.

Parallel execution can improve statement execution for SQL statements that involve full table scans or joins of large tables, creation of large indexes, and large Insert, Update and Delete statements.

Parallel execution is not limited to just completing disk I/O faster. Consider a SQL statement that involves aggregate functions such as *min* or *max*. Data needs to be sorted before the minimum or maximum value can be found. In this case, the parallel slaves will operate in two steps, or two *slave sets*. One that reads the data from disk, then another set to sort and aggregate the data, all before returning the results to the Query Coordinator.

If each of the four parallel threads finds the maximum value of its portion of data, then the QC only needs to determine the maximum of four values. The following diagram shows how the parallel slaves can work together to provide multiple levels to the parallel processing.

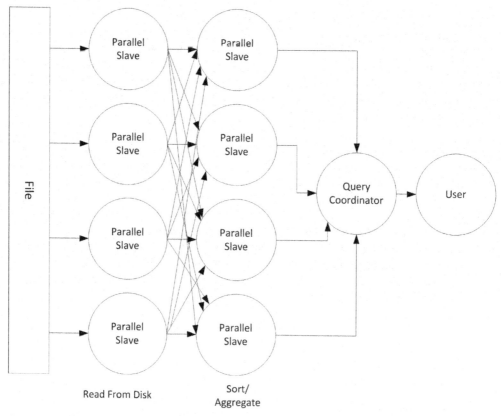

Read From Disk   Sort/
Aggregate

Figure 7.3 Multiple Parallel Levels

In the above diagram, the parallel slaves that are reading from disk are *producers* to the slaves on the next level. The slaves performing the sort/aggregation are *consumers* of the work performed by the producers. The producer does not need to complete its work before the consumer can start to use the results. As soon as the producer has data ready, it will pass it on to the consumer to promote *"Inter-Operation Parallelism"*. This helps speed up the parallel processing. The parallel slaves on the same level participate in *Intra-Operation Parallelism*. The consumer processes are not limited to sort and aggregate operations. Join operations can also be performed at the consumer level. Lastly, the producers have the capability to send their work on to any producer, which leads to all of the arrows between the producers and consumers in the diagram above.

So if a parallel degree of 4 works well, then why not a parallel degree of 10, 20, or even 100? The more parallel slaves, the better, right? Unfortunately, the server's physical resources have limits. For slaves performing disk I/O, there needs to be sufficient bandwidth from the storage subsystem to database server. Sorting operations are CPU intensive and too many slaves may start to push the CPU cores to their limits. If a very high parallel degree is used, there may be few resources for other users of the database, including those that are not performing parallel operations. Each slave process will need access to its own PGA memory. Parallel processing can struggle if the host does not have sufficient resources to support it.

The final sentence of the previous paragraph is where Oracle RAC can come to the rescue. You can scale the workload of parallel processing by spreading the load over multiple nodes in the cluster, thereby providing more resources. The following diagram shows how parallel processing might work in an Oracle RAC environment. If the single server does not have enough resources devoted to running the operation with parallel degree of 4, the processing can be moved to a two-node RAC cluster and run with parallel degree of 2 on each node.

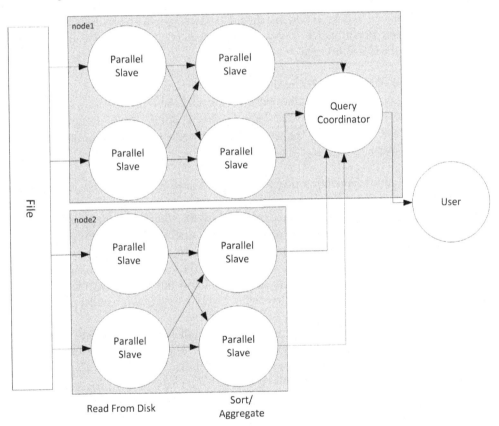

Figure 7.4 Parallel Operations on RAC

In the diagram above, each node has *producer* and *consumer* parallel slave processes. It should be noted that a producer is capable of sending results to any consumer across the network, to any RAC instance. The database engine does its best to distribute the work in an intelligent fashion in Oracle RAC to minimize the cross-instance communication between producers and consumers. The diagram above illustrates an ideal situation where there is no cross-instance traffic between producers and consumers but it is also likely that the producer slave processes will send results across the instance boundaries. As such, it is vital to have a well performing Cluster Interconnect to ensure optimal parallel execution in Oracle RAC systems.

The user's shadow process for the connection to the instance serves as the Query Coordinator. This process is either a dedicated or shared server process and can be identified from the *spid* column of the *v$process* view. Since the query coordinator will run on only one of the instances, the results from each parallel slave will need to be transferred across the Cluster Interconnect, whenever the slave is running on a different instance. Unlike single-instance databases, parallel operations in Oracle RAC can have poor performance if too much data needs to participate in global cache transfers to the QC's instance.

To reduce or eliminate global cache transfers for parallel operations in Oracle RAC, we can restrict the instances that will host parallel slave processes, a techniques that we will discussed in more detail later in this chapter. Keep in mind that doing segregating a RAC instance for parallelism will reduce the resource available to the parallel execution.

Parallel operations have one other feature when performed in Oracle RAC databases. By definition, all parallel slaves are on one instance in a single instance-database, accessing a singular Buffer Cache. In Oracle RAC, there are multiple Buffer Cache memory areas involved. When a parallel operation is performed and the *parallel_degree_policy* initialization parameter is set to AUTO, Oracle will access data from the different Buffer Cache memory areas. Without this feature, an instance that does not have the data block in the Buffer Cache would be forced to wait for a global cache transfer operation to complete, which would slow down parallel processing.

When a SQL statement is performed with parallel operations, the user's shadow process starts its role as the Query Coordinator. The QC then obtains the required number of parallel slave processes. The parallel slaves perform their work. Results from each slave are sent back to the QC. The QC performs any processing that could not be completed by parallel slaves. The QC puts together the final results and sends the results to the end user.

When an instance starts, a pool of parallel slave processes is automatically started. Initially, the number of slave processes in the pool is defined by the *parallel_min_servers* initialization parameter. If all of the slave processes from the initial pool allocation are being used and another parallel operation starts, more parallel slave processes are created until a maximum of *parallel_max_servers* processes have been reached. At this point, no more parallel processes can be spawned.

For most Oracle RAC deployments, the resources available in each node are similar. For example, each node would have the same number of CPU cores. In this case, the minimum and maximum number of slave processes should be configured identically for all instances.

If a node has twice as many CPU cores as another node, then you may consider allowing twice the number of parallel slave processes.

Determining the Degree of Parallelism

The *Degree of Parallelism* (DOP) defines how many slave processes will be utilized in the parallel execution. The DOP can be manually specified as a property of a table similar to the following.

```
SQL> alter table
  2      orders
  3      parallel 4;

Table altered.

SQL> alter table
  2      order_details
  3      parallel 8;

Table altered.
```

The DOP will be 4 for the first table shown above and 8 for the second table. When a SQL statement involves both tables, the higher degree of parallelism is used. If both producers and consumers are needed, then the total number of slave processes will be twice the DOP.

If the DOP is not explicitly specified, the default DOP for parallel operations is defined by the *cpu_count* and *parallel_threads_per_cpu* initialization parameters and the number of involved instances.

The following script can be used to compute the default DOP.

💾 default_dop_rac.sql

```
set serveroutput on

declare
    cpu_cnt    number;
    t_per_cpu number;
    inst_cnt   number;
 begin
    select
        value into t_per_cpu
    from
        v$parameter
    where
        name='parallel_threads_per_cpu';

    select
        value into cpu_cnt
    from
        v$parameter
    where
        name='cpu_count';

    select
        count(*) into inst_cnt
    from
        gv$instance;

    dbms_output.put_line('Default DOP: ' || cpu_cnt * t_per_cpu *
inst_cnt);

 end;
 /
```

```
Default DOP: 16

PL/SQL procedure successfully completed.
```

The script above will work for single-instance and Oracle RAC databases. The only difference is that the instance count will be one for single-instance databases. By default, the instance count is the number of instances up and running in the cluster. If Oracle services are used, the instance count is the number of instances available to the service.

The DOP can also be controlled by Optimizer hints. The *no_parallel* hint will effectively set the DOP to 1. This hint can be used to override any other DOP setting.

```
SQL> select
  2      /*+ no_parallel */
  3      o.order_id,
  4      count(od.item_id) as num_items
  5  from
```

```
 6       orders o
 7       join
 8       order_details od
 9       on o.order_id=od.order_id
10   group by
11       o.order_id;
```

The *parallel* hint by itself will use the default DOP for the objects involved.

```
SQL> select
 2       /*+ parallel */
 3       o.order_id,
 4       count(od.item_id) as num_items
 5   from
 6       orders o
 7       join
 8       order_details od
 9       on o.order_id=od.order_id
10   group by
11       o.order_id;
```

The *parallel* hint can be used to explicitly define the DOP for the SQL statement.

```
SQL> select
 2       /*+ parallel(16) */
 3       o.order_id,
 4       count(od.item_id) as num_items
 5   from
 6       orders o
 7       join
 8       order_details od
 9       on o.order_id=od.order_id
10   group by
11       o.order_id;
```

The order of precedence for determining the DOP to use is as follows:

1. Parallel-related optimizer hint
2. Manually defined DOP at the table level
3. Default DOP at the instance or session level.

You has many options when defining the DOP used for processing SQL statements. These options let you fine tune the number of parallel slaves in use for the SQL execution.

Parallel Query Parameters and RAC

As with most any aspect of an Oracle instance, there are a number of initialization parameters that you can configure. Remember, parallel processes can span multiple nodes of an Oracle RAC database. As a best practice, the parameters involved in parallel processing should be sized the same in all instances of the cluster. While not a complete list, the following initialization parameters are the most vital.

The *parallel_min_servers* initialization parameter defines the number of slave processes to initially spawn on instance startup. As slave processes are added and removed in response to changing demands on parallel processing, the number of slave processes in the instance will not fall below this parameter setting. Normally, the default value of this parameter is sufficient.

The *parallel_max_servers* initialization parameter defines the maximum number of slave processes available in the instance. For instances that will see a large number of concurrent parallel SQL statements, this parameter may need to be increased from its default value. Each session executing a parallel SQL statement will need a number of slave processes defined by the DOP for each slave set. This parameter should be sized to 2 * DOP * the number of concurrent sessions running parallel SQL statements. Increasing the maximum number of slave processes will increase the resource consumption on the server so you will need to understand the impact of raising this value without negatively impacting other users of the system.

The *parallel_degree_policy* initialization parameter defines whether automatic DOP and statement queuing will be enabled. The default value is MANUAL, which turns off automatic DOP and statement queuing. A value of AUTO turns on automatic DOP and statement queuing. If the parameter is set to ADAPTIVE, automatic DOP and statement queuing are enabled. The ADAPTIVE setting also provides performance feedback to the database engine so that subsequent executions of the same parallel SQL statement may run with a different DOP if the instance determines the automatic DOP value is not optimal.

Parallel Query Granules and RAC

The basic unit of work for a parallel slave is the *granule*. Once the slave process has completed processing the granule of data, the slave process will work on the next granule if more are available. The work continues until all granules have been processed.

A *partition granule* corresponds to each partition of a table. For example, assume a table with four partitions. In this case, there will be four granules to process. With a DOP of 4, each partition will be processed concurrently. If the table has eight partitions and the DOP is 4, each slave will process two partition granules.

As soon as the slave finishes its partition, it will move on to another partition. If the DOP is 8 and there are four partitions, then four slaves will work and four slaves will be idle. So it is important to set the DOP correctly when tables are partitioned. Partition granules work best when each partition is sized similarly. If one partition is very large and the others are very small, the slave processing the large partition will not complete until much later than the slaves processing the small partitions. It is desirable to have the partitions sized similarly to make the best use of parallel processing.

Partitions and the optimal degree of parallelism

When using both partitioning and parallel operations, it is important that the number of table partitions be an even multiple of the DOP involved. Consider the case where the DOP is 4 but there are six evenly sized partitions. During the first pass through the table, the four slaves will process four partition granules. During the second pass through the table, two slaves will process the remaining two partition granules while the other two slaves will sit idle. Hence, if the table had 8 partitions, all slave processes would be working. In addition, the partition granules could be smaller because the data would be spread over eight partitions instead of six which leads to quicker processing times. The Oracle documentation recommends that the number of partitions in the table be three times the DOP.

If a table is not partitioned, *block range granules* are used for the unit of work. The block range granule is computed by dividing the size of the table by the DOP. A 1-megabyte table with a DOP of 8 would result in block range granules of size 128 kilobytes each. Block range granules will not leave idle slave processes like partition granules can.

Parallel Statement Queuing and RAC

If the *parallel_degree_policy* initialization parameter is set to AUTO, Oracle will attempt to use parallel SQL whenever possible. The Query Coordinator will attempt to obtain the desired number of parallel slaves denoted by DOP for the involved segments as described earlier in this chapter. If there are not enough free parallel slaves, the parallel SQL statement is queued and will wait its turn for slave processes. Once enough slave processes are free and the SQL statement is at the front of the queue, the SQL statement is de-queued and the statement execution is allowed to proceed. The *resmgr:pq queued* wait event signals that the session's SQL statement is involved in parallel statement queuing. The *parallel_max_servers* initialization parameter defines the maximum number of parallel slaves. This parameter can be set to have different values for each Oracle RAC instance, but ideally each instance should have the same setting.

Parallel statement queuing can hamper performance so much that it may be more beneficial to run the SQL statement singularly. Remember that parallel statement queuing only occurs when there are not sufficient slave processes available. Later in this chapter we will see how to tune the number of parallel slave processes. However, if the application is seeing high occurrences of the *resmgr:pq queued* wait event, consider increasing the *parallel_max_servers* initialization parameter if the server can handle the additional workload.

The Resource Manager can also help with parallel statement queuing. Normally the parallel statements are in a traditional queue. The first one in the queue is the first one out. In Oracle 12c, the Resource Manager can be used to provide priority order for the parallel statement queue based on the consumer group. When creating a resource plan directive, the *parallel_server_limit* parameter can be used to constrain the consumer group so that it does not dominate slave process allocation. In Oracle 12c, the resource plan directive's *parallel_queue_timeout* parameter can be used to limit the time a parallel statement is queued. However, once the time has passed, the SQL statement is terminated and may need to be resubmitted. An existing plan can be modified similar to the following.

```
SQL> exec dbms_resource_manager.update_plan_directive( -
>    plan=>'BATCH_PLAN', -
>    new_parallel_queue_timeout=>3000, -
>    new_parallel_server_limit=>50);
```

With the above statement, a resource plan directive is modified to limit SQL statements to have a life of 3,000 seconds on the parallel statement queue before terminating. All of the consumers of this plan directive will use at most 50 parallel slave processes in the instance leaving the rest for other resource plans or users that are not constrained by the Resource Manager.

Tuning Parallel Execution

Parallel slave processes need additional memory to support communications between slave sets. The Oracle documentation goes to great lengths to indicate that the parallel message pool is in the Shared Pool memory component of the SGA. However, the parallel message pool may reside in the Large Pool, depending on how the SGA is defined, as can be seen in the following query.

```
SQL> select
  2      pool,
  3      name,
  4      bytes
  5  from
  6      v$sgastat
  7  where
  8      name='PX msg pool';

POOL          NAME                            BYTES
------------- ------------------------------- ----------
large pool    PX msg pool                     491520
```

If Automatic Memory Management is used, the PX message pool will be in the Large Pool, else it will be in the Shared Pool. The query above can be used to know for sure which memory component holds this pool. As more parallel SQL statements are executed concurrently, the PX message pool will need to grow accordingly. If there is insufficient memory for the PX message pool, one of the following two ORA-4031 errors will be raised.

```
ORA-04031: unable to allocate 2048024 bytes of shared memory ("large
pool","unknown object","large pool","PX msg pool")

ORA-04031: unable to allocate 16084 bytes of shared memory ("shared
pool","unknown object","shared pool heap","PX msg pool")
```

The error message will indicate the pool with the memory shortage. The fix is to increase the appropriate memory pool to support the PX message pool.

It is always better to be proactive rather than reactive. Waiting for the ORA-4031 error message before increasing the appropriate pool means that some end user is now seeing an error affecting their application. Instead, you should monitor the free space in the appropriate pool.

```
SQL> select
  2      pool,
  3      name,
  4      bytes
  5  from
  6      v$sgastat
  7  where
```

```
   8      name='free memory'
   9      and
  10      pool in ('shared pool', 'large pool');

POOL          NAME                                   BYTES
------------  ------------------------------   ----------
shared pool   free memory                        52741584
large pool    free memory                         7897088
```

If the free memory in the Shared Pool or Large Pool gets too low, the pool size should be increased.

Ideally, the Large Pool should be used for the PX message pool. Oracle will automatically use the Large Pool when the *sga_target* or *memory_target* initialization parameters are set. If those parameters are not set because you is manually sizing the various SGA components, the Large Pool will only be used when the *parallel_automatic_tuning* initialization parameter is set to a value of TRUE. Note that this parameter is now deprecated and is at the end of its life in Oracle 12c.

When a parallel slave needs to send its results to either another slave acting as a consumer, or to the Query Coordinator, the slave simply places the data in a table queue. The consumer slave can pull data from the queue as needed. The asynchronous passing of data between the levels helps speed up parallel statement execution considerably. The table queues are simply memory structures that have previously been labeled as the PX message pool. In a single-instance database, the table queue has three buffers. In an Oracle RAC database, the table queue has five buffers.

The buffers are sized by the *parallel_execution_message_size* initialization parameter. The default value of this parameter in Oracle 11.1 and earlier is 4096 bytes or less. In Oracle 11.2 and higher, the default value of this parameter is 16,384 bytes. For Oracle RAC, it is often beneficial to have the parameter sized to the largest value possible (up to 32 kilobytes on most platforms) and ensure that the Cluster Interconnect is configured with Jumbo Frames.

When increasing the *parallel_execution_message_size* parameter, the queue tables will be larger which means the PX message pool needs more space. As such, increasing the *parallel_execution_message_size* initialization parameter is often followed by an increase to the memory allocated for the Large Pool. All instances in an Oracle RAC database must have the same setting for the *parallel_execution_message_size* initialization parameter.

Oracle includes the *v$px_buffer_advice* view that shows parallel execution statistics for a running instance.

```
SQL> select
  2       statistic,
  3       value
  4  from
  5       v$px_buffer_advice
  6  order by
  7       statistic;

STATISTIC                        VALUE
------------------------------   ----------
Buffers Current Free                    445
Buffers Current Total                   500
Buffers HWM                             191
Estimated Buffers HWM                   765
Estimated Buffers Max                 19680
Servers Highwater                        31
Servers Max                             160
```

Note that the Servers Max statistic matches the *parallal_max_servers* initialization parameter. The Servers Highwater statistic shows the highest number of concurrent slave processes in use at any one time.

If the Servers Highwater value is near or equal to the Servers Max value, consider increasing the *parallal_max_servers* initialization parameter.

The Buffers Current Total value shows the maximum number of buffers in the PX message pool. The total number of buffers in use is Buffers Current Total – Buffers Current Free.

The maximum number of concurrent buffers used in the life of the instance is shown in the Buffers HWM value. If the Buffers HWM value is close to the Buffers Current Total value, this is another indicator that the appropriate SGA components, Shared Pool or Large Pool, need to be increased.

Many times when tuning applications, it is often beneficial to identify session details. Since this chapter is devoted to parallel operations, it is useful to determine the Query Coordinator process and its parallel slaves.

The *gv$px_session* view can provide this information as can be seen below.

parallel_sessions.sql

```
select
    ps.qcsid,
    ps.sid,
    p.spid,
    ps.inst_id,
    ps.degree,
    ps.req_degree
from
    gv$px_session ps
    join
    gv$session s
        on ps.sid=s.sid
            and
            ps.inst_id=s.inst_id
    join
    gv$process p
        on p.addr=s.paddr
        and
        p.inst_id=s.inst_id
order by
    qcsid,
    server_group desc,
    inst_id,
    sid;
```

QCSID	SID	SPID	INST_ID	DEGREE	REQ_DEGREE
84	84	15343	1		
84	39	5511	1	8	8
84	63	5552	1	8	8
84	66	5495	1	8	8
84	74	5469	1	8	8
84	80	18554	1	8	8
84	81	18560	1	8	8
84	82	18556	1	8	8
84	83	18558	1	8	8
84	11	6123	2	8	8
84	34	5015	2	8	8
84	40	5004	2	8	8
84	42	5013	2	8	8
84	57	5010	2	8	8
84	62	6121	2	8	8
84	68	6109	2	8	8
84	75	6115	2	8	8

The *qcsid* column shows the session identifier of the Query Coordinator. The first line of output shows the *sid* column has the same value as the *qcsid* column, which means the first line is the process that identifies the QC. Also note that for the QC process, the last two columns are null. The OS process identifier, shown in the *spid* column, should correspond to the user's shadow process on the host as can be seen below.

```
$ ps -ef|grep 15343

oracle   15343 15266  0 03:28 ?        00:00:00 oracleorcl1
(DESCRIPTION=(LOCAL=YES)(ADDRESS=(PROTOCOL=beq)))
oracle   18799 12748  0 03:37 pts/2    00:00:00 grep 15343
```

The remaining rows of output are the parallel slave processes. The *degree* column provides the DOP for this session while the *req_degree* column denotes the requested DOP. The actual DOP may be lower than the requested DOP if the Resource Master has constrained the session. In the output above, the DOP is 8 however there are 16 slave processes. When the number of parallel slaves equals twice the DOP, then half the slave processes are producers and half are consumers. Two of the slave OS process identifiers are verified below.

```
$ ps -ef|grep 5511

oracle    5511     1  1 03:16 ?        00:00:22 ora_p002_orcl1
oracle   18830 12748  0 03:37 pts/2    00:00:00 grep 5511

$ ps -ef|grep 5552

oracle    5552     1  1 03:16 ?        00:00:22 ora_p003_orcl1
oracle   18848 12748  0 03:37 pts/2    00:00:00 grep 5552
```

Also note by inspecting the *inst_id* column that half of the slave processes are executing on the first instance and half are on the second instance. Nothing special was done to force the parallel processes to spread over the instances. Oracle RAC automatically distributes the parallel slaves over the instances that run the QC session's service.

The *gv$ps_session* view can also show which sessions are producers and which are consumers. The *server_set* column will contain a value of '1' if the process is a producer and a value of '2' if the process is a consumer. If there are no consumers, the *server_set* column can only contain a value of '1'.

🖫 parallel_consumers_producers.sql

```
select
    qcsid,
    sid,
    inst_id,
    server_group,
    case server_set
        when 1 then 'Producer'
        when 2 then 'Consumer'
        when null then 'QC'
    end as slave_type,
    server#
from
    gv$px_session
order by
    qcsid,
    server_group desc,
    inst_id,
    server_set,
    server#;
```

QCSID	SID	INST_ID	SERVER_GROUP	SLAVE_TY	SERVER#
80	80	1		QC	
80	93	1	1	Producer	1
80	76	2	1	Producer	2
84	84	1		QC	
84	34	1	1	Producer	1
84	57	1	1	Producer	2
84	89	1	1	Consumer	1
84	90	1	1	Consumer	2
84	62	2	1	Producer	3
84	77	2	1	Producer	4
84	81	2	1	Consumer	3
84	70	2	1	Consumer	4

The output above shows two sessions with parallel operations. The session with a *qcsid* value of '80' only has producer slave processes. The session with a *qcsid* value of '84' has both producers and consumers.

As has already been stated throughout this chapter, parallel slave processes can be distributed across the nodes of an Oracle RAC cluster. As producers complete their work, their results may be sent across the Cluster Interconnect.

The database administrators can determine if the parallel execution is dominating the Cluster Interconnect traffic with the next script. This script is one of the rare ones that will access an X$ fixed view and will most likely need to be executed by a *sysdba* user.

```
select
    name,
    trunc(bytes_sent/1024/1024) as mb_sent,
    trunc(bytes_rcv/1024/1024) as mb_recv,
    trunc((bytes_sent+bytes_rcv)/1024/1024) as mb_total,
    to_char(round(100*(((bytes_sent+bytes_rcv)/1024/1024)/
        sum((bytes_sent+bytes_rcv)/1024/1024) over ()),2),'990.00') as
total_perc
  from
    sys.x$ksxpclient
  order by
    total_perc desc;
```

NAME	MB_SENT	MB_RECV	MB_TOTAL	TOTAL_P
cache	268609	236650	505259	59.48
ipq	94032	98765	192797	22.70
dlm	62596	78489	141085	16.61
diag	991	2375	3366	0.40
ksxr	505	2518	3024	0.36
cgs	1130	1112	2243	0.26
ping	808	808	1616	0.19
ksv	0	0	0	0.00
streams	0	0	0	0.00
internal	0	0	0	0.00
osmcache	0	0	0	0.00

The script above is the same script from Chapter 4 that discussed tuning the Cluster Interconnect. In the output above, the *ipq* traffic is the amount of data sent to and from this node for parallel execution. In the output above, the parallel query data on the private network accounts for 22.70% of all traffic on this node.

Note that there is no GV$ equivalent so the query will need to be run on all nodes individually. For those environments that have licensed the Diagnostics Pack, the *dba_hist_ic_client_stats* view shows the same information and this view does collect the statistics for all instances.

Next, let's look at local parallel operations.

Local Parallel Operations

As stated previously in this chapter, one of the greatest benefits of running parallel SQL statements in an Oracle RAC environment is the ability to distribute the parallel slaves over multiple nodes. However, doing so requires extra overhead than if the parallel slaves were all processed on the local node. There are times when the SQL statement will execute more quickly with multiple nodes at work and times when the

SQL statement will execute more quickly when run on a single node and avoid that extra overhead. Remember, each SQL statement is different as well as the system configuration it runs on, and parallel SQL statements should be tested to determine if a single node or multi-node execution works best for the specific environment. You should also be considering the impact of multiple parallel processes all running on the same node that could be impacting other processes competing for the same resources.

The *parallel_force_local* initialization parameter is used to control parallel SQL in Oracle RAC environments distribution over nodes other than the local, originating host. The default value for this parameter is FALSE and it is a best practice to leave this parameter at its default value. If this parameter is set to TRUE, then all parallel operations will only run on the local node. If this parameter does need to be set, it is best to do so at the session with the following command.

```
alter session set parallel_force_local=true;
```

To illustrate if forcing the parallel SQL to a specific node is beneficial or not, consider the following query.

```
select
   /*+ parallel */
   o.order_id,
   max(d.order_date) as max_date,
   count(*) as num_details
from
   orders o
   join
   order_details d
      on o.order_id = d.order_id
group by
   o.order_id;
```

The DOP for this statement is 8. The SQL statement execution was traced when running with parallel SQL across the cluster and when forcing the parallel slaves to all be local. The SQL statement completed in 35 seconds when executed across the cluster and in 20 seconds when forced locally. The wait events when executed across the cluster are shown below as captured from *tkprof* of a session trace file.

```
Event waited on                                  Times    Max. Wait  Total Waited
-----------------------------------------------  Waited   ---------  ------------
reliable message                                    2        0.01        0.02
enq: KO - fast object checkpoint                    2        0.00        0.00
KJC: Wait for msg sends to complete                 4        0.00        0.00
PX Deq: reap credit                               620        0.01        0.02
PX Deq: Join ACK                                   12        0.00        0.01
IPC send completion sync                            8        0.00        0.00
PX Deq: Parse Reply                                 8       12.35       12.35
resmgr:cpu quantum                                  2        0.01        0.01
SQL*Net message to client                        1315        0.00        0.00
PX Deq: Execute Reply                             250        1.13       19.77
```

SQL*Net message from client	1314	0.02	2.40
PX Deq: Signal ACK EXT	8	0.00	0.00
PX Deq: Slave Session Stats	8	0.00	0.00
enq: PS - contention	4	0.00	0.00

When executed all within the same node, the wait events look like the following.

Event waited on	Times Waited	Max. Wait	Total Waited
reliable message	1	0.00	0.00
enq: KO - fast object checkpoint	1	0.00	0.00
KJC: Wait for msg sends to complete	4	0.00	0.00
PX Deq: Join ACK	4	0.00	0.00
enq: PS - contention	1	0.00	0.00
PX Deq: Parse Reply	**4**	**0.00**	**0.00**
SQL*Net message to client	1315	0.00	0.00
PX Deq: Execute Reply	**115**	**2.52**	**20.57**
resmgr:cpu quantum	1	0.00	0.00
SQL*Net message from client	1314	0.01	2.93
PX Deq: Signal ACK EXT	4	0.00	0.00
PX Deq: Slave Session Stats	4	0.00	0.00

Notice that the *PX Deq: Execute Reply* wait events have very similar timings. This wait event is essentially the time that the QC waits for the slave processes to finish their work. The *PX Deq: Parse Reply* wait event has a total time of zero when executed locally and a total wait time of 12.35 seconds when executed across the nodes. The *PX Deq: Parse Reply* wait event differences account for almost all of the 15-second difference in runtimes. This wait even occurs when the QC process is waiting for the parallel slaves to receive and parse their work from the QC. When the processes are all local, the wait time is hardly noticeable and it makes sense that when some slave processes are on another note, it takes additional time to complete this operation.

If the local node has plenty of CPU resources and I/O bandwidth available to it, you may want the parallel SQL statement to run locally. Doing so would be no different than running a parallel SQL statement on a single-instance database. If you need the parallel SQL statement to enjoy the scale out capabilities of multiple nodes, then the overhead of distributing the parallel slaves can be overcome by the quicker time to completion for each parallel slave. In the end, the only way to know if running the parallel SQL statement locally or across the cluster is to run the statement both ways.

Controlling Slave Locations

By default in Oracle 10g RAC and beyond, slave processes will be equally distributed across all nodes in the cluster. Slave allocation in this manner can be beneficial by getting more resources involved. The previous section showed how to constrain the parallel slaves to the local instance with the *parallel_force_local* initialization parameter. In the days after Oracle 10g was released, the all or one approach may have worked well for most Oracle RAC deployments. Today's Oracle RAC is often deployed to consolidate database servers and their applications. It may be desirable to spread parallel execution of a SQL statement over more than one node, but less than all nodes in the cluster.

Prior to Oracle 11g, you could use the *instance_groups* and *parallel_instance_group* initialization parameters to help control parallel slave location. The *instance_groups* parameter defines the groups the instance is a member of. As an example, assume a four node Oracle RAC database has the following parameters defined.

```
orcl1.instance_groups='batch','oltp','single'
orcl2.instance_groups='batch','oltp'
orcl3.instance_groups='batch','dual'
orcl4.instance_groups='batch','dual'
```

The "batch" group is defined for all four instances. The "oltp" group is defined just for the first two instances. The "single" group, for parallel execution in a single instance, is just assigned to the first instance. The "dual" group is another two-instance group as well. An instance can have many parallel execution groups as defined by the database administrator.

With the group membership defined, the *parallel_instance_group* initialization parameter instructs the instance where to place the parallel slaves. Continuing with the example, assume the first instance has the following parameter setting.

```
orcl1.parallel_instance_group='oltp'
```

With this configuration, a parallel SQL statement initiated from the first instance would only spawn parallel execution slaves in instances 1 and 2. You can inadvertently cause problems if the instance's parallel execution group is not defined correctly. The code below defines the second instance's group.

```
orcl2.parallel_instance_group='single'
```

The problem is the group "single" is only available on the first instance. The database administrator has caused a problem because the QC will be on instance 2 and all of the parallel slaves would be on instance 1, which requires traffic on the Cluster Interconnect that would be unnecessary if the QC and parallel slaves were on the same node.

The application can also control the instance group in use at the session level as well. By setting at the session level, the instance's parameter can be overridden.

```
alter session set parallel_instance_group='dual';
```

Oracle 11g has made control parallel slave placement even easier with services. Services were first discussed in Chapter 3. A session connects to an Oracle RAC instance by through a service. When that session starts a parallel SQL statement, the slaves are distributed among all instances running that service. The *parallel_instance_group* parameter can now define a service as well as an *instance_groups* member.

Parallel Explain Plans and RAC

Any discussion of query performance tuning should have information on using the Explain Plan facility. Parallel SQL statements have additional Explain Plan nomenclature not seen in serial SQL statements. The following Explain Plan output has some columns removed (like Cost, Rows, Bytes) because they do not pertain specifically to parallel SQL statements. The columns in the output below will be discussed further to help see how Explain Plan output can assist in diagnosing how a parallel SQL statement is executed.

```
--------------------------------------------------------------------------------------------
| Id | Operation                      | Name         |Pstart|Pstop|   TQ  |IN-OUT| PQ Distrib |
--------------------------------------------------------------------------------------------
|  0 | SELECT STATEMENT               |              |      |     |       |      |            |
|  1 |  PX COORDINATOR                |              |      |     |       |      |            |
|  2 |   PX SEND QC (RANDOM)          | :TQ10005     |      |     | Q1,05 | P->S | QC (RAND)  |
|  3 |    HASH GROUP BY               |              |      |     | Q1,05 | PCWP |            |
|  4 |     PX RECEIVE                 |              |      |     | Q1,05 | PCWP |            |
|  5 |      PX SEND HASH              | :TQ10004     |      |     | Q1,04 | P->P | HASH       |
|  6 |       HASH GROUP BY            |              |      |     | Q1,04 | PCWP |            |
|* 7 |        HASH JOIN               |              |      |     | Q1,04 | PCWP |            |
|  8 |         PX RECEIVE             |              |      |     | Q1,04 | PCWP |            |
|  9 |          PX SEND HYBRID HASH   | :TQ10002     |      |     | Q1,02 | P->P | HYBRID HASH|
| 10 |           STATISTICS COLLECTO  |              |      |     | Q1,02 | PCWC |            |
| 11 |            VIEW                | VW_GBF_7     |      |     | Q1,02 | PCWP |            |
| 12 |             HASH GROUP BY      |              |      |     | Q1,02 | PCWP |            |
| 13 |              PX RECEIVE        |              |      |     | Q1,02 | PCWP |            |
| 14 |               PX SEND HASH     | :TQ10000     |      |     | Q1,00 | P->P | HASH       |
| 15 |                HASH GROUP BY   |              |      |     | Q1,00 | PCWP |            |
| 16 |                 PX BLOCK ITERATOR |           |      |     | Q1,00 | PCWC |            |
|* 17|                  TABLE ACCESS FULL | ORDERS   |      |     | Q1,00 | PCWP |            |
| 18 |         PX RECEIVE             |              |      |     | Q1,04 | PCWP |            |
| 19 |          PX SEND HYBRID HASH   | :TQ10003     |      |     | Q1,03 | P->P | HYBRID HASH|
| 20 |           VIEW                 | VW_GBC_6     |      |     | Q1,03 | PCWP |            |
| 21 |            HASH GROUP BY       |              |      |     | Q1,03 | PCWP |            |
| 22 |             PX RECEIVE         |              |      |     | Q1,03 | PCWP |            |
| 23 |              PX SEND HASH      | :TQ10001     |      |     | Q1,01 | P->P | HASH       |
| 24 |               HASH GROUP BY    |              |      |     | Q1,01 | PCWP |            |
| 25 |                PX PARTITION HASH ALL |        |  1   |  4  | Q1,01 | PCWC |            |
|* 26|                 TABLE ACCESS FULL |ORDER_DETAILS|  1 |  4  | Q1,01 | PCWP |            |
--------------------------------------------------------------------------------------------

Predicate Information (identified by operation id):
---------------------------------------------------

   7 - access("ITEM_1"="ITEM_1")
```

```
17 - access(:Z>=:Z AND :Z<=:Z)
26 - access(:Z>=:Z AND :Z<=:Z)

Note
-----
   - dynamic statistics used: dynamic sampling (level=AUTO)
   - automatic DOP: Computed Degree of Parallelism is 4 because of degree limit
```

The Explain Plan output above has some familiar pieces to it. Line 17 is showing a full table scan of the *orders* table. Line 26 is showing a full table scan of the *order_details* table. Additionally, line 26 is showing partitions 1 through 4 accessed in the table, seen in the *Pstart* and *Pstop* columns.

All of the parallel operations in the Explain Plan start with PX. Remember the section on granules? The *orders* table is not partitioned so *block range granules* are the only possible unit of work for the parallel slave processes. Line 16 shows that the *orders* table is accessed by *block range granules* with the *px block iterator* operation. The *order_details* table is partitioned so *partition granules* are used as can be seen in line 25 with the *px partition hash all* operation. The results of accessing the tables are fed to a *hash group by* operation in lines 15 and 24. Finally, the parallel slaves are ready to forward the results on to the next process. The *px send hash* operations on lines 14 and 23 are where the parallel slaves are finished and ready to send the results forward.

The *TQ* column of the Explain Plan output shows us the parallel slave groups in use. For lines 14 to 17, a group of parallel slaves known as *Q1,00* performed the operations. For lines 23 to 26, a group of parallel slaves known as *Q1,01* performed the operations.

In this output, there is a set of producer slaves and a set of consumer slaves. The producers are sending the output to the consumers in lines 14 and 23. The consumers are receiving the data in lines 13 and 22 with the *px receive* operation. Notice that the consumer slaves have different names, *Q1,02* and *Q1,03* respectively. The consumer slave processes perform the next sets of operations.

By now, we can see how the operations are moved through the parallel slaves in use. There are at most two parallel slaves groups, producer and consumer. Depending on the work that needs to be done by the slave groups, a consumer group may need to pass data on to another slave group. With only two slave groups, the consumers pass the data back to the original producers. In essence, the two groups switch roles. In the Explain Plan output above, the consumers denoted by *Q1,02* and *Q1,03* pass data to just group *Q1,04*. Group *Q1,04* was originally either group *Q1,00* or group *Q1,01* that has been repurposed. Group *Q1,04* eventually passes its work to group *Q1,05*. Group *Q1,05* is final parallel slave group. We know that data must end up at the Query Coordinator. In line 2, the *px send qc* operation is where the parallel slaves send the data on to the QC. Line 1 shows the *px coordinator* operation which is when the QC receives the results.

Remember that data sent between producers and consumers is done through a table queue. Also remember that any producer has the ability to send data to any consumer. The *PQ Distrib* column shows the method of how the data is passed between producer and consumer. The following table shows the values one can see in the *PQ Distrib* column.

PQ Distrib	Description
BROADCAST	Each producer sends all of its rows to all consumers.
BROADCAST LOCAL	A producer will send all rows to all consumers on the same node. This reduces the cross-instance traffic in Oracle RAC.
HASH	A hash algorithm is used to decide which consumer will receive the row of data
HYBRID HASH	New to Oracle 12c. Either BROADCAST or HASH is used, but it won't be known until runtime.
ONE SLAVE	New to Oracle 12c. All producers will send data to only one consumer process.
PARTITION KEY	The table's partition key will determine which consumer receives the data. This is used for partition-wise joins.
RANGE	A producer will send a range of rows to one consumer and then a range of rows to another consumer.
ROUND-ROBIN	Each row is sent to all consumers in round-robin fashion.
QC ORDER	The producer sends the data directly to the QC. The data is sent in a specific order to facilitate sorting.
QC RANDOM	The producer sends the data directly to the QC. The order is not important.

Table 7.1 PQ Distrib Values

The *IN-OUT* column shows the relationship between parallel operations. The following table summarizes the values seen in this column.

IN-OUT	Description
P->S	Parallel to Serial. Parallel processes send to a singular process, normally the QC.
P->P	Parallel to Parallel. Producer slave processes send rows to consumer slave processes.
PCWC	Parallel Combined With Child. The same slaves processes that perform this operation perform the child operation.
PCWP	Parallel Combined With Parent. The same slaves processes that perform this operation perform the parent operation.

S->P	Serial -> Parallel. A serial process sends rows to multiple parallel processes.
SCWC	Serial Combined with Child. The same serial process that performs this operation performs the child operation.
SCWP	Serial Combined with Parent. The same serial process that performs this operation performs the parent operation.

Table 7.2 IN-OUT Values

This section clarifies some of the more arcane terminology used in parallel SQL Explain Plan output. The *TQ* column shows the grouping of parallel slave processes. The granules used can be seen in the *Operation* column, which also shows parallel slave groups sending (producers) and receiving (consumers) rows of data.

Bloom Filters

This chapter has discussed parallel query execution in detail. By now, the reader understands the concepts of producer and consumer slave sets. It is possible for any producer to send rows to any consumer. In Oracle RAC, the consumer slave process may be on a different node than the producer slave process, requiring cross-instance traffic. To reduce cross-instance traffic, Oracle relies on *bloom filters*. Bloom filters, named after Burton Howard Bloom, are not new. Bloom filters were first implemented in Oracle 10gR2 to reduce the rows between producers and consumers when processing joins with parallel operations. Oracle 11gR1 allowed Bloom filters to be used to implement join-filter pruning.

A Bloom filter is an array that helps to indicate if an item is in a set. The array is a series of *m* bits. Multiple hash functions map a key value to multiple bits in the filter. To understand how the Bloom filter works, consider the following example illustrated in Figure 7.5. There are four hash functions applied to the key value.

For a value of "cat", function f1 returns 1, function f2 returns 6, function f3 returns 2, and function f4 returns 12. When the value of "cat" is found in a table, bits 1, 6, 2 and 12 are turned on, i.e. set to '1'.

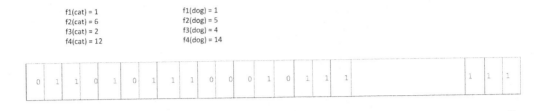

| 0 | 1 | 1 | 0 | 1 | 0 | 1 | 1 | 1 | 0 | 0 | 0 | 1 | 0 | 1 | 1 | 1 | | | | | | | | | | | | | 1 | 1 | 1 |

0 1 2 3 4 5 6 7 8 9 . . . . m

Figure 7.5 Bloom Filter

As stated earlier, Bloom filters let us know if a value is in a set. If we want to know whether "dog" is in the set, we apply the same hash function to the key value. As we can see in Figure 7.5, the value of "dog" is hashed to bits 1, 5, 4, and 14.

If these bits are all set to one, the Bloom filter is telling us that the value of "dog" is likely to be found in the set. If any of these bits is set to zero, then we know definitively that the value of "dog" is not in the set.

Notice that bit 5 is set to zero. The value of "dog" is not in the set. The Bloom filter can only tell is one of two conditions, the value is not present in the set or the value may be in the set.

The Bloom filter cannot definitively state that a value is in the set. Going back to the example, note that both "dog" and "cat" set bit 1 to true. A bit can be set by many key values. There is no inverse hash function that says if bits X and Y are set, the key value must be Z. As such, the Bloom filter cannot tell us definitively if a key value is in the set.

Bloom filters are very space efficient, which is why they are used to help determine set inclusion. The number of false positive hits from the Bloom filter depends on the size of the filter and the number of hash functions. Checking set inclusion with a Bloom filter is a function that is independent of the size of the set that makes using Bloom filters an efficient, quick operation.

Bloom filters are used in parallel SQL execution by a two-step process, creating the filter and then using the filter to indicate which rows will participate in a join operation. To see how Oracle uses bloom filters, consider the following excerpt from an Explain Plan.

```
-------------------------------------------------
| Id  | Operation             | Name      |
-------------------------------------------------
|   0 | SELECT STATEMENT      |           |
|   1 |  HASH JOIN            |           |
|   2 |   JOIN FILTER CREATE  | :BF0000   |
|   3 |    TABLE ACCESS FULL  | ORDERS    |
|   4 |   VIEW                | V1        |
|   5 |    HASH GROUP BY      |           |
|   6 |     JOIN FILTER USE   | :BF0000   |
|   7 |      TABLE ACCESS FULL| CUSTOMERS |
-------------------------------------------------
```

As we see above, the *orders* table has a full table scan performed on it in line 3. From this full table scan, the Bloom filter is created in line 2 with the *join filter create* operation. The *Name* column shows the filter is denoted by ":BF0000", i.e. Bloom Filter 0. The *customers* table has another full table scan in line 7. The Bloom filter created in line 2 is used in line 6, denoted by the *join filter use* operation, to filter out rows from the *customers* table that will not participate in the join.

When a Bloom filter is used in parallel join processing, the Explain Plan is not as clear that the Bloom filter was used. Below is an example of an Explain that does feature a Bloom filter. The example was trimmed for brevity.

```
---------------------------------------------------------------
| Id  | Operation                 | Name          |
---------------------------------------------------------------
|   0 | SELECT STATEMENT          |               |
|   1 |  PX COORDINATOR           |               |
|   2 |   PX SEND QC (RANDOM)     | :TQ10001      |
| * 3 |    HASH JOIN              |               |
|   4 |     PX RECEIVE            |               |
|   5 |      PX SEND BROADCAST    | :TQ10000      |
|   6 |       PX BLOCK ITERATOR   |               |
| * 7 |        TABLE ACCESS FULL  | ORDERS        |
|   8 |     PX BLOCK ITERATOR     |               |
| * 9 |      TABLE ACCESS FULL    | ORDER_DETAILS |
---------------------------------------------------------------

Predicate Information (identified by operation id):
---------------------------------------------------------------

   3 - access("O"."ORDER_ID"="OD"."ORDER_ID")
   7 - access(:Z>=:Z AND :Z<=:Z)
       filter("O"."ORDER_TYPE"='T1')
   9 - access(:Z>=:Z AND :Z<=:Z)
       filter(SYS_OP_BLOOM_FILTER(:BF0000,"OD"."ORDER_ID"))

Note
-----
   - Degree of Parallelism is 4 because of hint
```

The asterisk on line 9 of the Explain Plan signifies additional detail that follows the plan output. In the Predicate Information section, the presence of the Bloom filter is shown. The Bloom filter was created on the *order_id* column in this example.

The px_join_filter hint

The optimizer hint *px_join_filter* can be used to instruct the optimizer to use a Bloom filter. Similarly, if the optimizer is choosing a Bloom filter you can use the *no_px_join_filter* hint to run the SQL statement without it. Oracle includes the *v$sql_join_filter* view to provide information on how the Bloom filter is used.

```
SQL> select
  2      qc_session_id,
  3      qc_instance_id as inst_id,
  4      sql_plan_hash_value as plan_hash_val,
  5      length,
  6      filtered,
  7      probed
  8  from
  9      v$sql_join_filter;

QC_SESSION_ID INST_ID PLAN_HASH_VAL   LENGTH  FILTERED   PROBED
------------- ------- ------------- -------- --------- ---------
         1740       4    1322433283    16384    379666    412524
```

The *v$sql_join_filter* view shows the Query Coordinator session identifier and the Oracle RAC instance for this session. The *sql_plan_hash_value* column can be joined to *v$sql_plan* to obtain the SQL statement's Explain Plan. The *length* column shows the size of the Bloom filter. In the example above, the Bloom filter is only 16 kilobytes in size yet the tables involved in the SQL statement are multiple gigabytes each. This view illustrates how small Bloom filters can be.

The *probed* column tells us how many rows were examined with the Bloom filter. The *filtered* column shows how many rows were removed from consideration in the join operation. In the example above, 412,524 rows were examined and 379,666 rows were filtered out. Only 32,858 rows were sent to the consumer slaves for processing the join. The Bloom filter eliminated 92% of the rows. The bloom filter significantly reduced the producer to consumer transfer, and since this was run on Oracle RAC, will significantly reduce the transfers on the Cluster Interconnect.

Bloom filters are data structures used to determine set membership. They are most beneficial in determining if a value is not in a set in which case the row will not participate in a join so it no longer needs to be considered. While Bloom filters can be used in single-instance databases, they can really help in Oracle RAC where producer slaves may be sending rows to consumer slaves processes on another instance.

Summary

This chapter discussed parallel SQL processing in detail. Oracle RAC was built to scale by providing extra resources on multiple nodes. Parallel processing works well in Oracle RAC when multiple CPUs can all work together to significantly reduce the overall runtime of the SQL statement. The chapter started with a simple example of a query that ran faster when run in parallel before discussing how parallel execution works.

The first item when discussing tuning parallel execution focused on increasing the Large Pool memory area to support the PX message pool. Various initialization parameters and their impact were mentioned throughout the chapter. Being that this book focuses on Oracle RAC systems, the chapter spent time showing how to restrict parallel slave process to one or a few instances in the cluster.

The chapter finished with a discussion of reading Explain Plan output involving parallel SQL statements. The topic of Bloom filters finished the chapter, including what they are and how they work. Bloom filters can be very important for parallel SQL on Oracle RAC as they can reduce the rows sent between producer and consumer slave processes that may be on different nodes.

The next chapter is the first in a series focusing on Oracle RAC performance tuning tools and utilities. Oracle includes the ORAchk, OSWatcher, and Cluster Health Monitor utilities for you to use. Oracle 12c introduces the Grid Infrastructure Management Repository to assist with Oracle RAC performance.

RAC Support Tools

Performance tuning for Oracle RAC databases often involves using a variety of tools and utilities to collect diagnostic data that helps determine the root cause of the poor performance. It'd important to note that all of the tools the database administrator uses for single-instance databases are still valid for Oracle RAC databases. Fr example, to monitor CPU usage, the database administrator might use *top* in Unix or Linux or the Task Manager in Windows. Command line OS utilities such as *vmstat* and *sar* still work well for diagnosing OS resource utilization on Unix or Linux. Database administrators running Oracle on Windows can still use the PerfMon utility.

This book has already discussed a variety of performance tuning tools and utilities like *trcsess, iperf,* Orion, and more. Those utilities were discussed as they relate to the topics in those chapters. This chapter focuses on a bundle of tools released by Oracle Support for RAC performance tuning. Many of these utilities are focused on the OS level that the database administrator can use in conjunction with the OS utilities they are already familiar with using. These utilities were originally downloaded singly but more recently, Oracle Support now includes the tools as a bundle.

Most of the utilities in this chapter have many more features than are discussed in this book. There simply is not enough room in this chapter to discuss each tool in great detail. This chapter will provide more than enough information to start using the tool immediately and provide value to the database administrator. You are encouraged to explore each utility to see what else it can do for you.

RAC and DB Tools Bundle

As stated above, the tools in this chapter can be downloaded individually. In the past, the only way to obtain these utilities was one-by-one. Oracle Support now bundles the tools together in a single download. No matter if the database administrator downloads the utilities separately or as a bundle, they will need a valid support contract, as the utilities are only available on My Oracle Support Community. To download the bundle, go to MOSC Note 1594347.1 and click on the big download link. In the sections of this chapter that follow, the relevant My Oracle Support

Community note will be given if the database administrator wants to download that utility individually.

The RAC and DB Tools bundle contains the following utilities:

- ORAchk (formerly RACchk)
- Trace File Analyzer (TFA)
- OSWatcher
- Procwatcher
- Oratop
- SQLT

This chapter will additionally cover utilities not in the bundle, but still very useful to the Oracle RAC database administrator.

- Cluster Health Monitor (CHM)
- CHM OS Graphical (CHMOSG)
- Racdiag.sql script

Cluster Health Monitor

Oracle's Cluster Health Monitor (CHM), formerly known as the Instantaneous Problem Detector for Clusters (IPD/OS), automatically collects OS performance metrics on a regular basis to assist with diagnosing node evictions, server hangs, and other OS-related performance issues. The CHM will collect details on memory usage, processes, as well as CPU, I/O and network usage. In Oracle Grid Infrastructure 12c, CHM collects the OS metrics every five seconds, and in versions prior to 12c, CHM collects the metrics every second.

Oracle recommends installing the CHM on the cluster. Many times, Oracle Support will ask for CHM output when handling Service Requests for OS or cluster related issues. Installing CHM on the cluster prior to an incident is a great way to ensure diagnosis metrics are available when needed.

Beginning in Oracle Grid Infrastructure 11.2.0.2, CHM is bundled with the cluster software for Linux and Solaris Platforms. For AIX and Windows, CHM is bundled with Grid Infrastructure 11.2.0.3. For earlier Grid Infrastructure versions, down to 10.2, CHM is a standalone utility that can be downloaded from Oracle's Technet at the following URL.

http://www.oracle.com/technetwork/database/options/clustering/downloads/ipd-download-homepage-087212.html

That same URL also includes a download link for a graphical CHM interface that is not part of any installation. The graphical CHM is a recommended download as it makes working with CHM data much easier. This section will discuss the command line and graphical CHM functionality.

When integrated with the Grid Infrastructure software, the CHM is a managed resource in the cluster. To make things a little confusing, the resource is known as the Cluster Robustness Framework (CRF). As such, the resource name is *ora.crf* as can be seen below.

```
[oracle@host01 bin]$ ./crsctl stat res -t -init

----------------------------------------------------------------------
Name            Target  State         Server          State details
----------------------------------------------------------------------
Cluster Resources
----------------------------------------------------------------------
ora.asm         ONLINE  ONLINE        host01          Started,STABLE
ora.cluster_interconnect.haip
                ONLINE  ONLINE        host01          STABLE
ora.crf         ONLINE  ONLINE        host01          STABLE
ora.crsd        ONLINE  ONLINE        host01          STABLE
ora.cssd        ONLINE  ONLINE        host01          STABLE
ora.cssdmonitor
                ONLINE  ONLINE        host01          STABLE
ora.ctssd       ONLINE  ONLINE        host01          OBSERVER,STABLE
ora.diskmon     OFFLINE OFFLINE                       STABLE
ora.drivers.acfs
                ONLINE  ONLINE        host01          STABLE
ora.evmd        ONLINE  ONLINE        host01          STABLE
ora.gipcd       ONLINE  ONLINE        host01          STABLE
ora.gpnpd       ONLINE  ONLINE        host01          STABLE
ora.mdnsd       ONLINE  ONLINE        host01          STABLE
ora.storage     ONLINE  ONLINE        host01          STABLE
----------------------------------------------------------------------
```

Since the CHM is a managed cluster resource, it can be started and stopped just like other cluster resources.

```
[oracle@host01 bin]$ ./crsctl stop resource ora.crf -init

CRS-2673: Attempting to stop 'ora.crf' on 'host01'
CRS-2677: Stop of 'ora.crf' on 'host01' succeeded

[oracle@host01 bin]$ ./crsctl stat res -t -init

----------------------------------------------------------------------
```

```
Name              Target  State       Server               State details
--------------------------------------------------------------------------------
Cluster Resources
--------------------------------------------------------------------------------
ora.crf          OFFLINE OFFLINE                           STABLE
--------------------------------------------------------------------------------

[oracle@host01 bin]$ ./crsctl start resource ora.crf -init

CRS-2672: Attempting to start 'ora.crf' on 'host01'
CRS-2676: Start of 'ora.crf' on 'host01' succeeded
```

The output from the *crsctl status* command was trimmed to show only the CHM resource. It should be noted that starting and stopping the CHM resource manually is rarely done. Instead, the resource starts automatically when Grid Infrastructure starts and it typically stays up and running until Grid Infrastructure is shut down.

The CHM resource uses two processes on the server to collect and store the OS metric data. Each node will have an *osysmond* process that is responsible for the metric collection. This process sends the metrics to a master process called *ologgerd*. The *ologgerd* process is responsible compressing the metrics and storing the data from all nodes into the data store.

```
[oracle@host01 bin]$ ps -ef|grep osysmond

root       17114      1  1 16:46 ?        00:00:03
/u01/app/crs12.1.0.2/bin/osysmond.bin
oracle     18879   4279  0 16:50 pts/0    00:00:00 grep osysmond
 [oracle@host01 bin]$ ps -ef|grep ologgerd
root       17176      1  1 16:46 ?        00:00:03
/u01/app/crs12.1.0.2/bin/ologgerd -M -d /u01/app/crs12.1.0.2/crf/db/host01
oracle     18865   4279  0 16:50 pts/0    00:00:00 grep ologgerd
```

One node in the cluster will have the *ologgerd* master process. Another node can have a replica *ologgerd* process that can take over as the master should the master process abnormally terminate. Should the replica *ologgerd* process abnormally terminate, another one will be started on one of the nodes in the cluster. There is at most, one master and one replica *ologgerd* process across the entire cluster. The master node can be determined with the *oclumon* utility in *$GRID_HOME/bin*.

```
[oracle@host01 bin]$ ./oclumon manage -get master

Master = host01
```

A more complete description of the CHM topology on the cluster can be seen with the following command.

```
[oracle@host01 bin]$ ./oclumon manage -get alllogger -details
```

```
Logger = host01
Nodes = host01,host02
```

The master logger process is on host01 and nodes host01 and host02 have collection processes running.

As stated previously, the *ologgerd* process stores the OS performance metrics in a data store. Oracle 12c has a data store called the Grid Infrastructure Management Repository Database. In Oracle 12.1.0.2, the GI Management Repository Database is mandatory, and for Oracle 12.1.0.1, it is optional but highly recommended. If there is no Management Repository Database on the cluster, the CHM metrics are stored in a Berkeley database. The CHM repository path is easy to find with the *oclumon* utility.

```
[oracle@prod01 bin]$ ./oclumon manage -get reppath

CHM Repository Path = /u01/app/crs11.2.0.4/crf/db/prod01

 Done
```

The output above was obtained from an Oracle 11.2.0.4 Grid Infrastructure system. The repository path is shown as a directory on a file system. The next output shows the contents of that directory.

```
[oracle@prod01 bin]$ cd /u01/app/crs11.2.0.4/crf/db/prod01
[oracle@prod01 prod01]$ ls -l
total 10187828
-rw-r--r-- 1 root root   1773999 Jul  2 13:54 02-JUL-2014-13:54:50.txt
-rw-r--r-- 1 root root   1120665 Jul  2 14:00 02-JUL-2014-14:00:06.txt
-rw-r--r-- 1 root root     16953 Mar 25 19:51 25-MAR-2014-19:51:58.txt
-rw-r----- 1 root root 241414144 Sep  5 12:29 crfalert.bdb
-rw-r----- 1 root root 9277997056 Sep  5 12:29 crfclust.bdb
-rw-r----- 1 root root      8192 Jul  2 13:59 crfconn.bdb
-rw-r----- 1 root root 231993344 Sep  5 12:29 crfcpu.bdb
-rw-r----- 1 root root 224301056 Sep  5 12:29 crfhosts.bdb
-rw-r----- 1 root root 255447040 Sep  5 12:29 crfloclts.bdb
-rw-r----- 1 root root 166100992 Sep  5 12:29 crfts.bdb
-rw-r----- 1 root root     24576 Jul  2 13:54 __db.001
-rw-r----- 1 root root    401408 Sep  5 12:29 __db.002
-rw-r----- 1 root root   2629632 Sep  5 12:29 __db.003
-rw-r----- 1 root root   2162688 Sep  5 12:29 __db.004
-rw-r----- 1 root root   1187840 Sep  5 12:29 __db.005
-rw-r----- 1 root root     57344 Sep  5 12:29 __db.006
-rw-r----- 1 root root  16777216 Sep  5 12:28 log.0000005961
-rw-r----- 1 root root  16777216 Sep  5 12:29 log.0000005962
-rw-r--r-- 1 root root 120000000 Jul  2 13:55 nau-rac01.ldb
-rw-r----- 1 root root      8192 Jul  2 13:54 repdhosts.bdb
```

Notice that many of the files have a ".bdb" extension which signifies that this is a Berkeley database. If a Management Repository Database is used, the repository path will look different as can be seen below.

```
[oracle@host01 bin]$ ./oclumon manage -get reppath

CHM Repository Path =
+VOTE/_MGMTDB/FD9B43BF6A646F8CE043B6A9E80A2815/DATAFILE/sysmgmtdata.270.8550
70803
```

Most readers will recognize that the path is on an ASM diskgroup. The Management Repository Database name follows the diskgroup name in the path. The database name will always be "_MGMTDB" and will run on only one node of the Oracle RAC cluster.

The CHM will not keep the metric data forever. To see the CHM retention period, use the *oclumon* utility as below.

```
[oracle@host01 bin]$ ./oclumon manage -get repsize

CHM Repository Size = 136320 seconds
```

This system will keep data in the repository, no matter which data source is used, for 136,320 seconds or just under 38 hours. Depending on the problem needing resolution, the retention may need to be increased. The retention time is determined by the repository size. The *oclumon* utility can tell us how to size the repository to support the longer retention time.

```
[oracle@host01 bin]$ ./oclumon manage -repos checkretentiontime 259200

The Cluster Health Monitor repository is too small for the desired
retention. Please first resize the repository to 3896 MB
```

The repository is resized for the longer retention period.

```
[oracle@host01 bin]$ ./oclumon manage -repos changerepossize 3896

The Cluster Health Monitor repository was successfully resized. The new
retention is 259260 seconds.
```

The total size of the repository is a function involving the retention time and the number of nodes in the cluster. In Oracle 12c, the space required is approximately 700 megabytes per node per day. To store 3 days for a 4-node cluster would require about 201 gigabytes of storage space (700MB * 72 hours * 4 nodes).

To get an idea of metrics CHM is collecting, the *dumpnodeview* option for *oclumon* is used.

Oracle RAC Performance Tuning

```
[oracle@host01 bin]$ ./oclumon dumpnodeview -n host01

-------------------------------------------
Node: host01 Clock: '14-09-05 17.57.37 ' SerialNo:857
-------------------------------------------

SYSTEM:
#pcpus: 1 #vcpus: 1 cpuht: N chipname: Intel(R) cpu: 19.29 cpuq: 1
physmemfree: 94304 physmemtotal: 5081236 mcache: 940580 swapfree: 4024232
swaptotal: 4063228 hugepagetotal: 1000 hugepagefree: 22 hugepagesize: 2048
ior: 106 iow: 108 ios: 24 swpin: 0 swpout: 0 pgin: 106 pgout: 82 netr:
70.142 netw: 26.046 procs: 321 procsoncpu: 1 rtprocs: 13 rtprocsoncpu: N/A
#fds: 22496 #sysfdlimit: 6815744 #disks: 7 #nics: 5 nicErrors: 0

TOP CONSUMERS:
topcpu: 'asm_vktm_+asm1(4571) 2.79' topprivmem: 'java(4935) 156148' topshm:
'ocssd.bin(4275) 88904' topfd: 'oraagent.bin(4752) 258' topthread: 'console-
kit-dae(3496) 64'


-------------------------------------------
Node: host01 Clock: '14-09-05 17.57.42 ' SerialNo:858
-------------------------------------------

SYSTEM:
#pcpus: 1 #vcpus: 1 cpuht: N chipname: Intel(R) cpu: 51.75 cpuq: 3
physmemfree: 79528 physmemtotal: 5081236 mcache: 940848 swapfree: 4024232
swaptotal: 4063228 hugepagetotal: 1000 hugepagefree: 22 hugepagesize: 2048
ior: 939 iow: 137 ios: 98 swpin: 0 swpout: 0 pgin: 894 pgout: 94 netr:
46.047 netw: 36.686 procs: 321 procsoncpu: 1 rtprocs: 13 rtprocsoncpu: N/A
#fds: 22624 #sysfdlimit: 6815744 #disks: 7 #nics: 5 nicErrors: 0

TOP CONSUMERS:
topcpu: 'asm_vktm_+asm1(4571) 2.59' topprivmem: 'java(4935) 156148' topshm:
'ocssd.bin(4275) 88904' topfd: 'oraagent.bin(4752) 258' topthread: 'console-
kit-dae(3496) 64'
```

By default, the output will continue every five seconds until the user presses Control-C on Unix/Linux or Escape on Windows. The output above shows the timestamp the metrics were taken and various OS metrics including memory usage and CPU usage. Each section ends with the top consuming processes.

This section has discussed the Cluster Health Monitor, how it works, and provided an understanding of the metrics CHM collects. Beginning with Oracle 11.2.0.2, CHM is an integrated component of the Grid Infrastructure stack.

The next section will show how to leverage the metrics CHM collects to help the database administrator examine performance in their Oracle RAC database system.

CHMOSG

The real fun comes when you use the CHM OS Graphical interface, *chmosg*. For some reason, the Java-based GUI tool is not included with CHM. It can be downloaded from the Technet URL provided earlier in this chapter. The *chmosg* utility will need to be installed a machine that has Grid Infrastructure software. It is possible to run the utility remotely from the cluster being monitored, but most database administrators will run the utility on one of the cluster nodes directly. After downloading the utility from Technet, unzip the download file. In the newly created *install* subdirectory, run the *chmosg* installation utility.

```
[oracle@host01 install]$ export CRFPERLBIN=/usr/bin
[oracle@host01 install]$ ./chminstall -i /home/oracle/oracrf
ORACLE_HOME found. Using Java at /u01/app/crs12.1.0.2/jdk

Installation completed sucessfully at /home/oracle/oracrf...
```

With the *chmosg* utility installed, launching it is as simple as running the command line utility. For non-Windows platforms, the Java-based utility will need to be able to run X Windows programs.

```
[oracle@host01 bin]$ ./chmosg
Cluster Health Monitor V2.05

    Connect to Loggerd via node host01.localdomain
    ...waited 0.222s for a reply
  Node host01 up at 2014-09-06 00:28:47.791
    ...Connected to Loggerd on host01
```

On startup, a window with performance graphs will overlay a window with CHM information. Move the graph window to the side to reveal a window similar to the following.

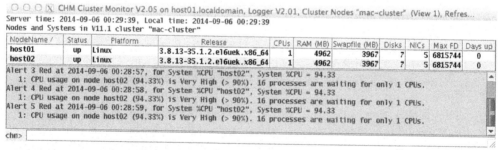

Figure 8.1 CHM Informational Panel

Oracle RAC Performance Tuning

The informational panel lists all the nodes in the cluster, their status, OS platform and version, number of CPUs, physical memory, swap size, and number of network interfaces. Any alerts due to high CPU, high swapping are displayed in the lower pane. Double click on a host in the informational panel to drill down in host-specific details, seen in the next figure.

CHM Cluster Monitor V2.05 on host01.localdomain, Logger V2.01, Node "host02" (View 3), Refresh rate: 1 sec

Server time: 2014-09-06 01:03:51, Local time: 2014-09-06 01:03:51
Total RAM: 5081236, Total SWAP: 4063228, CPUs: 1, Disks: 7, NICs: 5, SYSFDLIMIT: 6815744

Node	CPU	CPUQ	RAMFREE(KB)	MEMCACHE(KB)	SWAPFREE(KB)	IOR(KB/s)	IOW(KB/s)	IO/s	NETR(KB/s)	NETW(KB/s)	Procs	RTProcs	Files
host02	10.2	0	218976	1439812	4063228	55	78	19	17.04	30.63	265	10	19648

Top Consumers

Top user of	Process	PID	%CPU	Priv-MEM(KB)	Sh-MEM(KB)	Files	Threads	Priority	Nice	State

Process View

Process	PID	%CPU	Priv-MEM(KB)	Sh-MEM(KB)	Files	Threads	Priority	Nice	State
ora_vktm_orcl2	4884	3.8	2192	16892	12	1	-2	0	R
asm_vktm_+asm2	4532	3.4	2228	15984	12	1	-2	0	R
gipcd.bin	3900	1.8	23180	16252	157	8	20	0	R
ocssd.bin	4104	1.0	81876	88904	195	26	-100	0	S
ohasd.bin	3485	1.0	32724	30716	209	30	20	0	S
crsd.bin	4609	0.8	33088	30648	213	40	20	0	S
osysmond.bin	4592	0.6	31384	79920	116	12	-100	0	S
orarootagent.bi	3908	0.6	25520	23524	151	21	20	0	S
evmd.bin	3866	0.6	15700	17044	155	9	20	0	S
octssd.bin	4368	0.6	18140	15516	95	10	20	0	S
cssdmonitor	4076	0.4	34564	79920	62	17	-100	0	S
cssdagent	4092	0.4	35632	79924	62	17	-100	0	S
oraagent.bin	4676	0.4	31004	24108	205	27	20	0	S
oraagent.bin	3850	0.4	17964	22208	138	19	20	0	S
ora_lmon_orcl2	4906	0.4	16332	22536	15	1	20	0	S

Network Device View

DEVICE /	Read(KB/s)	Write(KB/s)	EffectiveBW(Kb/s)	ERR	Type	Latency(ms)
eth0	0.00	0.00	0.00	0	PUBLIC	-NA-
eth1	11.61	26.06	37.67	0	PRIVATE	-NA-
eth2	0.00	0.00	0.00	0	PUBLIC	-NA-
eth3	5.13	4.27	9.39	0	PRIVATE	-NA-
lo	0.30	0.30	0.60	0	PUBLIC	-NA-

Protocol Errors View

IPHdrErr	IPAddrErr	IPUnkProt	IPReasF	IPFragErr	TCPFailedConn	TCPEstRst	TCPRetraSeg	UDPUnkPort	UDPRcvErr
0	0	0	0	0	13	78	8	16	0

Disk Device View

DEVICE /	READ(KB/s)	WRITE(KB/s)	IO/s	QLEN	WAIT(ms)	TYPE
dm-0	0.0	32.8	7	0	0	SYS
dm-1	0.0	0.0	0	0	0	SWAP
sda	0.0	32.8	3	0	1	SYS
sdb	1.0	0.5	2	0	0	ASM,OCR,VOTING[ONLINE]
sdc	54.3	12.8	4	0	0	ASM
sdd	0.0	0.0	0	0	0	ASM
sde	0.0	0.0	0	0	0	SYS

chm>

Figure 8.2 CHM Host Drill Down

The host drill down screen shows a list of processes running on the node. The processes can be sorted by CPU usage, the default, memory used and more. Double clicking on network or disk devices lets the database administrator drill down even further into that device.

The window with multiple graphs shows various performance areas on all nodes in the cluster. An example is shown below.

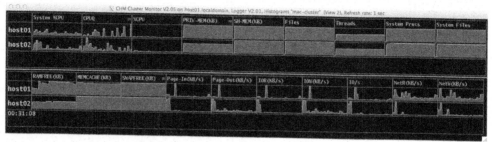

Figure 8.3 CHM Performance Graph

The performance graph shows all of the performance areas at a glance. One of the nice things about this utility is that it shows the performance areas for each node, which can be beneficial when trying to diagnose a performance problem. For instance, if slow performance is reported it can be easy for the database administrator to identify that host02 is experiencing a high degree of paging while the other node is not paging. This can help narrow down the root cause of the RAC problem. The figure above may be difficult to see in the book. The following figure is the subsection of the utility that pertains to CPU utilization

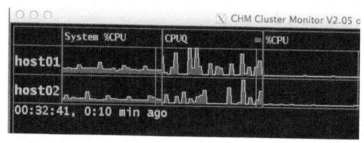

Figure 8.4 CHM CPU Utilization

Similarly, the next figure shows I/O utilization.

IOR(KB/s)	IOW(KB/s)	IO/s

Figure 8.5 CHM I/O Utilization

The I/O section shows I/O Read (IOR) and I/O Write (IOW) rates in kilobytes per second along with total I/O operations per second.

This real time performance graphs showing all nodes in the cluster can be beneficial if the database administrator is looking at the performance problem while it is happening. Unfortunately, many database administrators get the call to look at the problem after it has occurred. The *chmosg* utility can look back in the past with the –d parameter, specifying how far back to go. The –d argument takes values in the form "hh:mm:ss". For example, to go back 90 minutes ago, launch the utility similar to below.

```
[oracle@host01 bin]$ ./chmosg -d 01:30:00

Cluster Health Monitor V2.05
    ...reading 5400 sec from the past
```

The utility can go as far back as data is retained in the repository, which was discussed earlier in this section. While standard OS utilities can report much of the same information, few of them let the database administrator look at historical performance.

The Cluster Health Monitor is a highly recommended utility to have up and running on an Oracle RAC cluster. The tool is important enough that beginning with Grid Infrastructure 11.2.0.2, Oracle started including it automatically. The CHM will continually gather OS-related performs metrics which can help diagnose performance problems. The optional GUI tool, downloadable from Oracle's Technet, helps the database administrator see OS performance across all nodes at a glance. The GUI tool has a user manual located at the following URL which contains many more options than were discussed in this book.

http://www.oracle.com/technetwork/database/database-technologies/clusterware/downloads/chmosg-userman-1554904.pdf

OSWatcher

The OSWatcher utility captures performance metrics of the database host, very similar to the Cluster Health Monitor. While both tools are similar, they have their differences. The list below highlights some of the variances between the two.

- OSWatcher may not be able to collect metrics when the system is under a very heavy CPU load while CHM will still be able to gather the data.
- CHM gathers data every second or every 5 seconds depending on the version. By default, OSWatcher gathers data every minute. CHM provides more detail but OSWatcher requires less storage space.
- OSWatcher has an analyzer that can create performance graphs covering a much longer timeframe than CHM's GUI tool.
- CHM lets the database administrator see performance metrics for all nodes in the cluster while OSWatcher analyzes one node at a time.
- CHM runs on Windows but OSWatcher does not. For Windows platforms, use CHM only.
- OSWatcher contains data from *top*, *netstat*, and *traceroute* that is missing from CHM.
- Since CHM is a managed cluster resource, it starts automatically when Grid Infrastructure is started. OSWatcher needs to be manually started although one can certainly create a script to be used on server startup.

The CHM utility is preferred if one must be chosen over the other, primarily due to the first bullet point above. That being said, Oracle does recommend running both tools, if possible, to take advantage of their individual strengths.

The OSWatcher does not gather OS performance metrics on its own. Instead, it relies on the Unix or Linux utilities *top*, *ps*, *mpstat*, *ifconfig*, *vmstat*, *netstat*, *iostat*, and *traceroute*. On Linux, the utilities *meminfo* and *slabinfo* will also be used. When OSWatcher starts, it spawns data collector processes. One data collector process will run the *vmstat* utility, gather the output, store the results in a file, and then go to sleep until collection is needed again. Similar data collector processes work for the other OS utilities.

Unlike CHM, OSWatch is not integrated with any Oracle software, and you must download the utility and install it. The download link can be found in My Oracle Support Note 301137.1 for those that have a paid My Oracle Support Community (MOSC) contract. The download consists of a single tar file. OSWatcher was originally called OSWatcher Black Box. As such, references to the acronym *oswbb* will be found when working with this tool. Even the download file's name is of the form oswbb*xxx*.tar where *xxx* is a version number. Extracting the file's contents produces a directory named oswbb containing the OSWatcher utility.

```
[oracle@host01 ~]$ tar xvf oswbb730.tar
```

One of the benefits of OSWatcher is that it will also examine the Cluster Interconnect for the Oracle RAC Cluster. Looking at the private network is not set up by default. Before OSWatcher is started for the first time, the database administrator needs to create a file named private.net in the OSWatcher directory with the platform appropriate *traceroute* command. OSWatcher includes a file named *exampleprivate.net* that shows sample commands for each supported platform. The following shows the *private.net* file for a 2-node Linux cluster. This file exists on host01 and the *traceroute* command is to host02. The last line below changes the file's permissions to allow the file to be executable.

```
[oracle@host01 oswbb]$ cat private.net
echo "zzz ***"`date`
traceroute -r -F host02-priv
[oracle@host01 oswbb]$ chmod 755 private.net
```

If there were three nodes in the cluster, the file on host01 would contain a second *traceroute* command to host03-priv. Similarly, OSWatcher configuration on the other nodes in the cluster would contain traceroute commands to the other nodes in the cluster.

With OSWatcher configured for Oracle RAC, it is time to start the utility so that data can be collected. The *startOSWbb.sh* script is used to start data collection.

```
[oracle@host01 oswbb]$ ./startOSWbb.sh

Info...You did not enter a value for snapshotInterval.
Info...Using default value = 30
Info...You did not enter a value for archiveInterval.
Info...Using default value = 48
Setting the archive log directory to/home/oracle/oswbb/archive

Testing for discovery of OS Utilities...
VMSTAT found on your system.
IOSTAT found on your system.
MPSTAT found on your system.
IFCONFIG found on your system.
NETSTAT found on your system.
TOP found on your system.
Warning... /proc/slabinfo not found on your system.

Testing for discovery of OS CPU COUNT
oswbb is looking for the CPU COUNT on your system
CPU COUNT will be used by oswbba to automatically look for cpu problems

CPU COUNT found on your system.
CPU COUNT = 1

Discovery completed.

Starting OSWatcher Black Box v7.3.0  on Sat Sep 6 03:58:51 CDT 2014
With SnapshotInterval = 30
```

```
With ArchiveInterval = 48

OSWatcher Black Box - Written by Carl Davis, Center of Expertise,
Oracle Corporation
For questions on install/usage please go to MOS (Note:301137.1)
If you need further assistance or have comments or enhancement
requests you can email me Carl.Davis@Oracle.com

Data is stored in directory: /home/oracle/oswbb/archive

Starting Data Collection...

oswbb heartbeat:Sat Sep 6 03:58:56 CDT 2014
```

In the example above, OSWatcher was started with default values. Metrics will be obtained every 30 seconds and OSWatcher will retain 48 hours of data. When starting OSWatcher as done above, the utility maintains control of the session. Should the session terminate, so will data collection. Also, the screen will be filled with heartbeat information.

```
oswbb heartbeat:Sat Sep 6 03:59:56 CDT 2014
oswbb heartbeat:Sat Sep 6 04:00:26 CDT 2014
oswbb heartbeat:Sat Sep 6 04:00:56 CDT 2014
```

To remedy this situation, OSWatcher can be stopped. In another session, the stop script is executed as follows.

```
[oracle@host01 oswbb]$ ./stopOSWbb.sh
```

Next, OSWatcher will be started in the background:

```
[oracle@host01 oswbb]$ nohup ./startOSWbb.sh &
```

When OSWatcher is started for the first time, the archive directory is created. By default, this directory is a subdirectory of the main *oswbb* directory. The output below shows the contents of the archive directory.

```
[oracle@host01 oswbb]$ cd /home/oracle/oswbb/archive

[oracle@host01 archive]$ ls -l

total 40
drwxr-xr-x 2 oracle oinstall 4096 Sep  6 04:00 oswifconfig
drwxr-xr-x 2 oracle oinstall 4096 Sep  6 04:00 oswiostat
drwxr-xr-x 2 oracle oinstall 4096 Sep  6 04:00 oswmeminfo
drwxr-xr-x 2 oracle oinstall 4096 Sep  6 04:00 oswmpstat
drwxr-xr-x 2 oracle oinstall 4096 Sep  6 04:00 oswnetstat
drwxr-xr-x 2 oracle oinstall 4096 Sep  6 03:58 oswprvtnet
```

```
drwxr-xr-x 2 oracle oinstall 4096 Sep  6 04:00 oswps
drwxr-xr-x 2 oracle oinstall 4096 Sep  6 03:58 oswslabinfo
drwxr-xr-x 2 oracle oinstall 4096 Sep  6 04:00 oswtop
drwxr-xr-x 2 oracle oinstall 4096 Sep  6 04:00 oswvmstat
```

The archive directory contains one subdirectory for each process being captured. It should be easy to tell what each subdirectory contains simply by inspecting the directory name. Looking inside one of the directories, we can see the files that contain the metric data.

```
[oracle@host01 archive]$ cd oswtop

[oracle@host01 oswtop]$ ls -l

total 108
-rw-r--r-- 1 oracle oinstall 14307 Sep  6 03:59
host01.localdomain_top_14.09.06.0300.dat
-rw-r--r-- 1 oracle oinstall 86398 Sep  6 04:32
host01.localdomain_top_14.09.06.0400.dat
```

OSWatcher will create a new data file each hour. Each file contains a line with the string "zzz ***" followed by a timestamp. The lines that follow the timestamp are the output of the OS command. As an example, the following output shows the contents of the private network *traceroute* commands.

```
[oracle@host01 oswprvtnet]$ cat host01.localdomain_prvtnet_14.09.06.0300.dat

zzz ***Sat Sep 6 03:58:56 CDT 2014
traceroute to host02-priv (192.168.10.2), 30 hops max, 60 byte packets
 1  host02-priv.localdomain (192.168.10.2)  0.292 ms  0.166 ms  0.268 ms

[oracle@host01 oswprvtnet]$ cat host01.localdomain_prvtnet_14.09.06.0400.dat

zzz ***Sat Sep 6 04:27:41 CDT 2014
traceroute to host02-priv (192.168.10.2), 30 hops max, 60 byte packets
 1  host02-priv.localdomain (192.168.10.2)  0.363 ms  0.182 ms  0.108 ms
```

OSWatcher includes a File Manager process that will run once per hour to clean up any data files older than the retention period. The collection interval and retention period can be changed with the first two parameters, respectively, to the shell script that starts OSWatcher. The following starts OSWatcher to collect metrics every 120 seconds and store the data for 72 hours.

```
[oracle@host01 oswbb]$ ./OSWatcher 120 72
```

This section has provided the information for the database administrator to get the OSWatcher utility up and running. While very similar to the Cluster Health Monitor, the OSWatcher has enough differences to warrant using both tools. Just as CHM has a utility to help analyze the data, OSWatcher has its utility that is discussed in the next section.

OSWatcher Analyzer

It can be a daunting task to wade through the collected metric values in the data files to determine where a performance problem exists. Oracle created the OSWatcher Analyzer (*oswbba*) tool to parse the data and produce charts to help tell the RAC performance story. The Analyzer is a Java utility and on Unix or Linux needs an X Windows environment to execute. The java executable needs to be in the environment PATH.

```
[oracle@host01 bin]$ export PATH=$ORACLE_HOME/jdk/bin:$PATH
```

The *oswbba* is started as a Java program. The –i parameter is required to point to the OSWatcher archive directory.

```
[oracle@host01 oswbb]$ java -jar oswbba.jar -i /home/oracle/oswbb/archive

Starting OSW Analyzer V7.3.0
OSWatcher Analyzer Written by Oracle Center of Expertise
Copyright (c)  2014 by Oracle Corporation

Parsing Data. Please Wait...

Scanning file headers for version and platform info...


Parsing file host01.localdomain_iostat_14.09.06.0300.dat ...
Parsing file host01.localdomain_iostat_14.09.06.0400.dat ...
Parsing file host01.localdomain_iostat_14.09.06.0500.dat ...

Parsing file host01.localdomain_ps_14.09.06.0300.dat ...
Parsing file host01.localdomain_ps_14.09.06.0400.dat ...
Parsing file host01.localdomain_ps_14.09.06.0500.dat ...


Parsing Completed.


Enter 1 to Display CPU Process Queue Graphs
Enter 2 to Display CPU Utilization Graphs
Enter 3 to Display CPU Other Graphs
Enter 4 to Display Memory Graphs
Enter 5 to Display Disk IO Graphs

Enter 6 to Generate All CPU Gif Files
Enter 7 to Generate All Memory Gif Files
Enter 8 to Generate All Disk Gif Files
```

```
Enter L to Specify Alternate Location of Gif Directory
Enter T to Alter Graph Time Scale Only (Does not change analysis dataset)
Enter D to Return to Default Graph Time Scale
Enter R to Remove Currently Displayed Graphs

Enter A to Analyze Data
Enter S to Analyze Subset of Data(Changes analysis dataset including graph
time scale)

Enter P to Generate A Profile
Enter X to Export Parsed Data to File
Enter Q to Quit Program

Please Select an Option:
```

After starting the Analyzer, various data files will be parsed and processed. The longer the retention period, the longer the parsing phase will take to complete. Additionally, the more data files to be parsed, the more memory is required in the user's session. If a *java.lang.OutOfMemory* error is raised, start the Analyzer with a larger java heap size with the *–jar* parameter.

```
[oracle@host01 oswbb]$ java -jar –Xmx512M oswbba.jar -i
/home/oracle/oswbb/archive
```

After the data files are parsed, the user can select an option from the menu. If option 2 is selected to see CPU Utilization, the Analyzer utility will display a graph similar to the following.

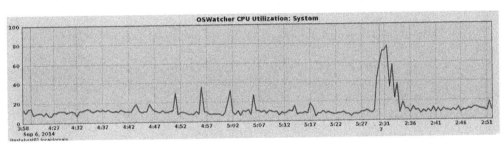

Figure 8.6 OSWatcher Analyzer CPU Chart

If the user were to choose option 5 to display the disk I/O utilization, the Analyzer utility will ask for the disk device.

```
The Following Devices and Average Service Times Are Ready to Display:

Device Name  Average Service Times in Milliseconds

sdd    0.73
sdb    0.67
sdc    0.36
sda    0.12
```

```
dm-0   0.06
dm-1   0.0

Specify A Case Sensitive Device Name to View (Q to exit):
```

After the user enters an appropriate device, the Analyzer generates a chart.

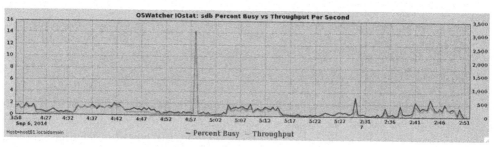

Figure 8.7 OSWatcher Analyzer Disk I/O Chart

The Analyzer will keep all charts open until the user presses R on the option menu to remove the charts or Q to quit the utility.

One way to reduce the initial parsing time is to start the Analyzer with a shorter time frame other than parse all available files. The database administrator can specify begin and end times for analysis with the –b and –e parameters respectively.

```
[oracle@host01 oswbb]$ java oswbba.jar -i /home/oracle/oswbb/archive -b Sep
06 05:00:00 2014 -e Sep 06 10:00:00 2014 -s
```

The example above restricts the analysis time from 5 a.m. to 10 a.m. on September 6, 2014. If the database administrator had already started the Analyzer session, menu option S lets the analysis timeframe be modified to a subset of the entire data retention period, similar to the following.

```
Please Select an Option:S

Specify Analysis Start Time. Valid entry between Sep 06 03:58:56 2014 and
Sep 07 19:30:09 2014
Example Format To Enter Time: Sep 06 03:58:56 2014   :Sep 06 05:00:00 2014

Specify Analysis End Time. Valid entry between Sep 06 03:58:56 2014 and Sep
07 19:30:09 2014
Example Format To Enter Time: Sep 07 19:30:09 2014   :Sep 06 10:00:00 2014

Dates accepted. Verifying valid begin/end data points...
```

The previous section discussed how to set up the OSWatcher to collect OS performance metrics from the system. This utility can complement but should not replace the Cluster Health Monitor. Included with the OSWatcher is the OSWatcher Analyzer utility that can help the database administrator wade through all of the data points to help diagnose performance problems.

RACDIAG

For those that have a valid My Oracle Support Community (MOSC) contract, Oracle supplies a nifty script called *racdiag.sql* that gathers Oracle RAC diagnostic information just by running a simple script in SQL*Plus. The script can be found by accessing Note 135714.1 from MOSC. In that note, there is a main section titled SCRIPT. We simply cut and paste the script from this note to a text editor and save the script as racdiag.sql in the database administrator's code library. This book does not have the rights to reproduce Oracle Corporation's intellectual property so the script will not be included in the book's code library.

When running the racdiag.sql script, run the script with a *sysdba* connection. The script provides performance-related information for the moment in time it is executed. However, the script does not collection performance metrics over a period of time like CHM and OSWatcher. The *racdiag.sql* script is very good at giving the database administrator a glimpse of what is happening right now. Running the script will produce an output file in the current directory with the filename of the form racdiag_*dbname_MonDD_hhmm*.out, portions of which can be seen below. The output can be very lengthy and contains information like the current wait event of every session and the current initialization parameter settings. While these may be important to the database administrator in diagnosing a performance problem, this book will trim back output to more interesting sections. The start of the output indicates the time the script was run and the instances for the Oracle RAC database.

```
TIME
--------------------
SEP-08-2014 13:43:28

1 row selected.


INST_ID INSTANCE_NAME HOST_NAME VERSION      STATUS   STARTUP_TIME
------- ------------- --------- ----------   -------  --------------------
      1 orcl1         host01    11.2.0.4.0   OPEN     SEP-04-2014 22:10:57
      2 orcl2         host02    11.2.0.4.0   OPEN     SEP-04-2014 22:10:56
      3 orcl3         host03    11.2.0.4.0   OPEN     SEP-04-2014 22:10:56

3 rows selected.
```

RAC Wait Chains

The next section shows Wait Chain information. A *wait chain* is a progression of sessions in the instances showing one session holding up another. The database administrator is most likely already familiar with transaction locks holding up sessions as can be seen in the *gv$lock* view. Locks will still be seen in wait chains, as enqueues waits are the most common blocking wait events. Other wait events may block sessions as well. The *v$wait_chain* view gives the database administrator information on which sessions are blocking others. The *racdiag.sql* output for wait chains may be similar to the following.

```
SQL> -- WAIT CHAINS
SQL> -- 11.x+ Only (This will not work in < v11
SQL> -- See Note 1428210.1 for instructions on interpreting.

Current Process: 24923                    SID                    INST #: 2
Blocking Process: <none> from Instance    Number of waiters: 1
Wait Event:
Seconds in Wait:                          Seconds Since Last Wait: 0
Wait Chain: 1: 'PX Deq Credit: send blkd'
Blocking Wait Chain: <none>

Current Process: 29285                     SID                    INST #: 1
Blocking Process: 24923 from Instance 2    Number of waiters: 0
Wait Event: 'enq: TX - contention'
Seconds in Wait: 33                        Seconds Since Last Wait: 0


2 rows selected.
```

From the wait chain above, we can see that session 24923 in instance 2 is holding up session 29285 in instance 1. The next section of the *racdiag.sql* output shows the sessions that are experiencing the longest wait events. The output from this session can be beneficial when trying to see who is waiting the longest time.

```
SQL> -- WAITING SESSIONS:
SQL> -- The entries that are shown at the top are the sessions that have
SQL> -- waited the longest amount of time that are waiting for non-idle wait
SQL> -- events (event column). You can research and find out what the wait
SQL> -- event indicates (along with its parameters) by checking the Oracle
SQL> -- Server Reference Manual

INST_ID SID  STATE   EVENT                          SECONDS
------- ---- ------- -------------------------- ----------
      1  655 WAITING Space Manager: slave idle       1274
      1 1253 WAITING PX Deq Credit: send blkd         571
      2  191 WAITING PX Deq Credit: send blkd         563
      3 1308 WAITING PX Deq: Table Q Normal          387
      2 1782 WAITING PX Deq Credit: send blkd         386
      1 1821 WAITING PX Deq: Table Q Normal          298
      3  761 WAITED  db file sequential read          178
```

RAC GES Blocking

One section of the *racdiag.sql* output shows Global Enqueue Services blocking activity. GES blocking was discussed in Chapter 2 of this book. In a single-instance database, a transaction making a change can block another session making a change to the same data. In Oracle RAC, transactions can still block other sessions but on a global scale, managed by GES.

```
SQL> -- GES LOCK BLOCKERS:
SQL> -- This section will show us any sessions that are holding locks that
SQL> -- are blocking other users.

INST_ID SID  SPID RESOURCE_NAME1                 GRANT_LEVEL     REQUEST_LEVEL
------- ---- ---- ----------------------------- --------------- ---------------
      1  575 2803 [0x4][0x0],[RF][ext 0x0,0x0]  S/Row-X (SSX)   S/Row-X (SSX)
      1  575 2803 [0x13][0x0],[RF][ext 0x0,0x0] Exclusive       Exclusive
      2    5 2782 [0x19][0x2],[RS][ext 0x0,0x0] Exclusive       Exclusive

3 rows selected.
```

If the sessions above are blocking another session, then some session must be waiting for those global locks to be released. The next section shows the sessions waiting on GES locks to be released. In the example below, they are all requesting Exclusive access to GES resources.

```
SQL> -- GES LOCK WAITERS:
SQL> -- This section will show us any sessions that are waiting for locks
SQL> -- that are blocked by other users.

INST_ID  SID SPID  RESOURCE_NAME1                GRANT_LEVEL REQUEST_LEVEL
------- ----- ----- ----------------------------- ----------- -------------
      3   575 26295 [0x13][0x0],[RF][ext 0x0,0x0] Null        Exclusive
      3   575 26295 [0x4][0x0],[RF][ext 0x0,0x0]  Null        Exclusive
      2   575 12266 [0x4][0x0],[RF][ext 0x0,0x0]  Null        Exclusive
      2   575 12266 [0x13][0x0],[RF][ext 0x0,0x0] Null        Exclusive
      2     5 12237 [0x19][0x2],[RS][ext 0x0,0x0] Null        Exclusive
      1     5 26275 [0x19][0x2],[RS][ext 0x0,0x0] Null        Exclusive

6 rows selected.
```

RAC Global Cache Consistent Read

Another section of the racdiag.sql script shows Global Cache Consistent Read performance. If the average receive time is more than a few milliseconds, it can indicate contention on the Cluster Interconnect.

```
SQL> -- GLOBAL CACHE CR PERFORMANCE
SQL> -- This shows the average latency of a consistent block request.

INST_ID GCS CR BLOCKS RECEIVED GCS CR BLOCK RECEIVE TIME AVG RCV TIME (ms)
------- ----------------------- ------------------------- ----------------
      1                 5160513                    492333              1.0
      2                 5518535                    580288              1.1
      3                 6082566                    686247              1.1

3 rows selected.
```

The next section shows the Global Cache lock performance. This section of the output shows how long, on average, sessions are waiting for a GES lock. The average time should be under 10 milliseconds.

```
SQL> -- GLOBAL CACHE LOCK PERFORMANCE
SQL> -- This shows the average global enqueue get time.

INST_ID  GLOBAL LOCK GETS GLOBAL LOCK GET TIME AVG GLOBAL LOCK GET TIME (ms)
-------- ---------------- -------------------- ----------------------------
       1        137153354               598625                           .0
       2         98605639               537118                           .1
       3        112418770               509176                           .0

3 rows selected.
```

RAC top-10 wait events

The *racdiag.sql* script provides a section detailing the top ten wait events across all instances. It would not be surprising to see the same wait event in more than one instance.

```
SQL> -- TOP 10 WAIT EVENTS ON SYSTEM
SQL> -- This view will provide a summary of the top wait events in the db.

  INST_ID EVENT                  TIME_WAITED TOTAL_WAITS TOTAL_TIMEOUTS
--------- ---------------------- ----------- ----------- --------------
        3 EMON slave idle wait     157536115      315066         315014
        2 EMON slave idle wait     157529147      315026         315003
        1 EMON slave idle wait     157526692      315419         314991
        3 DIAG idle wait            62825931     7100349        6122021
        2 DIAG idle wait            62824940     7081687        6108390
        1 DIAG idle wait            62770912     8404212        5893222
        3 Space Manager: slave idle 56668027      118815         111668
```

```
         1 Space Manager: slave idle      55032446      119345      108261
         2 Space Manager: slave idle      52235421      135298      102708
         3 wait for unread message o      34089990      346436      277898

10 rows selected.
```

After the top ten wait events section, a process reference is provided. As the comments state, this section assists in providing further information on the sessions identified in previous sections of the output. The information was trimmed in the output below for brevity.

```
SQL> -- SESSION/PROCESS REFERENCE:
SQL> -- This section is very important for most of the above sections to
find out
SQL> -- which user/os_user/process is identified to which session/process.

INST_ID SID  SERIAL# PID SPID  PROGRAM          USERNAME OS_USER
------- ---- ------- --- ----- ---------------- -------- -------
      1  161     435 632  7812 oracle@host01 SCOTT      oracle
      2  162    2379 296 21115 oracle@host02 HR         oracle
```

The *racdiag.sql* script contains much more information. This section illustrated key sections related to Oracle RAC performance tuning. You are encouraged to download the script from My Oracle Support to gain an understanding of the full breadth of information that this script can provide to assist in troubleshooting Oracle RAC performance problems.

The biggest benefit the *racdiag.sql* script offers is to quickly and easily generate a snapshot in time of Oracle RAC performance. This is no different than using many similar scripts the database administrator may already have in their library. The biggest downside to this script is that it will not track performance issues over time. If the database administrator is looking for similar functionality over a period of time, the Procwatcher utility can be used, which is discussed in the next section of this chapter.

Procwatcher

Where the Cluster Health Monitor and OSWatcher examine performance metrics of OS resources, the Procwatcher utility takes a look at performance from the perspective of the individual processes. Procwatcher can start stack traces of the processes and generate log files showing the waits, locks and latches hampering the processes performance. Procwatcher can also be used to diagnose memory issues that cause ORA-4030 and ORA-4031 errors to be raised. Note that Procwatcher will not run on Windows platforms.

Procwatcher is very similar to the *racdiag.sql* script discussed in the previous section. The racdiag.sql script captures its data at one time and generates a report. Procwatcher generates its data over a period of time. It will start data collection upon startup and continue until shutdown.

Procwatcher can be downloaded from My Oracle Support Community Note 459694.1 for those that have a valid Oracle Support contract. The download is a simple zip file. When unzipped, the result is a singular shell script, *prw.sh*. The script may need to be given execute permissions with the *chmod* command. This section of the chapter will discuss how to use Procwatcher but the reader is encouraged to go through the My Oracle Support note for more information.

For Oracle RAC systems, the first task is to deploy Procwatcher as a cluster resource.

```
[oracle@host01 procwatcher]$ ./prw.sh deploy
Registering clusterware resource
SETTING UP NODE host01
SETTING UP NODE host02
Copying Procwatcher to Node host02
prw.sh
100%  183KB 182.9KB/s   00:00
CRS-2672: Attempting to start 'procwatcher' on 'host02'
CRS-2672: Attempting to start 'procwatcher' on 'host01'
CRS-2676: Start of 'procwatcher' on 'host02' succeeded
CRS-2676: Start of 'procwatcher' on 'host01' succeeded

PROCWATCHER DEPLOYED

Checking Procwatcher Status:

Tue Sep 9 03:24:32 CDT 2014: PROCWATCHER VERSION: 12.1.13.11.1
Tue Sep 9 03:24:32 CDT 2014: ### Parameters ###
Tue Sep 9 03:24:32 CDT 2014: EXAMINE_CLUSTER=false
Tue Sep 9 03:24:32 CDT 2014: EXAMINE_BG=true
Tue Sep 9 03:24:32 CDT 2014: PRWPERM=777
Tue Sep 9 03:24:32 CDT 2014: RETENTION=7
Tue Sep 9 03:24:32 CDT 2014: WARNINGEMAIL=
Tue Sep 9 03:24:32 CDT 2014: INTERVAL=60
Tue Sep 9 03:24:32 CDT 2014: THROTTLE=5
Tue Sep 9 03:24:32 CDT 2014: IDLECPU=3
Tue Sep 9 03:24:32 CDT 2014: SIDLIST=
Tue Sep 9 03:24:32 CDT 2014: ### Advanced Parameters (non-default) ###
Tue Sep 9 03:24:32 CDT 2014: ### End Parameters ###

Tue Sep 9 03:24:32 CDT 2014: Procwatcher is currently running on local node
host01
Tue Sep 9 03:24:32 CDT 2014: Procwatcher files are be written to:
/u01/app/crs12.1.0.2/log/procwatcher

Tue Sep 9 03:24:32 CDT 2014: There are 0 concurrent debug sessions
running...

Tue Sep 9 03:24:33 CDT 2014: PROCWATCHER CLUSTERWARE STATUS:
```

```
NAME=procwatcher
TYPE=application
TARGET=ONLINE              , ONLINE
STATE=ONLINE on host02, ONLINE on host01
```

Procwatcher is now running on all nodes in the cluster. The database administrator should start Procwatcher as the 'root' user if trying to diagnose Grid Infrastructure issues but most often, Procwatcher will be started as the 'oracle' user to diagnose database performance issues. It should be noted that Procwatcher should not be run continuously. Instead, the database administrator will want to start the utility, reproduce the performance problem, and then stop the utility.

With Procwatcher up and running, you can check the status of the utility similar to the following commands.

```
[oracle@host01 procwatcher]$ ./prw.sh status
Tue Sep 9 19:44:17 CDT 2014: PROCWATCHER VERSION: 12.1.13.11.1
Tue Sep 9 19:44:17 CDT 2014: ### Parameters ###
Tue Sep 9 19:44:17 CDT 2014: EXAMINE_CLUSTER=false
Tue Sep 9 19:44:17 CDT 2014: EXAMINE_BG=true
Tue Sep 9 19:44:17 CDT 2014: PRWPERM=777
Tue Sep 9 19:44:17 CDT 2014: RETENTION=7
Tue Sep 9 19:44:17 CDT 2014: WARNINGEMAIL=
Tue Sep 9 19:44:17 CDT 2014: INTERVAL=60
Tue Sep 9 19:44:17 CDT 2014: THROTTLE=5
Tue Sep 9 19:44:17 CDT 2014: IDLECPU=3
Tue Sep 9 19:44:17 CDT 2014: SIDLIST=
Tue Sep 9 19:44:17 CDT 2014: ### Advanced Parameters (non-default) ###
Tue Sep 9 19:44:17 CDT 2014: ### End Parameters ###

Tue Sep 9 19:44:17 CDT 2014: Procwatcher is currently running on local node
host01
Tue Sep 9 19:44:17 CDT 2014: Procwatcher files are be written to:
/u01/app/crs12.1.0.2/log/procwatcher

Tue Sep 9 19:44:17 CDT 2014: There are 1 concurrent debug sessions
running...
Tue Sep 9 19:44:17 CDT 2014: Debug sessions:
ksh /u01/app/crs12.1.0.2/log/procwatcher/prw.sh sqlstart
/u01/app/crs12.1.0.2/log/procwatcher/PRW_SYS_host01/SQLvinstance oracle
orcl1 /u01/app/oracle/product/12.1.0.2

Tue Sep 9 19:44:17 CDT 2014: PROCWATCHER CLUSTERWARE STATUS:

NAME=procwatcher
TYPE=application
TARGET=ONLINE              , ONLINE
STATE=ONLINE on host02, ONLINE on host01
```

The status output shows the parameters in use and if the utility is up and running on the nodes. The parameter values can be changed with by editing the *prw.sh* script directly, but not before making a backup of the file first. With the utility up and running, Procwatcher will begin to monitor the processes on the nodes and generate diagnostic output for later analysis.

Procwatcher will place log files in the $GRID_HOME/log/procwatcher directory on each node. A subdirectory named PRW_SYS_*instance_name* will be created to hold all files Procwatcher produces for that instance.

In the instance's log directory, Procwatcher will create a file named pw_waitchains_*instance_date*.out which contains wait chain information similar to the racdiag.sql script in the previous section. The following is a sample of wait chain information captured by Procwatcher.

```
###############################################################################
SQL> SQL> V WAITCHAINS (top 100 rows) Snapshot Taken At: Tue Sep 9 04:18:47
CDT 2014
PROC 24988 : Current Process: 24988 SID: 82 SER#: 61122 INST orcl1 INST #: 1
PROC 24988 : Blocking Process: <none> from Instance     Number of waiters: 1
PROC 24988 : Final Blocking Process: <none> from Instance      Program:
PROC 24988 : Wait Event: SQL*Net message from client
PROC 24988 : Seconds in Wait: 36   Seconds Since Last Wait:
PROC 24988 : Wait Chain: 1: 'SQL*Net message from client'<='enq: TX - row
lock contention'
PROC 24988 : Blocking Wait Chain: <none>
--------------------------------
PROC 24910 : Current Process: 24910 SID: 34 SER#: 62559 INST orcl1 INST #: 1
PROC 24910 : Blocking Process: 24988 from Instance 1    Number of waiters: 0
PROC 24910 : Final Blocking Process: 24988 from Instance 1    Program:
oracle@host01.localdomain (TNS V1-V3)
PROC 24910 : Wait Event: enq: TX - row lock contention
PROC 24910 : Seconds in Wait: 23   Seconds Since Last Wait:
PROC 24910 : Wait Chain: 1: 'SQL*Net message from client'<='enq: TX - row
lock contention'
PROC 24910 : Blocking Wait Chain: <none>
--------------------------------
Elapsed: 00:00:00.08

----------blkr----------
Tue Sep 9 04:18:59 CDT 2014: Suspected final blocker is:  Process: 24988
SID: 82 SER#: 61122 INST orcl1 INST #: 1
-------end blkr---------
orcl1 Waitchains SessionCount:2-Instance:1
```

From the output above, process 24988 on instance 1 is blocking process 24910. The wait events tell us that process 24910 is waiting on an enqueue to be released and process 24988 is waiting on the user to press a button in the application and send a command back to the database. The Procwatcher file to show locks, pw_lock_*instance_date*.out, confirms this same information.

```
###############################################################################
Procwatcher lock report
###############################################################################
```

```
SQL> SQL> V LOCK Snapshot Taken At: Tue Sep 9 04:18:52 CDT 2014
PROC         PROC        TY    ID1       ID2      LMODE     REQUEST      BLOCK
----------   ----------  --  --------  --------  --------  ----------  ----------
PROC 24988 INST orcl1 TX     65569      4897        6          0           1
PROC 24910 INST orcl1 TX     65569      4897        0          6           0
Elapsed: 00:00:01.22
```

Process 24988 is holding a lock (*lmode* > 0) and process 24910 is requesting the lock (*request* > 0).

One of the better log files produced by Procwatcher has a file name of the form pw_ora_fg_*instance_pid_date*.out in the log directory. The output from the files above has already shown that process is 24910 is waiting on a lock. That corresponding foreground output file contains the lock information and wait chains seen in the individual files. The foreground output file also contains Active Session History wait events to show the wait events over time. Many times it can be difficult to know what the session was doing so the foreground output file also contains the current SQL statement similar to the following.

```
##########################################################################
SQL: Current SQL Report for Process 24910 ora_fg_orcl1

SQL> SQL> Snapshot Taken At: Tue Sep 9 04:19:07 CDT 2014

PROC 24910 - update orders set status='SHIPPED' where order_id=770145;
```

For those interested in the subject, the Procwatcher will also dump a complete Oracle kernel stack trace of the processes so that one can follow along with the internal operations.

You should copy any relevant log files generated by Procwatcher to another directory for safekeeping. When you are ready to stop Procwatcher, it can be easily de-installed from the RAC cluster.

```
[oracle@host01 procwatcher]$ ./prw.sh deinstall
CRS-2673: Attempting to stop 'procwatcher' on 'host02'
CRS-2673: Attempting to stop 'procwatcher' on 'host01'
CRS-2677: Stop of 'procwatcher' on 'host02' succeeded
CRS-2677: Stop of 'procwatcher' on 'host01' succeeded
De-registering procwatcher resource
DECONFIGURING NODE host01
DECONFIGURING NODE host02
Removing /u01/app/crs12.1.0.2/log/procwatcher directory
Procwatcher Deinstalled
```

As the output from the deinstall command shows, the log directory is automatically removed so the log files may need to be copied to another directory for future use.

The Procwatcher utility is very similar to the previously seen *racdiag.sql* script. If you want a quick and easy way to get a snapshot of performance, simply run the racdiag.sql script. Conversely, if you want to gather more information over a longer period of time, use the Procwatcher utility.

Oratop

The reader is most likely familiar with *top* utility on Unix and Linux platforms, which lets administrators see, at a glance, performance of processes on the server. Oracle has a companion product called *oratop* which may be of interest to database administrators.

Oratop does not sample processes on the OS level. Instead, it queries dynamic performance views from an Oracle instance and formats the results that look very similar to the standard *top* utility. The results are a good snapshot of the instance performance. Oratop is even RAC-aware which makes this utility a valuable tool for Oracle RAC database administrators.

Oratop can be downloaded from My Oracle Support Community Note 1500864.1 (for those with a valid Oracle Support contract). Oratop is written using Oracle's OCI libraries so it will require access to Oracle Client software, at a minimum. The utility does not need to be directly installed on the database server. This tool is only available on Linux platforms for Oracle 11.2 and higher, but can connect to Oracle instances running on other platforms. The Oratop utility, when downloaded, will have the database version and platform in the file name. Oracle Support wants the database administrator to rename the file to just "oratop" but a better practice is to create a softlink to the file instead. The file's permissions will need to be changed to make it an executable file.

```
[oracle@host01 oratop]$ ls -l

total 132
-rw-r--r-- 1 oracle oinstall 134796 Sep  9 20:16 oratop.RDBMS_12.1_LINUX_X64

[oracle@host01 oratop]$ ln -s oratop.RDBMS_12.1_LINUX_X64 oratop

[oracle@host01 oratop]$ chmod 755 oratop.RDBMS_12.1_LINUX_X64

[oracle@host01 oratop]$ ls -l

total 132
lrwxrwxrwx 1 oracle oinstall     27 Sep  9 20:23 oratop ->
oratop.RDBMS_12.1_LINUX_X64
-rwxr-xr-x 1 oracle oinstall 134796 Sep  9 20:16 oratop.RDBMS_12.1_LINUX_X64
```

The LD_LIBRARY_PATH environment variable must be set before launching the utility.

```
[oracle@host01 oratop]$ export LD_LIBRARY_PATH=$ORACLE_HOME/lib

[oracle@host01 oratop]$ ./oratop

oratop: Release 14.1.2 Production on Tue Sep  9 20:32:17 2014
Copyright (c) 2011, Oracle.  All rights reserved.

Connecting ...


oratop: Release 14.1.2 Production on Tue Sep  9 20:32:17 2014

Copyright (c) 2011, Oracle.  All rights reserved.

Enter username: system
Enter password:
```

The utility prompts for a userid and password. The user can provide the standard "*username*/*password*@*tns_alias*" as used in SQL*Plus and other utilities to connect oratop to a remote database. The TNS alias must exist in the tnsnames.ora configuration file. While Oratop is only supported on Linux platforms, it can monitor databases on any Oracle certified platform through TNS.

After oratop starts, it will display four sections of information, a header, instance activity, top database wait events, and process information. A sample of oratop output can be seen below.

```
Oracle 11g - orcl 15:38:20 up: 4.7d, 3 ins, 1.8k sn, 289 us, 61G mt,89.5% db
ID %CPU LOAD %DCU AAS ASC ASI ASW AST IOPS %FR  PGA UTPS UCPS SSRT   %DBT
 3   88    4   75 4.2   6   1   9  16  640  11 278M    9  463   1m   39.1
 1   47    2   31 3.6   1   1  10  12 1.1k  25 1.0G   14  562 677u   33.1
 2   41    4   43 4.8   5   0   9  13 1.0k  10 384M    9  258 759u   21.5
EVENT (C)                    TOT WAITS     TIME(s)   AVG_MS  PCT   WAIT_CLASS
DB CPU                                      733365             58
db file sequential read       1.107E+08     431461      3.9   34     User I/O
PX Nsq: PQ load info query       243583      47051    193.1    4        Other
log file parallel write        23524944      29097      1.2    2   System I/O
log file sync                   8629296      25651      3.0    2       Commit
ID  SID  SPID USR PROG S  PGA SQLID/BLOCKER OPN  E/T STA STE EVENT/*LA  W/T
 5 1314 20827 KWA eCro D  79M                PL/ 1.0s ACT WAI TCP Socke 1.1s
 6   60 17675 DMU eCro D  16M g2sk10q4gazub SEL      0 ACT I/O db file s  21m
 5  740  3720 SFA eCro D   9M az6utv7k4bqv7 SEL 2.0s ACT I/O db file s   8m
 4 1259 22347 JPO eCro D 8.8M d5m77kcvxz0qa INS 2.0s ACT I/O db file s   3m
 6 1252 19362 EWP eCro D 1.2M 3g61fxagxtb08 INS    0 ACT I/O db file s 809u
 5 1885  1796 BAC WcfM D 8.8M 981ks0qjy7fam SEL    0 ACT CPU cpu runqu  23u
```

Each section will be shown individually to help understand the contents.

```
Oracle 11g - orcl 15:38:20 up: 4.7d, 3 ins, 1.8k sn, 289 us, 61G mt,89.5% db
```

The first line in the output is the header line. It shows the database version, the database name, the uptime, and the number of instances. Right away, the Oratop utility is showing that it has connected to a 3-instance Oracle RAC database. After the header section is the instance activity.

ID	%CPU	LOAD	%DCU	AAS	ASC	ASI	ASW	AST	IOPS	%FR	PGA	UTPS	UCPS	SSRT	%DBT
3	88	4	75	4.2	6	1	9	16	640	11	278M	9	463	1m	39.1
1	47	2	31	3.6	1	1	10	12	1.1k	25	1.0G	14	562	677u	33.1
2	41	4	43	4.8	5	0	9	13	1.0k	10	384M	9	258	759u	21.5

Each of the three instances is shown. The instance id is shown on each line. The output is sorted by CPU percentage. The disk IOPS are shown along with the PGA allocation. The last column is the percentage of database time. The next section shows the top wait events across the cluster.

EVENT (C)	TOT WAITS	TIME(s)	AVG_MS	PCT	WAIT_CLASS
DB CPU		733365		58	
db file sequential read	1.107E+08	431461	3.9	34	User I/O
PX Nsq: PQ load info query	243583	47051	193.1	4	Other
log file parallel write	23524944	29097	1.2	2	System I/O
log file sync	8629296	25651	3.0	2	Commit

For each event, the total number of waits is shown along with the total time spent waiting. The output is sorted by the percent of total waits. The last section shows process information.

ID	SID	SPID	USR	PROG	S	PGA	SQLID/BLOCKER	OPN	E/T	STA	STE	EVENT/*LA	W/T
5	1314	20827	KWA	epro	D	79M		PL/	1.0s	ACT	WAI	TCP Socke	1.1s
6	60	17675	DMU	epro	D	16M	g2sk10q4gazub	SEL	0	ACT	I/O	db file s	21m
5	740	3720	SFA	epro	D	9M	az6utv7k4bqv7	SEL	2.0s	ACT	I/O	db file s	8m
4	1259	22347	JPO	weba	D	8.8M	d5m77kcvxz0qa	INS	2.0s	ACT	I/O	db file s	3m
6	1252	19362	EWP	epro	D	1.2M	3g61fxagxtb08	INS	0	ACT	I/O	db file s	809u
5	1885	1796	BAC	weba	D	8.8M	981ks0qjy7fam	SEL	0	ACT	CPU	cpu runqu	23u

For each process, the information contains the process's instance, session identifier, and OS process identifier. The first three letters of the username and first four letters of the program name, similar to the same columns in the *gv$session* view. The session's current SQL identifier is displayed. The last two columns are the session's current wait event and wait time.

While Oratop is running, pressing the 'h' key will bring up a help menu showing interactive commands.

```
oratop: Release 14.1.2
```

```
Interactive Keys: [default]
    d : toggle between [Cumulative (C)] & Real-Time (RT) (section 3)
    k : toggle between [EVENT/LATCH] & object FILE#:BLOCK# (proc section 4)
    m : Toggle between [USERNAME/PROGRAM] & MODULE/ACTION (proc section 4)
    s : switch to SQL mode (section 4)
    f : toggle between [standard] & detailed format (long)
    p : switch to [process] mode (section 4)
    t : tablespace information
    x : basic SQL plan table (requires sql_id input)
    i : refresh interval, requires value in seconds [5s]
    q : quit/ exit program (also, { Q | Esc | function keys })

Abbreviations:
    [N/B]: count(N)/ Byte(B) - (k)illo, (M)ega, (G)iga, (T)erra, [PEZY]
    [T]  : Time - (u)micro, (m)illi, (s)econd, (h)our, (d)ay, (y)ear
    [m/s]: stats interval size, (m) 1 minute, (s) 15s, else, Real Time
    [c]  : database service centric

Acronym Help Menu:
    Section 1 - DATABASE         .. [1]
    Section 2 - INSTANCE         .. [2]
    Section 3 - DB WAIT EVENTS   .. [3]
    Section 4 - PROCESS          .. [4]
    Quit Help                    .. (q|Q)

Enter selection Number:
```

Pressing the 'a' key displays the database's ASM information.

```
ASM DISKGROUP INFORMATION:

INST_ID  DISKGROUP_NAME  SIZE  FREE  %USED  HOTU  COLD  STATE       TYPE
-------  --------------  ----  ----  -----  ----  ----  ----------  ------
      1  DATA             40G   17G   57.4     0   23G  CONNECTED   EXTERN
      1  REDO            4.0G  2.4G   40.3     0  1.6G  CONNECTED   EXTERN
      1  VOTE            8.0G  1.8G   77.3     0  6.2G  MOUNTED     EXTERN
```

Similarly, pressing the 't' key will display tablespace information.

```
TABLESPACE INFORMATION:

TABLESPACE_NAME                    SIZE  USED  USE%  STATUS      BIG  NDBF
--------------------------------   ----  ----  ----  ----------  ---  ----
SOE                                 32T  1.9G     0  ONLINE      YES     1
SYSAUX                              32G  571M   1.7  ONLINE      NO      1
SYSTEM                              32G  394M   1.2  ONLINE      NO      1
TEMP                                32G     0     0  ONLINE      NO      2
UNDOTBS1                            32G   62M   0.2  ONLINE      NO      1
UNDOTBS2                            32G  145M   0.4  ONLINE      NO      1
USERS                               32G   10G  32.7  ONLINE      NO      1
--------------------------------   ----  ----  ----
Total:                              32T   13G     0
```

Pressing the 's' key will toggle the fourth section between showing session information, the default, and showing SQL statements as shown below.

```
ID USER SQL_ID        SQL_TEXT                X  ELAP  EXEC  ROWS  BH%  LOAD
 2 JJOH 2h6b007j5wvz5 SELECT SYSDATE FROM D   S  16s   1     100   85   1
 3 JJOH ds983rp2f0avj SELECT OWNER,TABLE_NA   C  4.2s  1     100   99   1
 1 CROP fbu07qx84amwy SELECT /*+ INDEX (COM   P  12s   4.6k  0     100  17
 1 CROP arm3ta00x3upk SELECT ORDER_ID,STATU   S  114m  1.0k  128   89   1
 3 CROP 13tg1d7mphxtt SELECT CUST_ID,NAME F   S  149m  1.6k  108   95   1
```

When showing SQL statements, the elapsed runtime and number of executions is shown. Pressing the 'x' key lets the database administrator see the Explain Plan for a given SQL identifier.

```
Enter sql_id: du5ahv8qrkauw

PLAN_TABLE_OUTPUT
-----------------------------------------------------------------------------
SQL_ID: du5ahv8qrkauw, child number 0
-----------------------------------------------
SELECT * FROM APPL_LOG WHERE LOG_ID > :1  ORDER BY LOG_ID

Plan hash value: 3590588800
-----------------------------------------------------------------------------
| Id | Operation                    | Name       | Rows | Cost | Stale |
-----------------------------------------------------------------------------
|  0 | SELECT STATEMENT             |            |      |   4  |       |
|  1 |   TABLE ACCESS BY INDEX ROWID | APPL_LOG   |  1   |   4  | YES   |
|  2 |    INDEX RANGE SCAN          | APPL_LG_PK |  1   |   3  | YES   |
-----------------------------------------------------------------------------
```

Having the ability to see top SQL statements and easily generate an Explain Plan all in the same tool makes the Oratop utility very useful for database administrators trying to resolve performance issues in real time.

Many administrators working on Unix/Linux systems are familiar with the regular *top* utility. Oratop takes the same idea and extends it to Oracle database sessions. Oratop is already RAC-aware and can help database administrators see performance information across the cluster.

ORAchk

The ORAchk (Oracle Check) utility was previously known RACchk. In its older incarnation, RACchk examined the Oracle RAC system's configuration looking for areas that needed improvement. Oracle Corporation decided to extend the utility to include more than just an Oracle database and focus on the entire Oracle stack of software. ORAchk now examines the following areas.

- Oracle Database (both RAC and single-instance)
- Enterprise Manager 12c Cloud Control
- Oracle Sun servers
- Oracle E-Business Suite

No matter which Oracle software component is being examined, ORAchk is scanning the configuration looking for problems. It can provide a report showing health risks. It is recommended that the database administrator run a report before and after software configuration changes to understand if those changes can cause future problems. Since this book is for Oracle RAC database performance, only the first Oracle component in the list above will be discussed. The other 3 software components are out of scope for this book.

The ORAchk utility can be downloaded from Note 1268927.1 on My Oracle Support. The download is a simple zip file. After downloading the file, use the OS unzip utility to extract its contents. The installation is complete after unzipping the file. Run the *orachk* executable to start the analysis. The 'oracle' user should be used to run the utility. By default, *orachk* will ask to verify the current Grid Infrastructure home. Next, *orachk* verifies ssh user equivalency.

```
[oracle@host01 orachk]$ ./orachk

CRS stack is running and CRS_HOME is not set. Do you want to set CRS_HOME to
/u01/app/crs12.1.0.2?[y/n] [y]y

Checking ssh user equivalency settings on all nodes in cluster
```

If ssh user equivalency fails, *orachk* can fix the situation temporarily or permanently. If the permanent fix is chosen, this will be the only time *orachk* will make any changes to the system. The next step is to select the databases to check.

```
Searching for running databases . . . . .

. .
List of running databases registered in OCR
1. orcl
2. None of above

Select databases from list for checking best practices. For multiple
databases, select 1 for All or comma separated number like 1,2 etc [1-
2] [1] .1
```

This system only has one database. The output gives options to verify multiple databases if the system has them. Next, *orachk* verifies that various software components are up and running.

```
Checking Status of Oracle Software Stack - Clusterware, ASM, RDBMS
```

```
. . .   . . . .   . . . . .   . . . . . .   . . . . .
-------------------------------------------------------------------
                      Oracle Stack Status
-------------------------------------------------------------------
HostName CRS Install RDBMS Install  CRS UP ASM UP RDBMS UP DB Instance Name

host01   Yes         Yes            Yes    Yes    Yes      orcl1
host02   Yes         Yes            Yes    Yes    Yes      orcl2
-------------------------------------------------------------------


Copying plug-ins

. . .   . . . .   . . . . .   . . . . . .   . . . . .
```

The *orachk* utility will need to run some checks as the root user. The database administrator will either need to supply the root password, have the user executing the utility configured with sudo access, or skip the root portion of the checks.

```
16 of the included audit checks require root privileged data collection . If
sudo is not configured or the root password is not available, audit checks
which  require root privileged data collection can be skipped.


1. Enter 1 if you will enter root password for each  host when prompted

2. Enter 2 if you have sudo configured for oracle user to execute
root_orachk.sh script

3. Enter 3 to skip the root privileged collections

4. Enter 4 to exit and work with the SA to configure sudo  or to arrange for
root access and run the tool later.

Please indicate your selection from one of the above options for root
access[1-4][1]:- 1
```

After answering the root collection question, the *orachk* utility goes to work. Following some period of time, the analysis is complete and a report is generated. The *orachk* utility will also create a zip file that can be uploaded to My Oracle Support Community if requested by a support engineer.

```
Detailed report (html) -
/home/oracle/orachk/orachk_host01_orcl_091214_235107/orachk_host01_orcl_0912
14_235107.html


UPLOAD(if required) -
/home/oracle/orachk/orachk_host01_orcl_091214_235107.zip
```

The generated report is an html file, which can obviously be opened in any web browser. The first part of the report contains a general summary

System Health Score is 87 out of 100 <u>(detail)</u>

Cluster Summary

Cluster Name	mac-cluster
OS/Kernel Version	LINUX X86-64 OELRHEL 6 3.8.13–35.1.2.el6uek.x86_64
CRS Home – Version	/u01/app/crs12.1.0.2 – 12.1.0.2.0
DB Home – Version – Names	/u01/app/oracle/product/12.1.0.2 – 12.1.0.2.0 – orcl
Number of nodes	2
Database Servers	2
orachk Version	2.2.5_20140530
Collection	orachk_host01_orcl_091214_235107.zip
Duration	43 mins, 10 seconds
Collection Date	13-Sep-2014 01:47:59

Figure 8.8 ORAchk Summary

The overall system health score is seen at the top. Many of the findings contain a hyperlink named "detail" or "View" which will jump to the documentation location that explains the analysis in much more detail.

The most important part of the ORAchk report is the section titled Findings Needing Attention. This section groups the findings into categories named FAIL, WARNING, ERROR and INFO. Many of the findings are not performance related, but rather they focus their attention on keeping the cluster and its database operational and following best practices. Some findings are performance related as can be seen in the last two findings of the figure below.

Findings Needing Attention

FAIL, WARNING, ERROR and INFO finding details should be reviewed in the context of your environment.

NOTE: Any recommended change should be applied to and thoroughly tested (functionality and load) in one or more non-production environments before applying environment.

Database Server

Status	Type	Message	Status On	Details
FAIL	SQL Check	Table AUD$[FGA_LOG$] should use Automatic Segment Space Management for orcl	All Databases	View
FAIL	SQL Check	Some bigfile tablespaces do not have non-default maxbytes values set	All Databases	View
WARNING	ASM Check	ASM memory_target is not set to recommended value for Linux	All ASM Instances	View
WARNING	ASM Check	ASM SGA_TARGET is not set to recommended value	All ASM Instances	View
WARNING	ASM Check	Linux Disk I/O Scheduler should be configured to [Deadline]	All ASM Instances	View
WARNING	OS Check	vm.min_free_kbytes should be set as recommended.	All Database Servers	View
WARNING	OS Check	Package unixODBC-devel-2.2.14-11.el6-x86_64 is recommended but NOT installed	All Database Servers	View
WARNING	OS Check	loopback address is NOT configured as recommended in /etc/hosts	All Database Servers	View
WARNING	OS Check	Network interfaces for cluster_interconnect are NOT on separate subnets	All Database Servers	View
WARNING	OS Check	Package unixODBC-devel-2.2.14-11.el6-i686 is recommended but NOT installed	All Database Servers	View
WARNING	OS Check	Package unixODBC-2.2.14-11.el6-i686 is recommended but NOT installed	All Database Servers	View
WARNING	OS Check	NTP is not running with correct setting	All Database Servers	View
WARNING	OS Check	OSWatcher is not running as is recommended.	All Database Servers	View
WARNING	OS Check	NIC bonding is NOT configured for public network (VIP)	All Database Servers	View
WARNING	OS Check	NIC bonding is not configured for interconnect	All Database Servers	View

Figure 8.9 ORAchk Findings

The last two findings above tell us that NIC bonding is not configured for the public network or the Cluster Interconnect. Each finding has more detail that can be seen by clicking on the View hyperlink. The last finding in the figure about would bring the detail screen seen below.

Interconnect NIC bonding config.

Success Factor	CONFIGURE NIC BONDING FOR 10G VIP (LINUX)
Recommendation	To avoid single point of failure for interconnect, Oracle highly recommends to configure redundant network for interconnect using NIC BONDING. Follow below note for more information on how to configure bonding in linux. NOTE: If customer is on 11.2.0.2 or above and HAIP is in use with two or more interfaces then this finding can be ignored.
Links	• Note: 298891.1 – Configuring Linux for the Oracle 10g VIP or private interconnect using bonding driver
Needs attention on	host01, host02
Passed on	–

Status on host01:
WARNING => NIC bonding is not configured for interconnect

```
DATA FROM HOST01 - INTERCONNECT NIC BONDING CONFIG.


eth1  192.168.10.0  global  cluster_interconnect
eth3  192.168.10.0  global  cluster_interconnect
```

Status on host02:
WARNING => NIC bonding is not configured for interconnect

```
DATA FROM HOST02 - INTERCONNECT NIC BONDING CONFIG.


eth1  192.168.10.0  global  cluster_interconnect
eth3  192.168.10.0  global  cluster_interconnect
```

Figure 8.10 ORAchk NIC Bonding Finding Detail

Each detail for each finding should include a My Oracle Support Note for even more details. While the details of this finding focus on high availability, we know from the chapter on tuning the Cluster Interconnect that this specific finding is performance related as well. The Cluster Interconnect can increase its bandwidth by NIC Bonding or HAIP. The finding shown below is obviously more performance related and was discussed in Chapter 3 of this book.

AUDSES$ sequence cache size

Success Factor	CACHE APPLICATION SEQUENCES AND SOME SYSTEM SEQUENCES FOR BETTER PERFORMANCE
Recommendation	Use large cache value of maybe 10,000 or more. NOORDER most effective, but impact on strict ordering. Performance. Might not get strict time ordering of sequence numbers. There are problems reported with Audses$ and ora_tq_base$ which are both internal sequences . Also particularly if the order of the application sequence is not important or this is used during the login process and hence can be involved in a login storm then this needs to be taken care of. Some sequences need to be presented in a particular order and hence caching those is not a good idea but in the interest of performance if order does not matter then this could be cached and presented. This also manifests itself as waits in "rowcache" for "dc_sequences" which is a rowcache type for sequences. For Applications this can cause significant issues especially with Transactional Sequences. Please see note attached. Oracle General Ledger - Version: 11.5.0 to 11.5.10 Oracle Payables - Version: 11.5.0 to 11.5.10 Oracle Receivables - Version: 11.5.10.2 Information in this document applies to any platform. ARXTWAI,ARXRWMAI Increase IDGEN1$ to a value of 1000, see notes below. This is the default as of 11.2.0.1.
Links	• Note: 561414.1 - Transactional Sequences in Applications in a RAC environment • Note: 432508.1 - High SQ Enqueue Contention with LOBs or Advanced Replication
Needs attention on	orcl
Passed on	-

Status on orcl:
WARNING => SYS.AUDSES$ sequence cache size < 10,000

audses$.cache_size = 10000

Figure 8.11 ORAChk Sequence Finding Detail

It is a good practice to run ORAChk regularly. Optionally, the report can be emailed to the database administrator. The following command will set the autorun interval to seven days and define the email address for the report.

```
[oracle@host01 orachk]$ ./orachk -set
"AUTORUN_INTERVAL=7d;NOTIFICATION_EMAIL=dba@acme.com"

Created AUTORUN_INTERVAL for ID[orachk.default]


Created NOTIFICATION_EMAIL for ID[orachk.default]
```

With the parameters set, the ORAchk daemon needs to be started.

```
[oracle@host01 orachk]$ ./orachk -d start
```

ORAchk will now run regularly and automatically send the finds to the database administrator.

A great strength of ORAchk is the ability to compare two reports. This feature is most important when used to determine if a maintenance activity has implemented a change that could negatively impact the cluster and its database. The following example instructs ORAchk to compare the difference between two reports.

```
[oracle@host01 orachk]$ ./orachk -diff orachk_host01_orcl_091214_235107
orachk_host01_orcl_091314_043033
Summary
Total   : 182
Missing : 0
New     : 8
Changed : 0
Same    : 174
File comparison is complete. The comparison report can be viewed in:
/home/oracle/orachk/orachk_091214235107_091314043033_diff.html
```

The resulting html file can be used to see the differences. Ideally, the differences show the configuration trending in a positive direction where the number of bad findings is decreasing over time.

The ORAchk utility replaces the RACchk tool used by database administrators in the past. The new name reflects the tools ability to check many different software components in the Oracle stack, but still includes Grid Infrastructure and Oracle RAC. Regularly scheduled runs of ORAchk can help the database administrator see deficiencies in the Oracle RAC configuration and hopefully show improvement. ORAchk can be a great tool to ensure that maintenance activities that change the configuration do not make the system worse.

SQLT

Many readers are familiar with Oracle's Explain Plan functionality to show how the Oracle database engine plans on executing a given SQL statement. Oracle also provides a utility named SQLTXPLAIN, affectionately known as SQLT. SQLT was created to fill in many gaps missing from the traditional Explain Plan. In addition to showing how the SQL statement will be executed, SQLT provides object statistics, object metadata, optimizer-related initialization parameters, and just about every bit of information the database administrator would want to know when tuning a SQL statement for optimal performance. SQLT produces an html file with many hyperlinks to all of the sections in that report.

SQLT can be downloaded from Note 215187.1 on My Oracle Support for those that have a valid Oracle Support contract. The utility comes as a simple zip file. Before SQLT can be used, it must be installed in the database. Installation will create two schemas, *sqltxplain* and *sqltxadmin*. The utility was unzipped to the directory

---

/home/oracle/sqlt and the installation is started below. The installation should be performed as a *sysdba* user.

```
SQL> connect / as sysdba
SQL> @/home/oracle/sqlt/install/sqcreate.sql

PL/SQL procedure successfully completed.
```

The installation can be performed in the local database by entering nothing for the Connect Identifier, or in a remote database by specifying a TNS alias.

```
Specify optional Connect Identifier (as per Oracle Net)
Include "@" symbol, ie. @PROD
If not applicable, enter nothing and hit the "Enter" key.
You *MUST* provide a connect identifier when installing
SQLT in a Pluggable Database in 12c
This connect identifier is only used while exporting SQLT
repository everytime you execute one of the main methods.

Optional Connect Identifier (ie: @PROD):
```

The password for the schema owner is provided.

```
Define SQLTXPLAIN password (hidden and case sensitive).

Password for user SQLTXPLAIN:
Re-enter password:


PL/SQL procedure successfully completed.

... please wait
```

The schema owner needs a permanent and a temporary tablespace. Note that the tablespace name is case sensitive.

```
TABLESPACE                     FREE_SPACE_MB
------------------------------ -------------
USERS                                  22064
SOE                                 33552498


Specify PERMANENT tablespace to be used by SQLTXPLAIN.

Tablespace name is case sensitive.

Default tablespace [UNKNOWN]: USERS

PL/SQL procedure successfully completed.
```

```
... please wait

TABLESPACE
------------------------------
TEMP


Specify TEMPORARY tablespace to be used by SQLTXPLAIN.

Tablespace name is case sensitive.

Temporary tablespace [UNKNOWN]: TEMP

PL/SQL procedure successfully completed.
```

Initially, one user is given the appropriate role to run SQLT in the database. If desired, additional users can run SQLT by granting them the *sqlt_user_role* role.

```
The main application user of SQLT is the schema
owner that issued the SQL to be analyzed.
For example, on an EBS application you would
enter APPS.
You will not be asked to enter its password.
To add more SQLT users after this installation
is completed simply grant them the SQLT_USER_ROLE
role.

Main application user of SQLT: SCOTT

PL/SQL procedure successfully completed.
```

SQLT can use the optional Diagnostic and Tuning packs provided they are licensed. If none of these are licensed, answer N to keep in compliance with current license agreements. In the example below, both packs will be used.

```
SQLT can make extensive use of licensed features
provided by the Oracle Diagnostic and the Oracle
Tuning Packs, including SQL Tuning Advisor (STA),
SQL Monitoring and Automatic Workload Repository
(AWR).
To enable or disable access to these features
from the SQLT tool enter one of the following
values when asked:

"T" if you have license for Diagnostic and Tuning
"D" if you have license only for Oracle Diagnostic
"N" if you do not have these two licenses

Oracle Pack license [T]: T
```

Specifying the licensing is the final question asked by the installation script. The script will now create all of the database objects, which may take some time. The installation is complete when the following messages appear.

```
SQLT users must be granted SQLT_USER_ROLE before using this tool.

SQCREATE completed. Installation completed successfully.
```

If the SQL statement to be tuned is in the Shared Pool and the *sql_id* value is known, the *sqlxtract.sql* script can be used to generate the report. The password for the *sqltxplain* user must be provided. Since the password was not provided as a parameter to the script, the script will prompt for it.

```
SQL> @/home/oracle/sqlt/run/sqltxtract.sql b5sgm4db0pjhj

PL/SQL procedure successfully completed.

Parameter 1:
SQL_ID or HASH_VALUE of the SQL to be extracted (required)

Paremeter 2:
SQLTXPLAIN password (required)

Enter value for 2: password

PL/SQL procedure successfully completed.

PL/SQL procedure successfully completed.


SQLT_VERSION
-----------------------------------------
SQLT version number: 12.1.09
SQLT version date   : 2014-06-13
Installation date   : 2014-07-24/11:24:45

... please wait ...
  adding: alert_orcl.log (deflated 91%)

NOTE:
You used the XTRACT method connected as PEASLAND.

In case of a session disconnect please verify the following:
1. There are no errors in sqltxtract.log.
2. Your SQL b5sgm4db0pjhj exists in memory or in AWR.
3. You connected as the application user that issued original SQL.
4. User PEASLAND has been granted SQLT_USER_ROLE.

In case of errors ORA-03113, ORA-03114 or ORA-07445 please just
re-try this SQLT method. This tool handles some of the errors behind
a disconnect when executed a second time.

To actually diagnose the problem behind the disconnect, read ALERT
log and provide referenced traces to Support. After the root cause
of the disconnect is fixed then reset SQLT corresponding parameter.

To monitor progress, login into another session and execute:
SQL> SELECT * FROM SQLTXADMIN.sqlt$_log_v;

... collecting diagnostics details, please wait ...
```

```
In case of a disconnect review log file in current directory
If running as SYS in 12c make sure to review sqlt_instructions.html first
```

At this point, SQLT will begin its data collection and will create a large zip file. The work is complete when messages similar to the following are shown.

```
  adding: sqlt_s34043_sqldx.zip (stored 0%)


SQLTXTRACT completed.
```

The zip file will have the SQL id number in the file name along with the type of SQLT utility that was run, xtract in this case.

```
[oracle@host01 ~]$ ls -l sqlt*.zip
-rw-r--r-- 1 oracle oinstall 1681777 Sep 15 11:28
sqlt_s34043_xtract_b5sgm4db0pjhj.zip
```

When the zip file is expanded, there will be a number of files but the one that starts the SQLT report is titled *sqlt_id_main.html* where *id* is the identifier number of the SQLT run. In the example above, the id is "s34043" so the file that starts the report is sqlt_s34043_main.html. The file can be opened in any web browser. The top of the file is the main area and contains a table of contents for the entire report.

215187.1 SQLT XTRACT 12.1.09 Report: sqlt_s34043_main.html

Global

- Observations
- SQL Text
- SQL Identification
- Environment
- CBO Environment
- Fix Control
- CBO System Statistics
- DBMS_STATS Setup
- Initialization Parameters
- NLS Parameters
- I/O Calibration
- Tool Configuration Parameters

Cursor Sharing and Binds

- Cursor Sharing
- Adaptive Cursor Sharing
- Peeked Binds
- Captured Binds

SQL Tuning Advisor

- STA Report
- STA Script

Plans

- Summary
- Performance Statistics
- Performance History (delta)
- Performance History (total)
- Execution Plans

Plan Control

- Stored Outlines
- SQL Patches
- SQL Profiles
- SQL Plan Baselines
- SQL Plan Directives

SQL Execution

- Active Session History
- AWR Active Session History
- SQL Statistics
- SQL Detail ACTIVE Report
- Monitor Statistics
- Monitor ACTIVE Report
- Monitor HTML Report
- Monitor TEXT Report
- Segment Statistics
- Session Statistics
- Session Events
- Parallel Processing

Tables

- Tables
- Statistics
- Statistics Extensions
- Statistics Versions
- Modifications
- Properties
- Physical Properties
- Constraints
- Columns
- Indexed Columns
- Histograms
- Partitions
- Indexes

Objects

- Objects
- Dependencies
- Fixed Objects
- Fixed Object Columns
- Nested Tables
- Policies
- Audit Policies
- Tablespaces
- Metadata

Figure 8.12 SQLT Main Report

Each section of the report can be reached by clicking on one of the hyperlinks that point to the relevant location in the document. Some items will not have hyperlinks if SQLT has chosen not to generate that section of the report. For instance, this query does not use bind variables so the Peeked Binds and Captured Binds sections were not generated. Every section in the report has a link at the bottom of that section that brings the user back to the top, or back to the section shown in the figure above.

The section after the main table of contents is often the most illuminating as to the performance of the query. The Observations section provides analysis SQLT has offered as the knowledge expert looking at all of the data collected for this query. An example of the Observations section can be seen below.

Observations

List of concerns identified by the health-check module. Please review. Some may require further attention.

#	Type	Name	Observation	Details
1	CBO PARAMETER	NON-DEFAULT	There are 2 CBO initialization parameters with a non-default value.	[+]
2	CBO PARAMETER	OPTIMIZER_FEATURES_ENABLE	DB version 11.2.0.4.0 and OPTIMIZER_FEATURES_ENABLE 11.2.0.3 do not match.	[+]
3	CBO PARAMETER	DB_FILE_MULTIBLOCK_READ_COUNT	MBRC Parameter is set.	[+]
4	DBMS_STATS	DBA_AUTOTASK_CLIENT	Automatic gathering of CBO statistics is enabled.	[+]
5	DBMS_STATS	DBA_AUTOTASK_CLIENT_HISTORY	Automatic gathering of CBO statistics is enabled but no job was executed in the last 8 days	[+]
6	PLAN	PLAN_HASH_VALUE	One plan was found for this SQL.	[+]
7	PLAN CONTROL	PLAN_CONTROL	None of the plans found was created using one of these: Stored Outline, SQL Profile, SQL Patch or SQL Plan Baseline.	
8	DBMS_STATS	SYSTEM STATISTICS	Single-block read time of .824 milliseconds seems too small.	[+]
9	DBMS_STATS	SYSTEM STATISTICS	Multi-block read time of 1.949 milliseconds seems too small.	[+]
10	MAT_VIEW	REWRITE_ENABLED	There is/are 3 materialized view(s) with rewrite enabled.	[+]

Figure 8.13 SQLT Observations

The user can click on the plus symbol in the Details column to the right of each observation to obtain more information.

When tuning SQL statements, the database administrator always wants to see the Explain Plan. It is no surprise that SQLT includes the Explain Plan in its report just for this information in the Execution Plan section. A sample Execution Plan section can be seen below.

Execution Plans

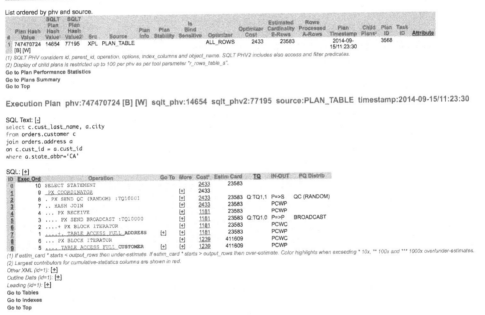

List ordered by phv and source.

Figure 8.14 SQLT Execution Plan

The SQLT report sample seen so far was generated with the *sqltxtract.sql* script. This script can only be used when the SQL statement is in the Shared Pool and the *sql_id* value can be determined. One of the benefits of the *sqltxtract.sql* script is that the SQL statement is not executed, which can be very useful when trying to analyze long running SQL statements. This extract method works great, but nothing gathers more information for SQLT than letting SQLT execute the statement and watching it in action. SQLT provides the *sqltxecute.sql* script to analyze a SQL statement that SQLT will execute. The SQL statement must be in a text file and contain a specific comment, seen below, in the text that SQLT will use to help identify it in the Shared Pool. The file my_query.sql below contains the query to be analyzed. Notice the comment in the SELECT clause. When running the *sqltxecute.sql* script, use this exact comment.

```
[oracle@host01 ~]$ cat my_query.sql

SELECT /* ^^unique_id */
 o.order_date, d.detail_id
FROM scott.orders o
JOIN scott.order_details d
ON o.order_id=d.order_id;
```

For those SQL statements that modify database, SQLT will create a savepoint and rollback the transaction to that savepoint upon completion. The *sqltxecute.sql* script is run very similarly to the *sqltxtract.sql* script, but instead of the *sql_id* value, the SQL script name is provided.

```
SQL> @/home/oracle/sqlt/run/sqltxecute.sql my_query.sql
```

The *sqltxtract.sql* and *sqltxecute.sql* scripts are the two most common methods to invoke SQLT. This section has provided what is only an introduction to SQLT. Since there is very little SQLT functionality just for Oracle RAC systems, this book will skip diving into SQLT in more detail. This section was provided because SQLT is part of the RAC Support Tools bundle from Oracle Support. The SQLT utility has lots of functionality in its arsenal and the reader is encouraged to further research this tool.

Summary

The Oracle RAC Support Tools bundle is very useful for Oracle RAC database administrators that need to tune the system for optimal performance. The Support Tools bundle includes the following utilities

- ORAchk (formerly RACchk)
- Trace File Analyzer (TFA)
- OSWatcher
- Procwatcher
- Oratop
- SQLT

The tools can be download in a large bundle or individually. Each of these utilities was discussed throughout the chapter. In addition, some very useful Oracle RAC performance tools were discussed that are not part of the bundle, including:

- Cluster Health Monitor (CHM)
- CHM OS Graphical (CHMOSG)
- Racdiag.sql script

With the knowledge in this chapter, the database administrator has a large collection of tools and utilities at their disposal to help diagnose performance issues with Oracle RAC databases. The next chapter discusses the Automated Workload Repository (AWR) as yet another utility in the database administrator's tool chest.

AWR, ADDM and ASH

Oracle Corporation provides a higher level of instrumentation than any other database platform on the market. There are two problems with all of the performance metrics generated by the database engine. One, the metrics need to be collected on a regular basis. Two, the metrics need to be collated so that meaningful information can be obtained from all of that data. Oracle provides the Automated Workload Repository (AWR) to help with both of these areas. Armed with the collected performance metrics, the Automatic Database Diagnostics Monitor (ADDM) takes the next step of providing expert performance tuning advice. Where AWR and ADDM look at database performance as a whole, Active Session History (ASH) provides a historical look at past performance on a session-level. Each of these features is available in single-instance databases as well as Oracle RAC.

Diagnostics Pack

The AWR is part of the optionally licensed Diagnostics Pack for Oracle Enterprise Edition. If the Diagnostics Pack is not licensed, you can use Statspack in place of AWR reports. However, Statspack's functionality is severely limited when compared to AWR, especially for Oracle RAC databases. Many companies do not like to pay for the extra, optional package, but the Diagnostics Pack is well worth the money. You can save so much time when trying to diagnose performance problems with the Diagnostics Pack compared to using Statspack, that it is very common for the Diagnostics Pack to pay for itself in a short period of time.

Out of the box, the AWR automatically captures performance metrics every hour. Some internal database operations, such as the Undo Advisor, use AWR data. The Diagnostics Pack does not have to be licensed to collect the metrics or use this advisor. The Diagnostics Pack will have to be licensed to run reports against the AWR, query any *dba_hist_*_* views, use ASH, leverage ADDM, or use the Performance page in Oracle Enterprise Manager, which will be discussed in the next chapter. Using the Diagnostics Pack in Enterprise Manager is often the biggest time saver.

AWR Retention and RAC

The Automated Workload Repository contains performance metrics gathered once per hour by default and stores the results in the *sysaux* tablespace. With Oracle RAC databases, the only difference is that the number of instances will linearly scale the AWR data volume. By default, AWR will keep eight days of data in the repository. Oracle includes a nice script, *$ORACLE_HOME/rdbms/admin/awrinfo.sql*, which can help you keep track of the AWR repository sizing.

The output of a sample *awrinfo.sql* script will be discussed in this section. The first portion of the script output shows some introductory information. Notice the snapshot interval and retention. Oddly, this script is warning that there is a non-default AWR setting but this database is out-of-the-box with no custom AWR configuration.

```
~~~~~~~~~~~~~~~~
AWR INFO Report
~~~~~~~~~~~~~~~~

Report generated at 11:44:21 on Sep 16, 2014 ( Tuesday ) in Timezone -06:00

Warning: Non Default AWR Setting!
-----------------------------------------------------------------------------
Snapshot interval is 60 minutes and Retention is 8 days


      DB_ID DB_NAME HOST_PLATFORM                    INST STARTUP_TIME
----------- ------- ------------------------------   ----- ----------------
* 2793090278 ORCL    host01 - Linux x86 64-bit          1 10:12:20 (08/28)
  2793090278 ORCL    host02 - Linux x86 64-bit          2 10:12:21 (08/28)
```

SYSAUX tablespace components

Section 1 of the report discusses the *sysaux* tablespace components. The total *sysaux* tablespace size is shown. Part 1a shows the breakdown by schema owner. Not surprisingly, the *sys* user accounts for the majority of the space utilization in that tablespace. These days, it seems it is too common for the *sysaux* tablespace to grow very large. Part 1b can help you get a handle on the functionality that is consuming the space. Where Part 1a may say that *sys* is the biggest holder of space, that schema will contain the AWR repository tables, Advisor findings and much more. Part 1b helps understand how the *sys* schema is really utilizing that space.

```
###########################################################
(I) AWR Snapshots Information
###########################################################
```

```
**********************************************************
(1a) SYSAUX usage - Schema breakdown (dba_segments)
**********************************************************
|
| Total SYSAUX size                          2,241.0 MB ( 7% of 32,768.0 MB MAX
with AUTOEXTEND ON )
|
| Schema   SYS          occupies        1,955.4 MB (  87.3% )
| Schema   XDB          occupies          126.9 MB (   5.7% )
| Schema   APEX_030200  occupies           77.4 MB (   3.5% )
| Schema   MDSYS        occupies           44.6 MB (   2.0% )
| Schema   SYSTEM       occupies           14.8 MB (   0.7% )
| Schema   ORDDATA      occupies           13.4 MB (   0.6% )
| Schema   EXFSYS       occupies            3.6 MB (   0.2% )
| Schema   WMSYS        occupies            3.5 MB (   0.2% )
| Schema   DBSNMP       occupies            1.0 MB (   0.0% )
| Schema   ORDSYS       occupies            0.4 MB (   0.0% )
|
**********************************************************
(1b) SYSAUX occupants space usage (v$sysaux_occupants)
**********************************************************
|
| Occupant Name          Schema Name              Space Usage
| -----------------      --------------------     ----------------
| SM/AWR                 SYS                       1,761.6 MB
| XDB                    XDB                         126.9 MB
| SM/OPTSTAT             SYS                         116.9 MB
| SDO                    MDSYS                        44.6 MB
| SM/ADVISOR             SYS                          34.5 MB
| ORDIM/ORDDATA          ORDDATA                      13.4 MB
```

Only the first few lines of Part 1b were shown for brevity. It is easy to see that the AWR repository is accounting for 1,761.6 megabytes of the 2,241.0 megabyte tablespace, by far the biggest consumer of space. If the *sysaux* tablespace seems to be growing rather large, the *awrinfo.sql* script can help determine the functional area of the database that is to blame.

Part 2 of the report helps you plan AWR space usage if the default interval or retention period is changed. This information is also useful when expanding the number of Oracle RAC nodes.

```
***************************************
(2) Size estimates for AWR snapshots
***************************************
|
| Estimates based on 60 mins snapshot INTERVAL:
|   AWR size/day         104.1 MB (4,443 K/snap * 24 snaps/day)
|   AWR size/wk          728.9 MB (size_per_day * 7) per instance
|   AWR size/wk        1,457.9 MB (size_per_day * 7) per database
|
| Estimates based on 24 snaps in past 24 hours:
|   AWR size/day         104.1 MB (4,443 K/snap and 24 snaps in past 24 hrs)
|   AWR size/wk          728.9 MB (size_per_day * 7) per instance
|   AWR size/wk        1,457.9 MB (size_per_day * 7) per database
|
```

From the output above, it is clear that each snapshot is taking 4,443 kilobytes of space. Changing the default collection interval to 30 minutes would double the total size from 1,457.9 megabytes to 2,915.8 megabytes. The database administrator can expand the *sysaux* tablespace accordingly if the data will be collected more often than the default. The information above also shows that each instance is holding 728.9 megabytes of data. You can now plan for AWR growth when adding one or more instances to the Oracle RAC database.

Part 3 of the script output breaks down space usage of AWR even more. If Part 2 is showing that AWR repository data is consuming large amounts of space, then Part 3 can be used to drill down into the problem area with more accuracy. Probably the best area to look at is Part 3b, which shows the usage by segment name. Only the first few lines of Part 3b are included in the output below. If the AWR is growing too large, it is Part 3b that is often the most helpful when working with Oracle Support to obtain a resolution. Note that when running the *awrinfo.sql* script, Part 3 can take a long time to complete.

```
*********************************
(3a) Space usage by AWR components (per database)
*********************************

COMPONENT    MB    % AWR  KB_PER_SNAP MB_PER_DAY MB_PER_WEEK TABLE% : INDEX%
---------  ------  ------ ----------- ---------- ----------- ----------------
FIXED      911.6   51.7      2,299       53.9       377.2    47% : 53%
EVENTS     527.6   29.9      1,331       31.2       218.3    44% : 56%
SQL        166.8    9.5        421        9.9        69.0    68% : 32%
SPACE       71.7    4.1        181        4.2        29.7    70% : 30%
RAC         44.8    2.5        113        2.6        18.5    53% : 47%
ASH         23.3    1.3         59        1.4         9.6    82% : 18%
SQLPLAN      9.0    0.5         23        0.5         3.7    67% : 33%
SQLTEXT      2.1    0.1          5        0.1         0.9    94% : 6%
SQLBIND      0.8    0.0          2        0.0         0.3    58% : 42%


*********************************
(3b) Space usage within AWR Components (> 500K)
*********************************

COMPONENT    MB  SEGMENT_NAME - % SPACE_USED                        SEGMENT_TYPE
---------  ----- --------------------------------------------       ----------------
FIXED      120.0 WRH$_LATCH.WRH$_LATCH_2793090278_0-94%             TABLE PARTITION
FIXED      112.0 WRH$_SYSSTAT_PK.WRH$_SYSSTA_2793090278_0-78%       INDEX PARTITION
FIXED       96.0 WRH$_LATCH_PK.WRH$_LATCH_2793090278_0 -80%         INDEX PARTITION
```

If a non-AWR component is taking up the space, then instead of using Part 3b, you will want to examine the information in Part 4 of the output. Only the first few lines of Part 4 are shown below for brevity.

```
**********************************
(4) Space usage by non-AWR components (> 500K)
**********************************

COMPONENT        MB  SEGMENT_NAME                         SEGMENT_TYPE
----------    ------- ----------------------------------  ----------------
NON_AWR        54.2  XDB.SYS_LOB0000069262C00025$$        LOBSEGMENT
NON_AWR        47.0  SYS.I_WRI$_OPTSTAT_H_OBJ#_ICOL#_ST   INDEX
NON_AWR        29.0  SYS.WRI$_OPTSTAT_HISTGRM_HISTORY     TABLE
NON_AWR        21.0  SYS.I_WRI$_OPTSTAT_H_ST              INDEX
```

Part 5 of the *awrinfo.sql* script output shows the snapshots in the AWR. Most of this is informational. As such, the output from Part 5 is not shown in this book. Part 6 provides the same interval and retention information seen in the report introduction. The last snapshot ID and time are also seen in this portion.

```
**********************************
(6) AWR Control Settings - interval, retention
**********************************

     DBID LSNAPID LSNAPTIME      LPURGETIME      INTERVAL           RETENTION
---------- ------- -------------- --------------- ----------------- -----------------
2793090278    1869 09/16 12:00:44 09/16 00:10:21 +00000 01:00:00.0 +00008 00:00:00.0
```

Setting the AWR Collection Interval

The *dbms_workload_repository* supplied package can be used to modify the collection interval and retention period. Both parameters are specified in minutes. The following example will change AWR to a thirty minute collection interval and keep the snapshot data in the repository for thirty days (30 days * 24 hours * 60 minutes = 43,200 minutes).

```
SQL> exec dbms_workload_repository.modify_snapshot_settings ( -
> interval=>30, retention=>43200);

PL/SQL procedure successfully completed.
```

You need to be mindful of the impact on the size of the *sysaux* tablespace as was discussed earlier in this section. The minimum interval is ten minutes and the maximum interval is one year, a value so large as to have no benefit when using automatic AWR snapshots to assist with performance analysis. Normally, the one-hour interval is sufficient for automatic collection. Many times, you will want a smaller time window for analyzing a specific performance issue. In those cases, it is recommended to gather the snapshots manually at the start and ending of the analysis window rather than to adjust the automated interval. The snapshot can be manually taken with the following command.

```
SQL> exec dbms_workload_repository.create_snapshot();

PL/SQL procedure successfully completed.
```

The minimal retention period is one day and the maximum is one hundred years. If the retention is set to zero, AWR will not automatically remove data from the repository, thus providing an infinite retention.

For the most part, the information in this section is not directly related to Oracle RAC performance tuning. However, the information in the AWR can directly impact how the database administrator uses the reports and information in the remainder of this chapter.

AWR Reports

This chapter assumes the reader has some level of familiarity with AWR reports. Much of what is in an AWR report applies to single-instance databases. The AWR report also has RAC-specific sections. For brevity, this chapter will skip most of the sections that are not RAC-specific that the reader is already familiar with and focus on the sections that are more relevant to an Oracle RAC performance-tuning book.

It should be noted that it is generally a bad idea to run the AWR report just hoping to find performance problems. The AWR report should be used when a specific performance problem needs attention. You should also be aware that the AWR report looks at overall instance or database performance. Depending on the performance problem, the AWR report may be the haystack hiding the needle. Too much information from a very high level may obscure the performance issue. If a single session is having a performance problem, SQL trace may be a better tool. If a single SQL statement is performing slowly, SQLT may be the utility to use. However, if end users are complaining about overall database performance and you are unsure where to start, AWR reports are a great way to start at a high level and drill down to an area of poor performance.

Invoking awrrpt.sql

Anyone generating an AWR report has most likely done so by executing the *awrrpt.sql* script located in the *$ORACLE_HOME/rdbms/admin* directory. Oracle's Enterprise Manager is capable of generating the same AWR report. The *awrrpt.sql* script is capable of producing a report in either text or html format. The html version has hyperlinks that can aid in navigation throughout the report. This chapter will show sections of a text version of the report only because that format is more conducive to the layout of the book.

The *awrrpt.sql* script can only generate a report for the current instance. If you have a SQL*Plus session connected to the *orcl1* instance but wants to generate a report from the *orcl2* instance, the session will need to be disconnected and subsequently instantiated to the other instance. Since the *awrrpt.sql* script is for a single instance, it is not capable of producing information about all instances of the Oracle RAC database.

The following shows the start of the *awrrpt.sql* script on one instance of the database. Notice that the script indicates at the very beginning that this execution is from the *orcl1* instance. The script asks for the report format and then displays all instances in the AWR repository. Lastly, the beginning and ending snapshots are defined after which the report is generated.

```
SQL> @?/rdbms/admin/awrrpt.sql

Current Instance
~~~~~~~~~~~~~~~~~

     DB Id DB Name       Inst Num Instance
----------- ------------- -------- ------------
 1543326278 ORCL                 1 orcl1

Specify the Report Type
~~~~~~~~~~~~~~~~~~~~~~~~~
Would you like an HTML report, or a plain text report?
Enter 'html' for an HTML report, or 'text' for plain text
Defaults to 'html'
Enter value for report_type: text

Type Specified:  text


Instances in this Workload Repository schema
~~~~~~~~~~~~~~~~~~~~~~~~~~~~~~~~~~~~~~~~~~~~~~~

     DB Id Inst Num DB Name     Instance     Host
----------- -------- ------------- ------------ ------------
 1543326278        1 ORCL        orcl1        host01
 1543326278        3 ORCL        orcl3        host03
 1543326278        2 ORCL        orcl2        host02

Using 1543326278 for database Id
Using          1 for instance number


Specify the number of days of snapshots to choose from
~~~~~~~~~~~~~~~~~~~~~~~~~~~~~~~~~~~~~~~~~~~~~~~~~~~~~~~~~
Entering the number of days (n) will result in the most recent
(n) days of snapshots being listed.  Pressing <return> without
specifying a number lists all completed snapshots.
```

```
Enter value for num_days: 1

Listing the last day's Completed Snapshots

                                                         Snap
Instance      DB Name        Snap Id   Snap Started      Level
------------  -------------  --------- ----------------- -----
orcl1         ORCL              49109  15 Sep 2014 00:00   1
                                49110  15 Sep 2014 01:00   1
                                49111  15 Sep 2014 02:00   1
                                49112  15 Sep 2014 03:00   1
                                49113  15 Sep 2014 04:00   1
                                49114  15 Sep 2014 05:00   1
                                49115  15 Sep 2014 06:00   1
                                49116  15 Sep 2014 07:00   1
                                49117  15 Sep 2014 08:00   1
                                49118  15 Sep 2014 09:00   1
                                49119  15 Sep 2014 10:00   1
                                49120  15 Sep 2014 11:00   1
                                49121  15 Sep 2014 12:00   1
                                49122  15 Sep 2014 13:00   1
                                49123  15 Sep 2014 14:00   1
                                49124  15 Sep 2014 15:00   1
                                49125  15 Sep 2014 16:00   1


Specify the Begin and End Snapshot Ids
~~~~~~~~~~~~~~~~~~~~~~~~~~~~~~~~~~~~~~~~
Enter value for begin_snap: 49119
Begin Snapshot Id specified: 49119

Enter value for end_snap: 49120
```

This section will show portions of the AWR report. Some sections of the report are applicable to both single-instance and Oracle RAC databases and will be omitted here. For example, the section showing the top 5 wait events and the section showing SQL ordered by elapsed time will not be shown as it is assumed that the reader is already familiar with these portions of the report. Since this is an Oracle RAC performance-tuning book, sections related to Oracle RAC performance will be shown here.

The first portion of the report to be discussed first appeared in Chapter 4 of this book when discussing how to tune the Cluster Interconnect. The Global Cache Load Profile provides statistics on global cache transfers along the private network, but only to and from this instance. A very important statistic is the estimated interconnect traffic. In the sample below, this instance is seeing over five megabytes per second on the private network. Generating similar reports for all instances will give you an idea of the total data volume on the Cluster Interconnect, which will need sufficient bandwidth to be able to support the global cache transfers.

```
Global Cache Load Profile
~~~~~~~~~~~~~~~~~~~~~~~~~~~             Per Second      Per Transaction
                                      ----------------  ---------------
       Global Cache blocks received:        279.76            21.86
        Global Cache blocks served:         305.77            23.89
         GCS/GES messages received:       1,352.73           105.70
             GCS/GES messages sent:       1,507.28           117.78
                 DBWR Fusion writes:          14.18             1.11
       Estd Interconnect traffic (KB)      5,242.81
```

Buffer Cache Access

After the Global Cache Load Profile is a breakdown of buffer cache access. A data block can be accessed from the local cache, from another instance via Cache Fusion, or from disk. In the sample below, 98.76% of all block access in this instance was from the local cache. In an ideal world, the accesses from the local cache should be very high as this is the most efficient block access path of the three. But just because the ratio is low does not mean a performance problem exists. Conversely, just because the ratio is high does not mean there are no performance problems.

```
Global Cache Efficiency Percentages (Target local+remote 100%)
~~~~~~~~~~~~~~~~~~~~~~~~~~~~~~~~~~~~~~~~~~~~~~~~~~~~~~~~~~~~~~~~~
Buffer access -  local cache %:     98.76
Buffer access - remote cache %:      1.09
Buffer access -        disk %:       0.14
```

Tuning SQL statements to use as few blocks as necessary may reduce the block access from a remote cache. Discussed in Chapter 3, Application Partitioning is another mechanism to reduce a high percentage of block access from another instance's cache.

The next portion of the AWR report details metrics on how quickly global cache operations are completed. The average time to acquire a global enqueue is the first metric. The average time should be very short, at most, a few milliseconds. High global enqueue get times are indicative of a private network having difficulties with its workload or high CPU utilization on the nodes. The average time to receive consistent read and current blocks from other instances should be no more than five milliseconds.

```
Global Cache and Enqueue Services - Workload Characteristics
~~~~~~~~~~~~~~~~~~~~~~~~~~~~~~~~~~~~~~~~~~~~~~~~~~~~~~~~~~~~~~~~
                   Avg global enqueue get time (ms):      0.0

        Avg global cache cr block receive time (ms):      0.6
   Avg global cache current block receive time (ms):      0.6

          Avg global cache cr block build time (ms):      0.0
           Avg global cache cr block send time (ms):      0.0
```

```
       Global cache log flushes for cr blocks served %:        25.9
            Avg global cache cr block flush time (ms):          1.4

           Avg global cache current block pin time (ms):        0.0
          Avg global cache current block send time (ms):        0.0
    Global cache log flushes for current blocks served %:       0.4
         Avg global cache current block flush time (ms):        2.5
```

If any of the average times above are more than five milliseconds, it can be indicative of a very busy Cluster Interconnect. Reducing the traffic on the private network or increasing the private network performance using techniques in Chapter 4 can reduce the average times of these metrics.

Average processing time for GCS and GES messages

The next portion of the AWR report shows average processing time for GCS and GES messages across the private network. If these average times are more than a few milliseconds, it is another indicator that the Cluster Interconnect is congested or not fast enough.

```
Global Cache and Enqueue Services - Messaging Statistics
~~~~~~~~~~~~~~~~~~~~~~~~~~~~~~~~~~~~~~~~~~~~~~~~~~~~~~~~~~~~~~
                 Avg message sent queue time (ms):        0.0
          Avg message sent queue time on ksxp (ms):       0.3
             Avg message received queue time (ms):        0.0
                Avg GCS message process time (ms):        0.0
                Avg GES message process time (ms):        0.0

                        % of direct sent messages:       46.28
                      % of indirect sent messages:       51.93
                    % of flow controlled messages:        1.79
        -------------------------------------------------------------
```

Cluster Interconnect Statistics

The AWR report includes configuration information on the Cluster Interconnect. This portion does not provide any performance metrics. It is informational only, but can assist you when targeting the private network as a performance bottleneck.

```
Cluster Interconnect
-> if IP/Public/Source at End snap is different a '*' is displayed
~~~~~~~~~~~~~~~~~~~~~
                                    Begin                           End
         --------------------------------------------------    ----------
-
Interface   IP Address      Pub Source                          IP  Pub Src
---------   --------------- ---  --------------------------     --- --- ---
eth1        192.168.80.210  N
```

Foreground Wait Class Statistics

The portion of the report on Foreground Wait Class is standard fare for the database administrator when examining AWR reports. What is new in this report is the *Cluster* classification of wait events. Global cache operations contribute to this wait event classification. Cluster events should not dominate the foreground wait times. Tuning the Cluster Interconnect and reducing the global cache transfer will go a long way towards reducing the effect of this classification. Note that the *Cluster* classification of wait events is discussed in more detail in Chapter 12.

```
Foreground Wait Class              DB/Inst: ORCL/orcls  Snaps: 49119-49120
-> s  - second, ms - millisecond -    1000th of a second
-> ordered by wait time desc, waits desc
-> %Timeouts: value of 0 indicates value was < .5%. Value of null is truly 0
-> Captured Time accounts for   81.3% of Total DB time     17,471.36 (s)
-> Total FG Wait Time:       7,145.16 (s)  DB CPU time:       7,061.84 (s)

                                                        Avg
                                 %Time    Total Wait    wait
Wait Class            Waits     -outs      Time (s)     (ms)   %DB time
----------------   ----------   -----   ------------   -----  --------
DB CPU                                          7,062             40.4
User I/O            7,461,669       0           5,209      1     29.8
Other              89,989,835     100             640      0      3.7
Network             1,886,997       0             494      0      2.8
Cluster             1,628,256       0             470      0      2.7
Application            80,996       0             124      2      0.7
Commit                 43,643       0             119      3      0.7
Concurrency            79,073       0              82      1      0.5
System I/O             10,331       0               7      1      0.0
Configuration             321      24               1      2      0.0
```

Service statistics

Further down in the AWR report, past the wait event histograms and other wait event metrics is a section showing metrics broken down by each service in this instance. CPU utilization and I/O read activity is shown for each service running in the instance.

```
Service Statistics                 DB/Inst: ORCL/orcl1  Snaps: 49119-49120
-> ordered by DB Time

                                                    Physical      Logical
Service Name          DB Time (s)   DB CPU (s)      Reads (K)    Reads (K)
```

```
-----------------------   ------------   ------------   ------------   ------------
hr_svc                           15,500          6,516          5,427      1,069,622
SYS$USERS                         1,953            529            196         19,393
orcl                                 12             13              0             30
SYS$BACKGROUND                        0              0             20          1,037
orclXDB                               0              0              0              0
                          -------------------------------------------------------------
```

If a service spans multiple instances, the information will need to be collected from each instance to understand the total impact on that service. You can use this information to help decide how to best distribute services across the cluster to make the most efficient use of the resources on each node.

Statistics by wait event

The next portion of the AWR report provides service statistics broken down by wait event classification. Unfortunately, not all wait event classifications are presented in this output. Remember that this information is from one instance's point of view. If a service spans multiple instances, AWR reports from other instances will be needed to amass a total picture.

```
Service Wait Class Stats          DB/Inst: ORCL/orcl1  Snaps: 49119-49120
-> Wait Class info for services in the Service Statistics section.
-> Total Waits and Time Waited displayed for the following wait
   classes:  User I/O, Concurrency, Administrative, Network
-> Time Waited (Wt Time) in seconds

Service Name
---------------------------------------------------------------------
 User I/O User I/O Concurcy Concurcy    Admin    Admin   Network   Network
Total Wts  Wt Time Total Wts  Wt Time Total Wts  Wt Time Total Wts  Wt Time
--------- -------- --------- -------- --------- -------- --------- --------
hr_svc
  7187183     4659    75241       70         0        0   1802802      494
SYS$USERS
   274019      555     3340       12         0        0     83911        0
orcl
      612        1      275        0         0        0       271        0
SYS$BACKGROUND
    11433       29   265482       14         0        0    129370       14
          -----------------------------------------------------------------
```

SQL Statements

The AWR report then proceeds with lots of information about SQL statements ordered by CPU usage, physical reads, total executions, elapsed time, and more. These sections of the AWR report are standard fare for single-instance databases. Within the SQL portion of the report is a section on SQL statements order by Cluster Wait Time. The sample below shows only one query in that portion of the report.

```
SQL ordered by Cluster Wait Time     DB/Inst: ORCL/orcl1  Snaps: 49119-49120
-> %Total - Cluster Time  as a percentage of Total Cluster Wait Time
-> %Clu   - Cluster Time  as a percentage of Elapsed Time
-> %CPU   - CPU Time      as a percentage of Elapsed Time
-> %IO    - User I/O Time as a percentage of Elapsed Time
-> Only SQL with Cluster Wait Time > .005 seconds is reported
-> Total Cluster Wait Time (s):           472
-> Captured SQL account for   28.8% of Total

        Cluster                     Elapsed
    Wait Time (s)  Executions %Total  Time(s) %Clu  %CPU   %IO  SQL Id
    ------------- ----------- ------ -------- ----- ----- ------ ------------
          19.3          227    4.1     183.7  10.5  16.0   57.9 fm5y9y9ud7gdg
SELECT MAX(order_id) FROM orders;
```

This portion of the report is very useful for identifying the SQL statements that heavily dominate global cache operations. SQL statements identified here should be tuned to ensure the queries are not returning excessive rows. If a query returns lots of rows that are eventually filtered out by the application, the query can be performing excessive global cache transfers. Another way to reduce the SQL statement's cluster wait time is to execute the query on one node so that no cluster waits are needed. Obviously, this is accomplished with services and application partitioning.

Global Cache Buffer Busy Events

Further down the AWR report is a section showing the most active segments experiencing Global Cache Buffer Busy events. Proper tuning of SQL statements may be able to reduce the blocks being transferred on the private network. If the top segments are from different applications, then application partitioning can reduce the global cache impacts. Keep in mind that application partitioning needs to be handled carefully as fewer resources will be available with fewer nodes supporting the application.

```
Segments by Global Cache Buffer Busy DB/Inst: ORCL/orcl1  Snaps: 49119-49120
-> % of Capture shows % of GC Buffer Busy for each top segment compared
-> with GC Buffer Busy for all segments captured by the Snapshot

                                                         GC
            Tablespace                  Subobject Obj.  Buffer   % of
  Owner       Name     Object Name        Name    Type   Busy  Capture
--------- ---------- ------------------ --------- ----- -------- -------
  HR        USERS    EMP_PK                       INDEX  49,809   25.52
  HR        USERS    EMPLOYEES                    TABLE  39,004   19.98
  ORDERS    USERS    ORDERS                       TABLE  26,434   13.54
```

```
ORDERS      USERS      ORDERS_PK                        INDEX      16,589    8.50
ACCTG       USERS      LEDGER_LINE                      TABLE      14,657    7.51
            ------------------------------------------------------------------------
```

The next portion of the AWR report shows the top segments ordered by Consistent Read Blocks Received. Remember from Chapter 2 that CR blocks are needed when a session in one instance needs to obtain a consistent read image of a block from another instance. Again, segregating block access to one node will eliminate the need for CR blocks to be shipped over the private network. Also, this portion of the report is showing info from one instance. The same segments may or may not show up in the same portion of the report that would be generated from another instance.

```
Segments by CR Blocks Received       DB/Inst: ORCL/orcl1  Snaps: 49119-49120
-> Total CR Blocks Received:             140,071
-> Captured Segments account for      36.6% of Total

                                                                 CR
            Tablespace                       Subobject  Obj.   Blocks
Owner       Name       Object Name           Name       Type   Received %Total
----------  ---------- --------------------  ---------- -----  -------- ------
HR          USERS      EMPLOYEES                        TABLE    15,369  10.97
ORDERS      USERS      ORDERS                           TABLE    10,718   7.65
ORDERS      USERS      ORDERS_PK                        INDEX     6,148   4.39
SYS         SYSTEM     SEQ$                             TABLE     2,995   2.14
ACCTG       USERS      LEDGER_LINE                      TABLE     1,836   1.31
            ------------------------------------------------------------------
```

The AWR report also includes a portion showing the top segments involved with Current block requests. Remember from Chapter 2, we noted that a current block transfer is where one instance obtains an unchanged block from another instance's Buffer Cache. Properly tuned SQL statements may reduce the need for global cache transfers involving these segments.

```
Segments by Current Blocks Received   DB/Inst: NCPP/ncpp4  Snaps: 49119-
49120
-> Total Current Blocks Received:         867,458
-> Captured Segments account for      55.2% of Total

                                                              Current
            Tablespace                       Subobject  Obj.   Blocks
Owner       Name       Object Name           Name       Type   Received %Total
----------  ---------- --------------------  ---------- -----  -------- -----
HR          USERS      EMPLOYEE_HISTORY                 TABLE    48,498   5.59
ORDERS      USERS      ORDER_DETAILS_PK                 INDEX    43,037   4.96
ORDERS      USERS      ORDER_DETAILS                    TABLE    39,960   4.61
HR          USERS      EMP_PK                           INDEX    32,844   3.79
ACCTG       USERS      LEDGER_LINE                      TABLE    32,521   3.75
            ------------------------------------------------------------------
```

Toward the end of the AWR report is a section on Global Messaging Statistics. Below is just a sample of the large number of statistics involving message traffic between the instances. In order to know if these statistics represent a problem, one would need a baseline for reference. With a baseline, you could determine if the metric has increased significantly, which would indicate a shift in utilization.

```
Global Messaging Statistics         DB/Inst: ORCL/orcl1  Snaps: 49119-49120

Statistic                           Total    per Second    per Trans
----------------------------  ----------------  ------------  -----------
acks for commit broadcast(actual)     138,240          38.4          3.0
acks for commit broadcast(logical     168,692          46.8          3.7
broadcast msgs on commit(actual)      269,944          75.0          5.9
broadcast msgs on commit(logical)     269,944          75.0          5.9
broadcast msgs on commit(wasted)       54,502          15.1          1.2
dynamically allocated gcs resourc           0           0.0          0.0
dynamically allocated gcs shadows           0           0.0          0.0
flow control messages received             46           0.0          0.0
flow control messages sent                 20           0.0          0.0
gcs apply delta                             0           0.0          0.0
gcs assume cvt                            112           0.0          0.0
gcs assume no cvt                     515,689         143.2         11.2
```

The next portion of the AWR report shows global cache requests this instance must serve to other instances. The number of CR and Current block requests handled by this instance is in the first two lines of this portion. The number of Errors, the last line of output, should be zero. A non-zero value can be indicative of issues with the Cluster Interconnect.

```
Global CR Served Stats              DB/Inst: ORCL/orcl1  Snaps: 49119-49120

Statistic                           Total
----------------------------  -------------------
CR Block Requests                    232,026
CURRENT Block Requests                33,090
Data Block Requests                  232,026
Undo Block Requests                    2,833
TX Block Requests                     12,143
Current Results                      146,173
Private results                        8,542
Zero Results                         106,646
Disk Read Results                      3,657
Fail Results                              67
Fairness Down Converts                53,686
Fairness Clears                        6,684
Free GC Elements                           0
Flushes                               67,696
Flushes Queued                             0
Flush Queue Full                           0
Flush Max Time (us)                        0
Light Works                            5,462
Errors                                     0
```

The next portion of the AWR report shows a histogram of the Current blocks served by this instance. Ideally, the majority of the statistics should be no more than ten

---

AWR Reports

milliseconds in duration. If these statistics spend time in the longer portions of the histogram, it can be indicative of a slow or congested Cluster Interconnect.

```
Global CURRENT Served Stats          DB/Inst: ORCL/orcl1  Snaps: 49119-49120
-> Pins    = CURRENT Block Pin Operations
-> Flushes = Redo Flush before CURRENT Block Served Operations
-> Writes  = CURRENT Block Fusion Write Operations

Statistic         Total    % <1ms  % <10ms % <100ms   % <1s   % <10s
----------    ----------   -------  ------- --------  -------  -------
Pins                 277    41.88    53.07     4.69     0.36     0.00
Flushes            3,483    64.69    32.01     3.04     0.26     0.00
Writes            51,065    17.37    64.50    15.57     2.55     0.00
              ------------------------------------------------------------
```

The next portion of the AWR report shows global cache transfers. Since this report was generated from the first instance, this portion will show the interactions with the other two instances of the 3-instance Oracle RAC database.

The database administrator will want to ensure the percentage of requests handled immediately is very high. If the *% Immed* value is low, it indicates that the other instance was not ready to send the global cache block transfer at that time. The other instance could be busy or have contention. The database administrator would need to obtain an AWR report from the other instance to determine the root cause of the problem. Both CR and Current block transfers are shown in this portion. Also notice that the blocks are classified by block type: data, undo, or other. It is normal for the data block classification to be the dominant block type involved in the transfers.

```
Global Cache Transfer Stats          DB/Inst: ORCL/orcl1  Snaps: 49119-49120
-> Immediate (Immed) - Block Transfer NOT impacted by Remote Processing
Delays
-> Busy       (Busy) - Block Transfer impacted by Remote Contention
-> Congested(Congst) - Block Transfer impacted by Remote System Load
-> ordered by CR + Current Blocks Received desc
```

| Inst | Block | CR | | | | Current | | | |
No	Class	Blocks Received	% Immed	% Busy	% Congst	Blocks Received	% Immed	% Busy	% Congst
3	data block	61,073	87.0	8.3	4.7	435,722	86.0	.9	13.2
2	data block	52,486	85.4	10.8	3.8	401,528	91.1	.7	8.2
2	Others	9,475	97.6	1.3	1.1	15,678	96.5	.9	2.6
3	Others	5,573	97.2	1.1	1.7	12,173	96.6	1.1	2.3
2	undo header	5,370	82.1	17.2	.7	1,306	93.7	5.4	.8
3	undo header	3,581	84.1	15.0	.9	1,094	96.0	3.4	.6
2	undo block	1,617	95.4	4.0	.7	0	N/A	N/A	N/A
3	undo block	901	90.5	8.4	1.1	0	N/A	N/A	N/A

While the portion above provides metrics on how many blocks were involved in the global cache transfers, the next portion shows the average time to transmit those blocks. Both of these portions of the AWR report go hand in hand. The database administrator will want to ensure that the average times are only a few milliseconds. Normally, the average times for immediate transfers will be very short. The busy and congested times are more indicative of issues with the other instance involved in the transfer. Again, you would need to investigate why the other instance was not responsive in receiving the block transfer.

```
Global Cache Transfer Times (ms)    DB/Inst: ORCL/orcl1  Snaps: 49119-49120
-> Avg Time - average time of all blocks (Immed,Busy,Congst) in ms
-> Immed, Busy, Congst -  Average times in ms
-> ordered by CR + Current Blocks Received desc


                     CR Avg Time (ms)            Current Avg Time (ms)
                ---------------------------  ----------------------------
Inst Block
No   Class        All   Immed   Busy  Congst    All   Immed   Busy  Congst
---- ------      -----  ------  -----  ------   -----  ------  -----  ------
  3  data blo    0.6    0.5     1.6    1.0      0.7    0.6     2.8    1.3
  2  data blo    0.6    0.4     2.1    1.3      0.6    0.5     2.7    1.1
  2  others      0.4    0.3     2.6    0.4      0.5    0.4     2.6    0.6
  3  others      0.5    0.5     2.5    0.5      0.5    0.5     2.2    0.5
  2  undo hea    0.7    0.5     1.8    0.6      0.3    0.2     2.2    0.6
  3  undo hea    0.6    0.4     1.7    0.3      0.4    0.3     3.6    0.2
  2  undo blo    0.4    0.4     1.6    0.5      N/A    N/A     N/A    N/A
  3  undo blo    0.4    0.4     1.0    0.3      N/A    N/A     N/A    N/A
                ---------------------------------------------------------
```

Global Cache Transfer Statistics

The next portion of the AWR report shows the immediate cache transfers, both consistent read and current, and how many instances were involved. Remember from Chapter 2 that a global block cache transfer can be 2-way or 3-way depending on how many instances are involved. This portion of the AWR report refers to the transfers as *2hop* and *3hop* instead. A 3-way global cache transfer will require slightly more time than 2-way transfers. The more instances in the cluster, the higher the chances for 3-way transfers.

```
Global Cache Transfer (Immediate)   DB/Inst: ORCL/orcl1  Snaps: 49119-49120
-> Immediate  (Immed) - Block Transfer NOT impacted by Remote Processing
Delays
-> % of Blocks Received requiring 2 or 3 hops
-> ordered by CR + Current Blocks Received desc


                                  CR                      Current
                         -------------------------  -------------------------
          Src Block    Blocks  Immed Blks     %       %   Immed Blks     %      %
          Inst Class    Lost   Received    2hop    3hop   Received    2hop   3hop
```

```
---- --------  ------  -----------  -------  -------  -----------  -------  -------
   3 data blo       0       53,121     70.4     29.6      374,573     76.8     23.2
   2 data blo       0       44,846     61.7     38.3      365,976     76.9     23.1
   2 others         0        9,246     80.4     19.6       15,135     75.0     25.0
   3 others         0        5,416     50.6     49.4       11,763     62.8     37.2
   2 undo hea       0        4,410    100.0      0.0        1,224    100.0      0.0
   3 undo hea       0        3,010    100.0      0.0        1,050    100.0      0.0
   2 undo blo       0        1,542    100.0      0.0            0      N/A      N/A
   3 undo blo       0          815    100.0      0.0            0      N/A      N/A
                           --------------------------------------------------------
```

Average time to complete 2-way and 3-way transfers

The next portion of the AWR report shows the average times to complete the 2-way and 3-way transfers. Not surprisingly, the average times should be at most, a few milliseconds. Since this portion is only concerned with immediate block transfers, high transfer times indicate a slow private network.

```
Global Cache Times (Immediate)      DB/Inst: ORCL/orcl1  Snaps: 49119-49120
-> Blocks Lost, 2-hop and 3-hop Average times in (ms)
-> ordered by CR + Current Blocks Received desc


                       CR Avg Time (ms)             Current Avg Time (ms)
                     ---------------------------   ---------------------------
   Src Block   Lost
   Inst Class  Time    Immed    2hop     3hop        Immed    2hop     3hop
   ---- -----  -----  -------- -------- --------   -------- -------- --------
      3 data blo        0.5      0.4      0.5         0.6      0.5      0.8
      2 data blo        0.4      0.4      0.5         0.5      0.5      0.6
      2 others          0.3      0.3      0.4         0.4      0.4      0.6
      3 others          0.5      0.4      0.5         0.5      0.4      0.5
      2 undo hea        0.5      0.5      N/A         0.2      0.2      N/A
      3 undo hea        0.4      0.4      N/A         0.3      0.3      N/A
      2 undo blo        0.4      0.4      N/A         N/A      N/A      N/A
      3 undo blo        0.4      0.4      N/A         N/A      N/A      N/A
                     -----------------------------------------------------------
```

The next portion of the AWR report shows pings from one instance to another on the private network. Notice that this instance even pings itself. The average time should be less than 1 millisecond as the Cluster Interconnect is high speed and low latency. If pings between the nodes were taking too long, it would be a guarantee that global cache transfers would suffer. Slow ping times are resolved by tuning the private network.

```
Interconnect Ping Latency Stats    DB/Inst: ORCL/orcl1  Snaps: 49119-49120
-> Ping latency of the roundtrip of a message from this instance to ->
target in
-> The target instance is identified by an instance number.
-> Average and standard deviation of ping latency is given in miliseconds
-> for message sizes of 500 bytes and 8K.
-> Note that latency of a message from the instance to itself is used as
```

```
-> control, since message latency can include wait for CPU

   Target 500B Pin Avg Latency       Stddev 8K Ping Avg Latency    Stddev
 Instance   Count     500B msg    500B msg   Count       8K msg    8K msg
 -------- ------- ----------- ----------- ------- ----------- -----------
        1     283         .20         .09     283         .19        .09
        2     283         .22         .09     283         .25        .18
        3     283         .28         .19     283         .33        .27
          ------- ----------- ----------- ------- ----------- -----------
```

The next portion shows the private network throughput for this instance. In the example below, the instance is sending 5.4 megabytes per second and receiving 7.08 megabytes per second. The global cache transfers and messaging for parallel query operations are dominating the traffic, which is to be expected. The information in this section, aggregated with the same information from all instances, can be used to determine the required Cluster Interconnect bandwidth.

```
Interconnect Throughput by Client  DB/Inst: ORCL/orcl1  Snaps: 49119-49120
-> Throughput of interconnect usage by major consumers
-> All throughput numbers are megabytes per second

                        Send    Receive
Used By            Mbytes/sec  Mbytes/sec
----------------   ----------- -----------
Global Cache            1.96        1.79
Parallel Query          3.03        4.90
DB Locks                 .40         .36
DB Streams               .00         .00
Other                    .01         .03
                   ----------------------------------------------------
```

The last section of the AWR report to be discussed in this chapter shows the private network interface its statistics. You will want to ensure that there are not send or receive errors and no send or receive drops. Any non-zero values in these columns indicate issues with the private network and its configuration.

```
Interconnect Device Statistics        DB/Inst: NCPP/ncpp4  Snaps: 49119-49120
-> Throughput and errors of interconnect devices (at OS level)
-> All throughput numbers are megabytes per second

Device Name      IP Address         Public Source
---------------  ----------------   ------ -------------------------------
                                    Send    Send
           Send      Send     Send  Buffer  Carrier
     Mbytes/sec    Errors  Dropped  Overrun  Lost
     ----------- -------- -------- -------- --------
                                    Receive Receive
        Receive   Receive  Receive  Buffer  Frame
     Mbytes/sec    Errors  Dropped  Overrun  Errors
     ----------- -------- -------- -------- --------
eth1             192.168.80.210     NO
            .00         0        0        0        0
            .00         0        0        0        0
                 -------------------------------------------------------
```

AWR Reports   **273**

This section of the chapter examined an AWR report run on one instance of an Oracle RAC database. Portions of the report that should be familiar to database administrators examining performance of single-instance databases were omitted form this section. This section focused on only on the portions of the AWR report that pertain to Oracle RAC databases. The reader should now have a better understanding on how to use the *awrrpt.sql* script to obtain and analyze performance of an Oracle RAC instance.

awrrpti.sql

As discussed earlier, the *awrrpt.sql* script will generate an AWR report for the current instance. If you want to generate a report for another instance, the *awrrpti.sql* script can be used instead. The script will ask for the database ID and the instance ID.

```
SQL> @?/rdbms/admin/awrrpti.sql

Specify the Report Type
~~~~~~~~~~~~~~~~~~~~~~~~~
Would you like an HTML report, or a plain text report?
Enter 'html' for an HTML report, or 'text' for plain text
Defaults to 'html'
Enter value for report_type: text

Type Specified:  text


Instances in this Workload Repository schema
~~~~~~~~~~~~~~~~~~~~~~~~~~~~~~~~~~~~~~~~~~~~~~

      DB Id Inst Num DB Name     Instance      Host
----------- -------- ------------ ------------ ------------
 2793090278        2 ORCL        orcl2         host02
* 2793090278        1 ORCL        orcl1         host01

Enter value for dbid: 2793090278
Using 2793090278 for database Id
Enter value for inst_num: 2
Using 2 for instance number
```

The asterisk shows the currently connected instance. You can choose to run the report for any of the instances of the database. At this point, the rest of the AWR report is no different than the *awrrpt.sql* script as discussed in the previous section of this chapter.

awrgrpt.sql

When using AWR reports to diagnose performance problems the standard *awrrpt.sql* script can be difficult to use as it examines the performance of only one instance of the Oracle RAC database. You can run reports in each instance, but then would have to manually collate the results from all reports. Oracle includes a global AWR report that gathers metrics for all instances of the database. The *awrgrpt.sql* script will create the global report.

```
SQL> @?/rdbms/admin/awrgrpt.sql

Current Database
~~~~~~~~~~~~~~~~

  DB Id     DB Name
----------- ------------
 2793090278 ORCL


Specify the Report Type
~~~~~~~~~~~~~~~~~~~~~~~~~
Would you like an HTML report, or a plain text report?
Enter 'html' for an HTML report, or 'text' for plain text
Defaults to 'html'
Enter value for report_type: text

Type Specified:  text


Instances in this Workload Repository schema
~~~~~~~~~~~~~~~~~~~~~~~~~~~~~~~~~~~~~~~~~~~~~~~

          DB Id   INST_NUM DB Name     INST_NAME         Host
----------- ---------- ------------ ----------------- ------------
* 2793090278          2 ORCL         orcl2             host01
* 2793090278          1 ORCL         orcl1             host02


Using 2793090278 for database Id
Using instances ALL (default 'ALL')
```

This section of the chapter will not discuss all of the report output as the reader should have an idea of the contents from the previous AWR examples in this chapter. The example below shows how the global report collates the metrics from multiple instances. Each instance is shown. The total, average, and standard deviation of each metric is provided as well.

```
System Statistics                   DB/Inst: ORCL/orcl1  Snaps: 1866-1867

        Logical    Physical   Physical     Redo    Block    User
  I#     Reads      Reads      Writes   Size (k) Changes   Calls     Execs    Parses  Logons     Txns
---- ---------- ---------- ---------- -------- -------- -------- -------- -------- ------- --------
    1     49,830     21,715        630    2,142    4,380    3,959    4,594    2,365     233       33
```

2	26,978	60	894	1,804	4,133	2,132	3,811	1,401	187	22
Sum	76,808	21,775	1,524	3,946	8,513	6,091	8,405	3,766	420	55
Avg	38,404	10,888	762	1,973	4,257	3,046	4,203	1,883	210	28
Std	16,159	15,312	187	239	175	1,292	554	682	33	8

The global AWR report can save you a lot of time when trying to diagnose performance issues across all instances of the Oracle RAC database. Many database administrators coming from an environment with only single-instance databases may not be aware of the *awrgrpt.sql* script for Oracle RAC databases.

This section of the chapter has discussed the scripts the database administrator will use when generating AWR reports for performance analysis. Much of the AWR report information is the same for single-instance databases as it is for a singular instance of an Oracle RAC database.

ADDM

The AWR is regularly capturing performance metrics with each snapshot. You can run an AWR report to obtain a ton of information about all of the performance areas shown in the report. Wading through all of this information can be daunting. The Automatic Database Diagnostics Monitor (ADDM) is a knowledge expert that uses decades of Oracle Corporation's expertise to analyze the AWR data and provide assistance in resolving performance problems.

The ADDM requires the optional Diagnostics Pack and Tuning Pack to be licensed. In order for ADDM to run, the *control_management_pack_access* initialization parameter must be set to a value of DIAGNOSTIC+TUNING.

```
SQL> show parameter control_management_pack_access

NAME                                 TYPE        VALUE
------------------------------------ ----------- ------------------------------
control_management_pack_access       string      DIAGNOSTIC+TUNING
```

Setting this parameter to NONE will disable ADDM. In addition, the *statistics_level* initialization parameter should be set to TYPICAL or ALL so that the AWR will have sufficient detail.

```
SQL> show parameter statistics_level

NAME                                 TYPE        VALUE
------------------------------------ ----------- ------------------------------
statistics_level                     string      TYPICAL
```

The ADDM works in three phases: analyze, diagnose, and recommend.

On a regular basis, ADDM analyzes the AWR metrics looking for problem areas. The ADDM diagnosis the root cause of performance problems. Finally, the ADDM recommends solutions to remediate the performance problem.

ADDM has one goal in mind, to reduce database time. From an end user's perspective, the total response time is the time spent for the database to finish the request. The database time is defined with the following formula.

```
DB Time = CPU Time + Wait Time
```

In order to reduce database time, ADDM will work to decrease the time spent on the CPU or the time spent waiting for events to complete, or both. Note that for Oracle RAC databases, database time is the time spent on all instances of the clustered database.

Performance tuning with ADDM can often involve multiple iterations. Implementing the ADDM recommendations will reduce or eliminate one bottleneck only to have another one take its place at the top of the list.

It is important that you know when to stop tuning with ADDM recommendations. Tuning efforts should cease when performance levels are acceptable to the end users. Additionally, since ADDM runs regularly, the database administrator should not be using ADDM findings just because they are generated. The database administrator should have a specific performance problem that needs attention. Not knowing when to stop tuning and tuning without a specific problem that needs remediation is referred to by today's Oracle DBA community as *"Compulsive Tuning Disorder"*.

For Oracle RAC systems, ADDM can run in three modes:

- Database
- Instance
- Partial

A *database* ADDM diagnosis will examine the performance of all instances. Not surprisingly, an *instance* ADDM diagnosis will examine the performance of one instance of the Oracle RAC database. The *partial* ADDM diagnosis will examine a subset of instances. It should be noted that the database ADDM diagnosis is the only one that will examine performance of the Cluster Interconnect.

The supplied *dbms_addm* package can be used to initiate a database level ADDM advisor task using two AWR snapshots. ADDM will examine the performance between those snapshots and create findings based on what it sees.

```
SQL> declare
  2      t_name varchar2(30);
  3  begin
  4      t_name := 'ADDM_RUN_350_351';
  5      dbms_addm.analyze_db(task_name=>t_name,
  6          begin_snapshot=>350,end_snapshot=>351);
  7  end;
  8  /

PL/SQL procedure successfully completed.
```

Once the ADDM task is complete, the *dbms_addm.get_report* procedure can be used to see the findings.

```
SQL> set long 9999999999
SQL> select
  2      dbms_addm.get_report('ADDM_RUN_350_351')
  3  from
  4      dual;
```

The first part of the report contains some introductory information including the AWR snapshots used to generate the ADDM report and start and end times of the analysis. Notice that this analysis is for all instances, which should be the case since *dbms_addm.analyze_db* was used to generate the ADDM run.

```
           ADDM Report for Task 'ADDM_RUN_350_351'
        -------------------------------------------------
Analysis Period
---------------
AWR snapshot range from 350 to 351.
Time period starts at 23-SEP-14 12.00.22 PM
Time period ends at 23-SEP-14 01.00.27 PM
Analysis Target
---------------
Database 'ORCL' with DB ID 1543326278.
Database version 12.1.0.2.0.
ADDM performed an analysis of all instances.
Activity During the Analysis Period
-----------------------------------
Total database time was 13674 seconds.
The average number of active sessions was 3.79.
```

The report then shows a high-level summary of the ADDM findings. In the case below, ADDM is showing four findings. Some findings have recommendations, but findings 1 and 4 do not. The findings are ordered by the percentage of activity over the analysis period. You should start by examining the top-most findings, i.e. the findings that contribute the most to the performance.

```
Summary of Findings
-------------------
  Description                                         Active Sessions   Recommendations
                                                      Percent of Activity
  ------------------------------------------------    --------------------   -----------
1 "User I/O" wait Class                               1.36 |  35.91          0
2 Top SQL Statements                                   .62 |  16.36          5
3 Top Segments by "User I/O" and "Cluster"             .15 |   4.01          1
4 Global Cache Messaging                               .14 |   3.65          0
```

After the findings summary, the report gives details on each finding. In the first
finding, ADDM is indicating that significant user I/O waits are causing problems.
Notice that for this Oracle RAC database, the ADDM finding is showing the impact
to each instance. If the finding showed impact to one or a few instances, the database
administrator could use that information to narrow down the performance analysis,
instead of looking database wide.

```
             Findings and Recommendations
             ----------------------------
Finding 1: "User I/O" wait Class
Impact is 1.36 active sessions, 35.91% of total activity.
-----------------------------------------------------------
Wait class "User I/O" was consuming significant database time.
The throughput of the I/O subsystem was not significantly lower than
expected.
Instances that were significantly affected by this finding:
   Number   Name    Percent Impact   ADDM Task Name
   ------   -----   --------------   --------------
     2      ORCL2   34.34            ADDM_RUN_350_351_2_350
     1      ORCL1   33.78            ADDM_RUN_350_351_1_350
     3      ORCL3   31.89            ADDM_RUN_350_351_3_350
   No recommendations are available.
```

The finding shown above had no recommendations from ADDM. The next finding
shows SQL statements that are consume the most database time. There can be
multiple SQL statements shown in this section of the report. The output below is
showing only one SQL statement for brevity.

```
Finding 2: Top SQL Statements
Impact is .62 active sessions, 16.36% of total activity.
-----------------------------------------------------------
SQL statements consuming significant database time were found. These
statements offer a good opportunity for performance improvement.
Instances that were significantly affected by this finding:
   Number   Name    Percent Impact   ADDM Task Name
   ------   -----   --------------   --------------
     2      ORCL2   49.56            ADDM_RUN_350_351_2_350
     1      ORCL1   26.99            ADDM_RUN_350_351_1_350
     3      ORCL3   23.45            ADDM_RUN_350_351_3_350
   Recommendation 1: SQL Tuning
```

```
Estimated benefit is .16 active sessions, 10.27% of total activity.
------------------------------------------------------------
Action
    Run SQL Tuning Advisor on the SELECT statement with SQL_ID
    "981ks0qjy7fam".
    Related Object
       SQL statement with SQL_ID 981ks0qjy7fam.
       SELECT MIN(ORDER_DATE) FROM
       ORDERS WHERE ORDER_FLAG=:B1
Rationale
    The SQL spent 100% of its database time on CPU, I/O and Cluster waits.
    This part of database time may be improved by the SQL Tuning Advisor.
Rationale
    Database time for this SQL was divided as follows: 100% for SQL
    execution, 0% for parsing, 0% for PL/SQL execution and 0% for Java
    execution.
Rationale
    SQL statement with SQL_ID "981ks0qjy7fam" was executed 60594 times and
    had an average elapsed time of 0.0062 seconds.
Rationale
    At least 2 distinct execution plans were utilized for this SQL
statement
    during the analysis period.
Recommendation 5: SQL Tuning
Estimated benefit is .1 active sessions, 2.61% of total activity.
```

The recommended course of action for SQL statements found by ADDM is to
always run the SQL Tuning Advisor. The next finding shows segments involved with
high I/O and global cache transfer rates. The segment name is provided so that you
know where to focus your attention. Many times, tuning SQL statements to be more
efficient will reduce the user I/O and global cache activity.

```
Finding 3: Top Segments by "User I/O" and "Cluster"
Impact is .15 active sessions, 4.01% of total activity.
------------------------------------------------------------
Individual database segments responsible for significant "User I/O" and
"Cluster" waits were found.
Instances that were significantly affected by this finding:
   Number  Name   Percent Impact  ADDM Task Name
   ------  -----  --------------  --------------
     2     ORCL2  40.68           ADDM_RUN_350_351_2_350
     1     ORCL1  33.9            ADDM_RUN_350_351_1_350
     3     ORCL3  25.42           ADDM_RUN_350_351_3_350
Recommendation 1: Segment Tuning
Estimated benefit is .15 active sessions, 4.01% of total activity.
------------------------------------------------------------
Action
    Investigate application logic involving I/O on INDEX
    "ORDERS.ORDERS_PK" with object ID 105906.
    Related Object
       Database object with ID 105906.
Action
    Look at the "Top SQL Statements" finding for SQL statements consuming
    significant I/O on this segment. For example, the SELECT statement
    with SQL_ID "djswbc1yvt1r4" is responsible for 59% of "User I/O" and
    "Cluster" waits for this segment.
```

```
Rationale
    The I/O usage statistics for the object are: 0 full object scans,
    222918 physical reads, 1818 physical writes and 0 direct reads.
Symptoms That Led to the Finding:
----------------------------------
    Wait class "User I/O" was consuming significant database time.
    Impact is 1.36 active sessions, 35.91% of total activity.
```

The next finding in this report focuses on global cache transfers. This finding is only available when a *database* ADDM analysis is performed. Reading the information below, it should be clear that global cache transfers are performing within acceptable limits. Yet ADDM still finds that the *cluster* wait class is consuming significant time.

This finding indicates that the private network is performing very well but sessions still have to wait for some network transfers to complete. If this finding were higher on the list and needed remediation, you would need to work towards reducing the need to transfer blocks on the Cluster Interconnect, as described in previous chapters of this book. Lastly, notice that instance 2 has the lowest impact for this finding. This should not be surprising because instance 2 was the highest for the *User I/O* wait class event in the previous finding. After blocks were read by instance 2, the blocks were transferred to the other instances via Cache Fusion.

```
Finding 4: Global Cache Messaging
Impact is .14 active sessions, 3.65% of total activity.
-----------------------------------------------------------
Inter-instance messaging was consuming significant database time.
The network latency of the cluster interconnect was within acceptable limits
of 1 milliseconds.
Read and write contention on database blocks was not consuming significant
database time in the cluster.
Global Cache Service Processes (LMSn) were performing within acceptable
limits of 1 milliseconds.
Waits on "buffer busy" events were not consuming significant database time.
Instances that were significantly affected by this finding:
   Number   Name    Percent Impact   ADDM Task Name
   ------   -----   --------------   --------------
   1        ORCL1   36.82            ADDM_RUN_350_351_1_350
   3        ORCL3   34.48            ADDM_RUN_350_351_3_350
   2        ORCL2   28.7             ADDM_RUN_350_351_2_350
No recommendations are available.
Symptoms That Led to the Finding:
----------------------------------
    Wait class "Cluster" was consuming significant database time.
    Impact is .14 active sessions, 3.66% of total activity.
```

After each finding is discussed, the ADDM report provides a synopsis of the findings, and the instances are shown with their activity impacts. This report concluded with other areas that ADDM checks but were not shown to be contributing significantly to the overall database performance:

```
~~~~~~~~~~~~~~~~~~~~~~~~~~~~~~~~~~~~~~~~~~~~~~~~~~~~~~~~~~~~~~~~~~~~~~~
        Additional Information
        --------------------
Instances that were analyzed:
----------------------------
  Number  Name   Host Name                Active Sessions  Percent of Activity
  ------  ----   --------------------     ---------------  -------------------
    2     ORCL2  host02                   1.49             39.28
    1     ORCL1  host01                   1.18             31.2
    3     ORCL3  host03                   1.12             29.52
Miscellaneous Information
-------------------------
Wait class "Application" was not consuming significant database time.
Wait class "Commit" was not consuming significant database time.
Wait class "Concurrency" was not consuming significant database time.
Wait class "Configuration" was not consuming significant database time.
The network latency of the cluster interconnect was within acceptable limits
of 1 milliseconds.
Session connect and disconnect calls were not consuming significant database
time.
```

In addition to database ADDM analysis runs, Oracle RAC systems can have *instance* or *partial* ADDM analysis runs. When performing an *instance* ADDM analysis you need to define the instance involved in the examination. The *dbms_addm.analyze_inst* procedure has an extra parameter to denote the instance number as seen below.

```
SQL> declare
  2      t_name varchar2(30);
  3  begin
  4      t_name := 'ADDM_INST_RUN_350_351';
  5      dbms_addm.analyze_inst(task_name=>t_name,
  6          begin_snapshot=>350,end_snapshot=>351,
  7          instance_number=>2);
  8  end;
  9  /

PL/SQL procedure successfully completed.
```

The *dbms_addm.analyze_partial* procedure lets you supply a comma-delimited list of instance numbers to include in the ADDM analysis.

```
SQL> declare
  2      t_name varchar2(30);
  3  begin
  4      t_name := 'ADDM_PARTIAL_RUN_350_351';
  5      dbms_addm.analyze_partial(task_name=>t_name,
  6          begin_snapshot=>350,end_snapshot=>351,
  7          instance_numbers=>'1,2');
  8  end;
  9  /

PL/SQL procedure successfully completed.
```

The database ADDM analysis is great for obtaining ADDM recommendations database-wide. However, if you know that application partitioning is being used and wants to focus the analysis to just the instance(s) supporting the application that is having performance problems, the instance or partial ADDM analysis will be used so that issues form other applications are not impacting the results. No matter which level of ADDM is started, the *dbms_add.get_report* procedure can still be used to see the recommendations.

All of the ADDM interactions can also be performed through Oracle's Enterprise Manager. A future chapter will discuss Enterprise Manager in more detail as it relates to Oracle RAC performance tuning. However, for this chapter's discussion, it should be noted that Enterprise Manager 12c Cloud Control now has Real-Time ADDM. ADDM performs a regular analysis after each AWR snapshot is collected. Real-Time ADDM can be run at any time without having to take an AWR snapshot. Real-Time ADDM's biggest benefit is to perform analysis of database hangs, or unresponsive instances, without having to restart the database. Real-Time ADDM can be found in Enterprise Manager 12c Cloud Control in the Performance menu for a database target. The following shows how Real-Time ADDM looks in Enterprise Manager.

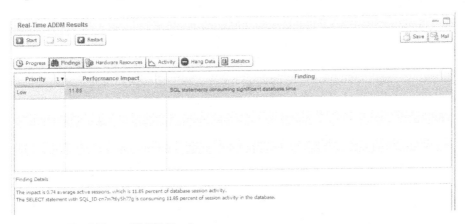

Figure 9.1 Real-Time ADDM Finding

Clicking the Start button will begin the ADDM analysis. The database administrator can then click on the Findings button to see the analysis results. If the Findings screen is empty, ADDM did not find any issues worthy of attention at this time. Clicking on each finding will show details for that entry.

Real-Time ADDM has two connection modes, *normal* and *diagnostic*. Many database administrators will use the normal connection mode, which connects through JDBC the same way Enterprise Manager connects to an instance. The diagnostic connection mode is used when the instance is unresponsive. This mode is used when the normal connection mode will not work, allowing the database administrator a chance to see what is happening to database performance.

ADDM

ASH for RAC

The AWR snapshots are captured once per hour, by default but you can run a report to glean performance information from these snapshots, as was discussed earlier in this chapter. This chapter also discussed how the ADDM advisor provides recommendations to improve performance.

For example, let's imagine a performance problem that lasts for fifteen minutes. Taking performance metrics over a one-hour window may contain forty-five minutes of data that will skew the results so as to help hide the true nature of the performance problem. Of course, you can take AWR snapshots with a smaller window, but this would have to be done in advance. Additionally, AWR reports focus on performance of the entire database and are not focused on the area of your performance issue..

The Active Session History (ASH) was initially created to help diagnose shorter duration performance issues that can go under-the-radar in an AWR report or an ADDM finding.

As the name implies, ASH focuses on the performance characteristics for each session. Many database administrators are finding that ASH keeps a treasure trove of performance data that can be used in a variety of ways. This section will provide some useful scripts utilizing ASH data. However, there is not enough space to provide scripts that can fully harness the power of the ASH data so the reader is encouraged to explore the topic further. Using ASH does require the optionally licensed Diagnostics Pack.

ASH metrics are sampled once per second for active sessions in the database. Right away, ASH provides more granular information than is found in the AWR snapshot collections. While there are gaps between the samples, the period between samples is very short. After all, any activity that only occurs between the samples exhibits sub-second performance and probably needs no analysis. If the ASH sample period is too large for the database administrator's analysis, then a SQL Trace of the session should be used instead.

Some readers may be asking if collecting performance metrics one per second will put a burden on the database system. First, metrics are collected only for sessions, whereas the AWR captures for the entire database. ASH won't capture metrics on Cluster Interconnect performance, SGA performance, or disk file performance. Secondly, ASH only captures metrics for active sessions. Idle sessions are not captured during the sampling. All of this greatly reduces the amount of information being collected.

ASH metrics are stored in a circular memory buffer in the SGA. This buffer is sized at two megabytes per CPU. The MMON Lite (MMNL) process gathers the metrics from *v$session* and *v$session_wait* and writes to the circular buffer. The contents of the circular buffer can be accessed from the *v$active_session_history* view. Obviously, for Oracle RAC, the *gv$active_session_history* view can be used to see the ASH data across all instances.

Every hour or when the circular memory buffer runs out of space, whichever comes first, one of every ten samples is written from the buffer to disk. By only writing one of every ten samples to disk, the historical ASH data volume is reduced. The historical ASH data can be accessed from the *dba_hist_active_sess_history* view. Keep in mind that when sampling ASH data from the historical view that the sample period is ten seconds, not one.

ASH metrics include the following:

- Session id and serial number
- Session module and action name
- Session consumer group
- Service hash identifier – can be joined to the *name_hash* column of *gv$services*.
- Wait event id and parameter values.
- SQL identifier – can be used to join to the *sql_id* column of *gv$sql*.
- SQL Plan hash value – can be used to join to the *plan_hash_value* column of *gv$sql_plan*.
- SQL Execution Plan information

Oracle includes a canned report for ASH data. Very similar to the *awrrpt.sql* script, the report can be generated by executing the *ashrpt.sql* script. The *ashrpt.sql* script generates information based on activity in the current instance. For Oracle RAC databases, the *ashrpti.sql* script can be used to generate a report for any instance. Unlike the AWR report scripts, there is no global or database-wide report.

The database administrator starts the *ashrpt.sql* script to generate the report. The script tells us that this is for the current instance. The script then asks for the report format.

```
SQL> @?/rdbms/admin/ashrpt.sql

Current Instance
~~~~~~~~~~~~~~~~~
```

```
   DB Id    DB Name      Inst Num Instance
----------- ------------ -------- ------------
 1543326278 ORCL                1 orcl1


Specify the Report Type
~~~~~~~~~~~~~~~~~~~~~~~~
Enter 'html' for an HTML report, or 'text' for plain text
Defaults to 'html'
Enter value for report_type: text

Type Specified:  text
```

Similar to the AWR report asking for the beginning and ending snapshot, the ASH report will ask for the start and end time of the analysis period. The script shows the oldest and most current time periods available. You can specify the time relative to *sysdate* if desired. To illustrate, in the example below the begin time is specified as "-1" which is one hour in the past. The end time will use the default to generate the report up to the current time.

```
ASH Samples in this Workload Repository schema
~~~~~~~~~~~~~~~~~~~~~~~~~~~~~~~~~~~~~~~~~~~~~~~~

Oldest ASH sample available:  18-Sep-14 01:44:09   [12041 mins in the past]
Latest ASH sample available:  26-Sep-14 10:25:37   [     0 mins in the past]


Specify the timeframe to generate the ASH report
~~~~~~~~~~~~~~~~~~~~~~~~~~~~~~~~~~~~~~~~~~~~~~~~~~~
Enter begin time for report:

--     Valid input formats:
--   To specify absolute begin time:
--     [MM/DD[/YY]] HH24:MI[:SS]
--     Examples: 02/23/03 14:30:15
--               02/23 14:30:15
--               14:30:15
--               14:30
--   To specify relative begin time: (start with '-' sign)
--     -[HH24:]MI
--     Examples: -1:15  (SYSDATE - 1 Hr 15 Mins)
--               -25    (SYSDATE - 25 Mins)

Defaults to -15 mins
Enter value for begin_time: -1
Report begin time specified: -1

Enter duration in minutes starting from begin time:
Defaults to SYSDATE - begin_time
Press Enter to analyze till current time
Enter value for duration:
```

The script will ask for a file name. In this case, the default file name is acceptable.

```
Specify the Report Name
~~~~~~~~~~~~~~~~~~~~~~~~~
The default report file name is ashrpt_4_0926_1032.txt.  To use this name,
press <return> to continue, otherwise enter an alternative.
Enter value for report_name:
```

After some time, the report is completed. Not surprisingly, the first part of the report
displays some introductory information, including instance details and

```
ASH Report For ORCL/orcl1

DB Name          DB Id      Instance Inst Num Release      RAC Host
------------ ----------- ------------ -------- ----------- --- ------------
ORCL         1543326278 orcl1                 1 11.2.0.4.0  YES host01


CPUs        SGA Size     Buffer Cache        Shared Pool   ASH Buffer Size
---- ----------------- ----------------- ----------------- -----------------
   4  20,389M (100%)    7,360M (36.1%)     5,188M (25.4%)      8.0M (0.0%)


              Analysis Begin Time:   26-Sep-14 09:37:00
              Analysis End Time:     26-Sep-14 10:37:27
                   Elapsed Time:     60.5 (mins)
              Begin Data Source:     V$ACTIVE_SESSION_HISTORY
                End Data Source:     V$ACTIVE_SESSION_HISTORY
                   Sample Count:     6,842
          Average Active Sessions:   1.86
    Avg. Active Session per CPU:     0.46
                  Report Target:     None specified
```

The next part of the report shows an aggregation of the top wait events for user
sessions and background processes.

```
Top User Events              DB/Inst: ORCL/orcl1  (Sep 26 09:37 to 10:37)

                                                          Avg Active
Event                        Event Class      % Event    Sessions
---------------------------- ---------------- ---------- ----------
CPU + Wait for CPU           CPU                   43.67       0.81
db file sequential read      User I/O              27.59       0.51
cursor: pin S wait on X      Concurrency            4.40       0.08
TCP Socket (KGAS)            Network                2.62       0.05
direct path read             User I/O               1.13       0.02
          ------------------------------------------------------------


Top Background Events        DB/Inst: ORCL/orcl1  (Sep 26 09:37 to 10:37)

                                                          Avg Active
Event                        Event Class      % Activity  Sessions
---------------------------- ---------------- ---------- ----------
CPU + Wait for CPU           CPU                    7.66       0.14
log file parallel write      System I/O             1.21       0.02
          ------------------------------------------------------------
```

The Top Event section, shown below, is interesting. The ASH report shows specific parameter values that can let you drill down into the event in more detail. For instance, in the report section below, the *db file sequential read* wait event has parameter values 1, 2819, 1 which correspond to starting at file number 1, block number 2819, and reading 1 block. This type of detail differs from the AWR report, which lacks wait event P1, P2 and P3 values.

```
Top Event P1/P2/P3 Values      DB/Inst: ORCL/orcl1  (Sep 26 09:37 to 10:37)

Event                      % Event  P1 Value, P2 Value, P3 Value % Activity
-------------------------- -------  ---------------------------- ----------
  Parameter 1                   Parameter 2               Parameter 3
-------------------------- --------------------  ---------------------------
db file sequential read       27.68                     "1","2819","1"      0.01
file#                     block#                         blocks

cursor: pin S wait on X        4.40 "3159891183","103079215104","      0.31
idn                       value                          where

TCP Socket (KGAS)              2.62                      "6","0","0"        2.62


log file parallel write        1.21                      "1","1","1"        0.31
files                     blocks                         requests

direct path read               1.13 "484","3595648","128"               0.03
file number               first dba                      block cnt

          ----------------------------------------------------------------
```

The next section of the report shows session activity broken down by service and module. Keep in mind that this report is for only one instance so only the services for that instance are shown. It is definitely possible for an Oracle RAC database to have services not part of an instance and those services would not show up in the ASH report.

```
Top Service/Module             DB/Inst: ORCL/orcl1  (Sep 26 09:37 to 10:37)

Service         Module              % Activity Action             % Action
--------------- ------------------- ---------- ------------------ ----------
hr_svc          HR                    36.22 UNNAMED                 36.22
                UNNAMED               25.58 UNNAMED                 25.58
SYS$USERS       DBMS_SCHEDULER        21.63 ORDERS_ROLLUP_JOB       21.47
SYS$BACKGROUND  UNNAMED               10.55 UNNAMED                 10.55
hr_svc          SQLPLUS                2.27 UNNAMED                  2.27
          ----------------------------------------------------------------
```

The Top SQL Command Types section is next in the report output. This section provides information not seen in the AWR report. The ASH metrics allow this report to be able to break down the SQL statements by type.

The information presented in this section of the report is mostly informational and there isn't much performance tuning done with this section, but it does help you understand the type of SQL activity performed in the sample period.

```
Top SQL Command Types          DB/Inst: ORCL/orcl1  (Sep 26 09:37 to 10:37)
-> 'Distinct SQLIDs' is the count of the distinct number of SQLIDs
      with the given SQL Command Type found over all the ASH samples
      in the analysis period

                                     Distinct            Avg Active
                                     SQLIDs % Activity    Sessions
SQL Command Type
----------------------------------  --------- ---------- ----------
SELECT                                    592      46.86       0.87
INSERT                                  1,281      22.70       0.42
PL/SQL EXECUTE                            178       7.07       0.13
UPDATE                                     25       4.12       0.08
DELETE                                     36       1.18       0.02
                                    -------------------------------------
```

The next section of the report shows the breakdown on SQL phases of execution. For most systems, the *SQL Execution* phase dominates the rest. If the parse phase accounts for a large amount of activity, it can be an indicator of too much dynamic SQL or a lack of bind variables. Or it may just be the norm, you will need to look at your application code to know for sure.

```
Top Phases of Execution        DB/Inst: ORCL/orcl1  (Sep 26 09:37 to 10:37)

                                          Avg Active
                                            Sessions
Phase of Execution              % Activity
----------------------------  ----------  ----------
SQL Execution                      81.64        1.52
Parse                              12.29        0.23
Hard Parse                          8.54        0.16
PLSQL Execution                     6.23        0.12
                              -------------------------------------
```

The next section shows top SQL statements by the top wait events, something that is unique to the ASH report. The example below only lists one SQL statement for brevity.

The sample below shows one query that spent its time either on the CPU or waiting for CPU cycles.

```
Top SQL with Top Events        DB/Inst: ORCL/orcl1  (Sep 26 09:37 to 10:37)

                                        Sampled #
         SQL ID     Planhash of Executions % Activity
-------------- ------------- ------------- ----------
Event                          % Event Top Row Source               % RwSrc
```

```
---------------------------------- ------- ---------------------------- -------
fbu07qx84amwy     2799396119              220      3.61
CPU + Wait for CPU                    2.09 SORT - GROUP BY                      0.82
SELECT MAX(ORDER_ID) FROM ORDERS
```

The ASH report also includes a section on top PL/SQL calls. This information can be useful when trying to determine the stored procedure calls that are accounting for the most activity.

```
Top PL/SQL Procedures          DB/Inst: ORCL/orcl1  (Sep 26 09:37 to 10:37)
-> 'PL/SQL entry subprogram' represents the application's top-level
      entry-point(procedure, function, trigger, package initialization
      or RPC call) into PL/SQL.
-> 'PL/SQL current subprogram' is the pl/sql subprogram being executed
      at the point of sampling . If the value is 'SQL', it represents
      the percentage of time spent executing SQL for the particular
      plsql entry subprogram

PLSQL Entry Subprogram                                        % Activity
-----------------------------------------------------------  ----------
PLSQL Current Subprogram                                      % Current
-----------------------------------------------------------  ----------
ORDERS.SHIP_ORDER                                                 21.47
   SQL                                                            20.20
```

The Top Sessions section of the ASH report provides information the sessions with the most activity. The top session is shown below. Note that this session accounts for 21.47% of activity in the sample period. The program, username, and wait event is also shown. Remember that ASH samples only active sessions. The output below shows that the top session was present in 754 of 3,687 samples.

```
Top Sessions                   DB/Inst: ORCL/orcl1  (Sep 26 09:37 to 10:37)
-> '# Samples Active' shows the number of ASH samples in which the session
      was found waiting for that particular event. The percentage shown
      in this column is calculated with respect to wall clock time
      and not total database activity.
-> 'XIDs' shows the number of distinct transaction IDs sampled in ASH
      when the session was waiting for that particular event
-> For sessions running Parallel Queries, this section will NOT aggregate
      the PQ slave activity into the session issuing the PQ. Refer to
      the 'Top Sessions running PQs' section for such statistics.

   Sid, Serial# % Activity Event                          % Event
--------------- ---------- -----------------------------  ----------
User                      Program                          # Samples Active  XIDs
----------------          -----------------------------   ------------------  -----
      1840,21419          21.47 CPU + Wait for CPU              11.02
JOBS_USER                 oracle@host01 (J000)             754/3,687 [ 20%]      1
```

Just like top sessions, the ASH report shows the top database objects by activity. This information is useful to not only show the hot segments in the sample period, but also to show the method of access by looking at the wait event.

```
Top DB Objects                    DB/Inst: ORCL/orcl1  (Sep 26 09:37 to 10:37)
-> With respect to Application, Cluster, User I/O and buffer busy waits
only.

        Object ID % Activity Event                                % Event
    --------------- ---------- ------------------------------- ----------
Object Name (Type)                                 Tablespace
----------------------------------------------------- -----------------------
         995504          5.60 db file sequential read             5.35
ORDERS.ORDERS (TABLE)                              USERS
```

The ASH report is easy to generate with a simple script, very similar to the AWR report. Most of the sections of the ASH report were shown above. Mining the ASH data can provide historical session-based performance information not seen in other reports or utilities, as was shown above.

One of the most exciting things to come about since ASH was introduced is the plethora of scripts to mine the ASH data. Many of today's database administrators are using specific queries, rather than the ASH report, to extract a wealth of information. For instance, you may want to know the top five sessions, or the top five SQL statements. Rather than run the entire report, you will often run a quick script from their library. One can look at the contents of the *ashrpti.sql* script to see how the ASH report is pulling information from the *v$active_session_history* view. Performing an Internet search for "oracle ash scripts" will provide other examples. The remainder of this section will walk through a few scripts from the books code library but the reader is encouraged to go beyond what is in this book.

The following script shows the top five SQL statements in the last hour. The script output shows the *sql_id* value which can be used to obtain the SQL statement from the *gv$sql* view.

💾 **ash_top_sql_last_hour.sql**

```
select
    *
from (
    select
        sql_id,
        count(*) as db_time,
        round(count(*)*100/sum(count(*)) over (), 2) as pct_activity
    from
        gv$active_session_history
    where
        sample_time >= sysdate - (1/24/60/60)*60
        and session_type <> 'BACKGROUND'
    group by
        sql_id
    order by
        count(*) desc)
where
    rownum <=5;
```

```
SQL_ID            DB_TIME PCT_ACTIVITY
-------------     ------- ------------
djswbc1yvt1r4          21        38.89
325p07d2t8dtv           7        12.96
az6utv7k4bqv7           4         7.41
6rumhhxm797x9           4         7.41
7ksjthxfcx8np           4         7.41
```

This next script shows the top five sessions in the last hour. The output from the script shows the *sid* and *serial#* columns from the *gv$session* view.

💾 **ash_top_sessions_last_hour.sql**

```
select
    *
from (
    select
        session_id||':'||session_serial# as "SID:SERIAL",
        count(*) as db_time,
        round(count(*)*100/sum(count(*)) over (), 2) as pct_activity
    from
        gv$active_session_history
    where
        sample_time >= sysdate - (1/24/60/60)*60
        and session_type <> 'BACKGROUND'
    group by
        session_id||':'||session_serial#
    order by
        count(*) desc)
where
    rownum <=5;
```

```
SID:SERIAL       DB_TIME PCT_ACTIVITY
---------------  ------- ------------
1719:3121              6        20.69
1800:13035             4        13.79
1870:26051             2          6.9
1299:21025             2          6.9
1222:21907             2          6.9
```

This next script shows the top objects involved in user I/O calls. The output from the script shows the current object number, which can be used to query the *dba_objects* view.

ash_top_objects_last_hour.sql

```
select
   *
 from (
    select
       current_obj#,
       count(*) as db_time,
       round(count(*)*100/sum(count(*)) over (), 2) as pct_activity
    from
       gv$active_session_history
    where
       sample_time >= sysdate - (1/24/60/60)*60
       and session_type <> 'BACKGROUND'
       and event in (select
                            name
                     from
                            v$event_name
                     where
                            wait_class='User I/O')
       and session_state='WAITING'
    group by
       current_obj#
    order by
       count(*) desc)
 where
    rownum <=5;
```

```
CURRENT_OBJ#    DB_TIME PCT_ACTIVITY
------------    ------- ------------
      523972          3        14.29
      961524          2         9.52
      960397          2         9.52
      960416          2         9.52
      524279          1         4.76
```

These scripts are just a start in using ASH data to solve performance problems. Because the scripts above query *gv$active_session_history*, only the most recent ASH data can be used. If you need to look further back in the past, simply change the source to *db_hist_active_sess_history* instead.

This section of the chapter has provided information on how Active Session History metrics are collected and how the data can be used to understand a session's performance problems. The ASH report was discussed and sections of that report were shown, sections that provide information different than what is seen from the AWR report. The database administrator can also use a variety of scripts to obtain performance-specific details. These scripts only scratch the surface of the wealth of information in the ASH data. In a later chapter, this book will show how Oracle's Enterprise Manager provides easy ASH analytic capabilities.

Summary

This chapter has discussed Oracle's latest and greatest approach to using performance metrics for Oracle RAC database tuning. The Automated Workload Repository captures database-wide performance metrics once per hour. The Automatic Database Diagnostic Monitor is a knowledge expert that can provide recommendations on its performance-related findings. Lastly, the Active Session History metrics samples data once per second to give you much more detail on session-level performance.

The next chapter will discuss benchmark utilities. With these tools, you can obtain information on how their system is performing. The utilities that will be discussed include Swingbench and HammerDB.

Benchmark Utilities for RAC CHAPTER

10

When making changes to any system, it is useful to have a method of providing a baseline before the change and measuring the performance after the change has been implemented. The difference in post-change metrics compared to the baseline can tell the database administrator if the change helped or hurt performance, or had minimal impact. In previous chapters, Iperf and Orion were discussed as these utilities can be used to measure network and disk performance respectively. Those utilities measured performance of specific components.

This chapter discusses utilities that can be used to benchmark overall RAC database performance. There are many vendors that are willing to sell their benchmark utilities. These are very good tools that work very well if the company is willing to pay the price. However, this chapter focuses on benchmark utilities that are freely available so that all readers of this book are able to use the tools that are discussed.

Swingbench

Swingbench is a load generation benchmark utility created by an Oracle employee, Dominic Giles. The tool is not an official Oracle product. As such, you cannot obtain support for it. But Swingbench is a nifty benchmark utility that many database administrators may find very useful. Swingbench can be found for download by pointing a web browser to http://dominicgiles.com/swingbench.html and clicking on the download link. The download is a simple zip file and can be unzipped with normal OS utilities. Swingbench is a Java program so it can be run on most any platform that supports Java. All of the Swingbench utilities can be invoked with command line options that facilitate scripting for multiple benchmark runs.

Order Entry Benchmark

The best way to learn Swingbench is to jump in and execute one of its benchmark runs. Swingbench includes an Order Entry application for one of its tests, simulating users placing orders for products not that much different than many shopping web sites prevalent on the Internet today. Before the benchmark can be taken, the database administrator needs to create some schema objects. Swingbench includes the *oewizard* utility in the *bin* directory to create the tables, indexes, and stored procedures that will be used. Upon launching the Order Entry installation wizard, the database administrator should see a screen similar to the following.

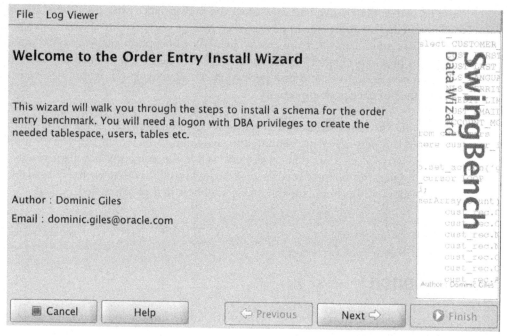

Figure 10.1 OE Install Wizard

After pressing the Next button, the benchmark version is defined. Unless there is a need to deviate, the best practice would be to use the latest and greatest version.

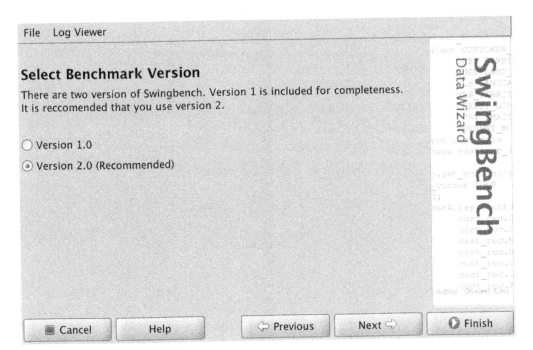

Figure 10.2 OE Wizard Benchmark Version

After pressing the Next button, there are choices to either create or to drop the Order Entry schema. Since this is the first run, the only sensible option is to create the schema.

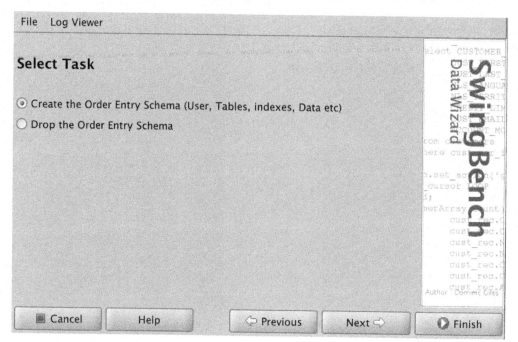

Figure 10.3 OE Wizard Task Selection

After pressing the Next button, the database details can be provided. Since this is an Oracle 12c RAC database, the connection string will use the SCAN VIP and a database service name. A user with the *dba* role will need to be provided.

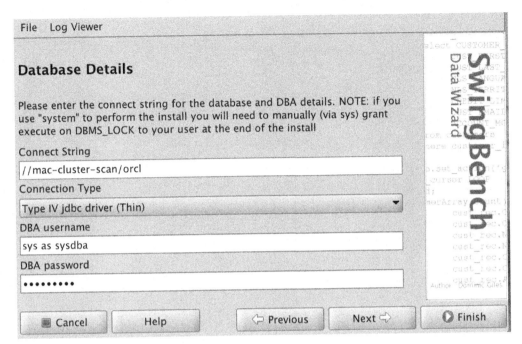

Figure 10.4 OE Wizard Database Details

After pressing the Next button, the benchmark schema's username and password can be provided. In the screenshots below, the default values for the Swingbench Order Entry (SOE) schema are used. The database administrator should provide a tablespace to hold the schema's segments.

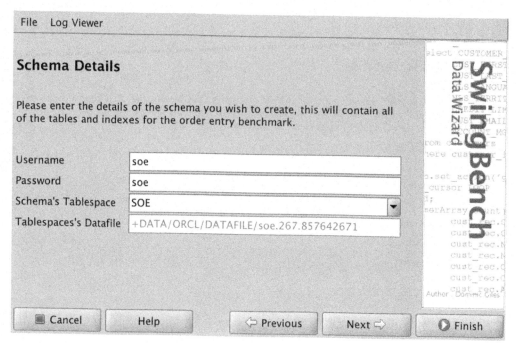

Figure 10.5 OE Wizard Schema Details

After pressing the Next button, the database administrator can specify certain options to be used including compression, partitioning, and the tablespace type.

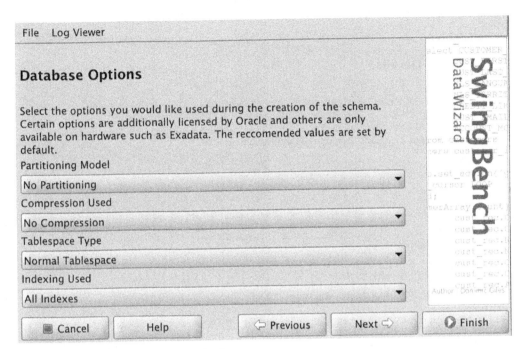

Figure 10.6 OE Wizard Database Options

After pressing the Next button, the database administrator can define the Swingbench sizing details. As the screen says, a smaller size will lead to a more CPU-intensive test while a large size will lead to a more I/O-intensive test. No matter which size is chosen, the bottom of the screen will show the required data and temporary tablespace sizes. It is important to note that no matter which size is chosen for a baseline test, the same size should be used for the post-change benchmark run so that the test size does not skew the results.

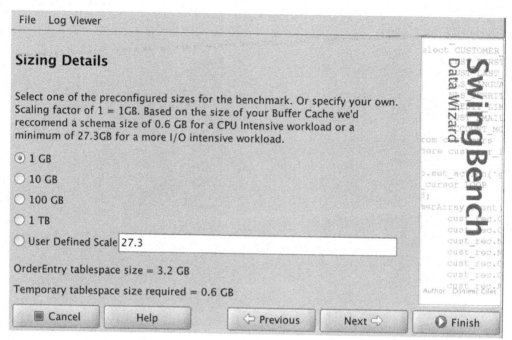

Figure 10.7 OE Wizard Sizing Details

After pressing the Next button, the database administrator can define the degree of parallelism used to create indexes and compute statistics when setting up the schema.

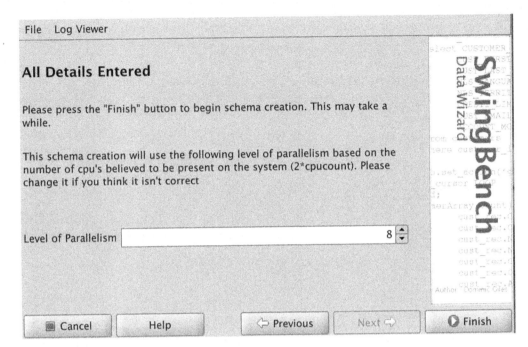

Figure 10.8 OE Wizard Parallelism

At this point, the database administrator can press the Finish button to start the wizard. A progress screen will be displayed, similar to the following.

Clear Events		
Type	Description	Time
ℹ	Inserting data into table ADDRESSES_562498	22:40:04
ℹ	Inserting data into table ADDRESSES_749997	22:40:04
ℹ	Inserting data into table ADDRESSES_187500	22:40:04
ℹ	Inserting data into table PRODUCT_INFORMATION	22:40:04
ℹ	Inserting data into table INVENTORIES	22:40:04
ℹ	Inserting data into table CUSTOMERS_874994	22:40:04
ℹ	Inserting data into table CUSTOMERS_499997	22:40:04
ℹ	Inserting data into table CUSTOMERS_624996	22:40:04
ℹ	Inserting data into table CUSTOMERS_1	22:40:04
ℹ	Inserting data into table CUSTOMERS_125000	22:40:04
ℹ	Inserting data into table CUSTOMERS_374998	22:40:04

Save to File

Figure 10.9 OE Wizard Progress Window

After a short period of time, the wizard will display the screen below that signifies the end of the schema creation.

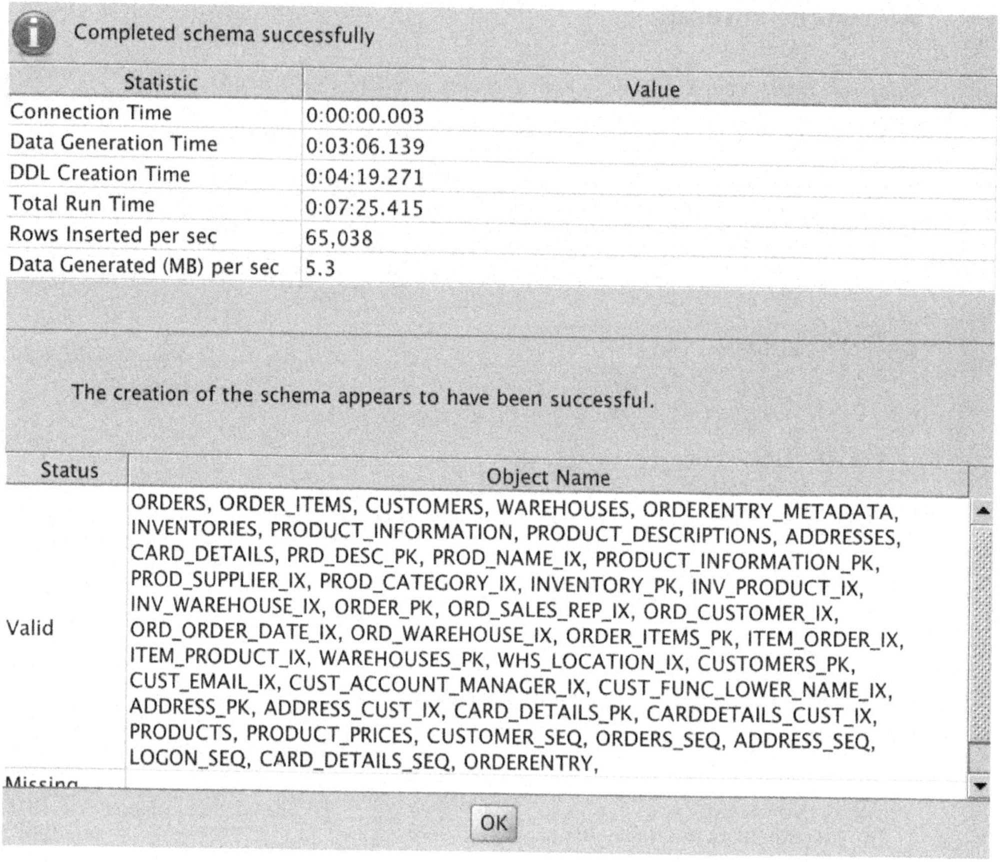

Statistic	Value
Connection Time	0:00:00.003
Data Generation Time	0:03:06.139
DDL Creation Time	0:04:19.271
Total Run Time	0:07:25.415
Rows Inserted per sec	65,038
Data Generated (MB) per sec	5.3

Completed schema successfully

The creation of the schema appears to have been successful.

Status	Object Name
Valid	ORDERS, ORDER_ITEMS, CUSTOMERS, WAREHOUSES, ORDERENTRY_METADATA, INVENTORIES, PRODUCT_INFORMATION, PRODUCT_DESCRIPTIONS, ADDRESSES, CARD_DETAILS, PRD_DESC_PK, PROD_NAME_IX, PRODUCT_INFORMATION_PK, PROD_SUPPLIER_IX, PROD_CATEGORY_IX, INVENTORY_PK, INV_PRODUCT_IX, INV_WAREHOUSE_IX, ORDER_PK, ORD_SALES_REP_IX, ORD_CUSTOMER_IX, ORD_ORDER_DATE_IX, ORD_WAREHOUSE_IX, ORDER_ITEMS_PK, ITEM_ORDER_IX, ITEM_PRODUCT_IX, WAREHOUSES_PK, WHS_LOCATION_IX, CUSTOMERS_PK, CUST_EMAIL_IX, CUST_ACCOUNT_MANAGER_IX, CUST_FUNC_LOWER_NAME_IX, ADDRESS_PK, ADDRESS_CUST_IX, CARD_DETAILS_PK, CARDDETAILS_CUST_IX, PRODUCTS, PRODUCT_PRICES, CUSTOMER_SEQ, ORDERS_SEQ, ADDRESS_SEQ, LOGON_SEQ, CARD_DETAILS_SEQ, ORDERENTRY,
Missing	

OK

Figure 10.10 OE Wizard Completion

At this point, the Swingbench tool is ready for its first run. To start the utility, run the *swingbench* executable from the *bin* directory. The top left section of the Swingbench screen contains the connection details. The Order Entry schema username and password is entered. In the Connection String field, enter "*//scan-vip//service_name*". The SCAN VIP is only available in Oracle 11gR2 and higher. With the SCAN VIP, Swingbench will be able to connect to all instances running the named service. If the database administrator is testing an earlier Oracle version, then the Swingbench cluster coordinator may need to be used, a feature that will be discussed later in this chapter. An alternative to the SCAN VIP and the cluster coordinator is to use the Oracle OCI driver and an alias in the *tnsnames.ora* configuration file that defines the connection to an Oracle RAC database.

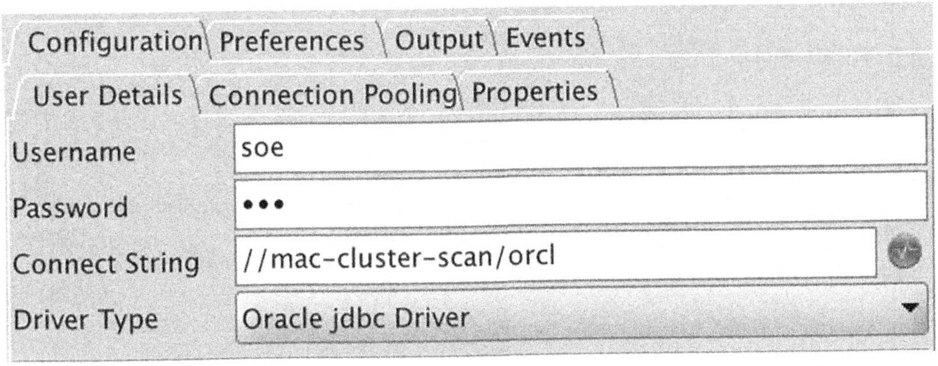

Figure 10.11 Swingbench Connection Details

Below the connection details is a section to automate AWR snapshots. It is always a good idea to collect snapshots at the start and end. With AWR snapshots, the database administrator can take a deep dive in to the benchmark performance. Even though the screen says for "10g/11g only", the snapshots work in Oracle 12c as well. The database administrator will need to enter a user with the *dba* role in this section.

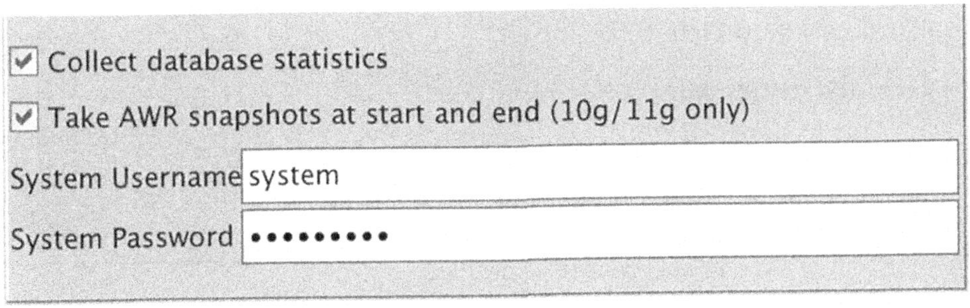

Figure 10.12 Swingbench AWR Snapshots

Continuing down the left side of the screen is the section on defining the load parameters. Here is where the database administrator denotes the number of users in the test and the benchmark runtime.

Load \ Environment Variables \ Distributed Controls \	
Number of Users	40
Min. Inter Delay Between Transactions (ms)	0
Max. Inter Delay Between Transactions (ms)	0
Min. Intra Delay Between Transactions (ms)	1,000
Max. Intra Delay Between Transactions (ms)	5,000
Logon Delay (milliseconds)	1
Logon Group	1
Wait Till All Sessions Log On	true
Logoff Post Transaction	false
Tx. per Reconnect	0
Benchmark Run Time (hh:min)	0	20
Record Statistics After (hh:min)	0	0
Stop Recording After (hh:min)	0	0

Figure 10.13 Swingbench Load Parameters

The example above will simulate 40 user with a runtime of 20 minutes. The test is now set up and ready to run. To start the test, press the green play button near the top left of the screen.

Figure 10.14 Swingbench Start

When the benchmark test is running, the Overview Chart provides nice information on the overall progress. This chart includes the number of transactions per minute and response time.

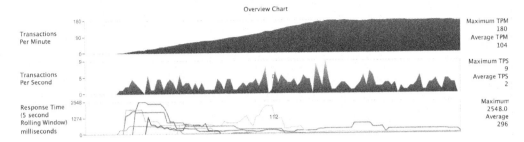

Figure 10.15 Swingbench Overview Chart

Above the Overview Chart is a pull down menu to select the Chart Type. The database administrator can choose the Transactions Per Minute (TPM) chart, a sample of which can be seen below.

Transactions Per Minute

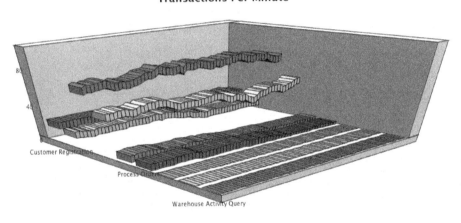

Figure 10.16 Swingbench TPM Chart

Another option is a chart that shows the Data Manipulation Language Operations Per Minute. This chart type is shown in the screen shot below.

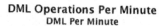

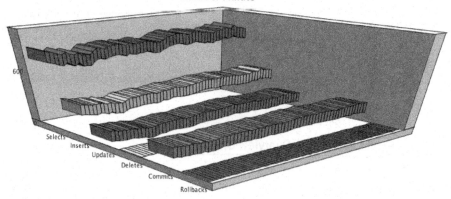

Figure 10.17 Swingbench DML Chart

At the completion of the load test, the Output tab contains an XML document with the test results.

```xml
<?xml version="1.0" encoding="UTF-8" standalone="no"?>
<Results xmlns="http://www.dominicgiles.com/swingbench">
    <Overview>
        <BenchmarkName>"Order Entry (PLSQL) V2"</BenchmarkName>
        <Comment>""</Comment>
        <TimeOfRun>Sep 28, 2014 11:37:40 PM</TimeOfRun>
        <TotalRunTime>0:20:46</TotalRunTime>
        <TotalLogonTime>0:00:02</TotalLogonTime>
        <TotalCompletedTransactions>3244</TotalCompletedTransactions>
        <TotalFailedTransactions>0</TotalFailedTransactions>
        <AverageTransactionsPerSecond>2.6</AverageTransactionsPerSecond>
        <MaximumTransactionRate>181</MaximumTransactionRate>
    </Overview>
```

The XML file concludes with wait events and database statistics for the load test. This information can be useful when comparing a post-change benchmark to the baseline results. The database administrator can get an idea of exactly where the change affected the outcome.

At this point, the Order Entry benchmark test from Swingbench is complete. The reader should now have a good idea on how to use Swingbench to perform simple benchmark testing for their system. Just remember that for Oracle RAC databases, use the SCAN VIP when connecting to the service so that the load is spread among all instances that support the service.

Calling Circle Benchmark

In addition to the Order Entry benchmark, Swingbench includes another load generator. The Calling Circle (CC) benchmark simulates a telecommunications company that lets its customers create a circle of friends and family members. When the customer calls someone in their circle, the call does not count against their plan. This benchmark simulates customers managing their Calling Circle.

Just like the OE benchmark, the database administrator needs to create a schema in advance. The *ccwizard* utility in the Swingbench *bin* directory is used to create the schema and populate it with data. It should be noted that the CC benchmark needs fresh data for each run. The *ccwizard* utility includes an option to generate new data between runs as can be seen below.

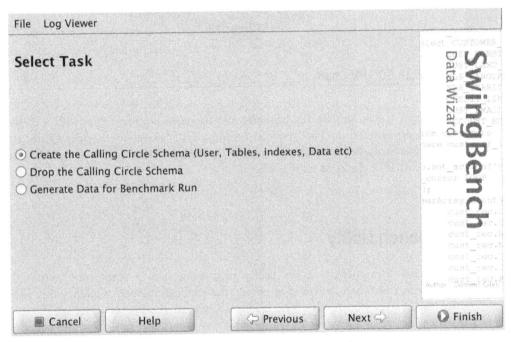

Figure 10.18 CC Wizard Task Selection

Aside from the screen above, the *ccwizard* utility is very similar to the *oewizard* tool.

The default username is "cc" instead of "soe". Aside from using a different username and password, the database administrator will use Swingbench the same way as for the OE load generation. When launching Swingbench, connect with the CC username and the utility will automatically perform the Calling Circle benchmark. Notice that

---

the Transactions Per Minute chart has different labels on the bottom axis compared to the OE load generation.

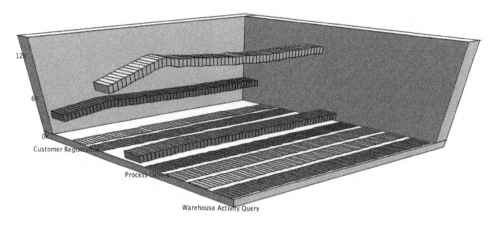

Figure 10.19 CC TPM Chart

The Calling Circle benchmark provides the database administrator with a different type of load generation. This test can be more CPU-intensive that the Order Entry benchmark. Swingbench can automatically detect the benchmark type by the schema objects owned by the connected user.

Charbench Utility

The regular Swingbench shows pretty pictures and is a great tool to use. One downside is that when launched remotely, the tool can introduce latency that has the potential to skew the results. The *charbench* utility in the *bin* directory eliminates the potential for result skewing and is a great way to programmatically run the benchmark for repeatable tests.

The following example shows the *charbench* utility in action. The connection string (-cs) is defined along with the userid (-u) and password (-p). Remember that connecting as the *soe* or *cc* user will run that appropriately named benchmark. This test will simulate forty concurrent users (-uc) and have a runtime of 20 minutes (-rt). The XML results (-r) will be written to the indicated file.

```
localhost$ ./charbench -cs //mac-cluster-scan/orcl -u soe -p soe -r
soe.results.txt -uc 40 -rt 20
Author   :   Dominic Giles
Version  :   2.5.0.932

Results will be written to soe.results.xml.
Hit Return to Terminate Run...

Time          Users   TPM     TPS

10:23:28 AM     40     4397    63
Completed Run.
```

Some database administrators will want to run the benchmark ten times. When running the same benchmark multiple times, the highest and lowest TPM results are often eliminated and the remaining results will be averaged. The *charbench* utility can be used similar to the following to automate the benchmark runs

```
./charbench -cs //mac-cluster-scan/orcl -u soe -p soe -r soe.results01.txt -
uc 40 -rt 20
./charbench -cs //mac-cluster-scan/orcl -u soe -p soe -r soe.results02.txt -
uc 40 -rt 20
./charbench -cs //mac-cluster-scan/orcl -u soe -p soe -r soe.results03.txt -
uc 40 -rt 20
./charbench -cs //mac-cluster-scan/orcl -u soe -p soe -r soe.results04.txt -
uc 40 -rt 20
./charbench -cs //mac-cluster-scan/orcl -u soe -p soe -r soe.results05.txt -
uc 40 -rt 20
./charbench -cs //mac-cluster-scan/orcl -u soe -p soe -r soe.results06.txt -
uc 40 -rt 20
./charbench -cs //mac-cluster-scan/orcl -u soe -p soe -r soe.results07.txt -
uc 40 -rt 20
./charbench -cs //mac-cluster-scan/orcl -u soe -p soe -r soe.results08.txt -
uc 40 -rt 20
./charbench -cs //mac-cluster-scan/orcl -u soe -p soe -r soe.results09.txt -
uc 40 -rt 20
./charbench -cs //mac-cluster-scan/orcl -u soe -p soe -r soe.results10.txt -
uc 40 -rt 20
```

If the commands are placed in a script, this benchmark activity becomes a simple push-button operation. You can start the script and come back tomorrow to collate the results. Using the *charbench* utility in this manner greatly simplifies the database administrator's work.

Another common benchmark activity is to see how the system handles an increasing number of concurrent users. At some point, the system will become saturated. The *charbench* utility can be used again to determine the number of concurrent users the system can handle before exhibiting a degradation of performance Notice in the example below that the number of users increases with each successive execution of the benchmark load, starting with 200 users on up to 2000 users.

```
./charbench -cs //mac-cluster-scan/orcl -u soe -p soe -r soe.results01.txt -
uc 200 -rt 20
./charbench -cs //mac-cluster-scan/orcl -u soe -p soe -r soe.results02.txt -
uc 400 -rt 20
./charbench -cs //mac-cluster-scan/orcl -u soe -p soe -r soe.results03.txt -
uc 600 -rt 20
./charbench -cs //mac-cluster-scan/orcl -u soe -p soe -r soe.results04.txt -
uc 800 -rt 20
./charbench -cs //mac-cluster-scan/orcl -u soe -p soe -r soe.results05.txt -
uc 1000 -rt 20
./charbench -cs //mac-cluster-scan/orcl -u soe -p soe -r soe.results06.txt -
uc 1200 -rt 20
./charbench -cs //mac-cluster-scan/orcl -u soe -p soe -r soe.results07.txt -
uc 1400 -rt 20
./charbench -cs //mac-cluster-scan/orcl -u soe -p soe -r soe.results08.txt -
uc 1600 -rt 20
./charbench -cs //mac-cluster-scan/orcl -u soe -p soe -r soe.results09.txt -
uc 1800 -rt 20
./charbench -cs //mac-cluster-scan/orcl -u soe -p soe -r soe.results10.txt -
uc 2000 -rt 20
```

The *charbench* utility helps the database administrator save time with its ability to script multiple executions together. Remember that when running the Calling Circle utility, the data needs to be refreshed before each run. The *ccwizard* utility can be run in command-line mode as well and would be run before each call to the *charbench* tool.

Clusteroverview for RAC

The Swingbench test harness was written before the release of Oracle 11gR2, which introduced the SCAN Listeners. For Oracle RAC testing, the database administrator could denote a traditional Virtual IP address in the connect string, but the connections would not be spread among multiple instances. If the database administrator is testing Oracle 11gR2 and higher, the SCAN Listener VIP can be specified which will ensure all instances handling the service will receive connections. The benchmark will spread out the load over the instances, which is precisely what the benchmark should be doing since this is an Oracle RAC database.

Since Swingbench was created before Oracle 11gR2 existed, a program was created called the *Clusteroverview* utility to help benchmark Oracle RAC systems. First, a coordinator needs to be started that will govern the benchmark activity. Next, one load generator per instance will be started. The load generators will be pointed to the coordinator. Finally, the *Clusteroverview* utility will be started to monitor the benchmark activity across the cluster.

Before the coordinator and load generators can be started, the database administrator needs to define connections to the instances in the *clusteroverview.xml* configuration file in the *bin* directory. The following shows the configuration for the two-instance test in this chapter to nodes *host01* and *host02*, which run instances *orcl1* and *orcl2* respectively. The rest of the XML file can remain at the default settings if desired.

```
<MonitoredNodes>
    <MonitoredNode>
      <GroupId>RAC1</GroupId>
      <DisplayName>RAC_host01</DisplayName>
      <ConnectString>host01:1521:orcl1</ConnectString>
    </MonitoredNode>
    <MonitoredNode>
      <GroupId>RAC2</GroupId>
      <DisplayName>RAC_host02</DisplayName>
      <ConnectString>host02:1521:orcl2</ConnectString>
    </MonitoredNode>
    <DBAUsername>system</DBAUsername>
    <DBAPassword>manager</DBAPassword>
    <DBADriverType>thin</DBADriverType>
  </MonitoredNodes>
```

With the configuration file defined correctly, the coordinator is started.

```
localhost$ ./coordinator -g
```

The –g parameter starts the coordinator in graphical mode. The utility will look similar to the following.

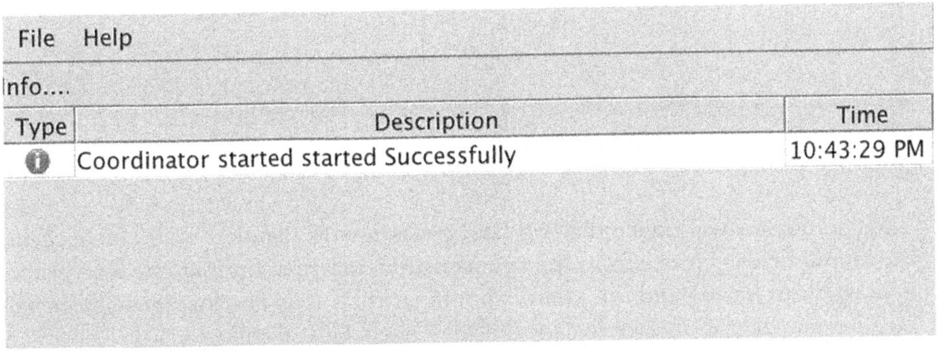

File	Help		
Info....			
Type	Description		Time
ⓘ	Coordinator started started Successfully		10:43:29 PM

Figure 10.20 Swingbench Coordinator

Next, the load generators will be started. There will be one load generator for each instance. In this section, the *minibench* utility will be used for the load generator, as it is more lightweight that Swingbench. The *minibench* utility will need the group ids specified in the *clusteroverview.xml* configuration file as well as the machine running the coordinator, which will be the local host in this example. The '&' symbol starts the utility in the background.

```
localhost$ ./minibench -g RAC1 -cs //host01/orcl1 -co localhost &
[1] 8779
localhost $ Running under Mac OS X... setting platform sepecific L&F
Started Minibench, Version 2.5.0.932. Using config file swingconfig.xml

localhost $ ./minibench -g RAC2 -cs //host02/orcl2 -co localhost &
[2] 8785
localhost $ Running under Mac OS X... setting platform sepecific L&F
Started Minibench, Version 2.5.0.932. Using config file swingconfig.xml
```

The result will be two minibench windows similar to the following.

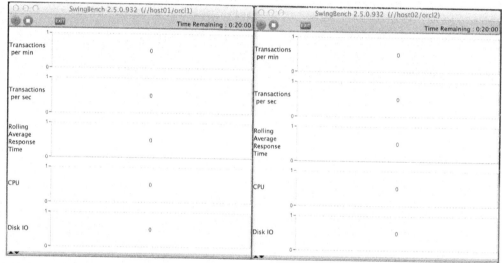

Figure 10.21 Minibench Windows

The coordinator will notice the two load generators as denoted by the new clients in the output below. Notice from the connect string information that one load generator is pointing to host01 and the other is pointing to host02. The load generators will be creating a workload on each instance of the Oracle RAC database.

Type	Description	Time
ⓘ	Added new client : id = 1 : connect string = //host02/orcl2	2:22:07 PM
ⓘ	Added new client : id = 0 : connect string = //host01/orcl1	2:21:30 PM
ⓘ	Coordinator started started Successfully	2:21:03 PM

File   Help

Connected clients = 2

Figure 10.22 Swingbench Coordinator With Loads

The database administrator is now ready to start the Clusteroverview tool.

```
localhost$ ./clusteroverview
```

The top left of the utility will show the load generators. Click on one of them and press the green "play" button to start the load on that instance. Then click on the next load generator and press the start button. Unfortunately, each load generator will need to be manually started in this fashion.

▶ 📊 ⬤ ⚙ ☑ Start In Order?

Databases \ Load Generators \ Events \

Database Name	Connect String	Status	TPM
RAC1_host01	host01:1521:orcl1	STOPPED	0
RAC2_host02	host02:1521:orcl2	STOPPED	0

Figure 10.23 Clusteroverview Start Load

Both load generators will show as status of *running*. The TPM column will provide the Transactions Per Minute throughput from each load generator.

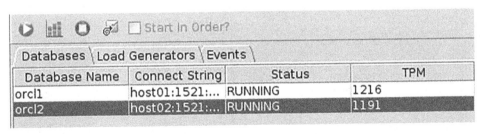

▶ 📊 ⬤ ⚙ ☐ Start In Order?

Databases \ Load Generators \ Events \

Database Name	Connect String	Status	TPM
orcl1	host01:1521:...	RUNNING	1216
orcl2	host02:1521:...	RUNNING	1191

Figure 10.24 Clusteroverview Load Running

Swingbench

The Oracle RAC database is now under load from multiple generators, one for each instance participating in the benchmark activity. The Clusteroverview shows fancy graphs indicating the load. The Transactions Per Minute graph shows each instance. The total TMP metric at the bottom right is the total of all participating instances.

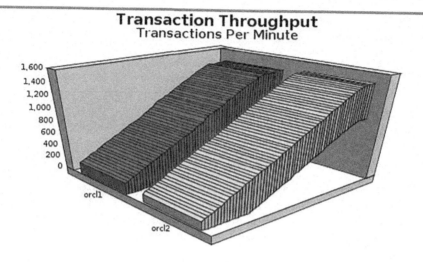

Transactions Per Minute : 2887

Figure 10.25 Clusteroverview TPM Chart

The two *minibench* screens should also show a load for each instance.

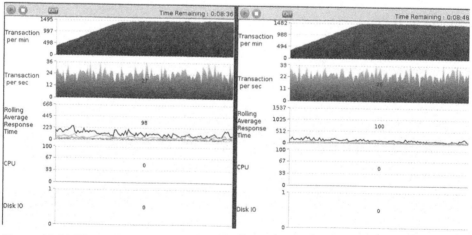

Figure 10.26 Minibench Graphs

Oracle RAC Performance Tuning

The Clusteroverview utility does not provide any ability to take AWR snapshots like Swingbench does. The database administrator will need to manually take the snapshots if they are needed.

Swingbench Summary

This chapter has shown many facets of Swingbench and how it can be used to benchmark Oracle RAC database systems. Database administrators looking to test older RAC deployments may want to use the Clusteroverview tool. Oracle RAC deployments of 11gR2 and higher now have the SCAN Listener which makes using Swingbench very easy. For a more push-button approach, the database administrator may choose to use the command-line based charbench utility for ease of scripting.

HammerDB

HammerDB is an open source benchmark utility for database systems. In the beginning, this tool went by the name HammerOra but it can now be used on other database platforms as well, hence the more generic name. HammerDB can be found at http://hammerora.sourceforge.net for the download files and the documentation. Installation is as easy as using an unzip utility to extract the contents.

TPC-C Benchmark

The easiest way to see HammerDB in action is to run the Transaction Performance Processing Council TPC-C benchmark, which simulates Online Transaction Processing (OLTP) order entry system, very similar to the Swingbench OE test. In the HammerDB unzip directory, run the *hammerdb.tcl* utility to start the program. After the program starts, expand the TPC-C folder under the Oracle heading, similar to the following.

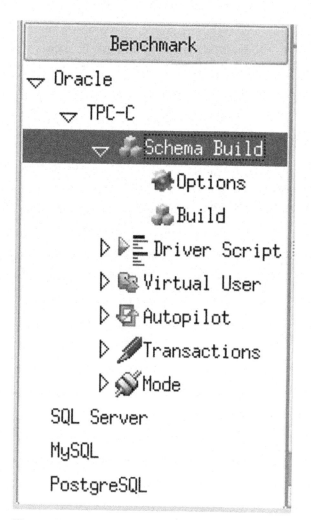

Figure 10.27 HammerDB TPC-C Options

Before the test can begin, the schema for the benchmark tool needs to be created. The database administrator can double click on the Options under the Schema Build section. This will bring up a dialog box to define the service name, dba user and password, the schema owner (tpcc) user and password, and a tablespace name, as seen in the next example. Note that the tablespace must previously exist which means the database administrator must manually pre-create it.

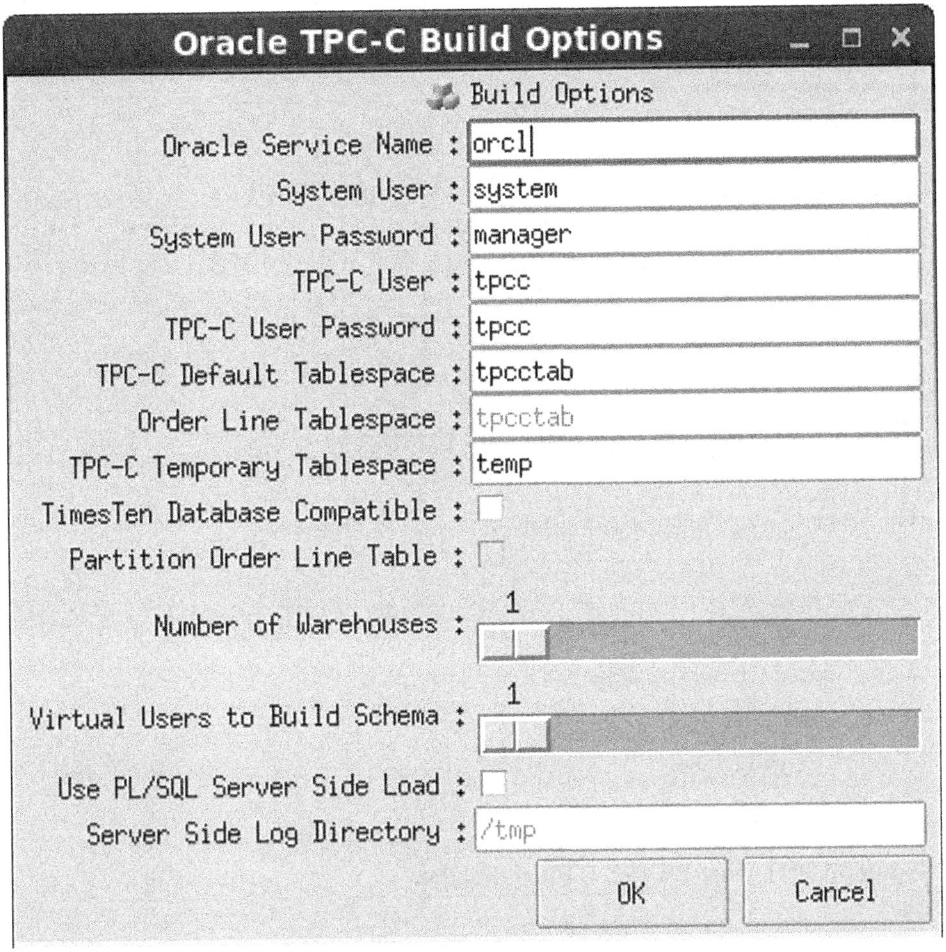

Figure 10.28 HammerDB TPC-C Build Options

Press OK to accept the build options. The database administrator will then need to double click on the Build item to begin the schema creation. Confirmation is needed before continuing, as seen below.

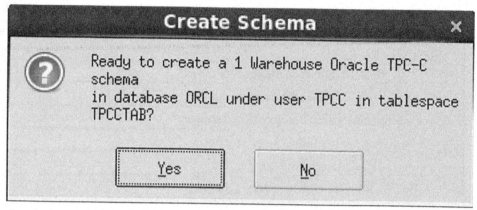

Figure 10.29 HammerDB TPC-C Build Confirmation

The Virtual User Output window shows the build progress.

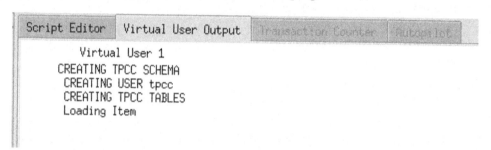

Figure 10.30 HammerDB TPC-C Build Creation

The schema creation will be complete when pane below the Virtual User Output window shows a value of '1' under the Complete column and the Status column shows a green check mark.

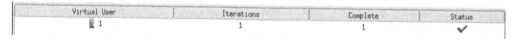

Figure 10.31 HammerDB TPC-C Build Complete

When complete, the database administrator will need to close the virtual user connection by pressing the red stop light icon in the toolbar, tenth icon from the left in the image below.

Figure 10.32 HammerDB Toolbar

Now that the test schema has been created, HammerDB needs a script to drive the benchmark test. The database administrator needs to open the Driver Script folder, as seen below.

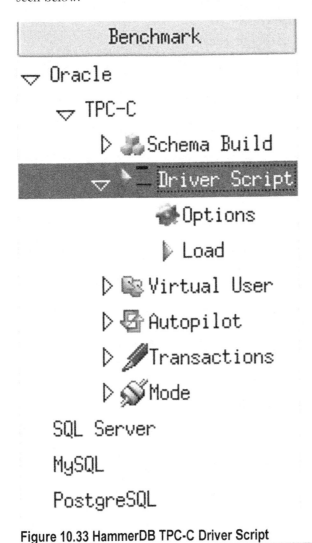

Figure 10.33 HammerDB TPC-C Driver Script

Double-clicking on the Options item lets the database administrator configure the options used to direct the test. For now, the default options are sufficient. Notice that the Driver Options section denotes a total number of transactions per user that will be executed.

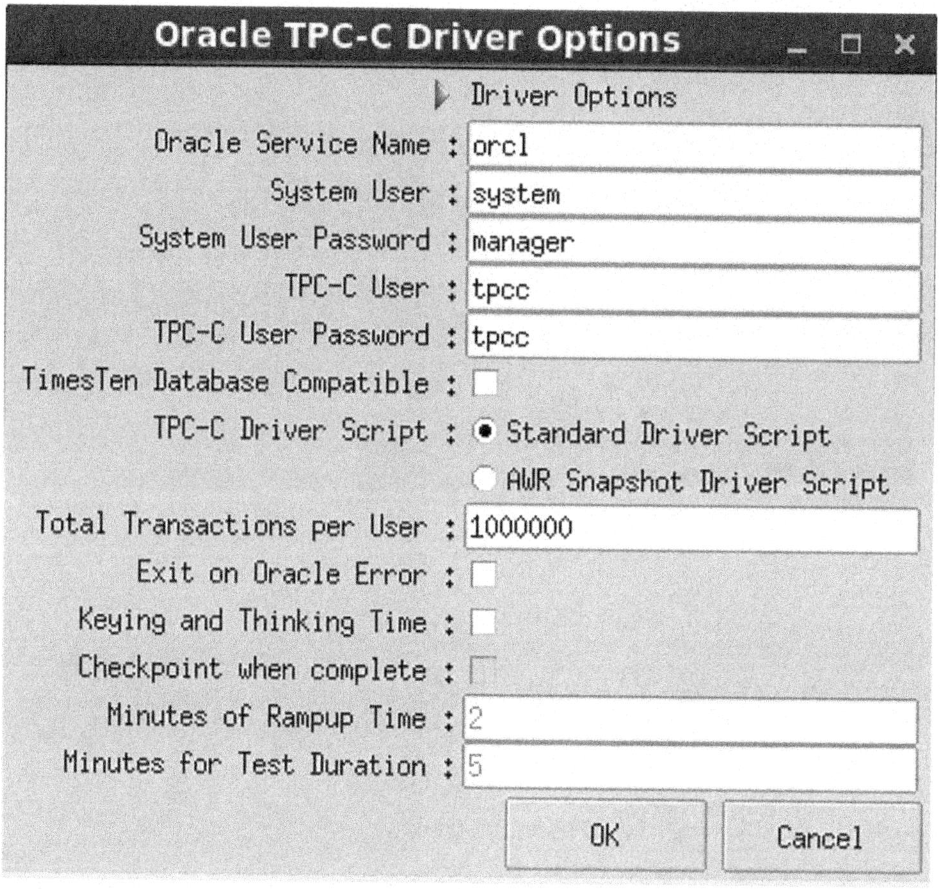

```
┌─────────────────────────────────────────────────────────────┐
│  Oracle TPC-C Driver Options              _  □  ✕            │
├─────────────────────────────────────────────────────────────┤
│                          ▶ Driver Options                    │
│          Oracle Service Name : │orcl                       │ │
│                  System User : │system                     │ │
│         System User Password : │manager                    │ │
│                   TPC-C User : │tpcc                       │ │
│          TPC-C User Password : │tpcc                       │ │
│   TimesTen Database Compatible : ☐                          │
│            TPC-C Driver Script : ⦿ Standard Driver Script    │
│                                  ○ AWR Snapshot Driver Script│
│     Total Transactions per User : │1000000                 │ │
│            Exit on Oracle Error : ☐                          │
│       Keying and Thinking Time : ☐                           │
│       Checkpoint when complete : ☐                           │
│          Minutes of Rampup Time : │2                       │ │
│       Minutes for Test Duration : │5                       │ │
│                          ┌──────────┐      ┌──────────┐     │
│                          │    OK    │      │  Cancel  │     │
│                          └──────────┘      └──────────┘     │
└─────────────────────────────────────────────────────────────┘
```

Figure 10.34 HammerDB TPC-C Driver Options

Next, the database administrator double-clicks on the Load item to place the driver script in the Script Editor window, as seen below.

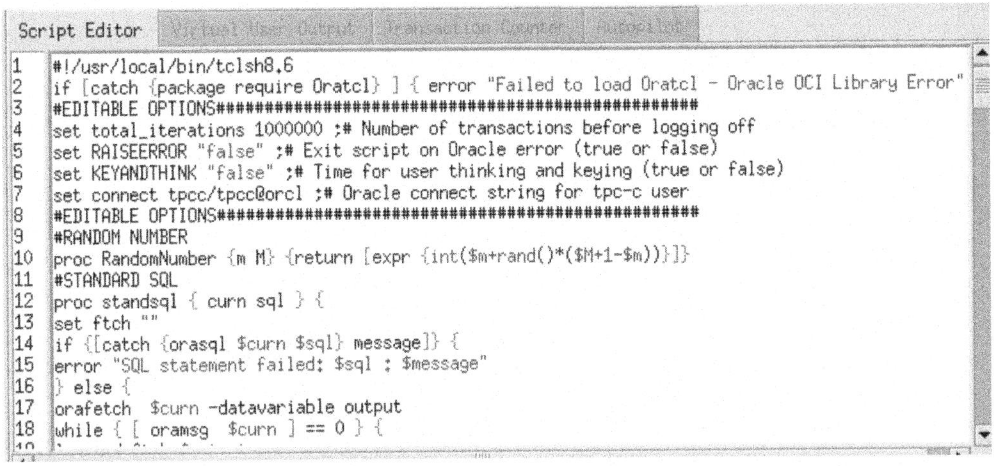

```
#!/usr/local/bin/tclsh8.6
if [catch {package require Oratcl} ] { error "Failed to load Oratcl - Oracle OCI Library Error"
#EDITABLE OPTIONS##################################################
set total_iterations 1000000 ;# Number of transactions before logging off
set RAISEERROR "false" ;# Exit script on Oracle error (true or false)
set KEYANDTHINK "false" ;# Time for user thinking and keying (true or false)
set connect tpcc/tpcc@orcl ;# Oracle connect string for tpc-c user
#EDITABLE OPTIONS##################################################
#RANDOM NUMBER
proc RandomNumber {m M} {return [expr {int($m+rand()*($M+1-$m))}]}
#STANDARD SQL
proc standsql { curn sql } {
set ftch ""
if {[catch {orasql $curn $sql} message]} {
error "SQL statement failed: $sql : $message"
} else {
orafetch  $curn -datavariable output
while { [ oramsg  $curn ] == 0 } {
```

Figure 10.35 HammerDB TPC-C Driver Script

At this point, the database administrator has created the database schema and created the script to define the benchmark tests. Next, the virtual users need to be defined. The database administrator needs to open the Virtual Users folder, similar to the following.

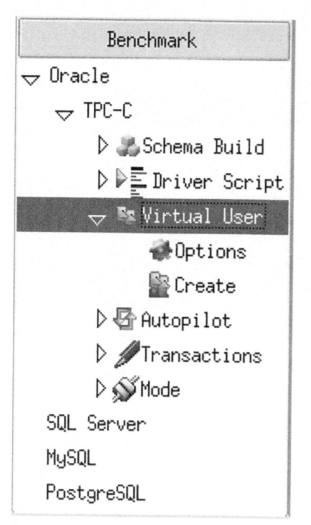

Figure 10.36 HammerDB TPC-C Virtual Users

Double-clicking on the Options item brings up a dialog box where the database administrator can define the number of virtual users to participate in the test. In the example below, forty users have been defined.

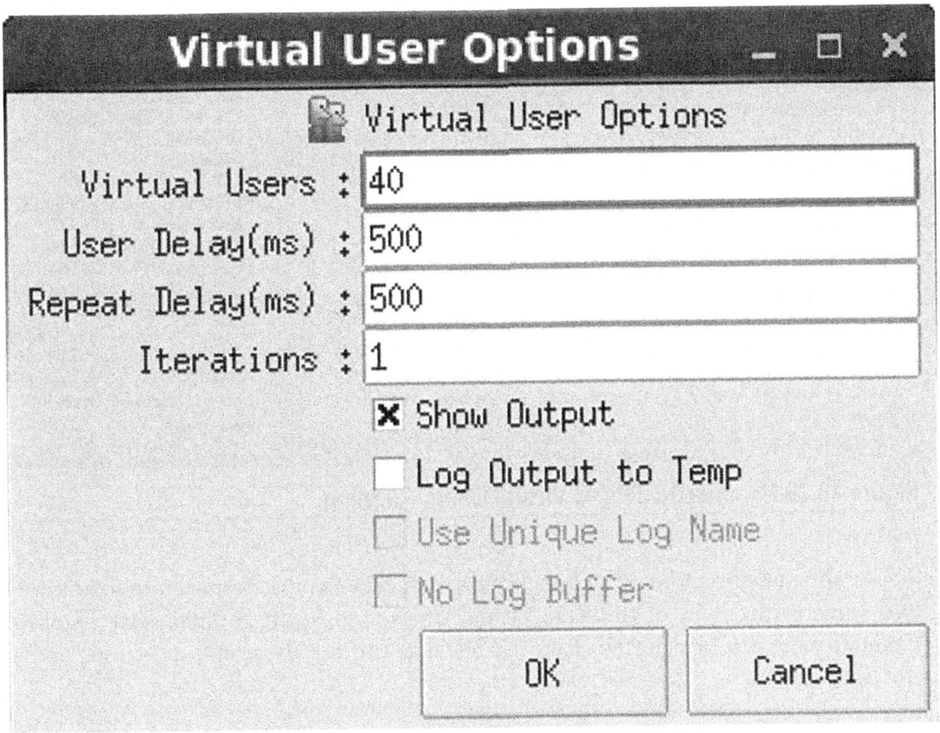

Figure 10.37 HammerDB TPC-C Virtual User Options

Next, the database administrator double-clicks on the Create item to create the virtual users. The virtual users will be shown in the tool as shown below. They will be idle.

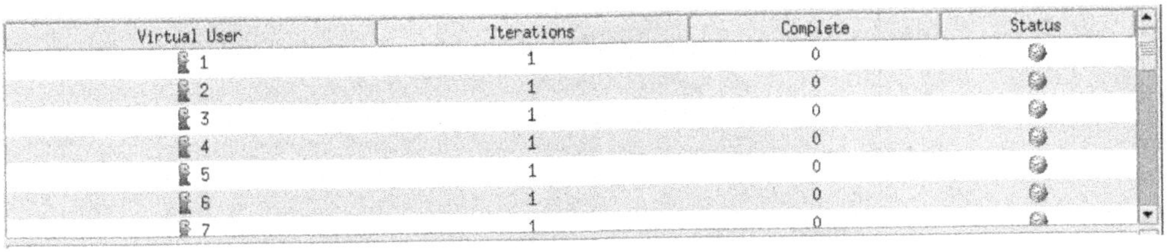

Virtual User	Iterations	Complete	Status
1	1	0	
2	1	0	
3	1	0	
4	1	0	
5	1	0	
6	1	0	
7	1	0	

Figure 10.38 HammerDB TPC-C Virtual Users

To begin the test, the database administrator will press the Run Virtual Users button (green arrow), which is immediately to the right of the Destroy Virtual Users button used after creating the schema. The Virtual User Output pane will show the work being done by the users.

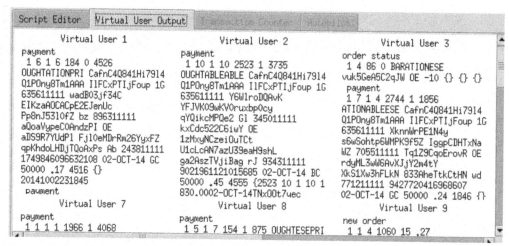

Figure 10.39 HammerDB TPC-C Virtual Users Running

To see the performance of the benchmark test, click on the Transaction Counter icon, two spots to the right of the Run Virtual Users icon in the toolbar. The Transaction Counter pane can be selected. Run the test again to see the graph in action, similar to the following.

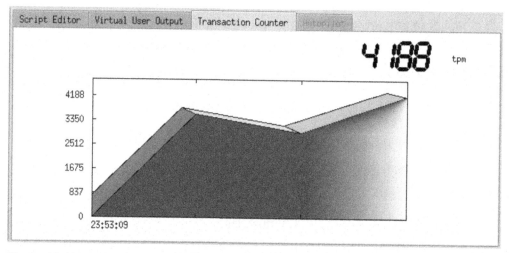

Figure 10.40 HammerDB TPC-C Transaction Counter

Unfortunately, other than the Transaction Counter graph, HammerDB does not provide metrics for the database administrator to use, which is the entire point of a benchmark anyway. The Transaction Counter graph provides a pretty picture to look

Oracle RAC Performance Tuning

at but for real use, the database administrator will want to leverage the AWR driver script in the next section.

AWR Driver Script

The standard driver script generated the load for The TPC-C benchmark in the previous section. The benchmark completed when each virtual user completed a pre-defined number of transactions. When using the AWR driver script, the database administrator can choose the benchmark runtime. In HammerDB, the database administrator will choose the Driver Options just as before. This time, the AWR Snapshot Driver Script option is chosen. The Minutes for Test Duration is set for five minutes, as seen below.

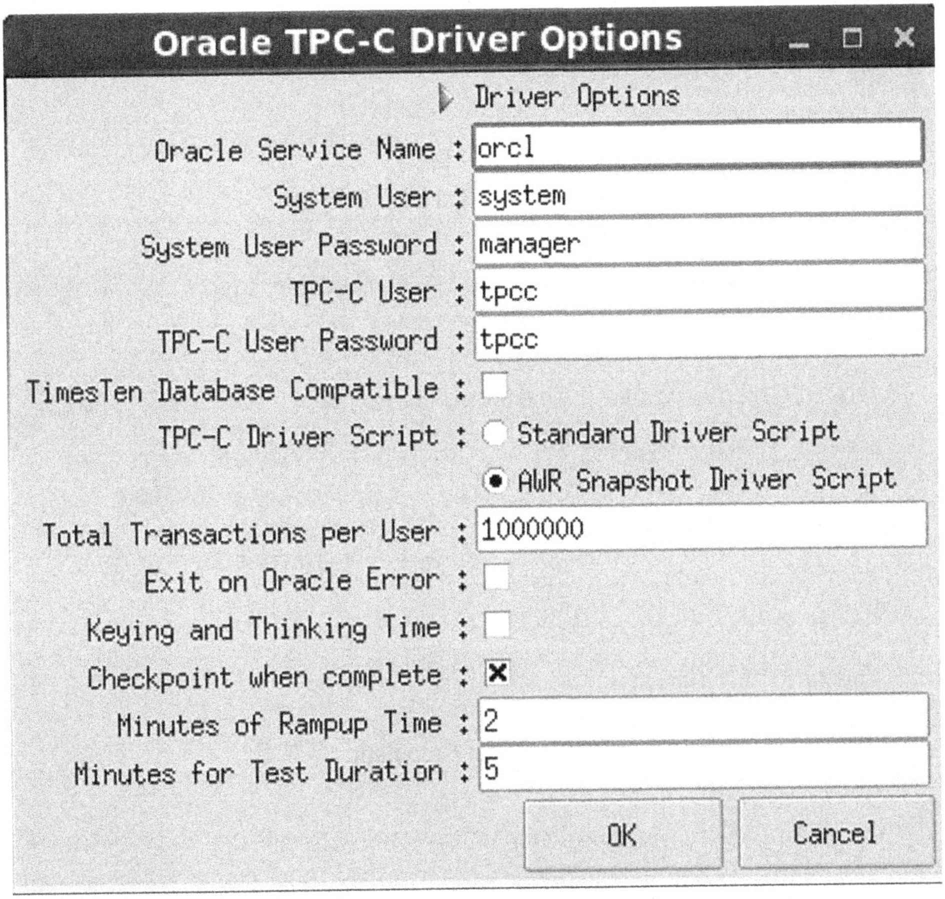

Figure 10.41 HammerDB TPC-C AWR Driver Options

Now that the options are defined, the database administrator loads the driver script, sets up the virtual users, and starts the benchmark run, just as was done in the initial TPC-C example.

The output from the virtual users looks different when running the AWR driver script. For starters, each virtual user has the output suppressed. Next, the first virtual user serves as the master and takes the AWR snapshots.

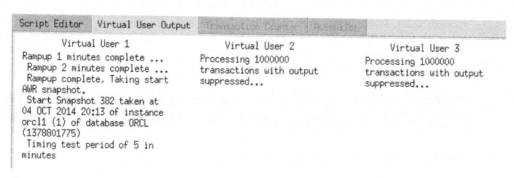

Figure 10.42 HammerDB AWR Driver Virtual User Output

When the benchmark is complete, the Virtual User 1 output shows the AWR snapshot identifiers as well as the TPM high water mark.

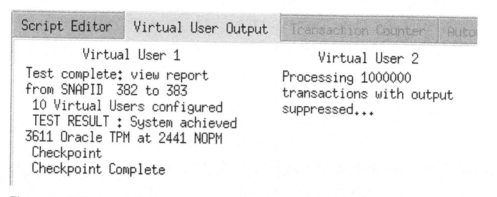

Figure 10.43 HammerDB AWR Driver Test Complete

At this point, you can generate the AWR report. The Load Profile section of the report is shown below. The output shows that 60.2 transactions were executed per second during the benchmark execution.

```
Load Profile                      Per Second    Per Transaction  Per Exec  Per Call
~~~~~~~~~~~~~~~                    -----------   ---------------  --------  ---------
           DB Time(s):                4.9                 0.1      0.00       0.10
            DB CPU(s):                0.4                 0.0      0.00       0.01
    Background CPU(s):                0.3                 0.0      0.00       0.00
     Redo size (bytes):         366,506.3             6,089.9
  Logical read (blocks):          5,585.5                92.8
        Block changes:            2,038.1                33.9
  Physical read (blocks):            10.9                 0.2
 Physical write (blocks):            35.8                 0.6
      Read IO requests:               9.7                 0.2
     Write IO requests:              18.9                 0.3
          Read IO (MB):               0.1                 0.0
         Write IO (MB):               0.3                 0.0
          IM scan rows:               0.0                 0.0
 Session Logical Read IM:
  RAC GC blocks received:            579.5                 9.6
    RAC GC blocks served:            609.4                10.1
             User calls:             47.5                 0.8
            Parses (SQL):            42.2                 0.7
       Hard parses (SQL):             1.8                 0.0
        SQL Work Area (MB):           6.0                 0.1
                  Logons:             0.3                 0.0
          Executes (SQL):          1,256.1                20.9
               Rollbacks:             0.1                 0.0
            Transactions:            60.2
```

The HammerDB AWR driver lets the database administrator obtain more information from the benchmark results than HammerDB provides on its own. Unfortunately, these results are only possible because of Oracle's AWR functionality, an optionally licensed feature that may not be available on all databases. Keep in mind that the standard AWR report is for one instance, as was shown in a previous chapter, and you will need to generate AWR reports for all instances involved in the benchmark activity.

TPC-H Benchmark

The Transaction Performance Processing Council TPC-H benchmark simulates a workload on a Decision Support System (DSS), commonly referred to as a data warehouse. HammerDB can run the TPC-H benchmark, but it is not very intuitive to find. After launching the HammerDB utility, you double-click on one of the non-Oracle databases in the Benchmark pane. This action will pop up a selection box to select the benchmark options. Make sure the radio button for Oracle is selected. Then ensure the TCP-H radio button is selected. Press the OK button to confirm.

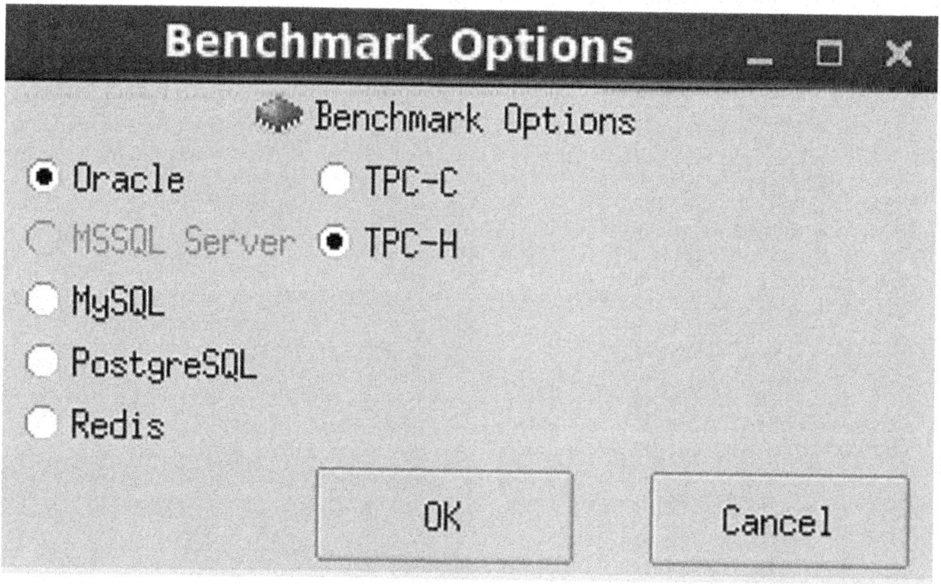

Figure 10.44 HammerDB Benchmark Options

The Benchmark pane in the HammerDB utility will change to show the TPC-H benchmark, similar to the following.

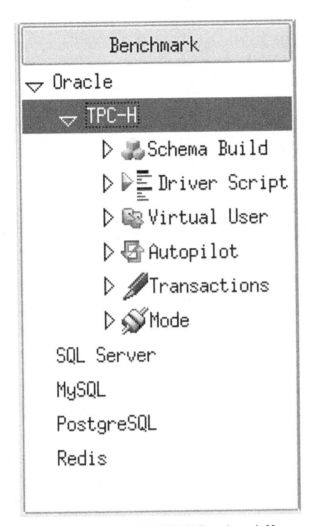

Figure 10.45 HammerDB TPC-H Benchmark Menu

A new schema needs to be created for the different benchmark type. In the Schema Build section, the database administrator double-clicks on the Options. Notice the schema owner defaults to "tpch". The default tablespace is now "tpchtab", which does need to be pre-created. Double-clicking on the Build option will create the test schema.

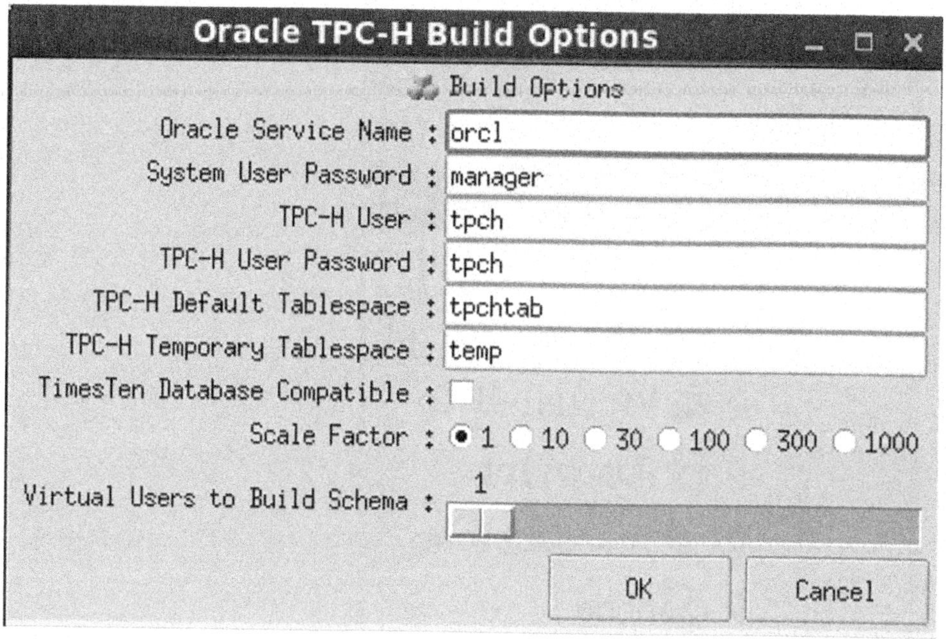

Figure 10.46 HammerDB TPCH Schema Build Options

The output from the user generating the schema will look different because, quite obviously, the schema is different. Once the schema is created, the rest of the benchmark run is similar to the TPC-C benchmark activity. However, there is no AWR driver for the TPC-H benchmark so the database administrator will need to manually initiate the AWR snapshots. The output from the virtual users looks different as well. The TPC-H comes with a set of predefined DSS queries that are executed by HammerDB.

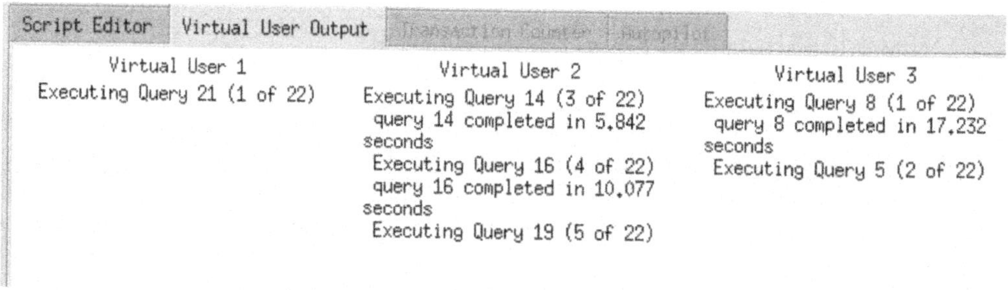

Figure 10.47 HammerDB TPC-H Benchmark Output

HammerDB Summary

The HammerDB benchmark utility can perform both OLTP and DSS benchmarks with the TCP-C and TPC-H loads, respectively. HammerDB was originally named HammerOra but was rebranded when the software was rewritten to handle more than just Oracle database systems. The TCP-C benchmark has a driver that lets the database administrator obtain AWR snapshots for more detailed information on the benchmark performance.

Summary

When discussing database performance, it is often helpful to use a benchmark utility and obtain throughput numbers. This chapter focused on two such utilities, Swingbench and HammerDB. Both benchmark tools are free. Other utilities exist for the database administrator to choose if desired.

Most of this chapter focused on how to use Swingbench, especially for Oracle RAC database systems. The standard Swingbench utility was shown. The *charbench* utility was discussed to be able to script multiple executions in a push-button fashion. The *Clusteroverview* functionality was discussed for running benchmarks against pre-11gR2 Oracle RAC instances. The HammerDB benchmark utility provides both OLTP and DSS benchmark load generation.

The next chapter discusses how to leverage Oracle's Enterprise Manager for performance tuning of Oracle RAC databases. Previous chapters have shown how to tune many aspects of an Oracle RAC system with scripts and command line utilities. The next chapter will show how to do much of the same in a graphical environment.

Enterprise Manager for RAC

11

Oracle's Enterprise Manager (EM) id s GUI tool that provides a management interface for many different systems including servers, applications, and of course, the RAC databases. Since this book is focused on Oracle RAC performance tuning, this chapter will concentrate on how to leverage Enterprise Manager to support the database administrators tuning efforts for Oracle's clustered databases. Other aspects of EM, while still very important, are out of scope for this chapter.

Just like many mature products, Enterprise Manager has changed greatly over the course of its lifetime. The earliest versions of EM were Java-based applications that connected to a single database. In contrast, today's EM is a web-based system. For Enterprise Manager 10g and 11g, the product is provided in two distributions, Database Control and Grid Control. Database Control can manage one and only one database. EM Database Control runs on the database server. If the company has multiple Oracle databases, they would need multiple instances of Database Control. Grid Control is a centralized version of Enterprise Manager capable of managing and monitoring multiple databases, even non-Oracle ones. Grid Control's centralized approach is best when the company has more than a few Oracle databases in their inventory.

Enterprise Manager 12c is the latest and greatest version of EM. With the new version comes a new name, Cloud Control. EM12c Cloud Control replaces Grid Control for centralized management. Oracle Database 12c's single database Enterprise Manager is now called Database Express. EM12c Cloud Control 12.1.0.4 is the most current version at the time this book was written and is used throughout this chapter. Much of the material in this chapter applies to other EM distributions including Database Express, Database Control, and Grid Control. The older EM versions have most of the functionality described here, just in a slightly different form or location within EM.

A lot of information in this chapter has been discussed throughout the preceding chapters in this book. AWR, ADDM, ASH Analytics, Cluster Interconnect throughput are just a few examples of the topics previously discussed. In all of the prior chapters, the information was presented without using Enterprise Manager. This chapter will show how to leverage EM to address the multitude of topics previously seen in this book.

Optional Packs

Enterprise Manager has many optionally licensed packs inside it. References to the optionally licensed Diagnostics Pack exist in many places throughout this book. The Tuning Pack has also been mentioned. For a complete list of the optional EM packs, go to Setup → Management Packs → License Information after signing on to EM. Each pack will be shown along with a brief description.

In Enterprise Manager 10g and 11g, it was too easy for the user to point and click their way into sections of EM that required an optional pack to be license. Without knowing it, the database administrator could use one of the packs. An audit from Oracle Corporation may reveal that the company is not in compliance with their licensing. EM12c improves pack access in two areas. From any page, the user can choose Setup → Management Packs → Packs For This Page. A popup window will appear indicating which packs need to be licensed to use the functionality on that page. In many cases, no packs are required as shown below.

Figure 11.1 EM Page Pack Info

The next example shows the Diagnostics Pack is needed.

> **Management Packs for this Page**   ×
>
> This Page requires either of the following pack(s):
>
> • Database Diagnostics Pack
>
> License Information
>
>   Close

Figure 11.2 EM Page Need Diagnostics Pack

Unfortunately, to obtain the page pack information, you must have chosen the page in advance, thus exercising the usage of that pack. To ensure that an optional pack is not used, the database administrator can navigate to Setup → Management Packs → Management Pack Access and allow or deny EM packs. Pack access can be configured differently for each database managed by EM .

Name ▲	Type	Host	Oracle Cloud Management Pack for Oracle Database	Database Diagnostics Pack		Oracle Database Lifecycle Management Pack	Data Masking Pack	Test Data Management Pack	Database Tuning Pack		Pack Access Agreed
-MGMTDB_host01	Database Instance	host01	✓	✓	🐞	✓	✓	✓	✓	🐞	☐
orcl	Cluster Database	host01	✓	✓	🐞	✓	✓	✓	✓	🐞	☐
orcl_orcl1	Database Instance	host01	✓	✓	🐞	✓	✓	✓	✓	🐞	☐
orcl_orcl2	Database Instance	host02	✓	✓	🐞	✓	✓	✓	✓	🐞	☐
repos	Database Instance	host03	✓	✓	🐞	✓	✓	✓	✓	🐞	☐

☑ **TIP** In Oracle Database 11g, you need to set the initialization parameter 'control_management_pack_access' to disable or enable Database Diagnostic and Tuning Packs.
☑ **TIP** For a detailed description of above functionality and where they can be used within the product refer to the Oracle Database Licensing Information document, the Oracle Application Server Licensing Information document or the Oracle Enterprise Manager Licensing Information document.

                Revert | Apply

Figure 11.3 EM Management Pack Access

With EM12c, the database now has the knowledge to understand the packs needed for each page in EM as well as the ability to limit usage of those packs before the company's Oracle licensing is violated.

The information in this chapter relies heavily on the Diagnostics and Tuning packs. Hopefully after finishing this chapter, the reader will have an understanding of how easy it is to obtain performance information using Enterprise Manager. The Diagnostics Pack coupled with EM saves the database administrator a large amount of time. This combination makes the Diagnostics Pack well worth the additional cost of the packs.

Cluster Topology

For the database administrator, it can be beneficial to know how the Oracle RAC system is laid out. Enterprise Manager can show the topology for the clustered database. Selecting Targets → Databases will show the list of databases managed by EM similar to the following.

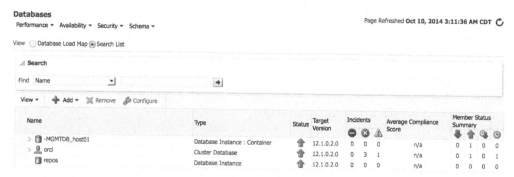

Figure 11.4 EM12c Database Targets

Notice that the 'orcl' database is denoted as a clustered database. Clicking on that database will take the user to database home page. The top of the page contains the database target's menu items. Notice that for an Oracle RAC database, the first menu item is *Cluster Database* instead of *Database Instance*.

Figure 11.5 EM12c Database Menus

Selecting Cluster Database → Cluster Topology will take the user to the topology screen. The example below is for a 2-node Oracle RAC database. More complex Oracle RAC deployments will have more intricate details. The slider bar on the left can be used to zoom in our out and pan through the diagram.

Cluster Topology

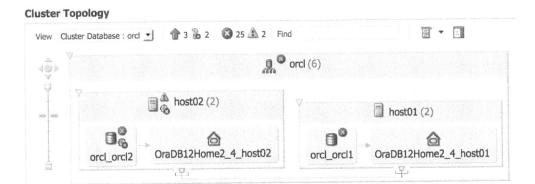

Figure 11.6 EM12c Database Topology

Looking at the topology, it can be seen that the *orcl* database spans two hosts and has two instances. The instances show a link to the home directory for the database software. The View pulldown menu can be used to change the point of view to the cluster itself. In addition to the *orcl* cluster database, this view shows the EM agents and other databases on the cluster.

Figure 11.7 EM12c Cluster Topology

The database administrator may find the topology information helpful when trying to diagnose problems. For instance, connections to the Oracle RAC database on the first host are experiencing performance problems but the instance doesn't seem overly busy. The topology reveals other instances on the node and upon further analysis, the database administrator is able to determine those instances are consuming large amounts of system resources.

Performance Home

When end-users call to complain about database performance problems, they rarely provide enough information to be able to help the database administrator pinpoint the root cause of the performance issue, and the user typically reports vague observations like "my database is running slow". When the database administrator receives a call like this, the EM Performance Home page is a great place to begin investigating the root cause of the problem.

This page below (Figure 11.8) provides an overview of how the database is performing. It is important to know that for Oracle RAC databases, the metrics on this page are summations of all active instances of the database. The screenshot below shows a database experiencing two areas of resource contention, CPU usage and user disk I/O. The colors of the graph help differentiate the different categories and match the legend to the right of the graph.

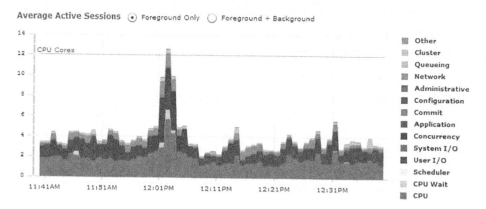

Figure 11.8 EM12c Performance Home Graph

The left side of the chart shows the number of CPU cores. There is a red line indicating the maximum number of CPU's available. In the example above, the red line is drawn at twelve CPU's. For Oracle RAC systems, this is the number of CPU's across the entire cluster. In the example above, the three nodes in the cluster have four cores each.

End users may start to experience performance problems when the performance graph crosses the red line, the Maximum CPU line. Note that some end-users may experience performance problems when the graph is below the Maximum CPU line. This graph is not always advantageous when looking for one user's performance, but it is useful when looking at the performance across the entire database cluster. The next screenshot (Figure 11.9) shows an Oracle RAC database that is heavily CPU burdened. The CPU utilization in the next figure is well above the red CPU Cores line.

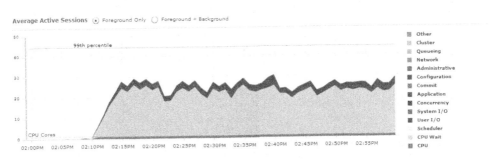

Figure 11.9 EM12c Performance Home CPU Bound

When looking at the Performance Home graph, you should focus on the areas of the graph that are bigger than the other areas. In the graph above (Figure 11.9), the User I/O and Concurrency sections contribute very little to the performance. The CPU and CPU Wait sections of the graph dominate everything else. Also notice that the graph is reaching almost 30 CPU cores, well above the red Maximum CPU line. When you have determined the problem area, clicking on that portion of the graph will drill down to provide more detail about the problem. In the image below, the User I/O is the dominant resource utilization and the database administrator has clicked on that portion of the graph to drill down to show the resource utilization by instance. As we see, this database is composed of two instances.

The new chart shows the breakdown of User I/O by instance of the Oracle RAC database. In printed form, it may not be very obvious in the chart below that almost all of the User I/O is coming from one of the two instances. Enterprise Manager has enabled the database administrator (with just a single click) to narrow down the performance pain to just one RAC instance. Literally within seconds, you learn a ton of information about the area of concern for the performance problem. Without EM, the database administrator would have to rely on AWR snapshots and run an AWR report, then sift through the report's contents to narrow down the problem area, a process that might take thirty minutes or more.

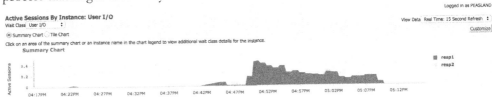

Figure 11.10 EM12c User I/O Drilldown

It can be difficult to see the graph instance by instance, especially when the chart looks similar to the figure above where one instance dominates the picture. Selecting the Tile Chart radio button will provide one graph per instance, similar to the following graph. The Tile Chart graph can be used to easily determine the instance by instance affect.

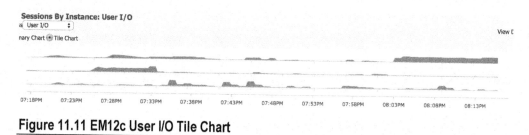

Figure 11.11 EM12c User I/O Tile Chart

After clicking on the instance that dominates the resource consumption, the database administrator is presented with a chart similar to the following.

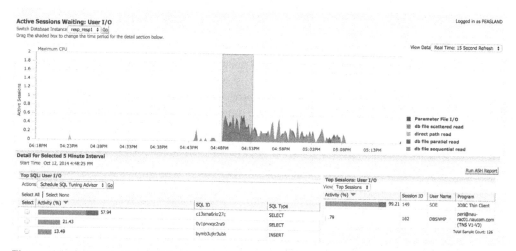

Figure 11.12 EM12c User I/O Instance Consumption

The User I/O consumption is broken down further by I/O type as can be seen in the chart's legend. You can drag the shaded box, (which represents a five-minute window) to the appropriate time period of interest. The information below the graph will change for that time window. It can be seen from this information that session number 149 accounted for 99.21% of all I/O activity in that small window. The SQL statements contributing to the I/O are also shown.

With just a few clicks, you can narrow-down a generic performance complaint to the exact instance having the problem and then click through to see the exact user behind the performance pain. Furthermore, the database administrator knows the SQL statements that user was executing. Oracle's Enterprise Manager, (along with the Diagnostics Pack that is needed to see these pages), has given the database administrator everything that is needed to determine the performance problem's root cause, quickly and effortlessly. This quick drilldown capability alone makes the Diagnostics Pack easily worth the additional cost.

ASH Analytics for RAC

Chapter 9 discussed Active Session History (ASH) and how it can be used to help diagnose performance problems in the past. Oracle's Enterprise Manager also provides the capability to use ASH data. After selecting the database target in question, select Performance → ASH Analytics. A screen similar to the following will be shown.

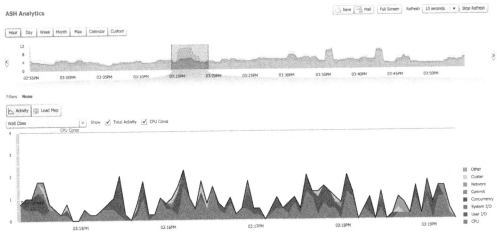

Figure 11.13 EM12c ASH Analytics

The database administrator can drag the shaded box in the top chart to a section of time indicating a performance issue. The second chart shows the activity of the selected time window. Quickly and easily, ASH analytics lets the database administrator focus on a performance issue in the past.

Another version of the second chart appears below. The first half of that chart clearly shows activity that went over the Maximum CPU line, thus indicating performance pain for the end users.

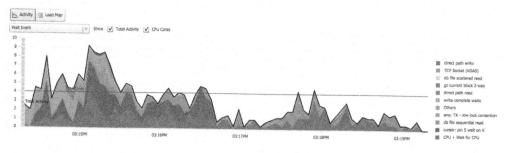

Figure 11.14 EM12c ASH Time Window Activity

Below this chart are two tables. The table on the left shows the SQL statements and their impact to the information in the chart. The table on the right shows the sessions from that time window.

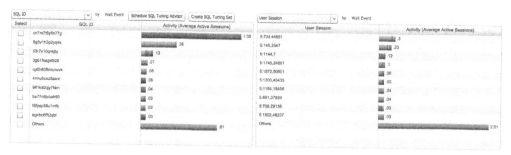

Figure 11.15 EM12c ASH SQL and Session Impacts

In the example above, one query stands out as a dominant contributor to the resource utilization. The query at the top has a bar that is much longer than the others. As such, efforts should be focused on tuning this query. In the table of user sessions, no singular session is standing out as a major contributor. This tells us that the one query is coming from multiple sessions. The problematic query should tuned to use less resources, which will bring benefit to all users executing that SQL statement.

Remember that ASH stores data for a recent period of time. The database administrator can use EM to go back as far as ASH has data available. In the screenshot below, the data is retained for one week.

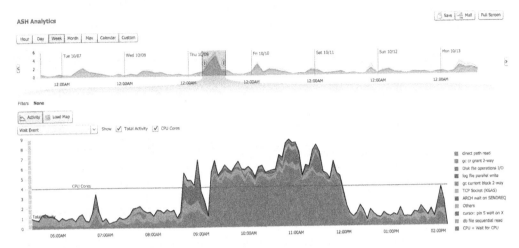

Figure 11.16 EM12c ASH Analytics Week View

When looking at the Week view, the time window defaults to one day. The shaded time window can be resized to narrow down to a smaller portion of the day, as was done above. Sizing the shaded time window to the area of focus removes extraneous data from the analysis.

With ASH Analytics, the database administrator can now answer the call when someone complains of performance issues last week. As with many graphical tools, EM will only show what is has been created to do. Many times, this is enough information for the database administrator to pinpoint the problem. Other times, EM12c's ASH Analytics will not show enough so the database administrator may need to query *dba_hist_** views directly, as shown in Chapter 9.

OEM Parallel Execution History

In the Performance Home section of Enterprise Manager, the bottom chart has five options. Selecting the Parallel Execution option brings up four charts showing parallel query execution, which was discussed in Chapter 7. The first chart shows the breakdown of serial sessions to parallel sessions. The second chart shows the number of parallel query coordinators and slave processes. The third chart shows the division of parallel SELECT statements, and DML and DDL operations. The fourth chart shows parallel statements that were had the number of slave processes downgraded. An example of this section is shown below.

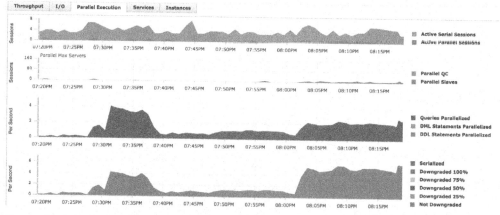

Figure 11.17 EM12c Parallel Execution Charts

Each of the four charts can be used to drill down further into the particular metric of interest. Remember that the metrics shown on the Performance Home page are for all instances of the Oracle RAC database. Drilling down will show the breakdown per instance.

AWR and RAC in EM

Chapter 9 discussed the Automated Workload Repository (AWR). Recall that the *awrrpt.sql* script will generate an AWR report for one instance. Chapter9 walked through sections of the report specific to Oracle RAC. To generate an AWR report for all RAC instances, the global *awrgrpt.sql* script is used. Oracle Enterprise Manager has the ability to generate the instance-specific and global AWR reports. To create an AWR report, go to Performance → AWR → AWR Report. A screen similar to the following will be shown.

Run AWR Report

Specify parameters for the report. You can either pick one baseline or a pair of snapshots.   Generate Report

◉ By Baseline

Baseline [   ] 🔍

◯ By Snapshot

Begin Snapshot [   ] 🔍

End Snapshot [   ] 🔍

▽ Hide Instances

Instances [   ] 🔍

☑ **TIP** Leave this field blank to run on all instances.

Figure 11.18 EM12c AWR Report

By default, EM will generate a global AWR report. Clicking on the Show Instances link will bring up the last field, under the newly renamed Hide Instances title, where you can choose the instance to appear in the AWR report output. When you are ready, clicking on the Generate Report button will bring up the report contents. The report will be in HTML format and can be saved to a local file if desired. Refer to Chapter 9 for more information on the AWR report contents.

Cluster Cache Coherency in EM

Chapter 2 discussed Cache Fusion operations. Other chapters throughout the book have referred to global cache transfers where appropriate. Enterprise Manager has a section that provides metrics on the performance of the Cluster Interconnect. The Cluster Interconnect metrics are available when choosing Performance → Cluster Cache Coherency. This section will provide a number of charts. The first chart shows the average time to receive current and CR blocks. The time should be a few milliseconds.

Figure 11.19 EM12c Block Receive Time

The next chart shows the number of current and CR blocks global cache blocks received by all instances.

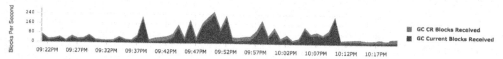

Figure 11.20 EM12c Blocks Received

The next chart shows the distribution of physical reads to global cache block transfers.

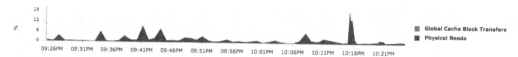

Figure 11.21 EM12c Global Cache Distribution

The last chart shows a breakdown of the different global cache transfer types, as discussed in Chapter 2. The grey slider box can be used to narrow down the analysis to a short time window. Below the chart will be top SQL and top sessions from the time period defined by the box, very similar to other shaded window selections in the Performance section of Enterprise Manager.

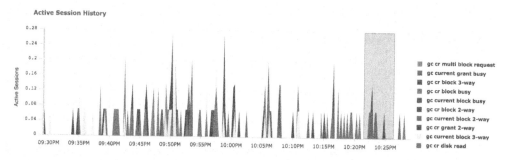

Figure 11.22 EM12c Global Cache Breakdown

If you suspect performance problems that are related to the Cluster Interconnect, the Cache Coherency section can be used to obtain information on the private network's performance. Unlike other charts, there is no capability to drill down to the instance level in this EM screen.

Oracle RAC Performance Tuning

Real Time ADDM in EM

Chapter 9 discussed Oracle's Automatic Database Diagnostics Monitor (ADDM), a knowledge expert to offer advice on performance related issues. Enterprise Manager 12c now provides a Real Time ADDM functionality the database administrator can use to obtain the advice, as the title says, in real time. You can start Real Time ADDM from the Performance menu, but note that using Real Time ADDM requires connecting to the database target with a *sysdba* connection. After establishing the connection, you can press the Start button and ADDM will execute.

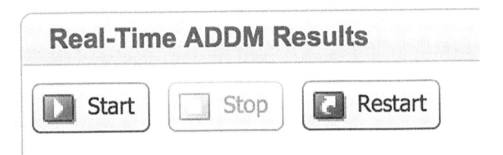

Figure 11.23 EM12c Real Time ADDM Start

After a short period of time, the ADDM analysis will be complete and Enterprise Manager will show the number of findings. In the example below, ADDM has detected one finding.

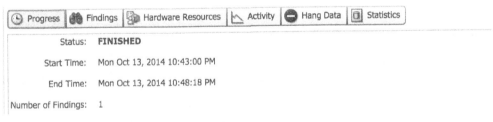

Figure 11.24 EM12c Real Time ADDM Summary

You can then click on the Findings tab to see the results, and then click on each finding to see the finding details. In the example below, ADDM found one SQL statement that was consuming significant database time.

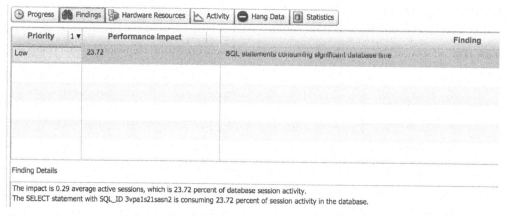

Priority	1 ▼	Performance Impact		Finding
Low		23.72	SQL statements consuming significant database time	

Finding Details

The impact is 0.29 average active sessions, which is 23.72 percent of database session activity.
The SELECT statement with SQL_ID 3vpa1s21sasn2 is consuming 23.72 percent of session activity in the database.

Figure 11.24 EM12c Real Time ADDM Findings

The Real Time ADDM feature of EM12c is a great way to get performance tuning advice from Oracle without having to wait for the command-mode ADDM run to complete. With a few simple clicks, Real Time ADDM has analyzed the current performance and offered its analysis. This feature can be a great time saver when the database administrator wants some analysis quickly. Real Time ADDM should be used when a performance problem is currently going on.

Search Sessions

Being able to find a session is important when tracking down performance problems. A user calls to complain that their session is hung. The database administrator needs to be able to find that session and see the session's activity. In Enterprise Manager, the database administrator can select Performance → Search Sessions. The first item on the page will be a pull down menu for the database administrator to choose the instance to search. This reveals one of the shortcomings for EM's ability to search for specific sessions. There is no way to search all instances of an Oracle RAC database. If the database administrator is unsure which instance to search, a quick query of *gv$sessions* can help.

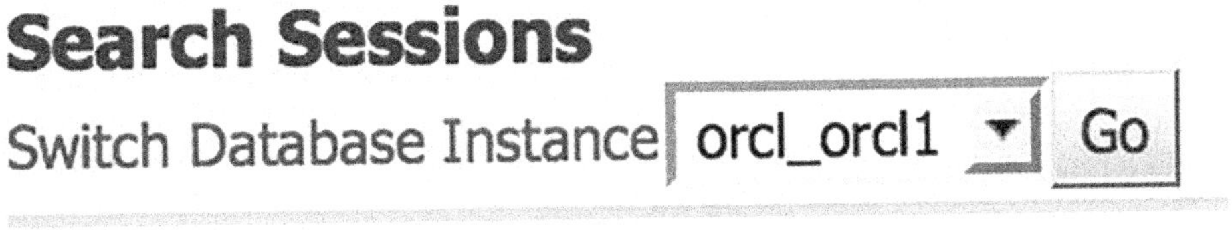

Search Sessions

Switch Database Instance orcl_orcl1 ▾ Go

Figure 11.26 EM12c Search Sessions Instance Picker

After the instance is chosen, the search criteria can be used. In the example below, the database administrator is looking for a specific user.

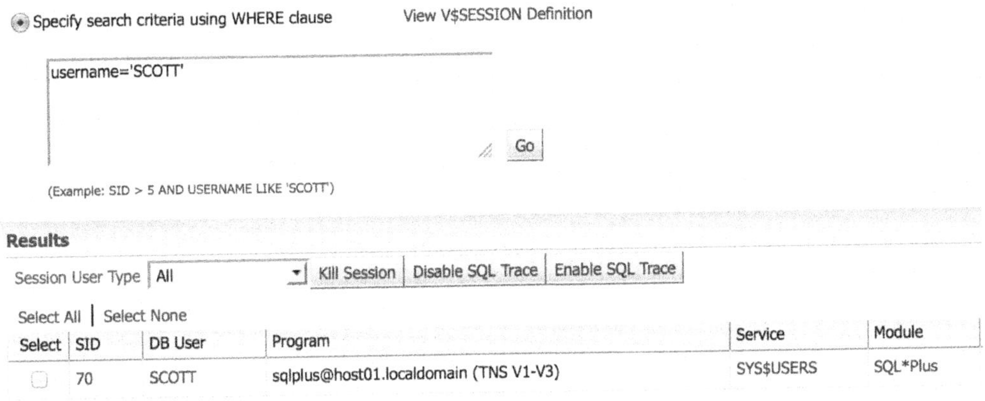

⦿ Specify search criteria using WHERE clause   View V$SESSION Definition

```
username='SCOTT'
```
Go

(Example: SID > 5 AND USERNAME LIKE 'SCOTT')

Results

Session User Type All ▾ | Kill Session | Disable SQL Trace | Enable SQL Trace

Select All | Select None

Select	SID	DB User	Program	Service	Module
☐	70	SCOTT	sqlplus@host01.localdomain (TNS V1-V3)	SYS$USERS	SQL*Plus

Figure 11.27 EM12c Search Sessions Results

Clicking on the *sid* value in the results section will bring up a screen with lots of details of the session. Remember that for Oracle RAC, Search Sessions can only search one instance at a time in EM12c. Many times, the database administrator will not know the instance holding the user's session so a query of *gv$session* will be needed similar to the following:

```
SQL> select
  2     inst_id,
  3     sid
  4  from
  5     gv$session
  6  where
  7     username='SCOTT';

  INST_ID        SID
---------- ----------
        1         70
```

If the database administrator is already in SQL*Plus to obtain the instance of the user's session, then why not use SQL*Plus to obtain more session details? The database administrator could certainly use SQL*Plus and query lots of different views, maybe with scripts from their library. However, EM provides an easy way to point and click to a large amount of session details. The following page shows some of those details for the session in question.

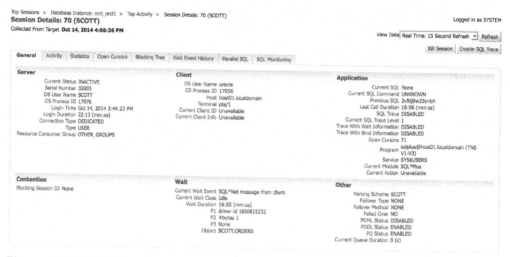

Figure 11.28 EM12c Session Details

From the above, the database administrator can see the login time, as well as the host and program. The current and previous SQL statements contain hyperlinks to the SQL details. Clicking on the SQL Monitoring tab lets you watch the session's SQL execution in near real time. Enterprise Manager's Search Sessions feature provides a ton of information about a session for the database administrator, quickly and easily.

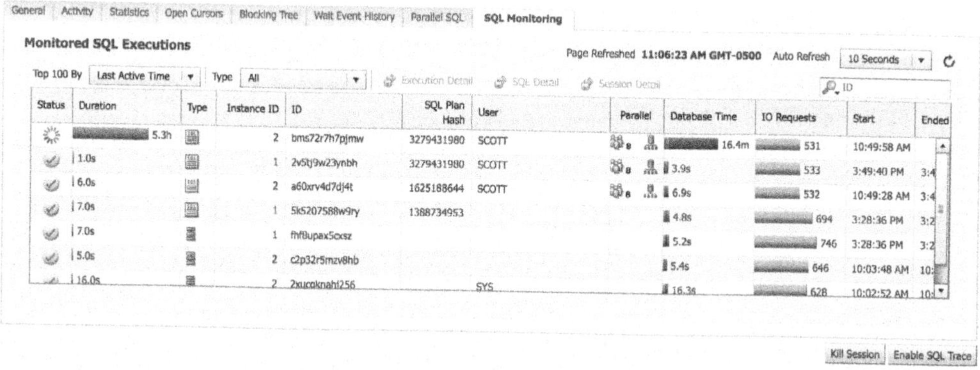

Figure 11.29 EM12c Session SQL Monitoring

As we have noted, EM provides the ability for you to search for sessions across all instances of the Oracle RAC database. There is little technical reason that EM cannot search *gv$session* for all instances and provide a column in the results that denotes the instance id, but it doesn't have this functionality. That being said, EM's Search Sessions capability is a great way to find many details about a specific session. Without EM, database administrators would normally use a number of scripts or queries against many V$ views in the database.

Blocking Sessions

Sometimes, one session is holding a lock. The database administrator would like to see the session holding the lock. In Enterprise Manager, go to Performance → Blocking Sessions to obtain this information.

Blocking Sessions   Page Refreshed **Oct 14, 2014 11:20:15 AM CDT** Refresh

Switch Database Instance orcl_orcl2 ▾ Go

View Session | Kill Session

Expand All | Collapse All

Select	Username	Sessions Blocked	Session ID	Serial Number	SQL ID	Wait Class	Wait Event	P1 Value	P2 Value	P3 Value	Seconds in Wait
	▽ Blocking Sessions										
⦿	▽	1	70	15593		Idle	Streams AQ: waiting for time management or cleanup tasks	0	0	0	763
○	SCOTT	0	44	55338	bms72r7h7pjmw	Application	enq: TX - row lock contention	1415053318	589827	4114	1816

Figure 11.30 EM12c Blocking Sessions

Just like Search Sessions, Blocking Sessions forces the database administrator to choose the instance to investigate. The example above shows a session in *orcl2* that is blocked. EM will now show this blocking session until the correct instance is chosen. Unfortunately, there is no indication from the output that the blocking session is running on a different instance.

Services

Chapter 3 discussed how to use services in support of application segregation. Enterprise Manager can assist the database administrator in managing and creating services. The database administrator will need to select the database target in EM, and then select the Availability → Cluster Managed Services menu option.

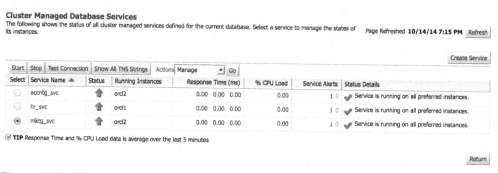

Figure 11.31 EM12c Database Services

From this screen, you can see the current status of each service of the Oracle RAC database. The services can be stopped or started. Clicking on the *Show All TNS Strings* button will provide aliases that can be used in any *tnsnames.ora* configuration file for client connections to that service.

Figure 11.32 EM12c Service TNS Strings

To create a new service, the database administrator will click on the *Create Service* button. Enterprise Manager will provide a screen with all of the questions that need to be answered. In the example below, the database administrator is creating a new Business Intelligence service that will run on *orcl1* (preferred) but can failover (available) to *orcl2* if necessary.

Create Service

Define a highly available service by specifying preferred and available instances. You can also specify service properties to customize failover mechanisms, monitoring thresholds and resource management.

* Service Name   bi_svc

☑ Start service after creation

☑ Update local naming parameter (tnsnames.ora) file

High Availability Configuration

Instance Name	Service Policy
orcl1	Preferred ▾
orcl2	Available ▾

☑ **TIP** Must select at least one preferred instance.

Service Properties

Transparent Application Failover (TAF) Policy   Preconnect ▾

☐ Enable Distributed Transaction Processing

Choose this option for all Distributed transactions including XA, JTA. Services with exactly one preferred instance can enable this.

Connection Load Balancing Goal   ◉ Long   ○ Short

Load balance connections based on number of sessions (Long) or elapsed time (Short).

Edition   None ▾

Figure 11.33 EM12c Create New Service

Using EM to create services can be easier than trying to use the command line *srvctl* utility. EM walks the database administrator through the process and asks all the appropriate questions.

Cluster Performance in EM

Oracle Enterprise Manager lets the database administrator see, on a single screen utilization trends for CPU, memory and disk I/O for all nodes in the cluster. To see these metrics, the database administrator will need to go to Targets → All Targets and then click on the Cluster target type.

Figure 11.34 EM12c Cluster Targets

Next, the database administrator will click on the desired cluster target name. In the next screen, the database administrator selects either Cluster → Performance or Cluster → Cluster Health Monitor. A RAC cluster resource utilization graphs will appear, similar to the following.

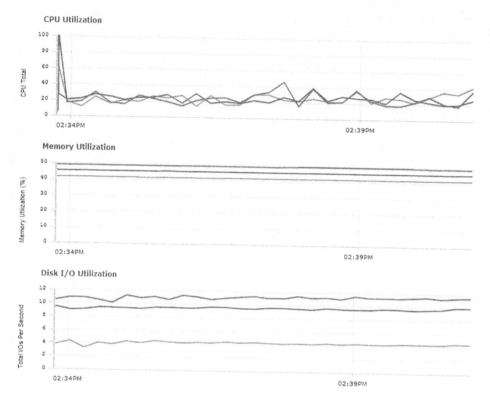

Figure 11.35 EM12c Cluster Performance

The graphs are purely informational, but they can help the database administrator see if one node in the cluster is utilizing more resources than the others.

Summary

This chapter has not provided much new content in the way of tuning Oracle RAC databases, but we have examined how Oracle Enterprise Manager 12c can be used to simplify the database administrator's tuning efforts. Enterprise Manager is a tool that can be used to address many of the topics seen in previous chapters of this book.

Keep in mind that the features shown in this chapter will require optionally licensed EM performance packs to be purchased. While these do have an extra cost, it should be obvious after reading the chapter that they are a great time saver to any database administrator responsible for performance tuning. A few simple clicks often provides the information needed to understand the root cause of the performance issue.

This chapter has shown how to use the Performance pages to quickly drill down into performance issues in real time. Enterprise Manager extends ADDM with the Real Time ADDM functionality. Active Session History becomes easier to access with the ASH Analytics section. This chapter also showed how to use EM to search for sessions and search for blocking sessions.

The next chapter discusses Oracle RAC wait events and locking. Many wait events were discussed in previous chapters when relevant. The next chapter will discuss these events and more.

Wait Events, Locks, and Statistics in RAC

Without a doubt, Oracle is the most instrumented relational database platform in existence. The database administrator can determine exactly what any session is doing at any point in time. A session is either processing on a CPU or waiting for something to happen. Oracle's wait event interface provides the ability to know what a session is waiting for. Database administrators can use this information to reduce bottlenecks, which improves performance. Readers can use this chapter to help understand how to reduce specific wait events common to Oracle RAC databases.

In any relational database system, locking prevents concurrent sessions from modifying the same row of data at the same time. Locking helps ensure the integrity of the data. Locking is more complex in Oracle RAC systems because the integrity of the data needs to be maintained across all instances. This chapter will discuss locking in Oracle RAC databases.

Wait Events

Readers already familiar with Oracle's wait event interface may skip to the next section of the chapter. This section will provide an introduction to Oracle's Wait Interface for those new to the topic, which will help make the rest of the chapter material more understandable.

From an end user's perspective the total response time is the time spent for the database to finish the request. The database time is defined with the following formula.

```
DB Time = CPU Time + Wait Time
```

If the response time is taking too long, the database administrator can improve performance by reducing the time spent using the CPU, reducing the time spent waiting, or both. In order to reduce the wait time, the database administrator must understand what the process is waiting for and how long.

Oracle 7 introduced the Wait Interface. From its beginning, the database administrator could determine if the user's processing was waiting on a full table scan (*db file scattered read* wait event) or an index lookup (*db file sequential read* wait event) or approximately one hundred other wait events. Each new release of the Oracle database has brought more wait events. Oracle 12.1.0.2 has more than 1,200 wait events.

To support the Wait Interface, Oracle has modified the kernel code to log the action the session is waiting on and the time it spends waiting for that action to complete. The database administrator can use the wait event information to determine the bottlenecks to application performance. As an example, consider the following script, created for Oracle RAC databases to determine the top five wait events for a specific session, that asks for the instance identifier and the session id as determined from *gv$session* or from Search Sessions in Oracle's Enterprise Manager.

💾 session_top5_events.sql

```
set verify off
accept v_instid prompt 'Enter Instance Id: '
accept v_sid    prompt 'Enter SID: '
select
    *
from (
    select
        event,
        to_char(time_waited,'999,999,999') as time_waited,
        to_char(round(ratio_to_report(time_waited) over ()*100,2),'990.00') as
"WAIT%"
    from
        gv$session_event
    where
        inst_id = &v_instid
        and
        sid = &v_sid
        and
        event not in (select
                        name
                    from
                        v$event_name
                    where
                        wait_class='Idle')
    order by
        time_waited desc)
where
    rownum <= 5;


Enter Instance Id: 2
Enter SID: 748

EVENT                           TIME_WAITED  WAIT%
------------------------------- ------------ -------
db file sequential read              65,953   87.49
SQL*Net more data to client           5,123    6.80
```

```
gc current block 2-way                    1,442    1.91
gc cr grant 2-way                         1,313    1.74
gc current block 3-way                    1,267    1.68
```

In the output above, it is clear that one wait event dominates the total time spent waiting. The database administrator could spend time trying to reduce the global cache wait events but they total less than six percent of the total time waited. Instead, the database administrator should be trying to reduce the time spent using an index to access data, as signified by the *db file sequential read* wait event. This event accounts for 87.49% of the total time spent waiting. Reducing this wait event by half will reduce the overall wait time by approximately 43%. The database administrator now has a good idea where to focus the tuning efforts, which is exactly what the Oracle wait events help determine.

The script above queries the *gv$session_event* view. This view shows a summary of all wait events for any active session. The *gv$session_wait* view provides information on what the session is waiting for at that specific point in time. The database administrator can repeatedly query this view to see the session advance from one event to another. Additionally, *gv$session_wait* provides more information on the specific wait occurrence. It has already been stated that the *db file scattered read* wait event indicates a session waiting on a full table scan to complete. The natural question to ask is, which table? The answer lies by examining the event description in the *v$event_name* view.

```
SQL> select
  2       parameter1,
  3       parameter2,
  4       parameter3
  5  from
  6       v$event_name
  7  where
  8       name='db file scattered read';

PARAMETER1 PARAMETER2 PARAMETER3
---------- ---------- ----------
file#      block#     blocks
```

For the *db file scattered read* event, the event parameters are the file number, block number, and number of blocks, in that order. Knowing what the parameters mean makes the queries from *gv$session_wait* more meaningful as can be seen below.

```
SQL> select
  2       event,
  3       p1,
  4       p2,
  5       p3
  6  from
  7       gv$session_wait
  8  where
```

```
   9      inst_id=1
  10      and
  11      sid=63;

EVENT                                         P1           P2           P3
--------------------------------     ----------   ----------   ----------
db file scattered read                         5       504064          128
```

The output from the query above shows that the session is waiting to read the table in file number 5, block 504064 and is reading 128 blocks. The database administrator can now query *dba_extents* to determine the table involved in this wait event.

All wait events have a classification that helps to group related events. For example, the *Idle* classification are those events where the instance is waiting on the application. From the instance's perspective, the session is idle. Many database administrators ignore wait events in the *Idle* classification. However, it is important to understand three important details about the *Idle* events

1. All wait events, even *Idle* events contribute to the end user's response time.

2. The idle wait events are from the perspective of the Oracle instance.

Tuning may still be needed on the application side if performance is unacceptable. Three, there are some wait events that while classified as *Idle* can still be tuned. For example, the *ges remote message* wait event is classified as *Idle*. The session is sitting idle waiting on a message to be returned from Global Enqueue Services on another instance. While there is nothing to be tuned on this instance, high CPU utilization on the remote instance may be contributing to the time for the GES message to return. Then there are wait events like *pmon timer*, which is raised when the *pmon* process has no work to do and it goes to sleep for a period of time. This is truly an idle event that can be ignored. If idle events are major contributors to the end user's response time, then they need to be addressed even if their classification says otherwise.

There are two classifications for input and output, *System I/O* and *User I/O*. The former is for background processes performing I/O to support internal operations. The latter is for application sessions performing I/O to satisfy SQL statements. The following output shows the number of wait events per classification in an Oracle 12.1.0.2 database. It is disturbing that half of the wait events are in the generic *Other* category, but this is what we are given.

```
SQL> select
  2      wait_class,
  3      count(*) as num_waits
  4    from
  5      v$event_name
  6    group by
```

```
  7      wait_class
  8  order by
  9      wait_class;
```

WAIT_CLASS	NUM_WAITS
Administrative	57
Application	17
Cluster	64
Commit	4
Concurrency	38
Configuration	26
Idle	121
Network	28
Other	1186
Queueing	9
Scheduler	9
System I/O	35
User I/O	56

```
13 rows selected.
```

Oracle's Enterprise Manager, discussed in the previous chapter, breaks down wait events by Wait Class in the Performance Home page. The classifications in the figure below are the same as the classifications shown above. Clicking on the graph to select one of the wait classes lets the database administrator drill down and see the cumulative waits for that classification.

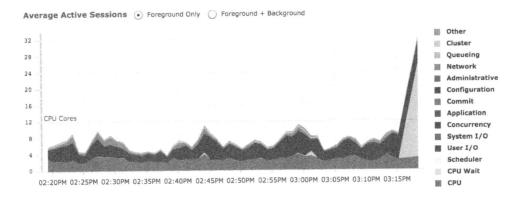

Figure 12.1 EM12c Wait Classes

Since this book is about Oracle RAC performance tuning, it should be no surprise that this chapter will devote a significant amount of time covering wait events in the *Cluster* classification. While there is not enough space in this book to cover all wait events from other classifications, this chapter will discuss events that are common to Oracle RAC deployments.

It is important to know that there is always a Top N list of wait events for every instance and for every session. If the database administrator can tune the session's work so as to eliminate the top event on the list, another event will take its place. Hopefully, the new event at the top of the list contributes less wait time than the previous top event. There will always be wait events for any session. There will always be a bottleneck. The database administrator must have a target to know when to stop the tuning efforts otherwise the work will never stop. For example, a query takes five minutes to complete which is unacceptable performance.

The target runtime may be defined as two minutes, which means the database administrator needs to trim three minutes off the runtime. The database administrator reduces the largest wait events and the query now runs in 2 minutes 30 seconds, short of the target time. The database administrator performs another iteration of tuning and the query now runs in 1 minute 45 seconds. At this point, even though the query still waits on events, the database administrator should stop the tuning efforts as the target runtime has been reached.

When working with wait events, the database administrator will often look at average wait times for various events. Consider the following query from *v$session_event* ordered by the *average_wait* column.

```
SQL> select
  2      event,
  3      total_waits,
  4      average_wait
  5  from
  6      v$session_event
  7  where
  8      sid=1947
  9  order by
 10      average_wait desc;
```

EVENT	TOTAL_WAITS	AVERAGE_WAIT
db file scattered read	2004	36.79
db file sequential read	64	1.24
PX Deq: Parse Reply	6	.45
Disk file operations I/O	1	.21
log file sync	1	.14
gc current block 3-way	2	.04
PX Deq: Join ACK	6	.04
row cache lock	32	.04
PX Deq: Execute Reply	21	.03
library cache lock	42	.03
gc cr block 2-way	1	.03
gc current block 2-way	5	.03
gc cr grant 2-way	42	.02

From the output above, the database administrator may conclude, based on the average wait time for the *db file scattered read* event, that a problem exists. Unfortunately, the average of any series of numbers loses the details about those values. For the *db file scattered read* event above, how many of the 2,004 total waits were near the average wait? How many occurrences were above or below the average? No one can answer those questions with the information provided. To help understand how averages hide the details, look at the following chart of values.

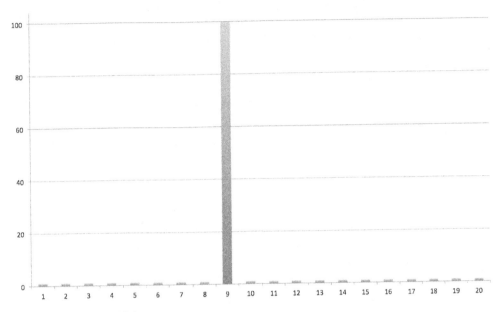

Figure 12.2 Twenty Values

In the chart above, there are twenty distinct values. Nineteen of the data points have a value of 1. One of the data points has a value of 100. The average of all values equals 5.95. If the highest and lowest values are thrown out, the average of the remaining eighteen values would equal 1, which is much more representative of the set of values. Let's assume that these values represent wait time. You could argue that the singular high value is skewing the overall average and that there is no performance problem. On the other hand, one could argue that there is a performance problem at one point, but the other values are hiding a performance issue for some user. This is the danger when looking at the average of a set of values is that the details are lost, details that may be relevant to the performance analysis.

To help provide more detail into average wait times for an event, Oracle has provided the *gv$event_histogram* view. This view can be used to show how many times a specific event waited for a precise time period. The following output shows the histogram for the *gc cr block 2-way* wait event, in milliseconds.

```
SQL> select
  2      event,
  3      wait_time_milli,
  4      wait_count
  5  from
  6      v$event_histogram
  7  where
  8      event='gc cr block 2-way'
  9  order by
 10      wait_time_milli;
```

EVENT	WAIT_TIME_MILLI	WAIT_COUNT
gc cr block 2-way	1	17638875
gc cr block 2-way	2	149450
gc cr block 2-way	4	51452
gc cr block 2-way	8	18295
gc cr block 2-way	16	3353
gc cr block 2-way	32	280
gc cr block 2-way	64	43
gc cr block 2-way	128	10
gc cr block 2-way	256	2

From the output above, the strong majority of the occurrences of this event were 8 milliseconds or less. The database administrator can see that there were a few occurrences where a session needed to wait 256 milliseconds.

At least now you have a good idea of the time distribution for this specific event. A number of occurrences more than 8 milliseconds will skew the average for this event.

This section has provided introductory information to Oracle's Wait Interface for those who may not be familiar with the concept. All wait events for single-instance Oracle databases are applicable to Oracle RAC databases.

Oracle RAC databases have additional waits like events for global cache transfers. Since this book is for Oracle RAC performance tuning, this chapter will discuss those wait events that are relevant to the clustered database.

Parallel Execution Wait Events in RAC

Executing SQL statements with parallel operations was discussed in Chapter 7 of this book. Many Oracle RAC implementations rely on parallel statement execution. A number of wait events can help understand where parallel execution is spending its time.

Parallel slave processes often exhibit wait events similar to user sessions. The parallel slave processes will read data from disk, sort data, join tables. So expect to see wait event related to user I/O and sort space requests. Additionally, the database administrator may see wait events for the following.

- *PX Deq: Table Q Normal* – This event shows a consumer slave processes that is waiting for data to arrive in the input table queue. High wait times can indicate that the workload is not balanced among all producer slaves or there is a slow Cluster Interconnect between the producers and the consumers.
- *PX Deq: Slave Session Stats* – At the completion of a parallel statement execution, the Query Coordinator will wait for statistics from the slave processes, thus posting this event. Reducing the degree of parallelism and ensuring the Cluster Interconnect is properly tuned can help alleviate this wait event.
- *PX Deq Credit: need buffer* – This event occurs when there are problems sending messages between parallel processes. A high number of messages can contribute to this event, so tune SQL statements to use a little data as possible. A slow Cluster Interconnect can contribute to this event as well. Finally, high CPU utilization on the server can be a contributor to this event.
- *PX Deq Credit: send blkd* – This wait event is essentially the same as the *PX Deq: need buffer* event.
- *PX Idle Wait* – After a slave process has completed its work and the parallel statement has completed its execution, the slave process will become idle. This event will be seen when the slave process is waiting to be acquired by a new Query Coordinator. This wait event can largely be ignored and considered an idle event. However, the database administrator may want to verify that the number of parallel slave processes is not over allocated, which could free up resources to be used elsewhere.
- *PX qref latch* – A latch protects the table queue used between the slaves and Query Coordinator. This event signifies processes are waiting to obtain the latch. Decreasing the degree of parallelism or increasing the *parallel_execution_message_size* initialization parameter can lessen these waits.

- **PX Queuing: statement queue** – If there are not enough slave processes available, the database administrator may choose to allow parallel statements to queue. This wait event shows how long the SQL statement has been waiting for slave processes to become available. The first thing to look at is to ensure parallel SQL statements are optimal so that they complete faster and return slave processes sooner. The second thing to consider is increasing the total number of slave processes.

With the wait events above, there are two events that can be an indicator of a slow Cluster Interconnect. The events can also indicate other problem areas as described above. However, the database administrator can run the script below to see if there is a need for further investigation. The average wait times should be low.

💾 px_cluster_interconnect_waits.sql

```
select
   event,
   sum(total_waits) as total_waits,
   sum(time_waited) as time_waited,
   round(avg(average_wait),2) as avg_wait
from
   gv$system_event
where
   event in ('PX Deq Credit: need buffer',
             'PX Deq Credit: send blkd')
group by
   event
order by
   event;
```

EVENT	TOTAL_WAITS	TIME_WAITED	AVG_WAIT
PX Deq Credit: need buffer	14161360	437105	.03
PX Deq Credit: send blkd	46022412	59242851	1.28

Remember that this script returns values from the lifetime of the instances. It is often better to use something like an AWR report to generate this information from a smaller time window.

Cluster Wait Class Events

Chapter 2 discussed Cache Fusion operations. A number of the wait events are centered on the global cache processing.

- ***gc buffer busy acquire*** – A session is trying to access a block. However, the session must wait for an open request for the Global Cache lock for this block to complete. If the session performing the open request is on the same instance as the session trying to access the block, the *gc buffer busy acquire* event is raised. High occurrences of this wait can indicate hot blocks being accessed with a high degree of concurrency. Tuning the SQL statements involving the blocks may help reduce this wait event. Application partitioning can also help. Additionally, a larger Buffer Cache may reduce the occurrences of this event.

- ***gc buffer busy release*** – A session is trying to access a block. However, the session must wait for an open request for the Global Cache lock for this block to complete. Unlike the previous event, the session performing the open request is on a different instance as the session trying to access the block. This event is handled the same as the *gc buffer busy acquire* event.

- ***gc buffer busy*** – Prior to Oracle 11g, the *gc buffer busy acquire* and *gc buffer busy release* events were lumped into this singular event. Oracle 11g split the events to provide a better understanding of where the open request was coming from. This event is handled the same as the other two events.

- ***gc cr block 2-way*** – This event occurs when a Consistent Read global cache transfer is needed and the resource master also holds the master copy of the block. This event is discussed in more detail in Chapter 2. Proper tuning of SQL statements can reduce the number of waits. A properly tuned Cluster Interconnect can reduce the transfer time.

- ***gc cr block 3-way*** – This event occurs when a Consistent Read global cache transfer is needed and the resource master does not hold the master copy of the block. This event is discussed in more detail in Chapter 2. Proper tuning of SQL statements can reduce the number of waits. A properly tuned Cluster Interconnect can reduce the transfer time.

- ***gc cr block busy*** – The session requested a Consistent Read block transfer, but the remote instance was too busy to send the block immediately. Common reasons for this wait event are that the remote instance was not able to provide the LMS process enough CPU resources or that the remote instance was experiencing an I/O bottleneck.

- ***gc cr block congested*** – The session requested a Consistent Read block transfer, but transfer is delayed. The LMS process on the remote node is not able to send the block immediately. When LMS is not able to immediately satisfy the transfer request, the request is placed in a queue. This wait event is often due to high CPU on the holding instance and LMS cannot obtain the CPU cycles it needs. Another method to remediate the waits for this event is to reduce the number of requests from LMS most often by application partitioning.

- ***gc cr block lost*** – A global cache transfer was requested, but the block was lost before its transfer could be completed. This event signifies the amount of time to retransfer the block. Normally, this event indicates either a network issue with the Cluster Interconnect, or high CPU utilization hampering the LMS process. This event was discussed in Chapter 4 and remediation for the event can be found there.

- ***gc cr disk read*** – This event occurs when a Consistent Read image is needed from another instance's Buffer Cache. Blocks from the Undo tablespace will be needed to construct a read-consistent image. If the undo block is not in the remote instance's Buffer Cache, the undo block must be read from disk. This event is the time to read that undo block from disk. This even can be reduced by a larger Buffer Cache or by reducing commit cleanouts.

- ***gc cr failure*** – This event occurs when a session initiates a global cache Consistent Read transfer but instead of receiving the block, the session receives a failure status message. The failure status could be because the instance holding the block has an invalid checksum or it is too busy to process the request. Verify the other instance is not overly busy. Verify the block does not have corruption on disk to ensure the data is still valid.

- ***gc cr grant 2-way*** – This event can also occur when the CPU count differs on the nodes as the number of LMS processes is not the same. The node with the higher number of CPUs can flood the other node with more requests than can be handled. In this case, set the *gcs_server_processes* initialization parameter to the same value in all instances rather than let it default.

- ***gc cr grant busy*** – A session intends to modify a block and needs to obtain a global grant on the resource and there is a delay in loading the block to the current instance's Buffer Cache. Most commonly, the delay is due to another instance. Application partitioning can help reduce this event.

- ***gc cr grant congested*** – The session requested a Consistent Read block transfer, but transfer is delayed due to high CPU on the holding instance. Reduce the CPU contention.

- ***gc cr multi block request*** – A session needs multiple Consistent Read blocks, similar to the familiar *db file scattered read* wait event. The first course of action to reduce this event is to tune the SQL statement to read as few blocks as possible. The second course of action is to ensure the Cluster Interconnect is tuned.

- ***gc cr request*** – A session sends a request for a Consistent Read block. This event is the time from the initial request until the LMS process on the remote instance acknowledges the request. Normally, this event is negligible. Should the event show significant wait times, it can be an indicator that either the Cluster Interconnect is saturated or LMS on the remote instance does not have the resources it needs, mostly CPU.

- *gc current block 2-way* – This event occurs when a Current global cache transfer is needed and the resource master also holds the master copy of the block. This event is discussed in more detail in Chapter 2. Proper tuning of SQL statements can reduce the number of waits. A properly tuned Cluster Interconnect can reduce the transfer time. This event can also occur when the CPU count differs on the nodes as the number of LMS processes is not the same. The node with the higher number of CPUs can flood the other node with more requests than can be handled. In this case, set the *gcs_server_processes* initialization parameter to the same value in all instances rather than let it default.

- *gc current block 3-way* – This event occurs when a Current global cache transfer is needed and the resource master does not hold the master copy of the block. This event is discussed in more detail in Chapter 2. Proper tuning of SQL statements can reduce the number of waits. A properly tuned Cluster Interconnect can reduce the transfer time. This event can also occur when the CPU count differs on the nodes as the number of LMS processes is not the same. The node with the higher number of CPUs can flood the other node with more requests than can be handled. In this case, set the *gcs_server_processes* initialization parameter to the same value in all instances rather than let it default.

- *gc current block busy* – The session requested a Current block transfer, but the remote instance was too busy to send the block immediately. Common reasons for this wait event are that the remote instance was not able to provide the LMS process enough CPU resources or that the remote instance was experiencing an I/O bottleneck. Another reason for this wait event is that the remote instance must wait for a committing transaction to write redo records to the online redo log before the changed block can be sent. If the commit is allowed to finish, a current block can be sent rather than a CR block.

- *gc current block congested* – The session requested a Current block transfer, but transfer is delayed. The LMS process on the remote node is not able to send the block immediately. When LMS is not able to immediately satisfy the transfer request, the request is placed in a queue. This wait event is often due to high CPU on the holding instance and LMS cannot obtain the CPU cycles it needs. Another method to remediate the waits for this event is to reduce the number of requests from LMS most often by application partitioning.

- *gc current block lost* – A global cache transfer was requested, but the block was lost before its transfer could be completed. This event signifies the amount of time to retransfer the block. Normally, this event indicates either a network issue with the Cluster Interconnect, or high CPU utilization hampering the LMS process. This event was discussed in Chapter 4 and remediation for the even can be found there.

- *gc current grant 2-way* – This event can also occur when the CPU count differs on the nodes as the number of LMS processes is not the same. The node with the higher number of CPUs can flood the other node with more requests than can be handled. In this case, set the *gcs_server_processes* initialization parameter to the same value in all instances rather than let it default.

- *gc current grant busy* – A session intends to modify a block and needs to obtain a global grant on the resource and there is a delay in loading the block to the current instance's Buffer Cache. Most commonly, the delay is due to another instance. Application partitioning can help reduce this event.

- *gc current grant congested* – The session requested a Current block transfer, but transfer is delayed due to high CPU on the holding instance. Reduce the CPU contention.

- *gc current multi block request* – A session needs multiple Current blocks, similar to the familiar *db file scattered read* wait event. The first course of action to reduce this event is to tune the SQL statement to read as few blocks as possible. The second course of action is to ensure the Cluster Interconnect is tuned.

- *gc current request* – A session sends a request for a Current block. This event is the time from the initial request until the LMS process on the remote instance acknowledges the request. Normally, this event is negligible. Should the event show significant wait times, it can be an indicator that either the Cluster Interconnect is saturated or LMS on the remote instance does not have the resources it needs, mostly CPU.

- *gc current retry* – A global cache transfer was requested, but the block was lost before its transfer could be completed. This event is similar to the *gc cr block lost* and *gc current block lost* wait events.

- *gc current split* – This wait event signifies contention for index block splits. If the index involved is populated with values from a sequence, refer to Chapter 3 for remediation suggestions.

- *gc remaster* – This event indicates that the session is waiting for a block re-mastering action to complete. Dynamic Resource Mastering (DRM) was discussed in Chapter 2. If an instance is terminated for some reason, it would be common to see some occurrences of this event until all blocks mastered by the now terminated instance are now mastered by a surviving instance. This even can occur sporadically as Oracle RAC performs automatic DRM operations. If this event is occurring more frequently then application partitioning can help reduce this wait event.

- **gc quiesce** – This event signifies a session is checking on the lock status of a resource and the resource is involved in Dynamic Resource Mastering. This event is not commonly seen as a top wait event.

With these wait events, you can see if there is significant time spent waiting for global cache transfers to complete. The following script breaks down the wait times for all instances.

💾 gc_block_transfer_waits.sql

```
select
   event,
   sum(total_waits) as total_waits,
   sum(time_waited) as time_waited,
   round(avg(average_wait),2) as avg_wait
from
   gv$system_event
where
   event like 'gc%block%-way'
group by
   event
order by
   event;
```

EVENT	TOTAL_WAITS	TIME_WAITED	AVG_WAIT
gc cr block 2-way	41936347	1194866	.03
gc cr block 3-way	14709248	631037	.04
gc current block 2-way	137944826	3344853	.02
gc current block 3-way	49426269	1997016	.04

The average waits for each event is pretty low so for the lifetimes of the instances, these events are not cause for concern.

Miscellaneous RAC Wait Events

This section contains miscellaneous wait events that are common in Oracle RAC databases.

- **cursor: mutex S** – A cursor is being parsed and trying to obtain a mutex in Shared mode. But it must wait because another session holds the mutex in exclusive mode. Contention can be introduced by a number of reasons: excessive parsing, an incorrect Shared Pool size, too many versions of cursors in the Shared Pool, not implementing Huge Pages. There are some known bugs with this wait event, especially in Oracle RAC. So it may be beneficial to file a Service Request to get to the bottom of it if this is a dominant wait event.

- **cursor: mutex X** – A cursor is being parsed and trying to obtain a mutex in eXclusive mode. But it must wait because another session holds the mutex in exclusive mode. Contention can be introduced by a number of reasons: excessive parsing, an incorrect Shared Pool size, too many versions of cursors in the Shared Pool, not implementing Huge Pages.

- **cursor: pin S** – A session is trying to obtain a mutex on a specific cursor in Shared mode. There is no holder of the mutex in exclusive mode. However, the mutex counter cannot be updated for this session because other sessions are trying to update the same mutex counter. Note that the other sessions are not necessarily trying to use the same cursor. High CPU utilization can contribute to the number of sessions waiting on this event. The P1 value for this wait event gives the hash value of the SQL statement waiting on this event. Use this hash value to get the SQL text from *gv$sqlarea*. If there are SQL statements that seemed to be involved more frequently than others, see if the application can be recoded to reduce the number of times the SQL statement is executed. For instance, if the SQL statement is inside a loop, see if a singular SQL statement can be created to encompass the loop.

- **cursor: pin S wait on X** – A session holds a mutex in shared mode and is trying to obtain the mutex in exclusive mode. This event can be caused by too many versions of the same SQL statement in the shared pool. Recoding the application to reduce the number of SQL versions can help reduce this event. Additionally, SQL statements that exhibit a high parse time can cause this wait event. Optimizer hints and plan management can reduce parse times. High CPU utilization can inflate parse times as well.

- **cursor: pin X** – A session is trying to obtain a mutex in exclusive mode. This event is handled similarly to the *cursor: pin S* wait event.

- **library cache: mutex S** – A session is trying to obtain shared access to a mutex protecting the library cache. This event can be caused by frequent hard parses. Using bind variables can reduce the hard parses. This event can also be caused by high versions of the same SQL statement. Recoding the application to reduce the number of SQL versions can help reduce this event. If a SQL statement is invalidated, it can cause this wait event. However, actions that would invalidate a SQL statement, like gathering object statistics or modifying the underlying objects, should be rarely done in a production system. Another cause of this wait event would be SQL reloads, which can be an indicator of a Shared Pool that is sized too small.

- **library cache: mutex X** – A session is trying to obtain exclusive access to a mutex protecting the library cache. This event is handled similarly to the *library cache: mutex S* wait event.

So far, this chapter has covered information related to wait events commonly seen in an Oracle RAC database. Wait event for parallel statement execution and global cache transfers were discussed. Mutex and pin wait events were presented in this section. Next, locking in Oracle RAC is shown. Additional wait events will be discussed as waiting on a lock manifests itself with an enqueue wait event.

RAC Locks

Database management systems are accessed concurrently by multiple users, each issuing their own transactions. In Oracle, transactions conform to the ACID properties: Atomic, Consistent, Isolated, and Durable. If two users are trying to modify the same record at the same time, it is incumbent on the database engine to make it seem like the users are acting in isolation, the 'I' in ACID. Like many database engines, Oracle uses locking to protect concurrent changes to the same data in a table. In Oracle terminology, locks are also called *enqueues*.

Locks often have two modes, *shared* and *exclusive*. Only one session can acquire an exclusive lock. Multiple sessions can acquire a shared lock. Oracle will never escalate a lock from shared to exclusive.

Oracle 12c has over 250 different lock types as can be seen below. Oracle 11g has less lock types, but still more than 200 different lock types.

```
SQL> select
  2      count(*)
  3  from
  4      v$lock_type;

  COUNT(*)
----------
       256
```

These lock types help protect many areas of the Oracle database, including but not limited to the control file, sort space, bloom filters, and the sequence cache. Out of all of the different locks, two types are most common, the TX and TM locks.

```
SQL> select
  2      type,
  3      name,
  4      description
  5  from
  6      v$lock_type
```

RAC Locks

```
    7   where
    8      type in ('TM','TX');

TYPE NAME
---- -----------
DESCRIPTION
------------------------------------------------------------------------
TM   DML
Synchronizes accesses to an object

TX   Transaction
Lock held by a transaction to allow other transactions to wait for it
```

As the *v$lock_type* view shows, the TM lock protects an object by signifying that DML is currently being executed. A TX lock protects data from being modified by a transaction. To show both lock types, consider a user who executes a simple DML statement similar to the following.

```
SQL> update
    2      orders
    3   set
    4      order_date=sysdate
    5   where
    6      order_id=22605;

1 row updated.
```

The transaction has not committed so the session is still holding on to its locks. Next, we need to determine the session's identifier from the *v$session* view.

```
SQL> select
    2      sid
    3   from
    4      v$session
    5   where
    6      audsid=sys_context('USERENV','SESSIONID');

       SID
----------
        84
```

The *v$lock* view will show the locks obtained by the session, as seen below.

```
SQL> select
    2      type,
    3      id1,
    4      id2,
    5      lmode,
    6      request
    7   from
    8      v$lock
    9   where
   10      sid=84;
```

```
TYPE        ID1        ID2      LMODE     REQUEST
----        ----       ----     -----     -------
TM        22975          0          3           0
TX       458753       4114          6           0
```

The single DML statement has obtained two locks for the session, a TX and a TM lock. The *lmode* column shows the lock mode. A value of 3 indicates a shared lock and a value of 6 shows an exclusive lock. The session has obtained an exclusive transaction lock to modify the row of data. The session has also obtained a shared lock for its DML operation. For a TM lock the *id1* column of *v$lock* points to the object id in the *dba_objects* view. Note that the TM and TX locks are in the instance only. Other instances of the Oracle RAC database will not see the session's locks. Instead, the other instances see the Global Enqueue Services locks on the resource, which will be shown later.

```
SQL> select
  2      owner,
  3      object_name
  4  from
  5      dba_objects
  6  where
  7      object_id=22975;

OWNER            OBJECT_NAME
----------       --------------------
SCOTT            ORDERS
```

The TM lock in this case is protecting the *orders* table. This lock ensures that the table cannot be dropped or altered while the transaction is still active. If a database administrator tries to drop the table, for example, an exclusive TM lock will not be obtained. Note that other sessions can obtain a shared lock on the same object to perform other DML operations.

For a TX lock, the *id1* and *id2* columns of *v$lock* point to the undo segment and transaction table, respectively for the transaction. When another session attempts to modify the same row, Oracle will try to generate a consistent read of the block and will run into the exclusive lock from the transaction, causing the other session to wait on the lock's release.

Another way to get the table involved in the transaction is to join the *v$locked_object* and *dba_objects* views.

```
SQL> select
  2      lo.object_id,
  3      o.owner,
  4      o.object_name
  5  from
  6      v$locked_object lo
```

```
 7      join
 8      dba_objects o
 9      on
10          lo.object_id=o.object_id
11  where
12      lo.session_id=84;

OBJECT_ID OWNER      OBJECT_NAME
--------- ---------- --------------------
    22975 SCOTT      ORDERS
```

In Oracle RAC, sessions in one instance can block a session in any other instance. To identify sessions waiting on transaction locks and their blockers, the database administrator can query *gv$lock*. The following script shows blockers and waiters for TX locks.

🖫 locked_sessions.sql

```
select
   inst_id,
   sid,
   type,
   id1,
   id2,
   case
      when lmode > 0
      then 'Blocker'
      else 'Waiter'
   end as action
from
   gv$lock
where
   (id1,id2) in (select
                    id1,
                    id2
                 from
                    gv$lock
                 where
                    type='TX'
                    and
                    request<>0)
order by
   id1,
   id2;

   INST_ID        SID TY        ID1        ID2 ACTION
---------- ---------- -- ---------- ---------- -------
         1        119 TX     196614       4189 Blocker
         2        102 TX     196614       4189 Waiter
```

Sessions with the same *id1* and *id2* values are involved lock contention. The script shows the instance and session identifier of the blocker and any waiting sessions.

Chapter 2 discussed GES blocking, as even a row is a managed shared resource in Oracle RAC databases. From that chapter, the *ges_blockers.sql* script shows GES locking involved in a transaction.

💾 ges_blockers.sql

```
select
   inst_id,
   pid,
   resource_name1 as resource_name,
   blocker,
   blocked,
   owner_node
from
   gv$ges_blocking_enqueue
order by
   resource_name;
```

INST_ID	PID	RESOURCE_NAME	BLOCKER	BLOCKED	OWNER_NODE
2	30421	[0xA7][0x5],[RS][ext 0x0,0x0]	1	0	1
1	29102	[0xA7][0x5],[RS][ext 0x0,0x0]	0	1	0
2	14494	[0x2000e][0x65a],[TX][ext 0x2,	0	1	1
1	29086	[0x2000e][0x65a],[TX][ext 0x2,	1	0	0

Remember that the first two lines show the resource being blocked on instance 1 from a session on instance 2. The blocker and blocked columns identify that instance 2 has the lock and is blocking the session on instance 1. The reader may wish to refer back to Chapter 2 for additional information.

Sessions waiting on locks to be released will have enqueue wait events. After all, the session is waiting for an action to be completed. The following is a list of some of the enqueue wait events that may be seen.

- ***enq: TX contention*** – This wait event is the typical TX lock shown so far in this chapter. Reducing this wait event is typically an application issue. The application needs to be examined to determine if the transaction is holding the lock too long or too often. In Oracle RAC, a transaction that causes an index block to split can result in an increase for this wait event. Converting the index to a reverse-key index or a hash-partitioned index can help in this case.
- ***enq: TX index contention*** – This wait event is seen for the reasons described above, a transaction causes an index block to split which is often worse in Oracle RAC environments. As stated above, a reverse-key index or a hash-partitioned index can help in this case.
- ***enq: HV contention*** – This event can occur when the *append* hint is used to insert rows above a table's High Water Mark (HWM). Inserting above the HWM in Oracle RAC systems can increase the wait time for this event due to

---

the global cache operations that need to be performed to support sessions on different instances. Normally, the *append* hint is used for bulk loading and should not be done by a high number concurrent sessions. Consider removing the hint if possible and if this wait event is a major contributor to the performance problem. Application partitioning can help if the sessions inserting above the HWM can be isolated to one or a few instances.

- **enq: SV contention** – This wait event occurs when sessions are competing for a sequence's next value. Refer to Chapter 3 for techniques on how to improve sequence performance in Oracle RAC databases.
- **enq: SS contention** – This wait event occurs when sessions are waiting on sort segment space in a temporary tablespace. Refer to Chapter 5 for information on how to tune the temporary tablespaces.

This section of the chapter has discussed locking in Oracle RAC databases. The chapter was largely focused on transaction (TX) enqueues, but did touch on GES blockers and referred the reader back to Chapter 2 for more information. This section concluded with a list of common enqueue wait events.

RAC Statistics

As stated at the start of this chapter, Oracle is the most instrumented relational database on the market. The first section of this chapter discussed the wait event interface to help support that claim. This section shows a variety of statistics available to the database administrator to help understand how the Oracle database is performing. Statistics relevant to a single-instance database are still applicable to an Oracle RAC database. This chapter will help the reader understand Oracle RAC statistics.

The current version of Oracle 12c has over one thousand different statistics. The *v$statname* view can provide us information on the statistics for the Oracle database.

```
SQL> select
  2      count(*) as num_stats
  3  from
  4      v$statname;


NUM_STATS
----------
      1178
```

Just like wait events, the statistics are grouped together by various classifications. The following table shows the different statistic classes.

Class	Description
1	User
2	Redo
4	Enqueue
8	Cache
16	OS
32	Real Application Clusters
64	SQL
128	Debug

Table 12.1 Statistics Classifications

Obviously, this book will discuss a number of statistics with in the Real Application Clusters classification. Oracle statistics may have multiple classifications as well. For example, a statistic in class 40 is for Real Application Cluster Caches (40=32+8). Any class number that has a value of 32 or 32 plus some number is for Oracle RAC. For Oracle 12.1.0.2, there are four classifications of statistics that fall in the Oracle RAC category.

```
SQL> select
  2      class,
  3      count(*) as num_stats
  4   from
  5      v$statname
  6   where
  7      bitand(class,32) <> 0
  8   group by
  9      class
 10   order by
 11      class;

    CLASS  NUM_STATS
---------- ----------
        32         35
        33          3
        34          1
        40         53
```

As can be seen above, the majority of the Oracle RAC statistics are class 32 (RAC) or 40 (RAC and Cache).

When an Oracle instance is started, all statistic values are zero. As activity occurs in the instance, Oracle automatically increases the appropriate statistic values to represent that activity. The statistic values will represent the intended measurement until the instance is terminated at which time the statistic value is lost. Statistic values do not survive instance shutdowns.

So let's look at an example of a statistic from an Oracle instance.

```
SQL> select
  2      value
  3  from
  4      v$sysstat
  5  where
  6      name='gc cr blocks received';

    VALUE
----------
 25381126
```

The statistic above shows how many Consistent Read blocks were received by the instance. The value by itself has little meaning. Twenty five million CR blocks were received. Is that a lot? A little? Without more information, one can't be sure. At this point, the statistic is just a value without meaning.

Normally, the database administrator needs to obtain the statistic value for a period of time. This involves sampling the statistic value at one point in time, then at another point in time. The difference in the two values represents the statistic measurement for the sample period. As an example, consider the two queries run below.

```
SQL> select
  2      to_char(sysdate,'HH24:MI') as sample_time,
  3      value
  4  from
  5      v$sysstat
  6  where
  7      name='gc cr blocks received';

SAMPL      VALUE
-----  ----------
12:17   25382427

SQL> select
  2      to_char(sysdate,'HH24:MI') as sample_time,
  3      value
  4  from
  5      v$sysstat
  6  where
  7      name='gc cr blocks received';

SAMPL      VALUE
-----  ----------
12:27   25723473
```

The two queries above were issued ten minutes apart. In those ten minutes a total of 341,046 CR blocks were received by the instance for an average of 34,105 blocks per minute. Just like wait events, this is just an average. This chapter has already shown how averages can skewed by very large or very small numbers.

This type of simple math is how many of the metric values are computed in an AWR report. Chapter 9 showed that an AWR report is generated using two snapshots. The snapshot captures all of the statistics at that time. A subsequent snapshot has new metric values. The AWR report knows the time the two snapshots were taken. The AWR report calculates the differences in the metric values and if applicable, provides an average over the sample period. When working with system statistics, it is often desirable to keep the sample window as short as possible for this reason, which means AWR reports with small windows are often most beneficial.

In the example above, the statistics indicates that 341,046 CR blocks were received by the instance in the ten-minute sample period. What is still unknown is if this value is high or low. To be able to answer that question, the database administrator must have a baseline. The AWR facility provides the ability to denote two snapshots that represent a baseline of good database performance. Comparing this value to the same statistic in the baseline helps to answer the question of whether the computed value is high or low. Without a baseline, we can only rely on our best guess.

The queries above obtain statistics from the *v$sysstat* view. For Oracle RAC, the *gv$sysstat* view is obviously useful. These views show statistic values from the current instance and from all instances, respectively. The *v$sesstat* and *gv$sesstat* views show statistic values for individual sessions. The *v$mystat* view shows statistic values for the current session only.

As stated in the start of this section, many statistics are applicable to both single-instance and Oracle RAC databases. With over a thousand statistics in Oracle 12c, there isn't enough room to talk about each one. Even the Oracle RAC statistics are too numerous to fit into this chapter. This chapter will discuss the most commonly used RAC-related statistics.

RAC Parallel Statistics

The first statistics discussed are all related to parallel operations.

- **DDL statements parallelized** – Shows the number of DDL (*create, alter,* etc) that were executed with parallel operations.
- **DML statements parallelized** – Shows the number of DML (*insert, update, delete*) that were executed with parallel operations.

- *queries parallelized* – Shows the number of *select* statements that were executed with parallel operations.

- *PX local messages recv'd* – Shows the number of messages received by parallel slave processes in this instance.

- *PX local messages sent* – Shows the number of messages sent to parallel slave processes in the same instance.

- *PX remote messages recv'd* – Shows the number of messages received by parallel slave processes from other instances.

- *PX remote messages sent* – Shows the number of messages sent to parallel slave processes in other instances.

- *Parallel operations downgraded 1 to 25 pct* – Shows the number of parallel statements that could not receive the requested number of slave processes. The slave processes in use were reduced by 1 to 25 percent of the initial request. The Resource Manager may also downgrade the operation per the resource policy. Ideally, this statistic should be zero.

- *Parallel operations downgraded 25 to 50 pct* – Shows the number of parallel statements that could not receive the requested number of slave processes. The slave processes in use were reduced by 25 to 50 percent of the initial request. The Resource Manager may also downgrade the operation per the resource policy. Ideally, this statistic should be zero.

- *Parallel operations downgraded 50 to 75 pct* – Shows the number of parallel statements that could not receive the requested number of slave processes. The slave processes in use were reduced by 50 to 75 percent of the initial request. The Resource Manager may also downgrade the operation per the resource policy. Ideally, this statistic should be zero.

- *Parallel operations downgraded 75 to 99 pct* – Shows the number of parallel statements that could not receive the requested number of slave processes. The slave processes in use were reduced by 75 to 99 percent of the initial request. The Resource Manager may also downgrade the operation per the resource policy. Ideally, this statistic should be zero.

- *Parallel operations downgraded to serial* – Shows the number of parallel statements that could not receive the requested number of slave processes and the statement was executed serially. The Resource Manager may also downgrade the operation per the resource policy. Ideally, this statistic should be zero.

- *Parallel operations not downgraded* – Shows the number of parallel statements that were able to receive the requested number of slave processes.

Armed with these statistics, you can find some interesting information about parallel statement executing in your Oracle RAC database. The script below shows the number of parallel statements issued since the instances were started.

💾 parallel_executions.sql

```
select
   name,
   sum(value) as total
from
   gv$sysstat
where
   name in ('DDL statements parallelized',
            'DML statements parallelized',
            'queries parallelized')
group by
   name;
```

```
NAME                                        TOTAL
----------------------------------------    ----------
DDL statements parallelized                        14
DML statements parallelized                        23
queries parallelized                          1451847
```

Obviously in the output above, this Oracle RAC database heavily favors parallelized *select* statements over the rest.

With other statistics, we can see how many parallel executions have been downgraded over the life of the instances.

💾 parallel_downgrades.sql

```
select
   sum(value) as total_downgraded
from
   gv$sysstat
where
   name like 'Parallel operations downgraded%';
```

```
TOTAL_DOWNGRADED
----------------
          53848
```

Over fifty thousand parallel operations have been downgraded since the instances were started. This number seems awfully high unless the instance has been running a very long time. It can be an indicator that not enough parallel slaves are available to support demand. The database administrator may want to investigate further.

Global Cache Statistics

This section shows statistics for global cache operations. As we already know, global cache operations are at the heart of Cache Fusion and Oracle RAC.

- **gc blocks corrupt** – Shows the number of blocks involved in a global cache transfer that were marked as corrupt. Ideally, this should be zero. A high number of non-zero values may indicate problems with the Cluster Interconnect.
- **gc blocks lost** – Shows the number of blocks involved in a global cache transfer that lost during the transfer. Ideally, this should be zero. A high number of non-zero values may indicate problems with the Cluster Interconnect.
- **gc cr block receive time** – Shows the amount of time to receive all global cache consistent read block transfers from other instances.
- **gc cr block send time** – Shows the amount of time to send all global cache consistent read block transfers to other instances.
- **gc cr blocks received** – Shows the total number of consistent read blocks received in a global cache transfer from all other instances.
- **gc cr blocks served** – Shows the total number of consistent read blocks sent in a global cache transfer to all other instances.
- **gc current block receive time** – Shows the amount of time to receive all global cache current block transfers from other instances.
- **gc current block send time** – Shows the amount of time to send all global cache current block transfers to other instances.
- **gc current blocks received** – Shows the total number of current blocks received in a global cache transfer from all other instances.
- **gc current blocks served** – Shows the total number of current blocks sent in a global cache transfer to all other instances.
- **gc kbytes sent** – Shows the number of kilobytes of data sent from this instance to satisfy global cache transfer requests.
- **gc local grants** – Shows the number of resource grants performed locally in this instance. See Chapter 2 for more details on resource grants.
- **gc remote grants** – Shows the number of resource grants performed remotely from other instances. See Chapter 2 for more details on resource grants.

With these statistics, the database administrator can gain a lot of knowledge into how busy global cache operations are for their Oracle RAC deployment. The following script shows the number of blocks lost or corrupt in global cache transfers.

gc_bad_transfers.sql

```
select
   days_up,
   blocks_lost,
   blocks_corrupt
from (select
         sum(value) as blocks_lost
      from
         gv$sysstat
      where
         name='gc blocks lost'),
      (select
         sum(value) as blocks_corrupt
      from
         gv$sysstat
      where
         name='gc blocks corrupt'),
      (select
         round(sysdate-min(startup_time),2) as days_up
      from
         gv$instance);


  DAYS_UP BLOCKS_LOST BLOCKS_CORRUPT
---------- ----------- --------------
    16.66          45              0
```

In more than sixteen days, forty-five block transfers were lost and zero blocks were corrupted during the transfer. These numbers are not terribly high if spread out over the sixteen day period. However, if all blocks lost occurred in a one-hour period of time, it could indicate a problem during that time period.

The next script shows the number of global cache blocks received by each instance of the Oracle RAC database.

gc_blocks_received.sql

```
select
   instance_name,
   sum(value) as blocks_received
from
   gv$sysstat ss
join
   gv$instance i
on
   ss.inst_id=i.inst_id
where
   name in ('gc cr blocks received',
            'gc current blocks received')
group by
   instance_name
order by
   instance_name;
```

```
INSTANCE_NAME    BLOCKS_RECEIVED
----------------  ----------------
orcl1                   154013801
orcl2                   132388034
orcl3                   150417560
```

The output from the script above can help the database administrator understand the demands on the Cluster Interconnect. If these statistics are sampled over a short duration, the average blocks per minute can easily be calculated to help determine the private network's throughput.

Summary

This chapter spent time discussing wait events, locking, and statistics. Wait events and locking can help the database administrator pinpoint where an application or session is experiencing performance problems.

The statistics provide even more information to help understand how the Oracle RAC database is performing. This chapter is a reference for the wait events and statistics common to Oracle RAC databases.

The next chapter delves into Oracle 12c's new flex architecture, namely Flex ASM and Flex Cluster.

Flex ASM and Flex Cluster

Oracle 12c has brought with it a few new features that may provide benefit to the Oracle cluster, namely Flex ASM and Flex Cluster. At a simple level, Flex ASM provides more elasticity for Oracle's Automatic Storage Management (ASM) in a cluster. Flex Cluster provides similar elasticity for nodes participating in the cluster. This chapter will discuss both of these new Oracle 12c options.

Flex ASM

In Oracle Grid Infrastructure, each node in the cluster has one ASM instance running on it. All database instances on that node that store files in ASM communicate with the ASM instance on that same node. If there are sixteen nodes in the cluster, there are sixteen ASM instances, a one-to-one correspondence.

Flex ASM eliminates the one-to-one ratio between nodes and ASM instances. Just like Grid Infrastructure 11gR2 provided up to three SCAN Listeners no matter how many nodes in the cluster, Grid Infrastructure 12c lets us use up to three ASM instances no matter how many nodes in the cluster. That three instance configuration is not a hard limit and can be configured differently should the database administrator desire the change.

The diagram below shows a standard ASM configuration in an Oracle cluster for a six-node Oracle cluster. This cluster has two databases, HR and FIN, each of which has an instance on three of the nodes.

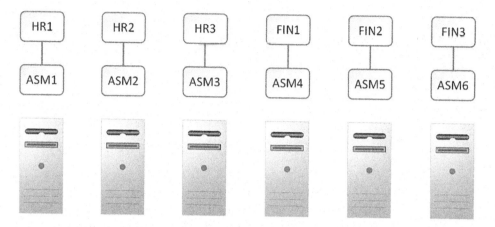

Figure 13.1 Standard ASM Architecture

Under a standard ASM configuration, if an ASM instance were to terminate, the Oracle RAC database instances on that node would terminate as well. In the diagram above, losing ASM4 also means losing instance FIN1.

The next diagram shows the same six-node cluster with the same database instances. However, this system is configured with Flex ASM. There are only three ASM instances on the nodes. Notice that instances running on nodes without ASM use an ASM instance from another node. The FIN3 instance is using ASM5 from node 5 even though FIN3 is running on node 6.

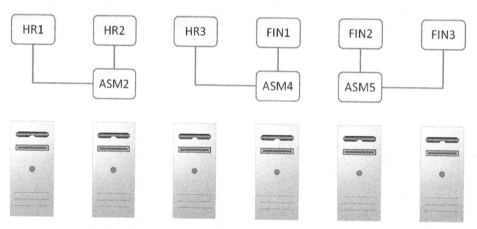

Figure 13.2 Flex ASM Architecture

When an ASM instance terminates, Grid Infrastructure will start ASM on another node. Any instances that were using the terminated ASM instance will now use another ASM instance.

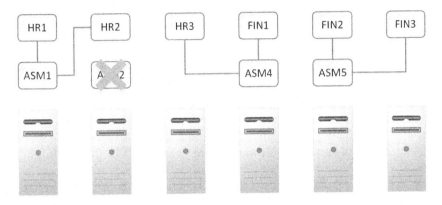

Figure 13.3 Flex ASM Failover

In the diagram above, the ASM2 instance has terminated for some reason. The instances HR1 and HR2 are now using the ASM1 instance that was not previously running.

One of the biggest benefits to using Flex ASM is higher availability. Flex ASM has other benefits as well. For Oracle Database 12c clients, Flex ASM now supports larger Logical Unit (LUN) sizes. The maximum number of disk groups has been increased to 511. Chapter 5 mentioned that Oracle recommends no more than two ASM diskgroups per instance. That chapter indicated that the database administrator often ignores this advice to help segregate I/O and to support Information Lifecycle Management (ILM) strategies. Also, clustered databases are getting larger, meaning more nodes in the cluster hence more instances for the database. Even if Oracle Corporation's recommendation is heeded, two disk groups per instance means the database administrator can have as many as 255 instances and still meet the recommendation. Flex ASM helps the database administrator scale the ASM diskgroups to handle the ability to scale the Oracle RAC deployment to many more nodes than before, which certainly helps to address Oracle RAC storage performance.

Another benefit of Flex ASM is the ability to use a private network for just ASM communications. Chapter 4 of this book discussed the Cluster Interconnect and how that network should remain truly private keep the Oracle RAC database performing at an optimal level. Flex ASM implements a new ASM network, just like the Cluster Interconnect. The ASM network is used for communication between ASM and its clients. With an ASM-only network, the ASM communications will not interfere and constrain the other networks in the cluster topology.

The following shows an example of three network interfaces in an Oracle RAC system to support the public, Cluster Interconnect, and ASM communications.

```
[root@host01 ~]# oifcfg getif
eth0 192.168.10.0 global public
eth1 10.0.1.0 global cluster_interconnect
eth2 10.0.2.0 global asm
```

All those benefits aside, you will want to test Flex ASM carefully before implementing in production. An instance leaving the current node to talk to an ASM instance on another node is certainly going to introduce latency that won't be present if the ASM instance were on the same node. You need to ensure the latency is not introducing a bottleneck to database performance. The end of this chapter shows a simple test where Flex ASM introduces negative performance on an instance.

Before Flex ASM can be used, it must be defined in a Grid Infrastructure environment. The next few sections show how to convert a Standard ASM install to Flex ASM as well as how to implement Flex ASM from an initial Grid Infrastructure installation.

Migrating to Flex ASM

If the Oracle cluster is already up and running and using standard ASM, the database administrator can migrate to Flex ASM very easily. First, we'll show that the Standard ASM is being used. The *srvctl* utility shows that ASM is running on both nodes of the cluster.

```
[oracle@host01 ~]$ srvctl status asm
ASM is running on host01,host02
```

Querying *gv$instance* from one of the ASM instances shows that ASM is running on both nodes as well.

```
SQL> select
  2      host_name,
  3      instance_name
  4  from
  5      gv$instance;
```

```
HOST_NAME                           INSTANCE_NAME
-------------------------------     -----------------
host01.localdomain                  +ASM1
host02.localdomain                  +ASM2
```

Lastly, the *asmcmd* utility shows that Flex ASM is not enabled.

```
[oracle@host01 ~]$ asmcmd

ASMCMD> showclustermode

ASM cluster : Flex mode disabled
```

To convert the Standard ASM, the database administrator will set the environment to the ASM instance on one of the nodes and launch the ASM Configuration Assistant (ASMCA). The *asmca* utility is a graphical tool so for Unix or Linux environments, X Windows needs to be used.

```
[oracle@host01 ~]$ . oraenv

ORACLE_SID = [orcl1] ? +ASM1

The Oracle base has been set to /u01/app/oracle

[oracle@host01 ~]$ asmca
```

When the *asmca* utility starts, the database administrator will want to click on the ASM Instances tab. This tab will show all ASM instances in the environment. Clicking the Convert to Flex ASM button in the bottom left starts the conversion wizard.

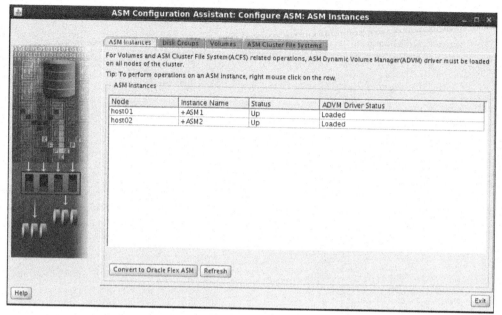

Figure 13.4 ASMCA Convert to Flex ASM

The database administrator will be presented with a screen asking for some basic information. If an ASM private network were to be used, it would be selected here. There is no way to create the ASM network from the wizard so it must be set up in advance. In the example below, the Cluster Interconnect is used for the ASM network as well.

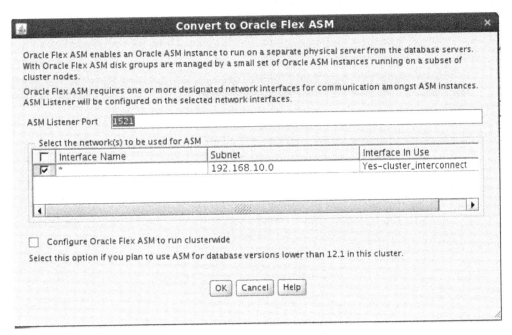

Figure 13.5 Flex ASM Conversion Wizard

The wizard asks for confirmation before proceeding. Notice that the confirmation informs that the Grid Infrastructure will be restarted, which means you need to arrange for downtime for the conversion of ASM.

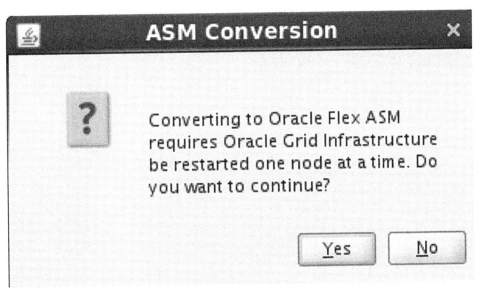

Figure 13.6 Flex ASM Conversion Confirmation

The wizard asks for a script to be run. For Linux or Unix, the "privileged user" means to run the script as root.

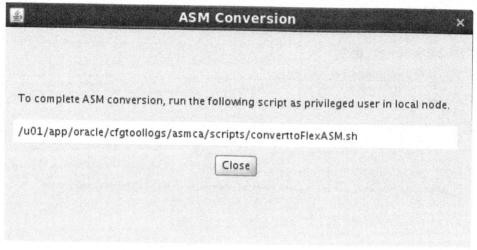

To complete ASM conversion, run the following script as privileged user in local node.

/u01/app/oracle/cfgtoollogs/asmca/scripts/converttoFlexASM.sh

Figure 13.7 Flex ASM Conversion Script

The script is asking to be executed on the local node. Running this script will perform the Grid Infrastructure restart on all nodes in the cluster. After the script has completed, *asmca* will provide confirmation that the conversion was successful.

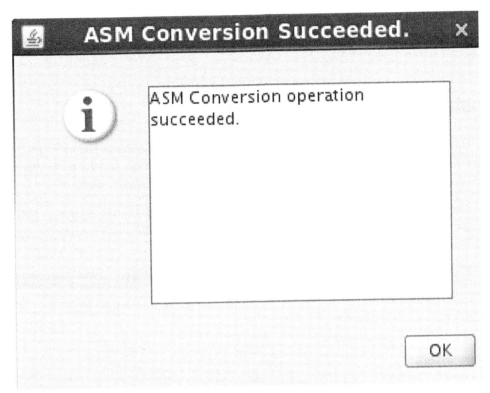

Figure 13.8 Flex ASM Conversion Complete

The *asmcmd* utility now confirms that Flex ASM is being used.

```
[oracle@host01 scripts]$ asmcmd

ASMCMD> showclustermode

ASM cluster : Flex mode enabled
```

The alert log further confirms that the instance is a Flex client. The alert log also shows the ASM instance in use for this Oracle database instance.

```
NOTE: ASMB registering with ASM instance as Flex client 0xffffffffffffffff
(reg:1085862955) (new connection)
NOTE: ASMB connected to ASM instance +ASM1 osid: 5375 (Flex mode; client id
0x10000)
```

The conversion is now complete and the Oracle RAC databases in the cluster are now using Flex ASM. The *asmca* utility provides a very easy way for the database administrator to convert from Standard ASM to Flex ASM. There is no documented method for converting from Flex ASM back to Standard ASM. Going back means that the cluster will need to be rebuilt.

Installing With Flex ASM

When installing Grid Infrastructure, the database administrator has the option of choosing Standard ASM or Flex ASM. The choice is a simple radio button and is all the database administrator needs to do to use Flex ASM from the start.

The Grid Infrastructure installation proceeds as normal. At the Installation Type screen, the database administrator needs to choose the Advanced Installation option as shown below.

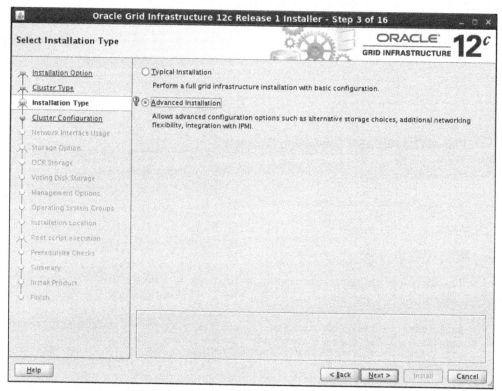

Figure 13.9 Grid Infrastructure Advanced Installation Selection

The rest of the Grid Infrastructure installation proceeds as normal for the environment. Eventually, the Storage Option select screen is displayed. The database administrator will choose the Use Oracle Flex ASM option on this screen.

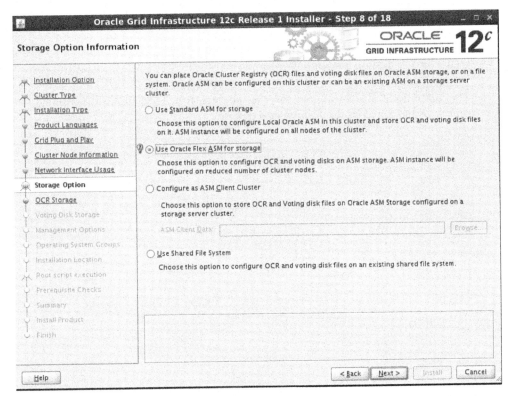

Figure 13.10 GI Installation Flex ASM Option

That's all there is to defining Flex ASM when installing Grid Infrastructure. Make sure the advanced installation option is chosen so that the Flex ASM option can be selected at the appropriate time. The Oracle Universal Installer will take care of the rest.

This section of the chapter, as well as the preceding section, showed how easy it is to implement Oracle 12c's new Flex ASM functionality. The database administrator can start using Flex ASM right away with the initial Grid Infrastructure installation or migrate if the cluster is using the standard ASM. The next section will show Flex ASM in action.

Using Flex ASM in RAC

With Flex ASM configured, it is now time to see it working in an Oracle RAC cluster. This section will show an Oracle RAC instance that does not have an ASM instance on the same node. The ASM instance will be terminated and this section will show the database instances survive the termination. All of this will build up to the next section that will show performance of instances using Flex ASM.

The three-node cluster in use for this chapter has ASM currently running on all nodes, as illustrated by the following query.

```
SQL> select
  2      instance_name,
  3      host_name
  4   from
  5      gv$instance;

INSTANCE_NAME      HOST_NAME
---------------    --------------------
+ASM1              host01.localdomain
+ASM2              host02.localdomain
+ASM3              host03.localdomain
```

Similarly, the database has three instances on the same nodes.

```
SQL> select
  2      instance_name,
  3      host_name
  4   from
  5      gv$instance;

INSTANCE_NAME      HOST_NAME
---------------    --------------------
orcl1              host01.localdomain
orcl2              host02.localdomain
orcl3              host03.localdomain
```

The cluster configuration for ASM shows that ASM is expecting three instances.

```
[oracle@host01 ~]$ srvctl config asm

ASM home: <CRS home>
Password file: +OCR/orapwASM
ASM listener: LISTENER
ASM instance count: 3
Cluster ASM listener: ASMNET1LSNR_ASM
```

To show Flex ASM in action, the instance count is lowered to one less than the total number of nodes in this cluster.

```
[oracle@host01 ~]$ srvctl modify asm -count 2

[oracle@host01 ~]$ srvctl config asm

ASM home: <CRS home>
Password file: +DB/orapwASM
ASM listener: LISTENER
ASM instance count: 2
Cluster ASM listener: ASMNET1LSNR_ASM
```

It should be noted that the minimum number of Flex ASM instances is two. Trying to configure ASM for less than two instances results in an error as seen below.

```
[oracle@host01 ~]$ srvctl modify asm -count 1

PRCA-1123 : The specified ASM cardinality 1 is less than the minimum
cardinality of 2.
```

At this point, there are two ASM instances on the three-node cluster.

```
SQL> select
  2      instance_name,
  3      host_name
  4  from
  5      gv$instance;

INSTANCE_NAME    HOST_NAME
---------------  --------------------
+ASM1            host01.localdomain
+ASM2            host02.localdomain
```

Note that ASM is not running on host03. When ASM was reconfigured, the *orcl3* instance, which we know is running on host03, showed the effect in its alert log. Below, we can see that the *asmb* background process registered as a Flex client to ASM instance *+ASM2*, which we know is running on host02.

```
Mon Dec 15 16:20:44 2014
NOTE: ASMB registering with ASM instance as Flex client 0x10002
(reg:317995479) (reconnect)
NOTE: ASMB connected to ASM instance +ASM2 osid: 17625 (Flex mode; client id
0x10002)
NOTE: ASMB rebuilding ASM server state
NOTE: ASMB rebuilt 1 (of 1) groups
NOTE: ASMB rebuilt 15 (of 15) allocated files
NOTE: fetching new locked extents from server
NOTE: 0 locks established; 0 pending writes sent to server
SUCCESS: ASMB reconnected & completed ASM server state
```

At this point, Flex ASM is up and running on two nodes of the three-node cluster. The *orcl3* instance does not have ASM on its same node. Next, we'll kill the ASM instance on host01.

```
[oracle@host01 ~]$ ps -ef|grep asm_smon

oracle      6488      1  0 16:41 ?         00:00:00 asm_smon_+ASM1
oracle      6610  22245  0 16:41 pts/1     00:00:00 grep asm_smon

[oracle@host01 ~]$ kill -9 6488

[oracle@host01 ~]$ srvctl status asm

ASM is running on host02
```

ASM is running on only one host. After a short period of time, Grid Infrastructure realizes that the ASM instance has been terminated and it restarts the instance automatically. The status now shows ASM instances running on two nodes again.

```
[oracle@host01 ~]$ srvctl status asm

ASM is running on host01,host02
```

Without Flex ASM, the instance *orcl1* would have been terminated along with the ASM instance on that note. We can see that the database's instances have all been running since before 4:00pm.

```
SQL> select
  2      instance_name,
  3      to_char(startup_time,'HH24:MI:SS') as startup_time
  4  from
  5      gv$instance;

INSTANCE_NAME    STARTUP_
---------------- --------
orcl2            15:48:37
orcl1            15:45:15
orcl3            15:51:18
```

Yet one of the ASM instances has a much more recent startup time.

```
SQL> select
  2      instance_name,
  3      to_char(startup_time,'HH24:MI:SS') as startup_time
  4  from
  5      gv$instance;

INSTANCE_NAME    STARTUP_
---------------- --------
+ASM2            15:48:25
+ASM1            16:42:01
```

The *v$asm_client* view shows the instances that are connected to the ASM instance. Remember that host03 had no ASM instance and the instance on host01 was terminated. Querying *v$asm_client* on +ASM2 shows all instances of the database connected the one ASM instance.

```
SQL> select
  2      instance_name,
  3      db_name,
  4      status
  5  from
  6      v$asm_client;

INSTANCE_NAME    DB_NAME   STATUS
---------------  --------  ------------
orcl1            orcl      CONNECTED
orcl2            orcl      CONNECTED
orcl3            orcl      CONNECTED
+ASM2            +ASM      CONNECTED
```

Here we see how Flex ASM has saved the day and provided for higher availability of the instances on the cluster. What needs to be seen next is how well Flex ASM performs for any instances that do not have a Flex ASM instance local to its node.

Flex ASM Performance in RAC

So far, this chapter has described Flex ASM and showed how it works. The big question remains, what happens to performance of an Oracle RAC instance that has no local ASM instance and must communicate with ASM across the Cluster Interconnect? The only way to know for sure is to test on your specific deployment of Flex ASM in an Oracle RAC environment.

This section of the chapter will set up a benchmark to test Flex ASM. Please keep in mind that this benchmark is run in a testbed system, so your mileage can and will vary. The reader can use the steps in this section to help design their own benchmark of Flex ASM.

Before testing can begin, we need to set up two services, one on an instance with ASM local to the node and another service on an instance with no local ASM.

```
[oracle@host03 trace]$ srvctl add service -d orcl -service asm_local_svc -
preferred "orcl2"
[oracle@host03 trace]$ srvctl add service -d orcl -service asm_non_local_svc
-preferred "orcl3"
[oracle@host03 trace]$ srvctl start service -d orcl -s asm_local_svc
[oracle@host03 trace]$ srvctl start service -d orcl -s asm_non_local_svc
[oracle@host03 trace]$ srvctl status service -d orcl
```

```
Service asm_local_svc is running on instance(s) orcl2
Service asm_non_local_svc is running on instance(s) orcl3
```

The database is now configured with two services that will be used for connections from the benchmark utility.

The Swingbench utility, discussed in Chapter 10, will be used to generate benchmark metrics. This benchmark wants to simulate I/O so the Order Entry benchmark will need to be sized correctly to impart more I/O on the load. On the Sizing Details screen, a larger size is chosen to generate a more I/O intensive workload.

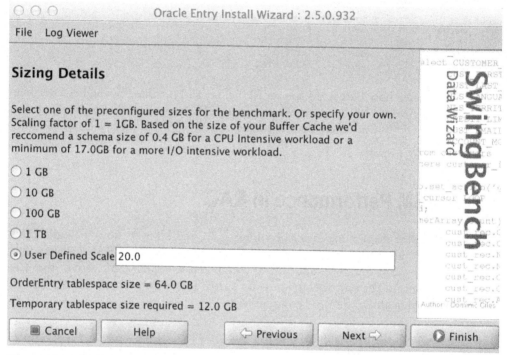

Figure 13.11 SOE Wizard Sizing Details

Even with the larger Swingbench sizing, not all interactions with the database will result in physical I/O. But as we will see shortly, the presence or lack of a local Flex ASM instance will impact the test results.

Swingbench will now be used to generate a workload with the two services set up earlier. When Swingbench connects to the *asm_local_svc* service, the benchmark activity will be run against a single instance that has ASM running on the same node. Similarly, the *asm_non_local_svc* will be used for a benchmark on a single instance that is a Flex ASM client. Restricting the benchmark runs to a single instance reduces the impact of Cache Fusion transfers that can skew the results. For this benchmark, the database had all of its instances restarted.

Swingbench was run five times against one service. The instances were bounced again and Swingbench was run five times against another service. The following diagram shows the load profile definition used in the Benchmark activity. The only thing that changed was the connection string to point to the correct service.

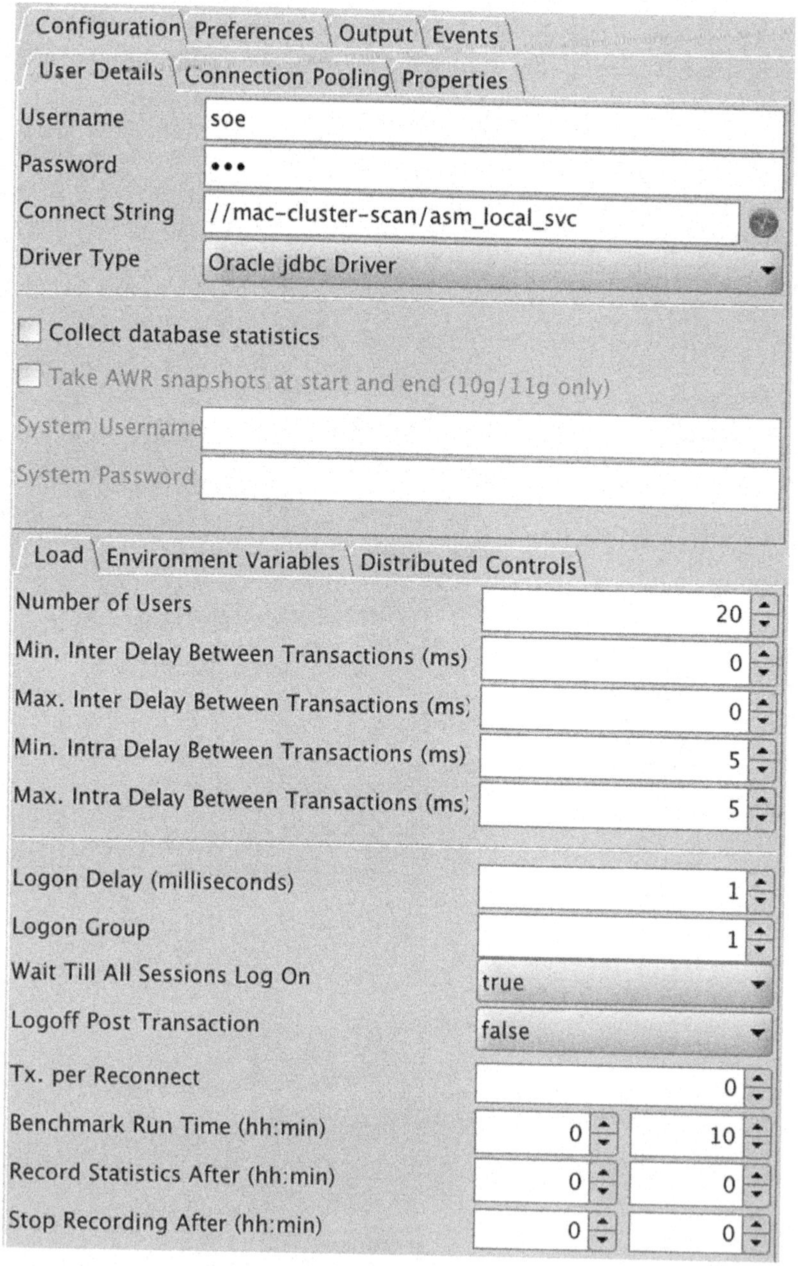

Figure 13.12 Swingbench Load Profile

As we stated, there were a total of ten Swingbench runs against the Order Entry schema, five with local ASM and five as Flex ASM clients. The following chart shows the maximum Transactions Per Minute (TPM) as noted by Swingbench for each run.

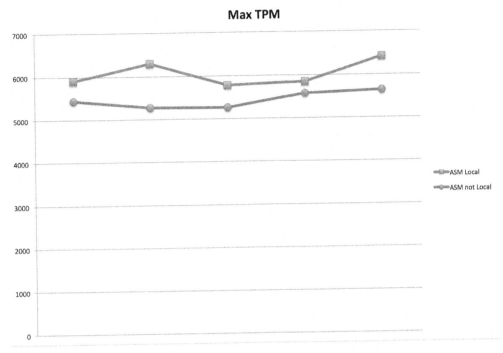

Figure 13.13 Flex ASM Max TPM Benchmark Results

The benchmark runs with local ASM on the node consistently exhibited a higher TPM than the runs without the local ASM. For this metric, higher is better. Maximum transactions per minute gives us a measure of the total capacity of the configuration, but what really matters to the end user is response time.

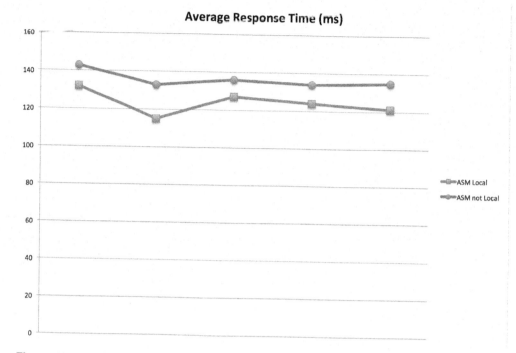

Average Response Time (ms)

ASM Local
ASM not Local

Figure 13.14 Flex ASM Benchmark Average Response Time

The chart above shows the average response time from each run. In this case, lower is better. The service with the local Flex ASM instance exhibited a better average response time for the benchmark runs.

Keep in mind that this benchmark is a simple test using a test application, not a real application. One should always test in their specific environment with their specific application before making a decision. This information is very useful for the database administrator thinking about using Flex ASM on systems that experience a high volume of disk I/O. You need to weigh the benefits of using Flex ASM with the potential increased response times that may come with it. Proper testing will need to be performed to know if Flex ASM will negatively impact application performance.

The results should not be surprising, as the instance without a local ASM instance would have some latency when trying to contact an ASM instance running on another node. The big question is if that latency is noticeable to the end user.

Remember that Flex ASM allows for more disk groups as well as the ability to dedicate a private network to just Flex ASM and reduces ASM resource requirements across the cluster. These factors may be enough to overshadow any additional latency

Flex ASM may experience. There are lots of variables that were not tested in the benchmark shown in this chapter. So test, test, and test your specific configuration to determine if Flex ASM is right for your deployment.

Flex Cluster

Oracle 12c introduced its new Flex Cluster option that had many in the Oracle community anticipating the possibilities. To understand what an Oracle Flex Cluster is, examine the following diagram.

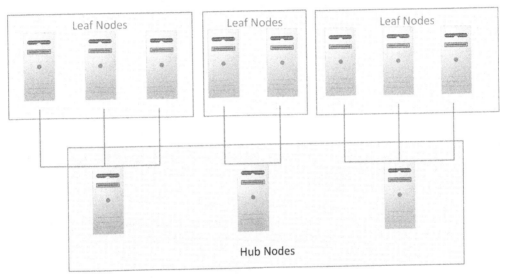

Figure 13.15 Flex Cluster Hub and Leaf Nodes

The *Hub Nodes* in Oracle's Flex Cluster is an architecture that the reader is already familiar with. The hub nodes have access to shared storage and are connected together via the Cluster Interconnect. Oracle RAC databases run on what would be the Hub nodes above. The *Leaf Nodes* in Oracle's Flex Cluster are servers that are part of the cluster configuration. However, the leaf nodes do not have direct access to the shared storage and do not need access to the private network.

A bug in the Oracle documentation when Oracle 12c was in beta testing led many to believe that an Oracle RAC database could run on the leaf nodes as well as the hub nodes. If this were true, it would mean great things to the database administrator responsible for the performance of an Oracle RAC deployment. It would be easy to

---

add a new leaf node to the cluster since that server does not need access to the shared storage or the private network. To the database administrator, a spike in activity could be handled by simply plugging in a new server to the cluster. When the period of high activity is over, the leaf node is disconnected and the configuration reverts back to its original state. Unfortunately, this is not the case and one cannot run an Oracle RAC instance on a leaf node.

To make matters worse, now that Oracle 12c is fully released, the Oracle documentation still isn't very clear on the subject. When this chapter was written, the Oracle 12c Clusterware Administration and Deployment Guide says in Chapter 4 the following:

"Oracle Flex Clusters provide a platform for a variety of applications, including Oracle Real Application Clusters (Oracle RAC) databases with large numbers of nodes"

Shortly after that sentence, the documentation further states:

"The number of Hub Nodes in an Oracle Flex Cluster can be as many as 64. The number of Leaf Nodes can be many more. Hub Nodes and Leaf Nodes can host different types of applications.

Hub Nodes are similar to Oracle Grid Infrastructure nodes in an Oracle Clusterware standard Cluster configuration: they are tightly connected, and have direct access to shared storage. In an Oracle Flex Cluster configuration, shared storage can be provisioned to Leaf Nodes independent of the Oracle Grid Infrastructure.

Leaf Nodes are different from standard Oracle Grid Infrastructure nodes, in that they do not require direct access to shared storage, but instead request data through Hub Nodes."

It appears that the Oracle documentation may easily mislead one into thinking that the shared storage can be accessed through the hub nodes and that Real Application Clusters databases can have instances on the leaf nodes. This configuration would open the doors to rapidly scaling an Oracle RAC database deployment but unfortunately, it is not possible to run an Oracle RAC instance on a leaf node in Oracle Flex Clusters. By this point in the book, the reader knows the importance of shared storage and the Cluster Interconnect for Cache Fusion operations to support an Oracle RAC database. If the leaf node does not directly access the shared storage and does not have access to the private network, then all blocks in the leaf node instance's Buffer Cache must be transferred through the public network of a hub node. Additionally, each instance must maintain its own thread of read and have its own undo tablespace, all of which would need to be accessed through the public network of a hub node. Obviously, this configuration would not provide a high performance solution.

It should be noted that nodes could be converted from hub to leaf and back again. Any leaf node that is converted to a hub node must be configured to have access to shared storage and the Cluster Interconnect. At that point, an Oracle instance can be created on the new hub node. Leveraging Flex Clusters in this way lets the database administrator quickly scale the hub nodes to support the Oracle RAC database by stealing one of the leaf nodes that may not be needed for an application server at that point in time and convert it to a hub node for supporting the Oracle RAC database.

The leaf nodes in an Oracle Flex Cluster environment are meant for applications and application servers, not for an Oracle RAC database. Don't be fooled into thinking that RAC instances can run on a leaf node. There have been rumors floating around that a future release will allow instances on leaf nodes, but at this point, it is just conjecture by some in the Oracle community.

Summary

This chapter has discussed two new features for Oracle 12c, Flex ASM and Flex Cluster. Flex ASM provides higher availability for ASM in a clustered environment. It also requires fewer ASM instances, which can free up resources to database instances. Flex ASM can also support more disk groups, which can let the administrator scale the shared storage solution. As was shown in this chapter, an instance that is a remote client to ASM may not exhibit the same performance as an instance that has ASM local to the node. Adequate testing should be performed before implementing Flex ASM.

Oracle's Flex Clusters allows for hub and leaf nodes in the cluster. Oracle RAC database instances can only run on hub nodes. Leaf nodes are for applications and application servers. However, the database administrator can quickly scale an Oracle RAC database by converting a leaf node into a hub node should a leaf node be available for the conversion.

Book Summary

This book has covered a lot of ground in each of the previous chapters. This final chapter will bring together some of the most important points from throughout the book and provide one last opportunity to reinforce and recap the material. The following is a list of top items every database administrator should address to keep their Oracle RAC applications performing at a high level.

RAC Areas of Focus

We have covered the following areas of RAC tuning, and our main focus has been on these central points:

- Tune the system as if it were a single-instance database. All of the single-instance tuning techniques still apply to Oracle RAC. An application that will not scale with a single-instance Oracle database will not scale with Oracle RAC.

- Remember the formula: *DB time = CPU time + wait time*

- Reducing database time involves reducing time spent on the CPU, time spent waiting for events to complete, or both.

- There will always be a bottleneck and a "Top N" list of wait events to deal with. Knowing when to stop tuning helps one avoid what is being known in Oracle circles as *Compulsive Tuning Disorder.*

- If global cache transfers are hampering application performance, the database administrator may want to leverage the concept of *application partitioning.* All or parts of an application's database sessions can be direct to one or a few instances by using database services.

- The database administrator does need to weigh the benefits of application partitioning against the scalability of spreading the application over multiple nodes. Application partitioning can significantly reduce the global cache transfers but will leave fewer resources available to the application's end users.

- Global cache transfers can be reduced by effective use of table compression, partitioning, and reverse key indexes.

- Sequence database objects need special attention when the application is deployed on Oracle RAC. It is a good idea to cache more sequence values in each instance and avoid *nocache* and *order* clauses when creating sequences.

- Two pieces of the architecture set Oracle RAC systems apart from any other database configuration: the Cluster Interconnect and the shared storage. Oracle RAC implementations that skimp on these two components or configure them incorrectly will soon show performance problems. These two components form the backbone of Oracle RAC, the foundation for its success.

- The Cluster Interconnect is often referred to as the private network. It must remain private.

- The Cluster Interconnect needs to be a high-bandwidth, low-latency network. In today's environment, this means 10 gigabit Ethernet or Infiniband.

- If possible, configure the private network with Jumbo Frames.

- Make sure that global cache transfer blocks are not being lost, which is most likely an indicator of a bad Cluster Interconnect.

- Using HAIP or NIC bonding not only provides fault tolerance on the private network, but offers better throughput as well.

- Each instance will have its own thread of redo so the database administrator will want to make sure that writing to the online redo logs will not cause contention that hampers performance.

- Similarly, each instance has its own undo tablespace. The database administrator will want to ensure that write activity to the Undo tablespace is not a source of contention for all instances.

- Temporary tablespaces are shared among the instances but each instance allocates its own extents within the temp tablespace. Each instance soft reserves extents that other instances will not be able to use. A temporary tablespace in Oracle RAC may need to be larger than in single-instance databases.

- Automatic Segment Space Management is a must for today's Oracle RAC systems. Databases with high rates of concurrent DML will enjoy the performance benefits of ASSM.

- Each Oracle RAC instance has its own memory structures. This book discussed that each of these memory structures, the Buffer Cache, the Shared Pool, etc. may need to be sized slightly larger just because this is an Oracle RAC database.

- The database administrator also needs to be mindful of application failover and its effect on these memory structures. The database administrator will want to size these to handle not only the current workload, but also any workload to support application failover.

- The database administrator will want to take advantage of the fact that a single SQL statement, largely transparent to the application, can be executed with parallel threads, not only on the originating instance, but also on all instances in the cluster, if desired.

- Enough slaves need to be available otherwise statement queuing can take place, which means a stoppage of the parallel execution.

- The database administrator needs to ensure that the Large Pool is sized correctly to support the message tables that facilitate communications between the slaves and to the Query Coordinator.

- If needed, the database administrator can constrain the parallel SQL slaves with instance groups or services. This will cut down on global cache transfers required to complete the parallel SQL statement, but will leave it with fewer resources.

- Today's Oracle RAC database administrator will want to download the support tools bundle from Oracle Support. This bundle is a convenient way to obtain ORAchk, OSWatcher, Cluster Health Monitor, and more.

- Increasingly, the Cluster Health Monitor is a tool that Oracle Support is relying on for helping customers with Oracle RAC performance problems, node evictions, and server hangs.

- Formerly called RACchk, the ORAchk utility can be used to diagnose the health of the cluster and its databases.

- More and more, SQLT is the tool of choice for Oracle Support when resolving performance issues with an SQL statement. This tool is not specific to Oracle RAC, but is included in the bundle. This tool is a knowledge expert and makes recommendations on how to tune a poorly performing SQL statement.

- If your company has not licensed the Diagnostics Pack, get them to do so. This optional, extra-cost item is well worth the price. The Diagnostics Pack gives the database administrator access to the AWR, ADDM, and ASH.

- The database administrator can run an AWR report, there are a few different ones to run for Oracle RAC, and obtain a very thorough listing of many different performance aspects of an Oracle database. The AWR reports are Oracle RAC aware and will provide performance metrics on global cache transfers, services, and more.

- The Automated Database Diagnostics Monitor is a knowledge expert that regularly examines the AWR data looking for areas of performance pain. Where SQLT makes recommendations on for a specific SQL statement, ADDM looks at the database as a whole.

- Enterprise Manager 12c now has Real Time ADDM, which lets the database administrator see performance remediation recommendations in real time.

- Active Session History is a great way to see performance history on just active sessions. Oracle includes an ASH report but many of today's database administrators are using scripts to generate a wealth of performance information from the ASH data.

- Oracle's Enterprise Manager, as a centralized management and monitoring tool, is now in its third major version. For purposes of performance tuning, the Performance Home page is the primary location in EM that the database administrator will want to visit. This page provides the ability to drill down into performance problems with a few simple clicks. No more scanning long AWR reports or running scripts.

That list is lengthy, but does cover the important points. There can always be debate on things that should have been included or taken off the list.

This book should not be the end of the reader's Oracle RAC performance tuning studies. There is so much more to Oracle RAC that could be crammed into this finite space. The reader is encouraged find other sources to enhance their knowledge.

In this last paragraph, I would like to thank the reader for purchasing this book and spending time with it. I hope that you have found this to be a useful reference that can help your Oracle RAC performance tuning efforts.

About the Author

Brian Peasland started his IT career at the age of 15, hanging magnetic tape and manually sorting punch cards, back in the days when monitors were big and the screens were green. He has over 25 years of IT experience, of which the last 17 years have been spent working as an Oracle database administrator.

Brian credits his education as the foundation for his career. He earned a Bachelor's of Science in Computer Science and Applied Mathematics from the University of North Dakota. Subsequently, he earned a Master's of Science in Computer Science from North Dakota State University where he focused his studies on database systems.

Brian has worked with Oracle since version 7. He has obtained Oracle Certified Professional DBA credentials for the 7.3, 8, 8i, 9i, and 10g versions. He has presented at IOUG conferences and been technical reviewer for a few Oracle-related books. Brian has shared his knowledge throughout his Oracle career, answering thousands of questions on the old Usenet newsgroups, the now defunct Quest Pipelines where he was a SysOp, as a panelist for SearchOracle.com's Ask The Expert, and most recently in the Oracle Technet and My Oracle Support Communities (username BPeasland). He can be followed on Twitter (@BPeaslandDBA) and tries to keep his blog current (http://www.peasland.net).

From the beginning of Brian's DBA career, he has been involved in performance tuning. He has managed Oracle RAC databases that were as small as 30 gigabytes on up to well over 100 terabytes in size. He has worked on projects that needed to grow by 2 terabytes per month or accommodate 100 million rows of new data, daily. Oracle RAC is one of his favorite Oracle technologies, but he is also very proficient in Data Guard as well. SQL*Plus used to be his favorite tool, but lately he is seen using SQL Developer and Enterprise Manager Cloud Control.

Brian has lived all over the world, from Asia to Europe. So it may be surprising to some that he now calls Fargo, North Dakota his home. He lives there currently with his wife Latana and his sons, Chay, and the twins Jace & Jenner.

Index

NIC, 109, 111, 112, 123
NIC bonding, 102, 414
NIC Bonding, 109, 243
NIC teaming, 102
no_parallel, 174, 184
no_px_join_filter, 205
nocache, 40, 41, 42, 45, 49, 50
node, 2, 4, 8
obj#, 19, 23
oclumon, 210, 211, 212, 213
OCR, 75
oifcfg, 77, 82, 104, 105, 107
ologgerd, 210, 211
OLTP, 70
OLTP test, 117, 118
on DEC VAX, 11, 13
onepass, 134
Online Transaction Processing, 70
OPS, 12, 173
ORA-4030, 229
ORA-4031, 229
orachk, 239, 240, 244, 245
ORAchk, 208, 238, 239, 241, 242, 243, 244, 245, 253, 415
Oracle 12c, 375, 380, 383, 388, 389, 399, 409, 410, 411
Oracle Diagnostics Pack, 151
Oracle Interface Configuration Tool, 77
Oracle Parallel Server, 12, 119, 173
Oracle Performance Pack, 151
Oracle's Times Ten, 164

Oracle's Wait Interface, 359, 366
Oratop, 208, 234, 235, 236, 238, 253
Orion, 114, 115, 116, 117, 118, 119, 126, 136, 143, 207, 295
OSWatcher, 208, 217, 218, 219, 220, 221, 222, 223, 224, 225, 229, 253, 415
oswbb, 218, 219, 220, 221, 222, 223, 224
oswbba, 219, 222, 223, 224
P1, 20, 33, 46
P2, 20, 33
pagefile., 153
paging, 153
parallel degree, 178, 180, 181
Parallel operations downgraded 1 to 25 pct, 384
Parallel operations downgraded 25 to 50 pct, 384
Parallel operations downgraded 50 to 75 pct, 384
Parallel operations downgraded 75 to 99 pct, 384
Parallel operations downgraded to serial, 384
Parallel operations not downgraded, 384
parallel parallelism, 173

RAID 0, 114
RAID 1, 113, 114
RAID 1+0, 114
RAID 5, 113, 114
RAT, 69
raw disks, 119, 120
Real Application Testing, 69
Real-Time ADDM, 283
redo log groups, 129, 132
Redundant Array of
  Independent Disks, 113
Relational Software, Inc, 11
response time, 5, 6
Response time, 5, 9
Result Cache, 159, 160, 161,
  162, 163
result_cache_max_size, 162, 163
Reverse Key index, 55
rmem, 87, 88, 89
-run parameter, 118
S.A.M.E, 114
SAN, 111, 112, 124
sar, 173
SAS, 111
SATA, 111, 139
scale out., 8, 9
scale up, 8, 9
scaling up, 7
SCAN Listener, 312, 317
SDL, 11
sequence, 40, 41, 42, 43, 44, 45,
  46, 47, 48, 49, 50, 51, 52, 53,
  54, 56, 74

sequence values, 40, 41, 42, 47,
  49, 50, 51
Serial ATA, 111, 139
Serial Attached SCSI, 111
serial#, 35, 36
serv_mod_act_trace_enable, 37, 40
server_set, 193, 194
SGA, 145, 147, 151, 154, 155,
  156, 157, 158, 159, 167, 177,
  189, 190, 191
sga_target, 123, 145, 162
shared lock, 375, 377
Shared Pool, 121, 123, 147,
  148, 149, 150, 151, 162, 172,
  373, 374, 415
shared_pool_size, 149, 162
sid, 35, 36, 45, 46
simulate I/O, 404
Single Instance RAC, 109
slave processes, 178, 182, 183,
  186, 187, 188, 189, 191, 193,
  194, 197, 200, 201, 202, 206
Solid State Disk, 111
SQL Execution phase, 289
SQL Trace, 35
sql_plan_hash_value, 205
SQLT, 208, 245, 246, 247, 248,
  249, 250, 251, 252, 253, 415,
  416
SS contention, 380
SSD, 111
ssh, 239
Statspack, 255
Storage Area Network, 111

CPSIA information can be obtained
at www.ICGtesting.com
Printed in the USA
BVOW04s1919280317

479675BV00007B/72/P

9 780986 119415